Charles A. Schott

Meteorological Observations

Charles A. Schott

Meteorological Observations

ISBN/EAN: 9783741144554

Manufactured in Europe, USA, Canada, Australia, Japa

Cover: Foto ©Thomas Meinert / pixelio.de

Manufactured and distributed by brebook publishing software
(www.brebook.com)

Charles A. Schott

Meteorological Observations

SMITHSONIAN CONTRIBUTIONS TO KNOWLEDGE.
146

METEOROLOGICAL OBSERVATIONS

ARCTIC SEAS.

BY

SIR FRANCIS LEOPOLD M'CLINTOCK, R. N.

MADE ON BOARD THE ARCTIC SEARCHING YACHT "FOX," IN BAFFIN BAY AND PRINCE REGENT'S INLET, IN 1857, 1858, AND 1859.

REDUCED AND DISCUSSED,

AT THE EXPENSE OF THE SMITHSONIAN INSTITUTION.

BY

CHARLES A. SCHOTT.
ASSISTANT U. S. COAST SURVEY.

[ACCEPTED FOR PUBLICATION, APRIL, 1861.]

CONTENTS.

CONTENTS

APPENDIX

ILLUSTRATIONS.

PLATES.

WOODCUTS.

PREFACE.

The following series of reduced meteorological observations have been prepared from the records kept on board the yacht "Fox," in 1857, '58, '59, during the expedition in search of Sir John Franklin, under the command of Captain M'Clintock,[1] R. N.

The records of these observations were presented by the commander of the expedition to the Institution, to be used in such manner as might be deemed best suited to advance the science of meteorology. They were accordingly placed in the hands of Mr. Charles A. Schott, of the U. S. Coast Survey, to be discussed in accordance with the plan proposed by Sir John Herschel in his work on meteorology, and which was adopted in regard to the records made during the voyage of Dr. Kane in the Arctic regions. These reductions form a part of a series of articles on the climatology of the Arctic portions of the North American continent, which are in the course of preparation and publication by the Smithsonian Institution. Of these the investigations relative to the winds of the Northern Hemisphere, by Prof. Coffin, the observations by Dr. Kane, and those by Dr. Hayes, form portions. It is to be hoped that an opportunity will be afforded for a thorough discussion of all the observations which have been made by the different Arctic explorers on a similar plan, since such a work would not only throw much light on the climatology of the continent of North America, but also on the meteorology of the globe.

The following brief account of the expedition of "the Fox," compiled from the narrative of the commander, and other sources, will perhaps be of service in rendering the observations more easily understood, as well as of interest to those who may not have ready access to the works from which the compilation has been made :—

Sir John Franklin was appointed in 1845 to the command of an expedition consisting of two ships, the *Erebus* and *Terror*, fitted out for a further attempt to discover a northwest passage. The expedition sailed from England on the 26th of May, 1845, and was last seen by a whaler in Baffin's Bay on the 26th of July following. In the autumn of 1847 public anxiety began to be manifest for the safety of the explorers, from whom nothing more had been heard, and several expeditions were sent from 1848 to 1854 in search of them. In these active exertions

[1] Now Sir Francis Leopold McClintock

Lady Franklin took the lead, and by her unwearied labors and sacrifices aroused the sympathy of the whole civilized world. Aid was offered by France and even by Tasmania. Citizens of the United States replied to her call by equipping two expeditions, the expense of which was principally borne by Mr. Henry Grinnell, of New York.

In August, 1850, traces of the missing explorers were discovered, where they had spent their first winter, but no further tidings were obtained until the spring of 1854, when Dr. Rae, of the Hudson's Bay Company, ascertained that they had been seen by the Esquimaux on the west coast of King William's Island, in the spring of 1850, and it was thought that they had all died on an estuary of the great Fish River. The attempt, in 1855, of the Hudson's Bay Company to explore this river resulted in obtaining but little additional information, and a few relics from the Esquimaux.

It was at this time that Lady Franklin, who had previously sent out three expeditions at her own expense, again earnestly urged the renewal of the search, that the fate of her husband and his companions might not be left in uncertainty, and in the spring of 1857 commenced the preparations for another expedition as a final effort to trace "the footsteps of these gallant men in their last journey upon earth," and, if possible, to rescue from entire loss some of the scientific results for which they had sacrificed their lives.

The small steamer Fox, of 177 tons burthen, was purchased for the service, and Lady Franklin was highly gratified in obtaining the willing service of Captain M'Clintock as commander of the expedition. This officer had signally distinguished himself in the voyages of Sir James Ross and Admiral Austin, and especially in his extensive journeys on the ice when associated with Captain Kellett.

The voyagers sailed from Aberdeen, July 1st, 1857, and after a favorable run across the Atlantic, passed Cape Farewell, the southern point of Greenland, on the 13th, and arrived at Frederickshaab on the 19th of the same month. After stopping to take in coal at Waigat, they reached Upernavik, the most northerly of the Danish stations in Greenland, and then bore away, on the 6th of August, directly westward for the purpose of crossing Baffin's Bay; but, on the evening of the 8th, their progress in that direction was stopped by impenetrable ice in Latitude 72° 40' and Longitude 59° 60' west. They then steered northward with the hope of finding a passage westward in a higher latitude, but in this they were disappointed, and, on the 19th of August, became entangled in the ice, and thus remained two hundred and forty-two days, until April, 1858. During this period, the "Fox" drifted from Latitude 75° north and Longitude 62° west, eleven hundred and ninety-four geographical miles in a southerly direction, almost to the lower extremity of Greenland. (See the accompanying map.)

On the 26th of April, the ice suddenly and almost entirely disappeared; the ship was again headed northward for another attempt, and arrived on the 19th of June in Melville Bay. They then again steered westward across Baffin's Bay, and, finally, entered Lancaster Sound in the beginning of August. They next sailed westerly and southerly until they reached the Longitude of 96° west, and about Latitude 73° north. From this point, they returned eastward through Barrow's

Straits, which they found clear of ice, and went southerly down Prince Regent's Inlet to the mouth of Bellot Straits, where they arrived on the 20th of August, and near which they were destined to remain for more than a year.

Bellot Strait, which is near Latitude 72° north, is the water communication between Prince Rupert's Inlet and that part of the western sea now known as Franklin Channel. It separates the extreme northern part of the continent of North America, or Boothia Felix, from North Somerset. The shores of this strait are faced in many places with lofty granite cliffs, and some of the adjacent hills rise to fifteen or sixteen hundred feet above the level of the sea. Through this channel the tide runs at the rate of six or seven knots an hour, and also frequent stormy winds blow from the west which probably affect the local meteorology of the country immediately around the eastern entrance.

At the time of the arrival of the expedition, this strait was choked up with masses of ice, but as the season advanced these obstacles so far gave way that the voyagers were enabled to work the ship through to the western outlet. But beyond this point they were unable to advance further in the same direction, and on account of the exposed position they were obliged to return and seek for safer winter quarters. These they found near the eastern entrance of the strait in a commodious harbor named Port Kennedy. At this place they remained frozen up from the 27th of September, 1858, until the 9th of August, 1859.

Early in the spring, three exploring parties set out from Port Kennedy in different directions, severally under the command of Captain M'Clintock, Captain Young, and Lieutenant Hobson. The routes traversed by these parties included the southern portion of the coast of Prince of Wales Island—the western coast of Boothia Felix, and the entire circumference of King William's Land. These explorations furnished important additions to the map of the Arctic regions as well as definite information relative to the fate of Sir John Franklin and his devoted companions. On the western coast of King William's Island, several relics of the lost mariners were found, and among the number a tin-case containing a record of the unfortunate explorers.

From this record, the following facts were obtained, namely, the Franklin Expedition spent the first winter after leaving England at Beechy Island near the south-western point of North Devon (see map). From this place it passed down Franklin Channel to within fifteen miles of the northwest coast of King William's Island (see the spot indicated on the map), where the ships were frozen in the ice, and finally abandoned on the 22d of April, 1848. Sir John Franklin died on the 11th of June, 1847, and several other deaths had occurred. The survivors, one hundred and five in number, under the command of Captain Crozier, landed on King William's Island, where all knowledge of their subsequent journeying ceases; they probably, however, all perished in their endeavor to reach a less inhospitable region.

Although the whole shore of King William's Island was three times patiently examined by Captain M'Clintock and Lieutenant Hobson, no vestige of the wrecks was seen, and it was doubted whether any portion of them remained above water.

After making the explorations above mentioned, the object of the expedition having been measurably attained, the explorers in the Fox waited for the advance of the season to be released from the ice, but though the summer at Port Kennedy was a warm one, they were not able to move before the 9th of August. At this time they commenced their homeward voyage and arrived at Portsmouth on the 23d of September following.

During the whole time of the exploration of "the Fox," a regular series of observations was made upon the temperature, the pressure and movements of the atmosphere, as well as upon the variations of the elements of terrestrial magnetism, the tides, &c.

The meteorological observations were under the care of Dr. David Walker, of Belfast, and were made at equal intervals of time during day and night. In winter they were generally taken at intervals of two hours; and in summer of four hours. Occasionally, there are found some irregularities in the time of observation, and omissions noted in the records, but these are of rare occurrence, and are corrected approximately in the reductions.

The reductions have been made at the expense of the Smithsonian Institution, by Mr. Schott, whose previous labors in the reduction of the observations of Dr. Kane have met with general approval.

The series of observations is divided into three parts, relating to the following subjects, namely:—

1. The temperature.
2. The direction and force of the winds.
3. The pressure of the atmosphere.

To these are added, in an appendix, miscellaneous phenomena, such as the face of the sky, appearance of plants and animals, auroras, &c.

The following remarks relative to the observations are from communications addressed by Captain M'Clintock to the Secretary of the Smithsonian Institution:—

"I have much pleasure in transmitting to you the meteorological records of my whole voyage in the Fox. I have had my two-hourly observations for the temperature and pressure of the air reduced according to the method adopted in Kane's observations, but they have not been published in any book, nor do I think they will be, the time required and the expense being an objection. Admiral Fitzroy has published in the fourth number of the Meteorological Papers of the Board of Trade a part of my observations (the temperature for noon, the face of the sky, and the specific gravity of sea water, &c., without reduction), which I fear will not be sufficient for your purpose. You are at full liberty to make any use you may think fit of the observations, and should you deem them worthy of publication, it would afford me much pleasure."

"I think it better to send the whole record than to make extracts which would increase the chance of error and perhaps not be sufficient after all. You will thus be able to trace my drift down Baffin's Bay and Davis' Straits and to compare it with De Haven's drift.

"My magnetical observations are in the hands of General Sabine. In the appendix of the second edition of my narrative, now published, you will see an article on the Tides, as also one upon the Geology, by Professor Haughton. Observations upon Halos, &c., with the Polariscope, have been sent to Professor Stokes; a series of earth temperatures, to Dr. Jos. Hooker, of Kew Botanic Gardens, as also the specimens of dried and living plants. Natural history specimens have also been made over to scientific friends of the Expedition, my sole object being, to render our labors subservient to scientific ends, and with the least possible delay."

"I quite agree with Kane's remarks as to the increase of cold during full moon. The fact was noticed as far back as 1829–30, by Sir John Ross, in the Victory.

"I also agree with you in opinion that the apparent quantity of ozone depends upon the velocity of the air which has free access to the box containing the prepared paper."

"I likewise think that when you have fully examined my data now in your possession you will in a great measure subscribe to my opinion as to the ice-movement [as connected with the wind]. I referred in my letter only to the winter movements of the ice when there is no discharge of water whatever from the land, and when the precipitation in the northern regions is reduced to its minimum. The Barrow Strait stream is almost lost in the vast expanse of Baffin's Bay, but its line is tolerably well indicated by De Haven's drift. The entire current which brings such quantities of ice round Cape Farewell, and up to about 65° N., appears to be deflected off shore to the westward by banks which lie in about the latitude of 67°. It sweeps very swiftly past Cape Walsingham, curves southward, and having united with Barrow Strait current continues its course downward along the Labrador coast; so that the Labrador current is not due, in my opinion, so much to water flowing from the upper part of Baffin's Bay as to the Arctic current which sets around Cape Farewell from the East."

"The long drift of the Terror through Hudson's Straits in 1836–37 appears to me to be another instance of the effect of wind upon the ice, as in this case it does not seem possible that any considerable current could always, that is to say all winter, set out of Hudson's Bay. But it is my anxious endeavor to bring to light facts instead of advancing hypotheses, and I do know from repeated observations in the Fox, in 1857, and in H. M. S. Bulldog during the past summer, that the Arctic currents (from around Cape Farewell) flow northward along the coast of Greenland—off Frederickshaab, for instance, at from eighteen to twenty-four miles daily, and that West India seeds have been borne by it as far north as Egedesminde, which is in about 68° of north latitude. Our observations, therefore, upon the volume of water setting out of Baffin's Bay [on the west side] should not be extended south of this point without making considerable allowance for the current which flows around Cape Farewell, and northward up the coast."

In one of his communications, Captain M'Clintock states that the beams of the aurora were most frequently seen in the direction of open water, or else in that of places where vapor was rising. In some cases, patches of light could be plainly seen a few feet above a small mass of vapor over an opening in the ice. This observation is in accordance with a deduction from an examination of a large number of notices of the aurora in the voyages of Arctic explorations by Peter Force, Esq., of Washington; published in Vol. VIII. of Smithsonian Contributions (in 1856), namely, "that on the Atlantic Ocean, and other open water, the aurora is most frequent and most brilliant." These facts would appear to favor the hypothesis that auroral displays are due to electrical discharges between the air and the earth, since such discharges would, at least in part, be interrupted by a stratum of non-conducting ice.

The accompanying map, to illustrate the voyage of the Fox, is drawn by Mr. Schott on the plan of the projection known as the polyconic, which is a development of the earth's surface on cones tangent to each parallel of latitude; the radius being the distance between the arc of the parallel and the earth's axis.

Points of intersection of the parallels and the meridians are, according to Mr. Schott, readily computed by substitution in the following formulæ, in which x and y are the co-ordinates for any difference of longitude, n, on any parallel of latitude, L, and N the normal ending at the polar axis.

$$x = N \cos L \left(n - \frac{n^3}{6} \sin^2 L + \ldots\right)$$

$$y = N \cos L \left(\frac{n^2}{2} \sin L - \frac{n^4}{24} \sin^3 L + \ldots\right)$$

This projection is used in the United States Coast Survey, and is described in the Report of the Superintendent, Dr. Bache, for 1859, Appendix, 32.

JOSEPH HENRY,
Secretary S. I.

SMITHSONIAN INSTITUTION,
WASHINGTON, December, 186[illegible]

PART I.

TEMPERATURES.

"On February 8th, 1858, the mercurial standard No. 19 fell steadily to —40°.2; then the mercury appeared to freeze, and descended into the bulb. Had the stem been graduated down to the neck of the bulb, it would then have indicated —70°. A globule of mercury corked up in a small test-tube remained fluid. Two other mercurial thermometers (good instruments) were exposed; one fell to —42°, the other to —40°.5. This was a very fair set of observations; the thermometers were taken to a distance from the ship, and freely suspended at five feet above the snow."

Taking the mean of the three Kew standards, Nos. 10, 8, and 6, and comparing the same with the readings of Newman, Nos. 11 and 7, we obtain the following corrections to each of the registering thermometers:—

	[illegible]	[illegible]	[illegible]	[illegible]	[illegible]	[illegible]	[illegible]	[illegible]	[illegible]	[illegible]	[illegible]	[illegible]	[illegible]	[illegible]	[illegible]	[illegible]	[illegible]	[illegible]
		+	—	—	—	—	—	—	—	—	—	—	—	—	—	—	—	—
Mean of Nos. 10, 8, and 6	31.4	2.3	9.5	10.0	18.4	12.2	14.1	18.6	24.5	25.7	34.6	38.0	39.1	39.6	41.8	41.3	46.2	53.8
Corr'n to Newman, No. 11	+0.1	—0.7	+0.7	+0.1	—0.1	—0.4	—0.1	—0.4	—0.5	—0.5	—0.8	..	—0.6	—1.3	—1.7	—1.1	—2.2	+0.3
Corr'n to Newman, No. 7	—1.4	—1.4	..	..	..	—1.2	..	—0.4	—0.3	..	..	—0.8	—0.9	—1.6	—2.1	—1.1	..	+0.1

From the above, it appears that the following small corrections may properly be applied, viz:—

For thermometer, Newman No. 11, used in winter 1857–58—

Between	0° and —30°,	—0°.3
" —30	" —48,	—1.6

For thermometer, Newman No. 7, used from Sept. 1858 to Aug. 1859—

Between	0° and —30°,	—0°.5
" —30	" —48,	—1.9

As remarked above, no correction is applied to the record, and to the results only when *specially* stated.

There were a number of other thermometers on board; but, since the numbers of these instruments are not given in connection with the observations, it suffices to show that their corrections are small. The following table is copied from p. 3 of the Meteorological Register in the fourth number of the papers published by authority of the Board of Trade:—

SPIRIT THERMOMETERS.

	Corrections at 32°	52°	72°	
Newman, No. 16,	+0.5	+0.7	+0.4	Compared at Kew, Nov. 1852.
Pastorelli, No. 19,	+1.9	+1.8	+0.1	
" No 23,	+0.1	+0.5	—0.3	

MERCURIAL THERMOMETERS

	Corrections at 45°	60°	75°		
Negretti, A 499,	−0.1	−0.1	−0.2	At departure.	Compared at Kew, Feb. 1867.
" 500,	0.0	−0.2	−0.5		
" 501,	−0.1	−0.2	−0.6		
" 502,	−0.1	−0.2	+0.1		
" 503,	−0.1	−0.2	−0.2		
" 504,	0.0	−0.2	−0.3		
Negretti, A 500,	−0.2	−0.3	−0.4	At return.	Compared at Kew Observatory.
" 501,	−0.1	−0.4	−0.4		
" 502,	−0.1	−0.1	−0.1		
" 503,	−0.4	−0.5	−0.4		
" 504,	−0.2	−0.5	−0.4		

The corrections in regard to the barometer are explained in the third part of the series, on page 79.

Temperature of the Air in Shade observed on board the Yacht Fox.
(Expressed in degrees of Fahrenheit's scale.)

July, 1857.

Day of the month.	Latitude north.	Longitude west of Greenwich.	4h	8h	Noon.	4h	8h	Midn't.	Mean.	[illegible] mean.
1	Aberdeen		..	..	..	..	..	..	..	..
2	57° 19'	2° 35'	..	..	..	..	57°	..	..	57.8°
3	58 56	6 10	..	57°	..	..	57.0	..	..	57.7
4	[illegible] 44	7 19	..	54	..	..	60	..	..	58.0
5	[illegible] 19	10 [illegible]	..	49.5	..	..	[illegible]	..	..	51.7
6	60 1	15 1	..	51.9	50°	50°	50.5	45°	..	50.1
7	60 9	15 [illegible]	54°	50	51	61	57	57	52.0°	..
8	60 [illegible]	19 [illegible]	[illegible]	54	59	50.5	[illegible]	54	57.9	..
9	61 17	[illegible]	56	55	57	57	[illegible]	51	56.0	..
10	61 19	[illegible]	52	53	[illegible]	54	54	54	53.7	..
11	61 0	[illegible]	[illegible]	54	[illegible]	53	[illegible]	51	52.8	..
12	[illegible] 27	[illegible] 44	[illegible]	55	50.9	50	[illegible]	47	49.8	..
13	[illegible] 19	41 [illegible]	[illegible]	[illegible]	[illegible]	44	44	[illegible]	46.3	..
14	[illegible] 34	44 [illegible]	44	40	44	47.9	44	44	47.5	..
15	[illegible] 9	[illegible] 19	44	43	41.6	43	41.6	42	43.3	..
16	[illegible] 34	[illegible]	43	41	43	44	39	41	41.9	..
17	[illegible]	[illegible]	36	[illegible]	37	34	[illegible]	[illegible]	35.0	..
18	[illegible] 57	50 31	[illegible]	[illegible]	34	35.5	37	[illegible]	34.4	..
19	Frederickshaab		[illegible]	..	..	..	..	..	..	41.9
20	=		44	40	41	40	41	[illegible]	40.3	..
21	...	...	[illegible]	41	43	43	..	31	..	38.4
22	63 [illegible]	51 5	34	36	[illegible]	34	37	37	36.5	..
23	Fiskernaes		34	41	42	[illegible]	40	40	44.6	..
24	63 [illegible]	52 10	43	40	41	41	41	[illegible]	41.6	..
25	Off Godthaab		39	36	41	41	41	[illegible]	38.5	..
26	64 7	53 10	39	41	41	41	41	[illegible]	40.3	..
27	64 44	[illegible] 0	40	36	40	39	36	34	38.9	..
28	65 1	55 30	36	37	36	38.5	35	39	35.6	..
29	67 [illegible]	55 [illegible]	36	35	38	42	39	39	38.3	..
30	69 [illegible]	56 12	39	45	43	41.9	40	41	41.8	..
31	Lievely		44	45	45	45	43	43	44.0	..
Mean	63.0	59.1	+44.72	+43.24	+44.46	+47.14	+43.30	+44.38	+45.00	

Correction to refer to mean from 24 observations in a day as −0°.[illegible].

August, 1857.

Day of the month.	Latitude north.	Longitude west of Greenwich.	4h	8h	Noon.	4h	8h	Midn't.	Mean.
1	In Disco Fiord		42°	45°	44°	44°	46°	42°	+43.7
2	69° 7'	[illegible]	42	44	46	46	45	45	44.0
3	Off [illegible] Point		43	44	45	49	44	41	44.5
4	At Rittenbenk		51	50	51	47	40	39	46.3
5	71 7	55 [illegible]	36	39	41	43	40	40	40.3
6	Off Upernavik		41	..	..	44	40	37	41.3
7	73 43	56 1	34	33	33	34	34	31	33.3
8	73 54	56 47	33	33	34	35	37.5	35	34.9
9	73 19	[illegible]	34	35.5	34	34	35	34	34.7
10	74 29	[illegible]	36	35	39	35.5	33	33	34.1
11	74 49	[illegible]	33	32	35	35	34	33	33.8
12	75 9	[illegible] 39	34	30	34	35	33	33	32.8
13	75 11	56 4	32.9	35	35	37	37	35	35.9
14	75 6	58 31	34	35	34.5	37	35	33	35.4
15	75 8	59 31	33	35	35	34	34	33	34.8
16	75 7	59 39	31	34	36	34.9	33	31	33.4
17	75 10	61 19	35	31	31	32.4	33	31	32.0
18	75 27	62 5	33	35	33	33	33	33	33.2
19	74 15	63 10	35.5	35	36	31.9	37	37	35.0
20	75 17	...	37.5	33	30	33	33	33	34.1
21	75 17	62 10	35	33	33	30	33	33	31.9
22	75 33	63 41	35	31.5	35	33.9	33	33	32.3
23	75 33	63 41	30	31	33.0	33	33	27	31.3
24	75 30	63 6	33	27	30	31	27	28	27.7
25	...	...	33	33	34	35	34	34	31.0
26	75 35	65 15	33	33	33.5	33.5	31.5	33.5	33.3
27	75 24	65 16	34	35	37	35	35	34	35.0
28	...	...	34.5	35	34	35	34	33	34.3
29	75 20	65 30	31	30	33	33	30	33	30.0
30	...	...	34	37	33.5	33.5	34	35	33.7
31	75 30	64 4	33	33.5	34	33	33	33	33.5
Mean	74.0	59.3	+33.15	+33.80	+33.80	+33.83	+34.74	+33.91	+34.30

Correction to refer mean of 6 observations to mean of 24 observations, 0°.[illegible].

Temperature of the Air in Shade observed on board the Yacht Fox.

(Expressed in degrees of Fahrenheit's scale.)

September, 1857.

Day of the month.	Lat. north.	Long. west of Green.	2h	4h	6h	8h	10h	Noon.	2h	4h	6h	8h	10h	Midn't.	Mean of 9 obs'ns.	Mean of 12 obs'ns.
1	73°29'	..	..	32°	..	28°	..	28°.5	..	32°	..	30°	..	29	+27°.8	+27°.2
2	..	..	..	31	..	34	..	34	..	38	..	32.8	..	28	32.7	30.2
3	..	..	..	29	..	25.9	..	30	..	32	..	30.5	..	29	29.2	29.1
4	..	..	..	32.5	..	29	..	25.9	..	36	..	34	..	43	31.0	30.6
5	74 27	64°21'	..	24	..	29	..	31	..	31	..	32	..	33	29.8	29.2
6	74 26	64 31	..	20	..	30	..	38	..	27.5	..	28	..	25	27.1	26.5
7	73 24	64 28	..	28	..	24.5	..	25.8	..	27	..	23.5	..	23	26.0	26.0
8	..	..	..	27	..	24.3	..	32	..	32	..	22	..	23	26.8	26.6
9	..	..	..	27.5	..	33	..	33	..	26	..	33	..	31	32.1	32.0
10	..	..	..	32	..	34	..	33.0	..	30	..	33.0	..	30	32.7	32.0
11	..	..	..	31	..	30.5	..	33	..	34	..	34	..	31	33.1	32.6
12	75 33	..	..	23	..	28	..	21	..	33	..	18	..	18.5	26.2	25.7
13	75 32	68 36	..	13	..	7	..	17	..	18	..	13	..	15	15.3	15.2
14	..	..	..	24	..	24	..	21	..	26	..	21	..	9	21.3	21.1
15	75 35	61 43	..	8	..	13.1	..	14.5	..	19	..	18	..	8	15.7	16.9
16	..	..	..	9	..	16.9	..	23	..	22.5	..	17.9	..	11	18.4	16.9
17	75 30	69 7	..	11.5	..	8	..	10	..	18	..	12	..	−3	7.1	7.0
18	75 30	66 25	..	6	..	8	..	7	..	14	..	12.8	..	11.0	8.7	8.5
19	75 29	66 32	..	12.3	..	9.5	..	15.6	..	17	..	9	..	7	11.4	11.5
20	75 21	66 24	..	6	..	8	..	13	..	16	..	16.9	..	10.9	10.9	10.9
21	75 17	66 21	..	13.5	..	17	..	25.5	27°	24.5	22°	21	21°	21	22.7	22.5
22	75 19	65 12	20°.5	23	20°	21.3	17°	13	17	16.3	16	16	17.0	15	18.7	18.8
23	75 10	65 5	17	12	12	12	15.9	17	16	17	9	5.5	5	5	13.4	12.8
24	75 9	65 20	9	8	9	1.6	10.9	10	13	13	8	8	3	4	8.1	7.8
25	75 6	65 21	6	3	6	0	12	14.9	10	16	10.8	2	7	3	7.8	8.0
26	75 4	65 26	3	5	0	3.6	11.5	12	13	14	11	4.5	2	2	6.3	6.1
27	75 3	..	8	7	8.5	12	14	14	19.5	20	20.8	20	13	13	15.3	14.8
28	..	..	13	10.5	10.8	10.5	15	10.5	21.5	16.9	15	16.9	12	13	15.7	15.8
29	73 2	..	10	16	17	12	22	21	27.6	12	14.5	12	11	21	18.3	17.9
30	..	..	12	13	11	14	14	16.9	15.5	15	16	19	11	15	15.1	15.1
Mean	75.5	65.9	+17.15	+17.23	+18.71	+16.28	+20.41	+22.07	+23.11	+23.10	+20.11	+19.03	+16.03	+17.38	..	+16.14

Correction to refer to mean of 24 observations = −0°.04.

October, 1857.

Day of the month.	Lat. north.	Long. west of Green.	2h	4h	6h	8h	10h	Noon.	2h	4h	6h	8h	10h	Midn't.	Mean.
1	..	..	+6°	+4°	+2°	+3°.7	+6°	+13°	+18°	+15°	+18°.8	+20°	+20°.8	+18°	+12°.0
2	..	..	19	11.8	17.8	20	28	22	19	21.9	8	14	7	8	+16.8
3	74° 10'	65° 12'	9	8	29	5	5	8.8	10	10	8	3	3	4	+ 7.4
4	74 31	..	7.5	8	8	11	15.8	17	15.8	10	13	12	12	4.3	+12.2
5	75 14	..	5.5	7.8	7	11	14	13	12	9	8	1	1	3	+ 7.9
6	74 12	63 43	−2	−3	19	14	13	17	15.8	14.9	12	8.9	1	−5	+ 8.0
7	74 32	63 42	−5	−8	−8	−3.1	−3.8	6	7	4	2	8	1	1.5	− 0.2
8	..	..	8	3	2	1	4	4	3.8	4.5	4	5.9	0	−3	+ 8.5
9	..	..	−1.5	−2	8	12	18	14	14	12.5	10	16.5	8	−1	+ 5.1
10	..	..	−3	−3	−3	3	9	9	−1.5	−1.5	−2.8	−7	−4	1	− 2.9
11	..	..	−1	−1	−1	−5	−5.8	6	−3	−5	−1	−2	0	0	− 1.1
12	74 32	..	0	0	6	6	14	15.0	15.5	16.5	15.6	13	2	3	+10.5
13	..	..	6	7	8	8	8.8	8.8	16	16.5	16.5	22	26.8	18	+13.9
14	..	..	20	22	24.8	30	32	32	30	28	21	23	24	26	+27.4
15	..	..	27	24	29.5	29	30.5	31	30	27	26	24	24	24	+27.8
16	..	..	22	28	28	26.5	28	26	27	25.8	26	26	22	21.5	+24.5
17	75 18	60 36	18	8	7	11	19	11	16	18.8	18	16	15	20	+14.7
18	..	..	21	21.5	20	17	14	13	13	13	13	11	21	11	+14.9
19	75 16	60 30	12	11	8	6.8	6.8	7	7	8.8	8	6.9	8	9	+ 7.6
20	..	..	8	7	8	8	16.9	16.9	11	16.5	10	11	16.5	11	+ 9.7
21	75 30	60 34	10	10	13	11.8	11	8	4	8	11.8	18	18	13	+11.5
22	..	..	13	11	8	8.8	2	3.8	6.8	4	4	8	1	1	+ 5.1
23	75 36	..	−3	−3	−1	−4	−1	−1	−0.8	−11	−11	−11	−13	−5	− 7.0
24	..	..	−3	−8	−1	−4	−3	−1	−3	−7.8	−8.8	−8.8	−10	−12.0	− 6.9
25	75 27	60 41	−10	−12	−9	−5	−5	−2.8	−3.8	−8	−6	−10	−10	−9	− 7.3
26	75 37	64 50	−7	−9	−1.9	−7.2	−9	−7	−6	−6	−5	−6	−4	−8	− 5.0
27	..	..	−7	−7	−7	−4.3	−3.8	−7	−3	−3	−3	−4	0	−1	− 3.9
28	75 37	..	−3	−1	−1	−1	−0.9	0	−6	−8	−9	−10	−11	−11	− 4.8
29	75 31	..	−12.5	−12	−13	−16	−10	−8	−10	−11	−9	−7	−9	−15	−10.6
30	75 33	65 40	−10	−11	−14	−14	−8.8	−8	−9	−8	−10	−12	−12.3	−12.0	− 7.8
31	..	..	−11.4	−9	−1	−4	−3.8	−6	−4	−4	−4	−6.4	−8	−6	− 6.3
Mean	75.38	65.9	+4.77	+4.31	+5.10	+5.29	+6.08	+7.38	+7.32	+6.10	+5.38	+5.23	+4.31	+4.32	+5.73

Correction to refer mean of 12 to mean of 24 observations in a day = +0°.02.

Temperature of the Air in Shade observed on board the Yacht Fox.

(Expressed in degrees of Fahrenheit's scale.)

November, 1857.

Day of the month	Lat. north	Long. west of Green.	2h	4h	6h	8h	10h	Noon	2h	4h	6h	8h	10h	Midn't.	Mean
1	75° 12′	61° 50′	− 4°	− 7°	−10°	−10°	− 8°	− 6°	− 1°	+ 2°	− 8°	− 8°	− 9°	− 6°.5	− 4°.7
2	. . .	. . .	− 4.5	− 3	− 4	− 7.9	− 7	− 7	− 6	− 3	− 4	+ 8	+ 3	− 1	− 3.5
3	75 18	63 30	− 7.5	− 8	− 6	−11	−11.5	− 7.5	−10.5	− 8	− 4	− 6.5	+ 1	+ 1.9	− 6.4
4	. . .	. . .	+ 2	+ 8	+ 4	+ 3	+ 4	+ 3	+ 4.5	+ 3	+ 8	+ 3	+ 2	+ 1	+ 3.1
5	. . .	. . .	− 1	− 4	− 7	− 6	− 9	− 3	− 5.5	− 7	− 7	− 6.9	− 6	− 6	− 5.7
6	. . .	. . .	− 8	− 9	− 8	− 3.5	+ 1.9	− 4	− 1	− 1	− 8	− 4.9	− 4	− 6	− 4.6
7	74 57	63 20	− 7	− 8	− 8	− 8	− 7	− 7	− 8	− 7	− 8	− 4	− 9	− 2.9	− 6.0
8	. . .	. . .	− 3	− 4	− 4	− 4	− 4	− 6	− 4	− 5	− 6	− 3	− 1	− 1	− 3.5
9	. . .	. . .	− 2	− 3	− 4.9	− 5	− 5	− 5	− 6	− 4	− 3	− 8	− 7	− 7	− 5.0
10	74 43	60 6	− 8	− 8.5	− 6	− 6	− 9	−11	−11.5	−13	−14.0	−16.5	−15	−14	−11.2
11	. . .	. . .	−12	− 9	− 6	− 7	− 4	− 7	− 6	− 6	− 7	− 5	− 7	− 4	− 7.0
12	74 36	. . .	− 7	− 7	− 4	− 8.2	− 9	− 6	− 9	− 9	−10	−10	−11	− 8	− 7.8
13	74 34	. . .	− 8.5	− 8	− 7	− 8	− 7	− 9.5	− 7	− 5	−10	−13	−10	−11.9	− 8.4
14	. . .	. . .	−10	− 4.9	− 5	− 3	− 1	− 1	0	− 1	+ 1	− 3	− 1	− 1	− 2.4
15	. . .	. . .	− 1	− 1	+ 1.5	+ 2.5	+ 7	+ 7.5	+ 6	+ 6	+ 5	+ 5.5	+ 5	+ 7	+ 4.5
16	. . .	. . .	+11	+14	+18	+15	+18	+14	+19	+14.9	+12	+11	9	− 2	+11.6
17	. . .	. . .	− 5	− 8	− 6	− 8	− 6	− 3	− 4	− 9	− 8	− 9	− 9	− 6	− 6.5
18	. . .	. . .	−10	−14.5	−11	−18	−18	− 5	− 3.5	− 5	− 7	− 6	− 5	− 9	− 8.6
19	74 47	. . .	− 8	− 6	− 8.5	−16	−10	−15	−13	−11	− 2.5	− 4	− 5	− 8	− 9.5
20	. . .	. . .	− 8	− 8	−10	−11	−11	−11.5	−16	−12	−10.5	−10	− 7	− 8	− 9.2
21	74 47	64 54	− 9	− 5	− 8	− 2	− 2.9	0	− 8	+ 2	+ 5	+ 8	+10	+15	+ 2.?
22	. . .	. . .	+15	+27	+23	+25	+30	+21	+20.5	+20.9	+23.5	+25	+22	+19	+22.0
23	. . .	. . .	+14	+12	+11	+10	+ 6	+ 7	+ 4	0	− 4	− 5	− 7	− 5	+ 3.0
24	75 2	70 22	− 3	− 6	− 6	− 5	− 6	− 3	− 1	+ 5	0	− 1	− 1	− 8	− 3.1
25	75 2	70 22	+ 6	+ 6	+ 6	+ 9	+ 6	+ 8	+ 9	+ 6	+ 5	+ 5	− 3	− 4	+ 4.6
26	. . .	. . .	− 7	− 7	− 6	−10	−10	− 6	−10	− 6	− 4.4	− 4.5	− 9	− 9	− 7.4
27	. . .	. . .	− 7.3	− 8	−10	−10	−11	−12	−12	−12.5	−16	−19	−10	−15	−12.1
28	74 44	69 38	−14	−17	−14	−18.5	−15	−20	−20	−21	−23	−22	−23	−23	−20.0
29	. . .	. . .	−20	−21	−22	−24	−29.5	−21	−20	−21	−23	−22	−22	−26	−21.6
30	. . .	. . .	−24	−24	−27	−24	−30	−30.5	−30.5	−31	−30	−27	−30	−33	−27.0
Mean	74.8	63.1	−4.83	−4.80	−4.88	−4.80	−4.43	−4.47	−4.48	−4.26	−4.72	−3.60	−3.77	−4.07	−4.16

Correction to reduce the mean of 12 to the mean of 24 readings = +0°.18.

December, 1857.

Day of the month	Lat. north	Long. west of Green.	2h	4h	6h	8h	10h	Noon	2h	4h	6h	8h	10h	Midn't.	Mean
1	74° 41′	69° 30′	−27°	−31°.5	−33°	−31°	−31°	−31°	−27°	−33°	−31°	−27°.5	−27°	−29°	−31°.4
2	. . .	. . .	23	30	30	30	30	33	30	32.5	23	33	30	33	−32.0
3	. . .	. . .	23	26	24	23	30	23	28	23	23	30.5	22	29	−27.0
4	. . .	. . .	27	28	30	28	28	30	26	27	27	26	31	22	−27.8
5	. . .	. . .	31	30.5	29	29	28	28	23	31	31	19	15	16	−24.6
6	. . .	. . .	17	17	16	14	17	17	23	21	23	23	23	23	−19.9
7	74 30	68 43	22	23	26	26	28	30	23	27	27	28	22.5	27	−27.5
8	. . .	. . .	28	23	21	19	19	23	23	23	21	21	16	21	−22.3
9	. . .	. . .	28	28	27	27	26	28	24	24	23.5	29	23.5	28	−26.7
10	74 31	68 21	27	29	28	28	27.9	27	26	23	24	27.5	28	29	−28.1
11	. . .	. . .	27	29	26	10	14	16.9	27.5	20	21	20	20	10	−21.1
12	. . .	. . .	17.5	24	19	16	17	14	14	13	13	10	13	18	−14.7
13	. . .	. . .	12	12.5	13	14	13	13	14	13	16	17	19	19	−14.6
14	74 11	67 10	20	22	22	22.9	22.8	22	24	23	23	25	24	24.5	−23.8
15	74 7	67 7	24	23	26	26	28	28	27	27	29	27	26.5	29.5	−26.9
16	. . .	. . .	27	27	27	27	23	25	26	19.5	14	16	14	12	−22.4
17	. . .	. . .	9	11.8	14	15.5	16	16	19	21	17.5	14	20	21	−14.8
18	. . .	. . .	21	22	23	22	22.8	22.5	28	22	22	24	24	27.5	−23.1
19	. . .	. . .	23	15	15.5	14	14	11.5	8	23	25	24	24.5	20	−19.8
20	74 5	66 27	17	10	14	13	11	10.5	11	12.5	8	6	8	7	−11.4
21	. . .	. . .	8	10.4	14	14	23	23.5	22.5	23	27.5	21	22	22	−22.5
22	. . .	. . .	24	24	21	23.6	23	22	23	22	20	17	14	14	−20.6
23	. . .	. . .	16	14	12	11	11.5	9.5	7.5	7.5	10	10	14	15	−12.1
24	. . .	. . .	22	20	27	22	20	20	20	22	22	22	21	20	−20.7
25	. . .	. . .	23	21.5	19	17.5	18	17	23	10	17.5	17	19	18	−19.8
26	. . .	. . .	18	17	16	15	12	17.0	17	10	19	20	14.5	16	−15.7
27	74 4	66 32	14	14	13	14	9	8	9.5	9	8.5	4	4	4	− 8.8
28	. . .	. . .	6	6	6	2.5	8	8	1	+ 3	+ 3	+ 5	9	7	− 1.8
29	. . .	. . .	8.9	6.6	11	15	16	22	22	24	25	24	27	24	−16.6
30	73 46	66 9	26	22.5	23	23.9	30	32	34	34	32	34	34	34	−31.7
31	. . .	. . .	33	35	35	36	36	34	36	36	36	35	35	35	−35.3
Mean	74.3	67.4	−22.09	−22.19	−21.47	−22.10	−21.[illegible]	−22.21	−22.48	−21.45	−22.44	−22.14	−22.16	−22.36	−22.16

Correction to reduce mean of 12 to mean of 24 observations = 0°.00.

Temperature of the Air in Shade observed on board the Yacht Fox.

(Expressed in degrees of Fahrenheit's scale.)

January, 1858.

Day of the month.	Lat. north.	Long. west of Green.	2h	4h	6h	8h	10h	Noon.	2h	4h	6h	8h	10h	Midn't.	Mean.
1	...	...	−36°	−35°	−36°.5	−35°	−35°	−33°.5	−35°	−37°	−33°	−31°.5	−30°	−27°	−37°.5
2	...	...	[illegible]	[illegible]	[illegible]	23	24	25	27	29	[illegible]	30	21.5	21	−30.0
3	...	...	25	29.5	27	24	25	21.5	30	20.5	23	22.5	24.5	25	−24.0
4	73° 43′	60° 43′	25	25	23	17	19	15	14.5	16	16	11	8.5	6	−18.6
5	...	...	6	5.5	10	10	9	10	20	10	12	21	22.5	23	−12.1
6	...	...	21.5	22	20	19	18	17.5	17	17	14.5	15	15	16	−15.0
7	...	...	15.5	15	15.5	16.5	14	19	16.5	14	15	15	15.5	15	−15.5
8	...	...	17	17.5	15	15	16	17	16	16.5	18.4	15	19	18.6	−17.5
9	...	...	15.0	16	18	20	20	19	20	25	24.5	24	24	23	−21.1
10	73 30	66 8	22	26	24	26	24	23	23	23	22	21	20	20	−23.1
11	...	...	18	14.5	18	18	18	16	18	21	11	24.5	24	24	[illegible]
12	73 34	63 34	27	25	27	25	23.5	23	20	21.5	27.5	26	20	24.5	−25.7
13	...	...	30	27.5	27	25	24	25	30	28	20.5	30	30	31	−27.7
14	...	...	31	31.5	33	35	36	34	34	33	27.5	23	20	29	−30.0
15	...	...	17	17	16.5	14	19	9.5	8	9	5	11.1	13	14	−13.4
16	...	...	14	13	18	18	11	18	14	15	15	17.5	17	17	−14.2
17	...	...	15	18	19	21	16	23	25	27	20	31	31	32	−24.1
18	73 5	63 25	34	35	35.5	35.5	38	36	30	37	38	34	34	32	−33.7
19	...	...	34	27	27.5	30.5	25	34	34	33	25	34	18	18	−30.1
20	...	...	6	9	6	9	8	4.5	9.5	19	17	19	11	11	−10.0
21	...	...	15	16	14	16.5	19	16	16	16.5	17	17.5	16	16	−16.0
22	...	...	16.5	19.5	20	26	27	30.5	31	30	29	29	29.5	29	−25.4
23	73 1	63 56	30	30	[illegible]	30	30.5	33	33	30	34	34.5	37.5	35	[illegible]
24	...	...	[illegible]	[illegible]	[illegible]	[illegible]	[illegible]	[illegible]	[illegible]	[illegible]	33	32	34	32.5	−31.5
25	...	...	[illegible]	[illegible]	[illegible]	[illegible]	[illegible]	[illegible]	34	[illegible]	37	37	36	35	−34.3
26	73 45	63 36	[illegible]	34.5	[illegible]	36	[illegible]	36	[illegible]	[illegible]	39	36	38	37	−38.1
27	...	...	[illegible]	[illegible]	34	33.5	[illegible]	[illegible]	41	31	33	34	35.5	34.5	−39.4
28	...	...	37	37	[illegible]	38.6	39	39	35	37.5	39.6	40	40.5	41.6	−39.4
29	...	...	[illegible]	39	35	35	41	41	40	43	44	44	43	43	−41.5
30	...	...	41	41	40	37	34.5	34	34.5	[illegible]	33.5	33	33	33	−34.0
31	...	...	35	34	34	34.5	31.5	36	35	34	33	35	33	31.6	−33.3
Mean	73.3	63.7	−25.61	−25.07	−24.82	−24.73	−25.20	−24.15	−24.53	−25.05	−24.57	−25.21	−25.06	−25.60	−24.94

Correction to reduce mean of 12 to mean of 24 readings = −0°.03.

February, 1858.

Day of the month.	Lat. north.	Long. west of Green.	2h	4h	6h	8h	10h	Noon.	2h	4h	6h	8h	10h	Midn't.	Mean.
1	...	...	−22°	−22°	−22°	−19°	−19°	−18°	−21°.5	−22°	−21°	−22°	−22°	−20°	−21°.0
2	72° 58′	61° 10′	20.5	20	17	16	11	10	11	5	12	15	17	19	−14.6
3	...	...	21.5	23	21.5	23.6	23	22.5	25	18	23	20	21	23	−21.4
4	72 55	61 10	30	31	22	28	26.5	25	28	27	29	29	28	28	−26.7
5	...	...	30	30	28	27	26	25	25	24	24	21	20	21	−25.1
6	...	...	21	15	19	19	16.5	15	15.5	13	14	15	17	22	−17.3
7	...	...	27.5	30	31	33	34	34	32	33	34	34	33.5	35	−32.5
8	72 53	61 33	33	34	35	37	38	39.5	39.6	38.5	38	37	37	35	−37.0
9	...	...	34	34	33	33	33.5	30	30.5	27.5	38	34	33	23	−33.5
10	...	...	24	23	20	18	16	15	12	11	10	10	8	6	−14.3
11	...	...	6	7	4.5	9	10.5	11	11.5	19	18	14	18	10	−10.0
12	...	...	6	5.5	7.5	5	6.6	7	15	16	17	17	15	14	−11.5
13	71 59	60 26	15	15	17	15	15	14	19	6	10.5	7	7.5	9	−11.6
14	...	...	6	6	6	7	7	5	5	5	5	6	7	1.5	− 5.9
15	72 20	61 01	6.5	10	10	10.5	5.0	6.5	11	11	11	19	19	11	−10.5
16	71 28	...	11	10	5	6.5	4	5	5	6	6	10	11	10	− 8.4
17	71 15	60 46	11	11	12	12	13	13	15	17	16	18	19	12	−16.1
18	71 6	...	13	13	12	11	10	8.5	6	10	10	11	11	10	−10.5
19	72 8	60 46	7	7	6	5	3	1	1	1.5	2	4	5	13	− 5.9
20	...	...	14	15	10	7	5.5	5.5	1	2	1	3	4	3	− 5.5
21	...	...	5	2	6	7	5	6	7.5	13	15	12	14	15	−10.5
22	...	...	16	15.5	10.5	17	17	19	15	18	15	16	14	14	−15.3
23	70 55	60 55	16	12	15	15	14.5	13	15	14.5	16	16	16	16	−15.0
24	...	...	15	13	11	21	12	12.5	13	21	19	23	11	13.5	−15.6
25	...	...	14	14	10	16	15	15	15	20	15	15	14	16	−14.5
26	...	...	15	16	10	15.5	13	5	7	10	15	21	14	20	−13.8
27	...	...	22.5	[illegible]	[illegible]	[illegible]	[illegible]	15	14	5.5	5.5	5	10	5	−15.7
28	69 50	66 43	5	+ 5	+ 6.5	+ 5.5	+10	+11	+ 7.5	+ 5	5	0	9	0.5	+ 4.0
Mean	71.5	60.5	−16.35	−16.15	−15.30	−15.56	−15.14	−14.11	−13.94	−14.60	−15.63	−15.94	−15.43	−15.79	−15.33

Correction to refer mean of 12 to mean of 24 observations = −0°.03.

TEMPERATURE OF THE AIR IN SHADE OBSERVED ON BOARD THE YACHT FOX.
(Expressed in degrees of Fahrenheit's scale.)

March, 1858.

Day of the month.	Lat. north.	Long. west of Green.	2h	4h	6h	8h	10h	Noon.	2h	4h	6h	8h	10h	Midn't.	Mean.
1	...	...	− 5°	− 5°	+ 4°	+ 5°	+ 5°.5	+ 5°.5	+10°	+15°.5	+16°	+15°	+ 6°	+ 3°	+ 7°.0
2	...	...	+ 8	+ 8	+ 9	+ 3	+ 2	+ 8	+ 2.9	+ 1.5	+ 0.5	+ 2	0	− 8	+ 1.9
3	...	...	− 7	− 7	−11	− 4.5	− 8	− 1	− 5	0	+ 2	+ 8	+ 8	+19	− 0.5
4	...	...	+13	+ 7	+ 4	+ 1	+ 1	0	− 8	− 1	− 7	− 8.5	−31	−18	− 1.7
5	70° 6'	55° 20'	−12.5	−12.9	−19	−18	−12.5	−10	− 9	− 8	−23	−18	−19	−22	−13.0
6	70 1	...	−22	−28	−25.5	−23	−18	−19	−14	−15	−19.5	−23.5	−23	−28	−27.5
7	69 55	59 11	−25	−24.5	−25	−23.5	−20	−24	−15	−18	−18	−16.8	−18	−29	−23.1
8	69 49	...	−18	−19	−11.9	−15.5	−14	−14.5	−18	−11.5	−17	−20	−18	−17	−14.2
9	...	...	−17	−17	−15	−12	− 6.6	− 3	+ 2.9	+ 2.5	+ 8	− 1	+ 1	+ 4	− 4.8
10	69 41	...	+ 4	+ 1	+ 8	+10	+22.5	+24.6	+22	+27	+20	+15	+20	+25	+17.4
11	...	...	+25.9	+25.7	+20	+28	+31	+32	+32	+30	+24	+20	+17	+17	+28.1
12	...	...	+19	+22	+18	+20	+26	+21.9	+27.9	+15	+19	+11	+11	+ 8	+20.5
13	...	...	+10	+11	+11	+11.5	+10	+15	+10	+18	+ 2	− 6	− 8	−10	+ 1.8
14	68 55	60 6	− 8	− 8	− 8	− 7	− 7	− 6.5	− 4	− 9	−15	−14	−15	−17	− 9.4
15	...	...	−25	−20	−18	−18	−16.5	−15	−14	−18	−18	−18	−19	−18	−17.4
16	68 28	58 14	−18	−20	−20	−14	−14.5	−18	−10	−10	−11.5	−18	−11	−11	−14.9
17	68 31	...	−11.8	−10.5	− 4	− 2.5	− 9.5	− 4	− 8	− 9	− 2.9	−10	−11	−29	− 8.8
18	68 25	55 56	−12	−12	−18	−12	− 7.5	− 6	− 3	− 8	− 6	− 5.9	− 6.0	− 7	− 7.5
19	68 20	...	− 9	− 8	− 9	− 5	− 8	− 4	− 8	− 2.5	− 2.5	− 8	−10	− 3	− 6.5
20	68 16	56 43	− 4	− 5	− 1	− 4	− 6	+ 1	+ 2.5	+ 2.5	0	− 8	− 8	−18	− 2.5
21	68 14	...	−21.5	−15	−11	−25	− 4	− 5.6	− 1	+ 2	− 8	− 8	0	0	− 4.7
22	...	...	+ 1	+ 2	+ 6	+ 6	+ 8	+12	+14	+14.5	+17	+16.5	+22	+28	+12.5
23	...	...	+25	+24	+29	+20.5	+25	+29	+20	+15	+11	+ 8.5	+ 2.0	+ 9	+15.9
24	...	...	+ 7	+ 7	+ 7	+ 8.5	+10	+10	+ 8.5	+ 2.9	+ 7	+ 8	+ 8	+ 9	+ 7.8
25	68 10	55 50	+ 1	− 8	− 3	+ 8	+ 6	+ 4	+ 5	+ 2.9	+ 1.5	0	0	− 1	+ 1.8
26	68 09	...	− 1	− 8	− 8	− 8	− 7	− 7.9	− 7	− 2.5	− 8	−18	−19	−20	− 7.7
27	68 44	56 57	−31.5	−16	−27	−24	−25	−13.5	−21	−21	−22	−14	−15	−17.9	−14.1
28	68 36	...	−13.5	−15.5	−16	−21	− 8	− 8.5	− 8	− 4	− 7	− 7	− 2	−22	− 8.8
29	68 37	55 29	−15	−12	−15	− 7	− 7	− 6.5	− 8	− 8	−20	−15	−14	−15	−10.3
30	68 28	56 31	−14	−13.5	−21.5	− 5	+ 3.5	+ 4.5	+ 4	− 2	− 4	−19	−14	−18	− 6.7
31	68 20	...	−22	−35	−28.1	−22	−31	−29	−16.8	−19	−20	−29.9	−23.0	−27	−22.7
Mean	69.4	58.1	−5.05	−4.82	−5.05	−1.44	−1.24	+0.41	+0.14	−0.13	−2.48	−4.79	−5.57	−6.62	−2.81

Correction to solar mean of 12 to mean of 24 observations = +0°.22.

April, 1858.

Day of the month.	Lat. north.	Long. west of Green.	2h	4h	6h	8h	10h	Noon.	2h	4h	6h	8h	10h	Midn't.	Mean of 6 obs'ns.	Mean of 12 obs'ns.
1	68° 17'	59° 10'	−35°	−37°	−35°	−13°	− 5°	− 7°	− 4°.5	− 8°	− 9°.5	−17°	−17°	−17°	−14°.2	−14°.8
2	68 17	...	−19	−20	−15	−12	−10.5	− 8.5	− 6	− 2.6	−15	−11	−16	−18	−12.7	−12.0
3	68 5	58 55	−15	−15	−10.2	−14	− 6	− 7.4	− 8	− 8	−11.4	−18	−14	−14	−11.5	−11.8
4	...	...	−15	−18	−18	−14.8	−12.5	−11	− 5.5	− 8	−10	−15	−21.8	−18.5	−18.0	−13.3
5	...	...	−12.8	−12	−11	− 6	− 4	− 1	+ 3	− 4	− 7	− 5.9	− 9	−20	− 8.0	− 7.3
6	67 18	58 17	− 5	− 9	− 8	− 4	− 9	0	+ 2	+ 4.5	− 8	− 6	− 9	− 8	− 4.1	− 4.5
7	...	...	− 5	− 5	− 6	+ 3	+18	+10.0	+15	+ 9	+ 9	+ 4	+ 4	+ 4	+ 6.2	+ 4.0
8	...	...	+ 4	+ 4	+ 2.5	+ 6	+ 1	+ 1	+ 4	− 2	− 2	− 5	− 7	− 0.6	− 0.4	0.0
9	66 52	58 31	− 8	−10	− 8	− 3.5	0	+ 1	+ 1.5	0	− 8	− 4	− 8	− 9	− 2.7	− 3.9
10	66 46	58 20	− 9	− 7	− 9	− 1	+ 8	+ 9	+19	+ 9	+ 2.6	+ 3	− 1.9	− 1.9	+ 2.7	+ 2.4
11	66 45	...	− 8	− 7	− 1	+ 9	+11	+20	+19	+18	+24	+ 6.5	+ 1	+ 4	+ 9.0	+ 7.8
12	66 33	58 9	0	− 1	− 2.0	− 3	− 2.6	− 1	0	− 1.9	− 5.5	− 7.4	− 8	−19	− 4.0	− 3.4
13	66 28	58 18	−10.8	−10	− 5	− 3	+ 1	+ 5	+ 9	+10	+ 5.5	+ 9	+ 1.9	− 8	+ 0.9	+ 0.7
14	64 53	56 4	− 5	− 3	+ 1	+ 8	+10	+17	+12	+11	+ 6	+ 4	+ 1	0	+ 6.0	+ 4.5
15	64 17	57 55	+ 1	+ 1.5	+ 8	+ 2.6	+ 3	+ 5.5	+ 5.5	+ 4.9	+ 4	+ 1.6	0	− 0.5	+ 3.5	+ 3.5
16	65 58	...	0	− 1.5	+ 1	+ 4.5	+ 8	+10	+11.5	+14	+10	+ 9	+ 5	+ 8	+ 7.6	+ 7.4
17	65 55	56 24	+ 7	+ 2.5	+ 7	+ 6	+14	+18	+18	+15	+15	+16	+14	+14	+10.1	+12.0
18	64 50	55 36	..	+11	..	+13	..	+18.5	..	+18	..	+17	..	+16	+15.2	+15.1
19	64 15	...	..	+16	..	+15.9	..	+18	..	+16	..	+20	..	+ 8	+15.8	+13.1
20	64 23	55 48	..	+ 9	..	+18	..	+16	..	+14	..	+18	..	+19	+15.7	+12.6
21	64 10	55 46	..	+12	..	+13	..	+17	..	+17	..	+ 8.1	..	+ 7	+12.0	+12.4
22	63 31	54 56	..	+ 9	..	+ 6	..	+15	..	+15.5	..	+18	..	+ 7	+ 8.7	+ 8.6
23	63 41	55 56	..	+ 2	..	+12	..	+ 8.6	..	+22	..	+18.9	..	+19	+14.6	+14.7
24	...	...	..	+17	..	+25	..	+20.5	..	+33	..	+33	..	+30	+17.0	+27.0
25	63 40	55 36	..	+25	..	+30	..	+34	..	+31	..	+25	..	+23	+29.9	+27.8
26	63 47	53 28	..	+29	..	+28.6	..	+30.5	..	+28	..	+25	..	+24	+28.0	+28.1
27	63 14	53 41	..	+28	..	+25	..	+20	..	+30	..	+26	..	+23	+28.4	+26.7
28	63 29	53 20	..	+28	..	+26	..	+29	..	+26	..	+25	..	+26	+26.8	+26.3
29	63 20	53 30	..	+21	..	+22	..	+20	..	+26	..	+26	..	+23	+24.7	+24.7
30	63 20	53 30	..	+27	..	+31	..	+35	..	+30	..	−36	..	+34	+32.5	+32.4
Mean.	65.0	57.7	+2.05	+8.35	+4.13	+7.10	+10.34	+12.63	+13.37	+12.46	+10.30	+7.77	+6.14	+5.30	..	+8.04

Correction to solar mean of 12 to mean of 24 daily readings = +0°.[illegible].

Temperature of the Air in Shade (observed on board the Yacht Fox.)
(Expressed in degrees of Fahrenheit's scale.)

May, 1858.

Day of the month.	Latitude north.	Longitude west of Greenwich.	[illegible]	[illegible]	Noon.	[illegible]	[illegible]	Midnight.	Mean.
1	[illegible]	[illegible]	[illegible]	[illegible]	[illegible]	[illegible]	[illegible]	[illegible]	[illegible]
2	[illegible]	[illegible]	[illegible]	[illegible]	[illegible]	[illegible]	[illegible]	[illegible]	[illegible]
3	[illegible]	[illegible]	[illegible]	[illegible]	[illegible]	[illegible]	[illegible]	[illegible]	[illegible]
4	[illegible]	[illegible]	[illegible]	[illegible]	[illegible]	[illegible]	[illegible]	[illegible]	[illegible]
5	[illegible]	[illegible]	[illegible]	[illegible]	[illegible]	[illegible]	[illegible]	[illegible]	[illegible]
6	[illegible]	[illegible]	[illegible]	[illegible]	[illegible]	[illegible]	[illegible]	[illegible]	[illegible]
7	[illegible]	[illegible]	[illegible]	[illegible]	[illegible]	[illegible]	[illegible]	[illegible]	[illegible]
8	[illegible]	[illegible]	[illegible]	[illegible]	[illegible]	[illegible]	[illegible]	[illegible]	[illegible]
9	[illegible]	[illegible]	[illegible]	[illegible]	[illegible]	[illegible]	[illegible]	[illegible]	[illegible]
10	[illegible]	[illegible]	[illegible]	[illegible]	[illegible]	[illegible]	[illegible]	[illegible]	[illegible]
11	Whalefish Islands		[illegible]	[illegible]	[illegible]	[illegible]	[illegible]	[illegible]	[illegible]
12	[illegible]	[illegible]	[illegible]	[illegible]	[illegible]	[illegible]	[illegible]	[illegible]	[illegible]
13	[illegible]	[illegible]	[illegible]	[illegible]	[illegible]	[illegible]	[illegible]	[illegible]	[illegible]
14	[illegible]	[illegible]	[illegible]	[illegible]	[illegible]	[illegible]	[illegible]	[illegible]	[illegible]
15	[illegible]	[illegible]	[illegible]	[illegible]	[illegible]	[illegible]	[illegible]	[illegible]	[illegible]
16	[illegible]	[illegible]	[illegible]	[illegible]	[illegible]	[illegible]	[illegible]	[illegible]	[illegible]
17	[illegible]	[illegible]	[illegible]	[illegible]	[illegible]	[illegible]	[illegible]	[illegible]	[illegible]
18	[illegible]	[illegible]	[illegible]	[illegible]	[illegible]	[illegible]	[illegible]	[illegible]	[illegible]
19	[illegible]	[illegible]	[illegible]	[illegible]	[illegible]	[illegible]	[illegible]	[illegible]	[illegible]
20	[illegible]	[illegible]	[illegible]	[illegible]	[illegible]	[illegible]	[illegible]	[illegible]	[illegible]
21	[illegible]	[illegible]	[illegible]	[illegible]	[illegible]	[illegible]	[illegible]	[illegible]	[illegible]
22	[illegible]	[illegible]	[illegible]	[illegible]	[illegible]	[illegible]	[illegible]	[illegible]	[illegible]
23	[illegible]	[illegible]	[illegible]	[illegible]	[illegible]	[illegible]	[illegible]	[illegible]	[illegible]
24	[illegible]	[illegible]	[illegible]	[illegible]	[illegible]	[illegible]	[illegible]	[illegible]	[illegible]
25	[illegible]	[illegible]	[illegible]	[illegible]	[illegible]	[illegible]	[illegible]	[illegible]	[illegible]
26	[illegible]	[illegible]	[illegible]	[illegible]	[illegible]	[illegible]	[illegible]	[illegible]	[illegible]
27	[illegible]	[illegible]	[illegible]	[illegible]	[illegible]	[illegible]	[illegible]	[illegible]	[illegible]
28	[illegible]	[illegible]	[illegible]	[illegible]	[illegible]	[illegible]	[illegible]	[illegible]	[illegible]
29	[illegible]	[illegible]	[illegible]	[illegible]	[illegible]	[illegible]	[illegible]	[illegible]	[illegible]
30	[illegible]	[illegible]	[illegible]	[illegible]	[illegible]	[illegible]	[illegible]	[illegible]	[illegible]
31	Off Upernivik		[illegible]	[illegible]	[illegible]	[illegible]	[illegible]	[illegible]	[illegible]
Mean	[illegible]	[illegible]	[illegible]	[illegible]	[illegible]	[illegible]	[illegible]	[illegible]	[illegible]

[illegible]

June, 1858.

Day of the month.	Latitude north.	Longitude west of Greenwich.	[illegible]	[illegible]	Noon.	[illegible]	[illegible]	Midnight.	Mean.
1	Off Upernivik		[illegible]	[illegible]	[illegible]	[illegible]	[illegible]	[illegible]	[illegible]
2	[illegible]	[illegible]	[illegible]	[illegible]	[illegible]	[illegible]	[illegible]	[illegible]	[illegible]
3	[illegible]	[illegible]	[illegible]	[illegible]	[illegible]	[illegible]	[illegible]	[illegible]	[illegible]
4	[illegible]	[illegible]	[illegible]	[illegible]	[illegible]	[illegible]	[illegible]	[illegible]	[illegible]
5	[illegible]	[illegible]	[illegible]	[illegible]	[illegible]	[illegible]	[illegible]	[illegible]	[illegible]
6	[illegible]	[illegible]	[illegible]	[illegible]	[illegible]	[illegible]	[illegible]	[illegible]	[illegible]
7	[illegible]	[illegible]	[illegible]	[illegible]	[illegible]	[illegible]	[illegible]	[illegible]	[illegible]
8	[illegible]	[illegible]	[illegible]	[illegible]	[illegible]	[illegible]	[illegible]	[illegible]	[illegible]
9	[illegible]	[illegible]	[illegible]	[illegible]	[illegible]	[illegible]	[illegible]	[illegible]	[illegible]
10	[illegible]	[illegible]	[illegible]	[illegible]	[illegible]	[illegible]	[illegible]	[illegible]	[illegible]
11	[illegible]	[illegible]	[illegible]	[illegible]	[illegible]	[illegible]	[illegible]	[illegible]	[illegible]
12	[illegible]	[illegible]	[illegible]	[illegible]	[illegible]	[illegible]	[illegible]	[illegible]	[illegible]
13	[illegible]	[illegible]	[illegible]	[illegible]	[illegible]	[illegible]	[illegible]	[illegible]	[illegible]
14	[illegible]	[illegible]	[illegible]	[illegible]	[illegible]	[illegible]	[illegible]	[illegible]	[illegible]
15	[illegible]	[illegible]	[illegible]	[illegible]	[illegible]	[illegible]	[illegible]	[illegible]	[illegible]
16	[illegible]	[illegible]	[illegible]	[illegible]	[illegible]	[illegible]	[illegible]	[illegible]	[illegible]
17	[illegible]	[illegible]	[illegible]	[illegible]	[illegible]	[illegible]	[illegible]	[illegible]	[illegible]
18	[illegible]	[illegible]	[illegible]	[illegible]	[illegible]	[illegible]	[illegible]	[illegible]	[illegible]
19	[illegible]	[illegible]	[illegible]	[illegible]	[illegible]	[illegible]	[illegible]	[illegible]	[illegible]
20	[illegible]	[illegible]	[illegible]	[illegible]	[illegible]	[illegible]	[illegible]	[illegible]	[illegible]
21	[illegible]	[illegible]	[illegible]	[illegible]	[illegible]	[illegible]	[illegible]	[illegible]	[illegible]
22	[illegible]	[illegible]	[illegible]	[illegible]	[illegible]	[illegible]	[illegible]	[illegible]	[illegible]
23	[illegible]	[illegible]	[illegible]	[illegible]	[illegible]	[illegible]	[illegible]	[illegible]	[illegible]
24	[illegible]	[illegible]	[illegible]	[illegible]	[illegible]	[illegible]	[illegible]	[illegible]	[illegible]
25	[illegible]	[illegible]	[illegible]	[illegible]	[illegible]	[illegible]	[illegible]	[illegible]	[illegible]
26	[illegible]	[illegible]	[illegible]	[illegible]	[illegible]	[illegible]	[illegible]	[illegible]	[illegible]
27	[illegible]	[illegible]	[illegible]	[illegible]	[illegible]	[illegible]	[illegible]	[illegible]	[illegible]
28	[illegible]	[illegible]	[illegible]	[illegible]	[illegible]	[illegible]	[illegible]	[illegible]	[illegible]
29	[illegible]	[illegible]	[illegible]	[illegible]	[illegible]	[illegible]	[illegible]	[illegible]	[illegible]
30	[illegible]	[illegible]	[illegible]	[illegible]	[illegible]	[illegible]	[illegible]	[illegible]	[illegible]
Mean	[illegible]	[illegible]	[illegible]	[illegible]	[illegible]	[illegible]	[illegible]	[illegible]	[illegible]

[illegible]

Temperature of the Air in Shade observed on board the Yacht Fox.
(Expressed in degrees of Fahrenheit's scale.)

July, 1858.

Day of the month.	Latitude north.	Longitude west of Greenwich.	4h	8h	Noon.	4h	8h	Midn't.	Mean.
1	75° 5[illegible]'	67° 26'	33°	36°	37°	41°	34°	33°	+36°.7
2	75 13	67 11	33	34	41	40	34	31	35.8
3	75 31	70 42	32.5	33	34	34	31.5	31	32.7
4	75 34	70 56	33	39	33	34	31.5	33	33.1
5	76 44	70 28	35	36	36	35	35	37	35.7
6	75 17	73 35	33	33	34	33	31	33	32.7
7	76 28	72 33	34	36	37	36	36	34	35.3
8	75 30	73 57	35	31.5	36	36	33	34	34.4
9	75 17	75 47	33	35	35	36	34	34	35.0
10	76 28	75 46	35	37	38	38	35	38	37.5
11	75 9	74 46	36	37	39	40	36	34	36.7
12	74 41	78 56	33	33	33	38	33	33	34.0
13	74 56	80 40	33	31	33.5	33	35	34	33.2
14	...	...	35	36	40	36	36	33	36.0
15	74 28	80 57	35	36	37	33	33	35	35.3
16	74 24	81 56	33	36	38.5	36	36	34	35.6
17	74 8	83 0	36	37	44	37	36	33	36.9
18	73 46	78 10	33	38	38	38	33	31	34.8
19	73 46	74 38	32	38	37	38	36	34	36.2
20	73 58	76 33	38	38.5	46	46	36	37	40.1
21	73 56	75 38	36	36	44	43	38	36	39.8
22	74 0	76 6	39	40	46	44	39.5	36	40.9
23	74 6	77 43	34	36	43	46	41	37	39.3
24	73 54	74 56	37	46	43	46	42	39	43.0
25	73 36	77 0	34	46	47.5	43	42	36	41.4
26	73 6	75 40	36	45	49	46	40	37	42.2
27	...	...	37	33	41	40	42	36	38.3
28	73 40	...	33	38	42	38	36	33	37.6
29	73 61	76 39	34	35	35	35	33	34	35.3
30	73 13	76 13	34	36	35	36	33	33	35.5
31	73 57	...	37	38	40	36	36	36	37.5
Mean	74.6	73.4	+34.57	+36.39	+39.16	+38.44	+36.14	+34.74	+36.61

Correction to refer mean of 6 to mean of 24 observations = —0°.03.

August, 1858.

Day of the month.	Latitude north.	Longitude west of Greenwich.	4h	8h	Noon.	4h	8h	Midn't.	Mean.
1	73° 47'	77° 9'	34°	37°	36°	38°	39°	33°	+36°.5
2	73 49	75 56	37	38	36	40	38	37	37.7
3	73 45	76 34	36	38	36.5	39	37	38	37.4
4	73 44	...	37	37	39.5	40	39	38	38.4
5	73 44	76 30	37	38	40	37	38	36	37.8
6	73 54	75 30	35	35	38	40	37	36	37.3
7	73 40	77 15	36	37	36	36	33	34	36.0
8	73 55	79 23	33	33	35	35	36	33	34.3
9	74 16	87 30	34	33	36	34	34	34	33.8
10	74 17	88 30	35	34	34	33	36	33	35.0
11	...	...	33	34	36	36	37	36	36.3
12	...	...	32	33	41	44	43	38	40.0
13	...	...	35	43	40	38	36	35	38.7
14	...	...	33	46	41	40	34	36	39.8
15	...	...	30	39	40	36	36	33	37.3
16	...	...	33	37	33	35	36	34	33.7
17	74 11	86 35	33	34	38	33	33	31.5	34.3
18	74 19	92 33	31.5	31	32	30.5	34	32	32.8
	Port Leopold								
19			36	33	33	32	33	32	33.0
20	73 41	91 56	33	33	33	33	33	32	32.7
21	73 30	94 9	33	35	33	34	33	31	32.8
	In Depot Bay								
22			33	31.5	34	33	32	33	32.9
	In Bellot Straits								
23			33	32	35	30	32	33	34.1
24	71 56	94 36	31	33	33	33	33	32	32.6
25	73 30	94 6	35	35	36	34	30	32	33.5
26	73 54	96 13	30.5	33	33	31	33	33	32.3
27	71 56	93 57	32	35	33	31	34	33	31.7
28	71 50	93 39	33	33	29.5	30	30	31	32.1
	Depot Bay								
29			33	33	33	33	31	30	32.3
30	73 00	94 16	34.5	34	30	33	33	37	33.1
31	Port Kennedy		35	30	30	30	29	33	29.3
Mean	73.1	84.5	+33.56	+34.44	+35.40	+35.13	+34.35	+33.57	+34.53

The correction to refer mean of 6 to mean of 24 observations becomes zero for this month.

TEMPERATURE OF THE AIR IN SHADE OBSERVED ON BOARD THE YACHT FOX.

(Expressed in degrees of Fahrenheit's scale.)

September, 1858.

Day of the month.	Latitude north.	Longitude west of Greenwich.	4h	8h	Noon.	4h	8h	Midn't.	Mean.
1	Head of Port Kennedy		[illegible]	[illegible]	[illegible]	[illegible]	[illegible]	[illegible]	+30°.6
2	"	"	[illegible]	[illegible]	[illegible]	[illegible]	[illegible]	[illegible]	27.0
3	"	"	[illegible]	[illegible]	[illegible]	[illegible]	[illegible]	[illegible]	[illegible]
4	"	"	[illegible]	[illegible]	[illegible]	[illegible]	[illegible]	[illegible]	[illegible]
5	"	"	[illegible]	[illegible]	[illegible]	[illegible]	[illegible]	[illegible]	[illegible]
6	Near Possession Bluff		[illegible]	[illegible]	[illegible]	[illegible]	[illegible]	[illegible]	[illegible]
7	"	"	[illegible]	32.9	[illegible]	[illegible]	[illegible]	[illegible]	[illegible]
8	"	"	[illegible]	[illegible]	30.3	[illegible]	31.5	[illegible]	[illegible]
9	[illegible]	[illegible]	[illegible]	[illegible]	[illegible]	[illegible]	[illegible]	[illegible]	[illegible]
10	[illegible]	[illegible]	[illegible]	[illegible]	[illegible]	[illegible]	[illegible]	[illegible]	[illegible]
11	Port Kennedy		[illegible]	[illegible]	[illegible]	[illegible]	[illegible]	[illegible]	[illegible]
12	[illegible]	[illegible]	[illegible]	[illegible]	[illegible]	[illegible]	[illegible]	[illegible]	[illegible]
13	[illegible]	[illegible]	[illegible]	[illegible]	[illegible]	[illegible]	[illegible]	[illegible]	[illegible]
14	[illegible]	[illegible]	[illegible]	[illegible]	[illegible]	[illegible]	[illegible]	[illegible]	[illegible]
15	[illegible]	[illegible]	[illegible]	[illegible]	[illegible]	[illegible]	[illegible]	[illegible]	[illegible]
16	[illegible]	[illegible]	[illegible]	[illegible]	[illegible]	[illegible]	[illegible]	[illegible]	[illegible]
17	[illegible]	[illegible]	[illegible]	[illegible]	[illegible]	[illegible]	[illegible]	[illegible]	[illegible]
18	Bellot Straits		[illegible]	[illegible]	[illegible]	[illegible]	[illegible]	[illegible]	[illegible]
19	"	"	[illegible]	[illegible]	[illegible]	[illegible]	[illegible]	[illegible]	[illegible]
20	"	"	[illegible]	[illegible]	[illegible]	[illegible]	[illegible]	[illegible]	[illegible]
21	"	"	[illegible]	[illegible]	[illegible]	[illegible]	[illegible]	[illegible]	[illegible]
22	"	"	[illegible]	[illegible]	[illegible]	[illegible]	[illegible]	[illegible]	[illegible]
23	"	"	[illegible]	[illegible]	[illegible]	[illegible]	[illegible]	[illegible]	[illegible]
24	"	"	[illegible]	[illegible]	[illegible]	[illegible]	[illegible]	[illegible]	[illegible]
25	"	"	[illegible]	[illegible]	[illegible]	[illegible]	[illegible]	[illegible]	[illegible]
26	"	"	[illegible]	[illegible]	[illegible]	[illegible]	[illegible]	[illegible]	[illegible]
27	72 16	"	[illegible]	[illegible]	[illegible]	[illegible]	[illegible]	[illegible]	[illegible]
28	Port Kennedy		[illegible]	[illegible]	[illegible]	[illegible]	[illegible]	[illegible]	[illegible]
29		"	[illegible]	[illegible]	[illegible]	[illegible]	[illegible]	[illegible]	[illegible]
30		"	[illegible]	[illegible]	[illegible]	[illegible]	[illegible]	[illegible]	[illegible]
Mean	72.0	94.4	[illegible]	[illegible]	[illegible]	[illegible]	[illegible]	[illegible]	[illegible]

Correction to make mean of 6 to mean of 24 readings [illegible].

October, 1858.

Day of the month.	Latitude north.	Longitude west of Greenwich.	4h	8h	Noon.	4h	8h	Midn't.	Mean.
1	Port Kennedy		[illegible]	[illegible]	[illegible]	[illegible]	[illegible]	[illegible]	[illegible]
2	72° 01'	94° 14'	[illegible]	[illegible]	[illegible]	[illegible]	[illegible]	[illegible]	[illegible]
3	Winter Quarters		[illegible]	[illegible]	[illegible]	[illegible]	[illegible]	[illegible]	[illegible]
4	"	"	[illegible]	[illegible]	[illegible]	[illegible]	[illegible]	[illegible]	[illegible]
5	"	"	[illegible]	[illegible]	[illegible]	[illegible]	[illegible]	[illegible]	[illegible]
6	"	"	[illegible]	[illegible]	[illegible]	[illegible]	[illegible]	[illegible]	[illegible]
7	"	"	[illegible]	14.5	[illegible]	[illegible]	[illegible]	[illegible]	[illegible]
8	"	"	[illegible]	[illegible]	[illegible]	[illegible]	[illegible]	[illegible]	[illegible]
9	"	"	[illegible]	[illegible]	[illegible]	[illegible]	[illegible]	[illegible]	[illegible]
10	"	"	[illegible]	[illegible]	[illegible]	[illegible]	[illegible]	[illegible]	[illegible]
11	"	"	[illegible]	[illegible]	[illegible]	[illegible]	[illegible]	[illegible]	[illegible]
12	"	"	[illegible]	[illegible]	[illegible]	[illegible]	[illegible]	[illegible]	[illegible]
13	"	"	[illegible]	[illegible]	[illegible]	[illegible]	[illegible]	[illegible]	[illegible]
14	"	"	[illegible]	[illegible]	[illegible]	[illegible]	[illegible]	[illegible]	[illegible]
15	"	"	[illegible]	[illegible]	[illegible]	[illegible]	[illegible]	[illegible]	[illegible]
16	"	"	[illegible]	[illegible]	[illegible]	[illegible]	[illegible]	[illegible]	[illegible]
17	"	"	[illegible]	[illegible]	[illegible]	[illegible]	[illegible]	[illegible]	[illegible]
18	"	"	[illegible]	[illegible]	[illegible]	[illegible]	[illegible]	[illegible]	[illegible]
19	"	"	[illegible]	[illegible]	[illegible]	[illegible]	[illegible]	[illegible]	[illegible]
20	"	"	[illegible]	[illegible]	[illegible]	[illegible]	[illegible]	[illegible]	[illegible]
21	"	"	[illegible]	[illegible]	[illegible]	[illegible]	[illegible]	[illegible]	[illegible]
22	"	"	[illegible]	[illegible]	[illegible]	[illegible]	[illegible]	[illegible]	[illegible]
23	"	"	[illegible]	[illegible]	[illegible]	[illegible]	[illegible]	[illegible]	[illegible]
24	"	"	[illegible]	[illegible]	[illegible]	[illegible]	[illegible]	[illegible]	[illegible]
25	"	"	[illegible]	[illegible]	[illegible]	[illegible]	[illegible]	[illegible]	[illegible]
26	"	"	[illegible]	[illegible]	[illegible]	[illegible]	[illegible]	[illegible]	[illegible]
27	"	"	[illegible]	[illegible]	[illegible]	[illegible]	[illegible]	[illegible]	[illegible]
28	"	"	[illegible]	[illegible]	[illegible]	[illegible]	[illegible]	[illegible]	[illegible]
29	"	"	[illegible]	[illegible]	[illegible]	[illegible]	[illegible]	[illegible]	[illegible]
30	"	"	[illegible]	[illegible]	[illegible]	[illegible]	[illegible]	[illegible]	[illegible]
31	"	"	[illegible]	[illegible]	[illegible]	[illegible]	[illegible]	[illegible]	[illegible]
Mean	72.0	94.2	[illegible]	[illegible]	[illegible]	[illegible]	[illegible]	[illegible]	[illegible]

Correction to make mean of 6 to mean of 24 readings [illegible].

TEMPERATURE OF THE AIR IN SHADE OBSERVED ON BOARD THE YACHT FOX.
(Expressed in degrees of Fahrenheit's scale.)

November, 1858.

Day of the month.	Lat. north.	Long. west of Green.	2h	4h	6h	8h	10h	Noon.	2h	4h	6h	8h	10h	Midn't.	Mean.
1	Port Kennedy		+6°	+5°	+5°	+9°	+10°	+12°	+12°	+9°	+2°	+11°	+11°	+11°	+8.3
2	72° 01'	94° 14'	+10	+12	+12	+10	+3	−3	−1.6	−11	−12	−12	−8	−7	−1.0
3	Winter Quarters		−6	−5	−5	−8	−9	−15	−14	−8	−4	−15	−15	−15	−9.7
4	″	″	−14	−14	−11	−14	−13	−16	−11	−11	−11	−11	−10	−11	−12.3
5	″	″	−11	−12	−14	−12	−15.5	−15	−16	−16	−16	−15	−16	−11	−14.0
6	″	″	−10	−9	−5	−3	+5	+8	+6	+5	−4	−4	−4	−2	−0.6
7	″	″	−16	−16	−16	−16	−15	−15	−11	−13	+1	−9	−12	−12	−12.5
8	″	″	−12	−12	−13	−12	−12	−10	−11	−11	−11	−11	−11	−11	−11.4
9	″	″	−14	−14	−14	−12	−11	−9	−9	−7	−7	−7	−8	−12	−10.3
10	″	″	−12	−14	−16	−17	−14	−17	−20	−21	−16	−17	−17	−17	−16.8
11	″	″	−16	−15	−14	−14	−13	−12	−12	−12	−9	−9	−7	−7	−11.4
12	″	″	−7	−7	−10	−12	−10.5	−13	−14	−13	−13	−13	−15	−16	−12.0
13	″	″	−13	−10	−9	−8	−7	−7	−7.6	−9	−10	−11	−10	−9	−9.2
14	″	″	−7	−7	−11	−8	−11	−13	−16	−17	−24	−27	−21	−20	−17.0
15	″	″	−30	−23	−21	−21	−21	−20	−23	−20	−21	−21	−20	−24	−20.1
16	″	″	−24	−24	−22	−22	−20	−21	−11	−16	−16	−14	−13	−11	−17.9
17	″	″	−6	−2	+1	+4	+6	+2	−6	−6	−4	+1	+3	+6	−0.3
18	″	″	+6	+7	+9	+11	+11	+10	+8	+8	+10	+10	+10	+7	+8.1
19	″	″	+8	+7	+13	+12	+13	+13	+11	+18	+13	+11	+9	+6	+11.0
20	″	″	+2	+9	+11	+10	+12	+12	+4	+2	−8	−3	−8	−8	+3.6
21	″	″	−8	−5	+8	−1	−8	+3	+1	+6	+4	+3	−1	−8	−0.3
22	″	″	−7	−10	−10	−14	−16	−17	−17	−18	−23	−23	−22	−23	−16.6
23	″	″	−21	−22	−21	−20	−12	−21	−22	−21	−22	−25	−21	−25	−21.9
24	″	″	−24	−25	−27	−27	−22	−22	−23	−23	−23	−26	−26	−26	−23.7
25	″	″	−28	−21	−25	−26	−22	−23	−22	−25	−25	−26	−28	−29	−24.6
26	″	″	−26	−24	−26	−26	−29	−28	−25	−27	−27	−27	−29	−21	−24.9
27	″	″	−25	−22	−21	−21	−21	−21.5	−23	−27	−27	−27	−24	−28	−21.8
28	″	″	−25	−25	−21	−20	−20	−20	−19	−19	−17	−16	−16	−16	−19.6
29	″	″	−16	−16	−18	−16	−14	−11	−10	−10	−10	−9	−8	−8	−12.0
30	″	″	−6	−9	−10	−9	−7	−7	−7	−7	−7	−7	−8	−11	−4.2
Mean	72.0	94.2	−11.53	−11.29	−10.60	−10.33	−10.03	−10.32	−11.07	−11.57	−11.07	−12.17	−12.23	−12.07	−11.39

Correction = +0°.12.

December, 1858.

Day of the month.	Lat. north.	Long. west of Green.	2h	4h	6h	8h	10h	Noon.	2h	4h	6h	8h	10h	Midn't.	Mean.
1	Port Kennedy		−16°	−18°	−18°.6	−19°	−16°	−17°	−17°	−22°	−21°	−31°	−30°	−30°	−18.90
2	72° 01'	94° 14'	32	31	32	25	27	30	30	31	33	32	30	30	27.4
3	Winter Quarters		26	27	24	23	30	25	25	26	26	28	26	26	32.0
4	″	″	25	30	30	35	33	41	30	34	37	37	37	37	33.4
5	″	″	30	34	35	33	32	31	32	32.5	30	33	32	31	32.6
6	″	″	26	26	30	32	33	32	32	30	33	31	30	32	30.9
7	″	″	30	30	31	31	31	33	30	31	24	33	31	34	31.3
8	″	″	23	29	33	30	24	36	33	33	27	33	34	34	27.9
9	″	″	33	32	33	37	32	31	22	25	32	33	33	30	30.0
10	″	″	22	25	30	17	17	18	18	31	32	35	27	30	22.8
11	″	″	31	33	33	34	33	33	34	39	41.6	40	40	40	35.8
12	″	″	34	37	37	32	36	34	34	34	30	35	37	38	36.5
13	″	″	34	37	32	30	36	36	31	34	36	37	36	37	35.3
14	″	″	34	33	36	34	33	34	36	33	33	34	36	36	33.9
15	″	″	31	34	33	33	33	37	33	32	37	38	34	33	34.1
16	″	″	33	40	43	43	43	44	43	43	43	41	43	43	41.9
17	″	″	43	41	43	41	34	36	36	35	37	37	33	31	36.5
18	″	″	33	33	33	33	34	34	34	33	35	33	34	34	33.4
19	″	″	33	33	33	33	30	36	30	33	31	33	33	33	31.7
20	″	″	30	34	30	13	37	23	21	15	14	15	16	10	23.5
21	″	″	13	14	10	24	25	20	23	35	33	34	35	36	27.7
22	″	″	37	36	34	33	33	34	33	31	30	30	30	32	32.3
23	″	″	33	36	30	37	33	35	34	35	35	37	33	32	33.4
24	″	″	36	37	33	41	41	41	44	41	44	44	44	43	41.0
25	″	″	44	45	43	43	44	45	44	42	44	43	43.5	47	44.5
26	″	″	47	47	44	44	44	44	43	40	40	34	34	33	42.3
27	″	″	33	33	30	33	33	30	33	33	31	33	33	35	31.5
28	″	″	33	33	33	33	33	31	37	31	30	30	31	31	31.1
29	″	″	35	31	37	33	34	35	37	30	34	35	37	34	34.6
30	″	″	37	31	33	40	30	34	37	36	41	42	43	43	37.1
31	″	″	30	37	34	35	31	31	30	36	30	34	30	36	34.2
Mean	72.0	94.2	−32.53	−32.41	−32.60	−32.23	−32.7	−32.94	−33.74	−33.10	−33.57	−33.15	−33.40	−33.69	−32.97

Correction in order to mean of 24 observations in a day = 0°.00.

TEMPERATURE OF THE AIR IN SHADE OBSERVED ON BOARD THE YACHT FOX.

(Expressed in degrees of Fahrenheit's scale.)

January, 1859.

Day of the month.	Lat. north.	Long. west of Green.	2h	4h	6h	8h	10h	Noon.	2h	4h	6h	8h	10h	Midn't.	Mean.
1	Port Kennedy		[illegible]	−37°	−37°	−37°	[illegible]	[illegible]	[illegible]	−37°	[illegible]	[illegible]	−41°	[illegible]	[illegible]
2	72° 01' [illegible]	[illegible]	[illegible]	[illegible]	[illegible]	[illegible]	[illegible]	[illegible]	[illegible]	[illegible]	[illegible]	[illegible]	[illegible]	[illegible]	[illegible]
3	Winter Quarters		[illegible]	[illegible]	[illegible]	[illegible]	[illegible]	[illegible]	[illegible]	[illegible]	[illegible]	[illegible]	[illegible]	[illegible]	[illegible]
4	"	"	[illegible]	[illegible]	[illegible]	[illegible]	[illegible]	[illegible]	[illegible]	[illegible]	[illegible]	[illegible]	[illegible]	[illegible]	[illegible]
5	"	"	[illegible]	[illegible]	[illegible]	[illegible]	[illegible]	[illegible]	[illegible]	[illegible]	[illegible]	[illegible]	[illegible]	[illegible]	[illegible]
6	"	"	[illegible]	[illegible]	[illegible]	[illegible]	[illegible]	[illegible]	[illegible]	[illegible]	[illegible]	[illegible]	[illegible]	[illegible]	[illegible]
7	"	"	[illegible]	[illegible]	[illegible]	[illegible]	[illegible]	[illegible]	[illegible]	[illegible]	[illegible]	[illegible]	[illegible]	[illegible]	[illegible]
8	"	"	[illegible]	[illegible]	[illegible]	[illegible]	[illegible]	[illegible]	[illegible]	[illegible]	[illegible]	[illegible]	[illegible]	[illegible]	[illegible]
9	"	"	[illegible]	[illegible]	[illegible]	[illegible]	[illegible]	[illegible]	[illegible]	[illegible]	[illegible]	[illegible]	[illegible]	[illegible]	[illegible]
10	"	"	[illegible]	[illegible]	[illegible]	[illegible]	[illegible]	[illegible]	[illegible]	[illegible]	[illegible]	[illegible]	[illegible]	[illegible]	[illegible]
11	"	"	[illegible]	[illegible]	[illegible]	[illegible]	[illegible]	[illegible]	[illegible]	[illegible]	[illegible]	[illegible]	[illegible]	[illegible]	[illegible]
12	"	"	[illegible]	[illegible]	[illegible]	[illegible]	[illegible]	[illegible]	[illegible]	[illegible]	[illegible]	[illegible]	[illegible]	[illegible]	[illegible]
13	"	"	[illegible]	[illegible]	[illegible]	[illegible]	[illegible]	[illegible]	[illegible]	[illegible]	[illegible]	[illegible]	[illegible]	[illegible]	[illegible]
14	"	"	[illegible]	[illegible]	[illegible]	[illegible]	[illegible]	[illegible]	[illegible]	[illegible]	[illegible]	[illegible]	[illegible]	[illegible]	[illegible]
15	"	"	[illegible]	[illegible]	[illegible]	[illegible]	[illegible]	[illegible]	[illegible]	[illegible]	[illegible]	[illegible]	[illegible]	[illegible]	[illegible]
16	"	"	[illegible]	[illegible]	[illegible]	[illegible]	[illegible]	[illegible]	[illegible]	[illegible]	[illegible]	[illegible]	[illegible]	[illegible]	[illegible]
17	"	"	[illegible]	[illegible]	[illegible]	[illegible]	[illegible]	[illegible]	[illegible]	[illegible]	[illegible]	[illegible]	[illegible]	[illegible]	[illegible]
18	"	"	[illegible]	[illegible]	[illegible]	[illegible]	[illegible]	[illegible]	[illegible]	[illegible]	[illegible]	[illegible]	[illegible]	[illegible]	[illegible]
19	"	"	[illegible]	[illegible]	[illegible]	[illegible]	[illegible]	[illegible]	[illegible]	[illegible]	[illegible]	[illegible]	[illegible]	[illegible]	[illegible]
20	"	"	[illegible]	[illegible]	[illegible]	[illegible]	[illegible]	[illegible]	[illegible]	[illegible]	[illegible]	[illegible]	[illegible]	[illegible]	[illegible]
21	"	"	[illegible]	[illegible]	[illegible]	[illegible]	[illegible]	[illegible]	[illegible]	[illegible]	[illegible]	[illegible]	[illegible]	[illegible]	[illegible]
22	"	"	[illegible]	[illegible]	[illegible]	[illegible]	[illegible]	[illegible]	[illegible]	[illegible]	[illegible]	[illegible]	[illegible]	[illegible]	[illegible]
23	"	"	[illegible]	[illegible]	[illegible]	[illegible]	[illegible]	[illegible]	[illegible]	[illegible]	[illegible]	[illegible]	[illegible]	[illegible]	[illegible]
24	"	"	[illegible]	[illegible]	[illegible]	[illegible]	[illegible]	[illegible]	[illegible]	[illegible]	[illegible]	[illegible]	[illegible]	[illegible]	[illegible]
25	"	"	[illegible]	[illegible]	[illegible]	[illegible]	[illegible]	[illegible]	[illegible]	[illegible]	[illegible]	[illegible]	[illegible]	[illegible]	[illegible]
26	"	"	[illegible]	[illegible]	[illegible]	[illegible]	[illegible]	[illegible]	[illegible]	[illegible]	[illegible]	[illegible]	[illegible]	[illegible]	[illegible]
27	"	"	[illegible]	[illegible]	[illegible]	[illegible]	[illegible]	[illegible]	[illegible]	[illegible]	[illegible]	[illegible]	[illegible]	[illegible]	[illegible]
28	"	"	[illegible]	[illegible]	[illegible]	[illegible]	[illegible]	[illegible]	[illegible]	[illegible]	[illegible]	[illegible]	[illegible]	[illegible]	[illegible]
29	"	"	[illegible]	[illegible]	[illegible]	[illegible]	[illegible]	[illegible]	[illegible]	[illegible]	[illegible]	[illegible]	[illegible]	[illegible]	[illegible]
30	"	"	[illegible]	[illegible]	[illegible]	[illegible]	[illegible]	[illegible]	[illegible]	[illegible]	[illegible]	[illegible]	[illegible]	[illegible]	[illegible]
31	"	"	[illegible]	[illegible]	[illegible]	[illegible]	[illegible]	[illegible]	[illegible]	[illegible]	[illegible]	[illegible]	[illegible]	[illegible]	[illegible]
Mean	72.0	[illegible]	[illegible]	[illegible]	[illegible]	[illegible]	[illegible]	[illegible]	[illegible]	[illegible]	[illegible]	[illegible]	[illegible]	[illegible]	[illegible]

Correction to refer to mean of 24 observations = [illegible]

February, 1859.

Day of the month.	Lat. north.	Long. west of Green.	2h	4h	6h	8h	10h	Noon	2h	4h	6h	8h	10h	Midn't.	Mean.
1	Port Kennedy		[illegible]	[illegible]	[illegible]	[illegible]	[illegible]	[illegible]	[illegible]	[illegible]	[illegible]	[illegible]	[illegible]	[illegible]	[illegible]
2	72° 01' [illegible]	[illegible]	[illegible]	[illegible]	[illegible]	[illegible]	[illegible]	[illegible]	[illegible]	[illegible]	[illegible]	[illegible]	[illegible]	[illegible]	[illegible]
3	Winter Quarters		[illegible]	[illegible]	[illegible]	[illegible]	[illegible]	[illegible]	[illegible]	[illegible]	[illegible]	[illegible]	[illegible]	[illegible]	[illegible]
4	"	"	[illegible]	[illegible]	[illegible]	[illegible]	[illegible]	[illegible]	[illegible]	[illegible]	[illegible]	[illegible]	[illegible]	[illegible]	[illegible]
5	"	"	[illegible]	[illegible]	[illegible]	[illegible]	[illegible]	[illegible]	[illegible]	[illegible]	[illegible]	[illegible]	[illegible]	[illegible]	[illegible]
6	"	"	[illegible]	[illegible]	[illegible]	[illegible]	[illegible]	[illegible]	[illegible]	[illegible]	[illegible]	[illegible]	[illegible]	[illegible]	[illegible]
7	"	"	[illegible]	[illegible]	[illegible]	[illegible]	[illegible]	[illegible]	[illegible]	[illegible]	[illegible]	[illegible]	[illegible]	[illegible]	[illegible]
8	"	"	[illegible]	[illegible]	[illegible]	[illegible]	[illegible]	[illegible]	[illegible]	[illegible]	[illegible]	[illegible]	[illegible]	[illegible]	[illegible]
9	"	"	[illegible]	[illegible]	[illegible]	[illegible]	[illegible]	[illegible]	[illegible]	[illegible]	[illegible]	[illegible]	[illegible]	[illegible]	[illegible]
10	"	"	[illegible]	[illegible]	[illegible]	[illegible]	[illegible]	[illegible]	[illegible]	[illegible]	[illegible]	[illegible]	[illegible]	[illegible]	[illegible]
11	"	"	[illegible]	[illegible]	[illegible]	[illegible]	[illegible]	[illegible]	[illegible]	[illegible]	[illegible]	[illegible]	[illegible]	[illegible]	[illegible]
12	"	"	[illegible]	[illegible]	[illegible]	[illegible]	[illegible]	[illegible]	[illegible]	[illegible]	[illegible]	[illegible]	[illegible]	[illegible]	[illegible]
13	"	"	[illegible]	[illegible]	[illegible]	[illegible]	[illegible]	[illegible]	[illegible]	[illegible]	[illegible]	[illegible]	[illegible]	[illegible]	[illegible]
14	"	"	[illegible]	[illegible]	[illegible]	[illegible]	[illegible]	[illegible]	[illegible]	[illegible]	[illegible]	[illegible]	[illegible]	[illegible]	[illegible]
15	"	"	[illegible]	[illegible]	[illegible]	[illegible]	[illegible]	[illegible]	[illegible]	[illegible]	[illegible]	[illegible]	[illegible]	[illegible]	[illegible]
16	"	"	[illegible]	[illegible]	[illegible]	[illegible]	[illegible]	[illegible]	[illegible]	[illegible]	[illegible]	[illegible]	[illegible]	[illegible]	[illegible]
17	"	"	[illegible]	[illegible]	[illegible]	[illegible]	[illegible]	[illegible]	[illegible]	[illegible]	[illegible]	[illegible]	[illegible]	[illegible]	[illegible]
18	"	"	[illegible]	[illegible]	[illegible]	[illegible]	[illegible]	[illegible]	[illegible]	[illegible]	[illegible]	[illegible]	[illegible]	[illegible]	[illegible]
19	"	"	[illegible]	[illegible]	[illegible]	[illegible]	[illegible]	[illegible]	[illegible]	[illegible]	[illegible]	[illegible]	[illegible]	[illegible]	[illegible]
20	"	"	[illegible]	[illegible]	[illegible]	[illegible]	[illegible]	[illegible]	[illegible]	[illegible]	[illegible]	[illegible]	[illegible]	[illegible]	[illegible]
21	"	"	[illegible]	[illegible]	[illegible]	[illegible]	[illegible]	[illegible]	[illegible]	[illegible]	[illegible]	[illegible]	[illegible]	[illegible]	[illegible]
22	"	"	[illegible]	[illegible]	[illegible]	[illegible]	[illegible]	[illegible]	[illegible]	[illegible]	[illegible]	[illegible]	[illegible]	[illegible]	[illegible]
23	"	"	[illegible]	[illegible]	[illegible]	[illegible]	[illegible]	[illegible]	[illegible]	[illegible]	[illegible]	[illegible]	[illegible]	[illegible]	[illegible]
24	"	"	[illegible]	[illegible]	[illegible]	[illegible]	[illegible]	[illegible]	[illegible]	[illegible]	[illegible]	[illegible]	[illegible]	[illegible]	[illegible]
25	"	"	[illegible]	[illegible]	[illegible]	[illegible]	[illegible]	[illegible]	[illegible]	[illegible]	[illegible]	[illegible]	[illegible]	[illegible]	[illegible]
26	"	"	[illegible]	[illegible]	[illegible]	[illegible]	[illegible]	[illegible]	[illegible]	[illegible]	[illegible]	[illegible]	[illegible]	[illegible]	[illegible]
27	"	"	[illegible]	[illegible]	[illegible]	[illegible]	[illegible]	[illegible]	[illegible]	[illegible]	[illegible]	[illegible]	[illegible]	[illegible]	[illegible]
28	"	"	[illegible]	[illegible]	[illegible]	[illegible]	[illegible]	[illegible]	[illegible]	[illegible]	[illegible]	[illegible]	[illegible]	[illegible]	[illegible]
Mean	72.0	[illegible]	[illegible]	[illegible]	[illegible]	[illegible]	[illegible]	[illegible]	[illegible]	[illegible]	[illegible]	[illegible]	[illegible]	[illegible]	[illegible]

Correction to refer mean of 12 to mean of 24 observations = [illegible]

TEMPERATURE OF THE AIR IN SHADE OBSERVED ON BOARD THE YACHT FOX.
(Expressed in degrees of Fahrenheit's scale.)

March, 1859.

Day of the month.	Lat. north.	Long. west of Greenw.	2h	4h	6h	8h	10h	Noon.	2h	4h	6h	8h	10h	Midn't.	Mean.	Mean of 6 obs'ns.
1	Port Kennedy 72° 01′	94° 14′	−31°	[illegible]	−31°	[illegible]	[illegible]	−30°	[illegible]	−27°	[illegible]	[illegible]	[illegible]	[illegible]	[illegible]	[illegible]
2	Winter Quarters		[illegible]	[illegible]	[illegible]	[illegible]	[illegible]	[illegible]	[illegible]	[illegible]	[illegible]	[illegible]	[illegible]	[illegible]	[illegible]	[illegible]
3	"	"	[illegible]	[illegible]	[illegible]	[illegible]	[illegible]	[illegible]	[illegible]	[illegible]	[illegible]	[illegible]	[illegible]	[illegible]	[illegible]	[illegible]
4	"	"	[illegible]	[illegible]	[illegible]	[illegible]	[illegible]	[illegible]	[illegible]	[illegible]	[illegible]	[illegible]	[illegible]	[illegible]	[illegible]	[illegible]
5	"	"	[illegible]	[illegible]	[illegible]	[illegible]	[illegible]	[illegible]	[illegible]	[illegible]	[illegible]	[illegible]	[illegible]	[illegible]	[illegible]	[illegible]
6	"	"	[illegible]	[illegible]	[illegible]	[illegible]	[illegible]	[illegible]	[illegible]	[illegible]	[illegible]	[illegible]	[illegible]	[illegible]	[illegible]	[illegible]
7	"	"	[illegible]	[illegible]	[illegible]	[illegible]	[illegible]	[illegible]	[illegible]	[illegible]	[illegible]	[illegible]	[illegible]	[illegible]	[illegible]	[illegible]
8	"	"	[illegible]	[illegible]	[illegible]	[illegible]	[illegible]	[illegible]	[illegible]	[illegible]	[illegible]	[illegible]	[illegible]	[illegible]	[illegible]	[illegible]
9	"	"	[illegible]	[illegible]	[illegible]	[illegible]	[illegible]	[illegible]	[illegible]	[illegible]	[illegible]	[illegible]	[illegible]	[illegible]	[illegible]	[illegible]
10	"	"	[illegible]	[illegible]	[illegible]	[illegible]	[illegible]	[illegible]	[illegible]	[illegible]	[illegible]	[illegible]	[illegible]	[illegible]	[illegible]	[illegible]
11	"	"	[illegible]	[illegible]	[illegible]	[illegible]	[illegible]	[illegible]	[illegible]	[illegible]	[illegible]	[illegible]	[illegible]	[illegible]	[illegible]	[illegible]
12	"	"	[illegible]	[illegible]	[illegible]	[illegible]	[illegible]	[illegible]	[illegible]	[illegible]	[illegible]	[illegible]	[illegible]	[illegible]	[illegible]	[illegible]
13	"	"	[illegible]	[illegible]	[illegible]	[illegible]	[illegible]	[illegible]	[illegible]	[illegible]	[illegible]	[illegible]	[illegible]	[illegible]	[illegible]	[illegible]
14	"	"	[illegible]	[illegible]	[illegible]	[illegible]	[illegible]	[illegible]	[illegible]	[illegible]	[illegible]	[illegible]	[illegible]	[illegible]	[illegible]	[illegible]
15	"	"	[illegible]	[illegible]	[illegible]	[illegible]	[illegible]	[illegible]	[illegible]	[illegible]	[illegible]	[illegible]	[illegible]	[illegible]	[illegible]	[illegible]
16	"	"	[illegible]	[illegible]	[illegible]	[illegible]	[illegible]	[illegible]	[illegible]	[illegible]	[illegible]	[illegible]	[illegible]	[illegible]	[illegible]	[illegible]
17	"	"	[illegible]	[illegible]	[illegible]	[illegible]	[illegible]	[illegible]	[illegible]	[illegible]	[illegible]	[illegible]	[illegible]	[illegible]	[illegible]	[illegible]
18	"	"	[illegible]	[illegible]	[illegible]	[illegible]	[illegible]	[illegible]	[illegible]	[illegible]	[illegible]	[illegible]	[illegible]	[illegible]	[illegible]	[illegible]
19	"	"	[illegible]	[illegible]	[illegible]	[illegible]	[illegible]	[illegible]	[illegible]	[illegible]	[illegible]	[illegible]	[illegible]	[illegible]	[illegible]	[illegible]
20	"	"	[illegible]	[illegible]	[illegible]	[illegible]	[illegible]	[illegible]	[illegible]	[illegible]	[illegible]	[illegible]	[illegible]	[illegible]	[illegible]	[illegible]
21	"	"	[illegible]	[illegible]	[illegible]	[illegible]	[illegible]	[illegible]	[illegible]	[illegible]	[illegible]	[illegible]	[illegible]	[illegible]	[illegible]	[illegible]
22	"	"	[illegible]	[illegible]	[illegible]	[illegible]	[illegible]	[illegible]	[illegible]	[illegible]	[illegible]	[illegible]	[illegible]	[illegible]	[illegible]	[illegible]
23	"	"	[illegible]	[illegible]	[illegible]	[illegible]	[illegible]	[illegible]	[illegible]	[illegible]	[illegible]	[illegible]	[illegible]	[illegible]	[illegible]	[illegible]
24	"	"	[illegible]	[illegible]	[illegible]	[illegible]	[illegible]	[illegible]	[illegible]	[illegible]	[illegible]	[illegible]	[illegible]	[illegible]	[illegible]	[illegible]
25	"	"	[illegible]	[illegible]	[illegible]	[illegible]	[illegible]	[illegible]	[illegible]	[illegible]	[illegible]	[illegible]	[illegible]	[illegible]	[illegible]	[illegible]
26	"	"	[illegible]	[illegible]	[illegible]	[illegible]	[illegible]	[illegible]	[illegible]	[illegible]	[illegible]	[illegible]	[illegible]	[illegible]	[illegible]	[illegible]
27	"	"	[illegible]	[illegible]	[illegible]	[illegible]	[illegible]	[illegible]	[illegible]	[illegible]	[illegible]	[illegible]	[illegible]	[illegible]	[illegible]	[illegible]
28	"	"	..	[illegible]	..	[illegible]	..	[illegible]	..	[illegible]	..	[illegible]	..	[illegible]	[illegible]	[illegible]
29	"	"	..	[illegible]	..	[illegible]	..	[illegible]	..	[illegible]	..	[illegible]	..	[illegible]	[illegible]	[illegible]
30	"	"	..	[illegible]	..	[illegible]	..	[illegible]	..	[illegible]	..	[illegible]	..	[illegible]	[illegible]	[illegible]
31	"	"	..	[illegible]	..	[illegible]	..	[illegible]	..	[illegible]	..	[illegible]	..	[illegible]	[illegible]	[illegible]
Mean	72.0	94.2	−21.[illegible]	−21.09	−21.57	−19.45	−14.79	−11.42	−12.03	−13.77	−1[illegible].4[illegible]	−12.2[illegible]	−19.[illegible]	−20.06	−17.7[illegible]	

Correction to reduce mean to 24 observations = [illegible].

April, 1859.

Day of the month.	Latitude north.	Longitude west of Greenwich.	4h	8h	Noon.	4h	8h	11h	Mean.
1	Port Kennedy 72° 01′	94° 14′	−11°	[illegible]	−6	[illegible]	−10°	−9°	−9.7
2	Winter Quarters		−2	+2	+2	+4	+2	+3	+2.0
3	"	"	+1	[illegible]	+6	+11.6	+6	+3.5	+5.6
4	"	"	+3	+6	+12	+4.5	+2	−2.5	+4.7
5	"	"	−5	−8	9	−3	−13	−15	[illegible]
6	"	"	−20	−20	−19	−16	−22.5	−22	−20.3
7	"	"	−5	−8	−5	−6	−15	−24	−10.7
8	"	"	−22	−11.6	−5	−8	−13	−21	−13.6
9	"	"	−17	−6	−2	0	−6	−16	[illegible]
10	"	"	−6	−4	−11	−18	−19	−22	−13.3
11	"	"	−21	−14	−13	−16	−22	−27	−18.8
12	"	"	−14	−15	−13	−15	−18	−22	−16.2
13	"	"	−19	−14	−10.5	−18	−17	−19	[illegible]
14	"	"	−13	−15	−10	−2	−10	−13	−10.8
15	"	"	−3	−1	[illegible]	+5	−4	−8	[illegible]
16	"	"	−5	−7	[illegible]	−2.5	−5	−6	−4.5
17	"	"	−6	0	+5	+10	+1	+4	+3.3
18	"	"	+14	[illegible]	[illegible]	+12.5	+21	+15	[illegible]
19	"	"	+6	+5	+3	[illegible]	−3.5	−6	[illegible]
20	"	"	−7	−7	−4	−6	−6	−4.8	−6.1
21	"	"	−1	+2	+2	[illegible]	−1	+3	+2.0
22	"	"	+11	+16	+16	+16	+20.5	[illegible]	+11.3
23	"	"	0	−1	0	+1	−1.3	0	−0.3
24	"	"	−5	−3	−5	0	−6	−11.5	−6.2
25	"	"	−12	−10	−5	−5	−11	−11	−10.0
26	"	"	−6	−4	[illegible]	0	−1	+0.6	−1.6
27	"	"	−2	[illegible]	[illegible]	+15	+10	[illegible]	+7.7
28	"	"	+12.5	[illegible]	+16	+16.8	+12.1	[illegible]	[illegible]
29	"	"	+11	[illegible]	+12	[illegible]	[illegible]	[illegible]	[illegible]
30	"	"	−11	[illegible]	+21	+17	+8	+1	[illegible]
Mean	72.0	94.2	−1.[illegible]	−5.77	+1.25	+0.60	−4.07	−5.93	−2.65

Correction to reduce observed mean to mean from 24 observations = −0°.17.

Temperature of the Air in Shade observed on board the Yacht Fox.
(Expressed in degrees of Fahrenheit's scale.)

May, 1859.

Day of the month.	Latitude north.	Longitude west of Greenwich.	3h	9h	Noon.	3h	6h	11h	Mean.
1	Port Kennedy		6°	3°.5	4°	3°.5	3°	6°	+ [illegible]
2	72° 01'	94° 14'	5	8.5	11	14.5	8.5	1	8.1
3	Winter Quarters		3	5.5	9.5	5	7	1.5	1.7
4	"	"	3	7.5	5.5	6.5	3.8	0	4.7
5	"	"	4	8	19	17.5	6.5	0	6.0
6	"	"	4	9	9	6.5	3.5	−0.5	5.2
7	"	"	3	8	6.5	4	3	0	4.1
8	"	"	5	11.5	14	14	6	8.5	9.2
9	"	"	3	6	9	9	4	8.5	6.1
10	"	"	7	16.5	18	16.5	14.8	8.5	11.5
11	"	"	14	22.5	19	19	14.5	8.5	16.0
12	"	"	14	20.5	14	17	15	18	16.0
13	"	"	10	12	13.6	15.5	14	13	13.0
14	"	"	21	23	27.6	19	19.5	17.6	20.4
15	"	"	17	19.6	24	29	23.5	21.5	22.4
16	"	"	23	24.5	16	19.6	12.5	13	11.4
17	"	"	15.5	19	21.6	20	17	13	17.7
18	"	"	20	23	23	23	14	7	18.8
19	"	"	14	15.6	23	23	12.8	18	18.7
20	"	"	19	23	18	15	14	14	17.5
21	"	"	19	21.6	22.5	20	13	11	17.9
22	"	"	9	8	17	13	16	15	13.8
23	"	"	17.5	19	23	21.6	19	16	19.5
24	"	"	18	23	23	21.5	17	11.5	19.0
25	"	"	18	16	20	17	20	23	19.1
26	"	"	24.5	20	27.5	27.5	22.6	20.6	24.0
27	"	"	19	30	31	28.6	28	20.6	24.1
28	"	"	20	23	33	30.5	24	23	23.4
29	"	"	24	28	25.5	20	20.5	19.6	24.7
30	"	"	21	32.5	25.6	23	21.6	21	24.1
31	"	"	20	21	24.6	24	22.5	17	21.2
Mean	72.0	94.3	+13.34	+16.50	+18.81	+19.71	+14.28	+11.30	+15.43

Correction to refer observed mean to mean from 24 observations = −0°.38.

June, 1859.

Day of the month.	Latitude north.	Longitude west of Greenwich.	3h	9h	Noon.	3h	6h	11h	Mean.
1	Port Kennedy		30°	34°	37°.6	35°	34°.6	30°.5	+ [illegible]
2	72° 01'	94° 14'	19	31	35	27.5	25.5	23	27.7
3	Winter Quarters		31.5	36	43.6	34	30	27.5	32.7
4	"	"	31	35	42.5	34	30	25	34.1
5	"	"	30	33.6	44.6	33	30.5	23.5	33.6
6	"	"	27	34.5	39.5	34	34.6	27.5	32.8
7	"	"	33	30	36	34.5	33	29	32.9
8	"	"	33	37.5	38	37	32.6	31	34.6
9	"	"	34	36.5	40	30.6	31.6	31.5	35.5
10	"	"	33	36	35.5	34.6	33	29.6	33.6
11	"	"	35	35.6	39.5	36	37	34	33.3
12	"	"	36	46	43.5	36	34.5	31	34.2
13	"	"	34	41	41.6	39	34	29.6	37.3
14	"	"	33.6	37	36.5	34	34	30.5	35.1
15	"	"	36	47	43	44.6	34.6	36	41.2
16	"	"	36	38.5	43	43	39	33	38.3
17	"	"	36	47.5	40.6	43	34	33	40.5
18	"	"	34.5	38.5	39.5	36	38	34.5	36.3
19	"	"	36	42.6	37.6	39	34.6	32.5	36.3
20	"	"	34	43	49	38	32.5	33	38.3
21	"	"	36	37.5	47.6	40	37.6	34.5	38.6
22	"	"	35	39	37	37	35.6	33	38.1
23	"	"	33	44.5	37	33	34.6	33	34.7
24	"	"	35	38	39	35.5	35	32.6	34.9
25	"	"	36	41	41	37	34.6	32.6	37.3
26	"	"	35	36.5	39.6	38	37.5	34	36.6
27	"	"	34.5	35	37	36.5	36	33.6	35.4
28	"	"	33	40	39.5	37	35	34.6	36.0
29	"	"	37	40	35.5	37	36	37	37.6
30	"	"	38	44.5	41	37	35.5	34	35.3
Mean	72.0	94.3	+33.53	+38.06	+39.92	+36.93	+33.93	+31.10	+ [illegible]

Correction to refer mean of 6 to mean of 24 observations = −0°.41.

TEMPERATURE OF THE AIR IN SHADE OBSERVED ON BOARD THE YACHT FOX.

(Expressed in degrees of Fahrenheit's scale.)

July, 1859.

Day of the month	Lat. north.	Long. west of Green.	2h	4h	6h	8h	10h	Noon	2h	4h	6h	8h	10h	11h Midn't.	Mean.	Mean of 4 obs'ns
1	Port Kennedy		..	37°.5	..	45°	..	43°.5	..	40°	..	41°	..	40°	+40°.8	+40°.8
2	72° 01'	94° 14'	..	43	..	50	..	46	..	47	..	43.5	..	37.5	43.1	43.7
3	Winter		..	36	..	40	..	41.5	..	38	..	34	..	33.5	37.4	37.6
4	Quarters		..	38	..	42.5	..	41.5	..	40	..	37.5	..	38	39.9	39.1
5	"		..	37	..	43	..	44	42°	40.5	37°.5	38	35°	32.5	39.2	
6	"		35°	38	37°	37.5	40°	43	41	39.5	34.5	37	38	38	37.9	
7	"		35.5	38	38	38	41.8	41.5	42.5	41.5	37	36	35	34.5	38.3	
8	"		33	33	32	43	40.8	39.5	36.5	39.5	37	36.5	33	35	36.5	
9	"		34.6	33	36	36	37	43	37.5	38	37.8	34	33.6	34	36.7	
10	"		34	37	33	36.5	41	40	36.5	35.5	35	38	35	36	35.4	
11	"		33	34.5	34	39	39	39	41	41.5	40	37	37	35.3	38.0	
12	"		34	35	36	36.6	38	37	34	39	38	36.5	34	37	36.7	
13	"		37	40	40	40	39	42	38	37	40.8	39	37	33	38.7	
14	"		35.5	38	38	43	43	42	43	39.5	40	39	36.5	35	39.1	
15	"		34	34	36	34	34.5	38	43	38	38	37.5	36	35	36.3	
16	"		35	37	36.5	38	42	43	40	39	37.8	37	36	35	37.8	
17	"		35	38	40	40	44	43	45	43	39	39	36	35	40.0	
18	"		34	33	34	37	37	37	31.5	37	37	37	36	34	35.9	
19	"		34	35	35.5	37	40.8	40.3	39	39	38	37	35	35	37.3	
20	"		35	38	37	43	47.5	42	48	42.5	42	40	38	37.5	39.8	
21	"		37	38	38	39	40	41	40	40	41	41	40	39	39.6	
22	"		37	41	43	45	49	49	45	46	46	45	44	38	44.0	
23	"		44	45	46	47	44.5	47	47	43.5	43	40	37	36	43.3	
24	"		35	39	43	44	40	53	41	43	45	44	43	40.5	44.0	
25	"		37	38	42	44	42	44	43	43	43	41	41	40	41.5	
26	"		39	42	46	44	50	53	42	46	46	46	43	43	45.3	
27	"		40	39	43	43	45	49	41	41	47	40	44	37	41.8	
28	"		38	40	44	49	49	43	42	47	43	42	41	37	42.9	
29	Off Observation Point		38	38	38	49	50	55	55	54	55	53	45	41	46.7	
30			41	41	43	45	45	48	47	50	49	45	47	49	45.7	
31	"		43	39	45	45	44	46	50	50	48	47	47	41	45.3	
Mean	72.0	94.2	+36.31	+37.34	+39.24	+41.29	+42.[illegible]	+43.4[illegible]	+42.34	+41.98	+41.47	+40.02	+38.36	+38.[illegible]	+40.13	

Correction to refer mean of 12 to mean of 24 observations = −0°.01.

August, 1859.

Day of the month	Latitude north.		Longitude west of Greenwich.		4h	8h	Noon.	4h	8h	Midn't.	Mean.	
1	Port Kennedy				41°	42°	43°	45°	47°	40°	+42°.5	
2	"		"		39	37	38	38	35	35	36.2	
3	"		"		34	34	36	41	40	39	37.5	
4	"		"		35	40	41	41	45	34	39.2	
5	"		"		33	37	38	39	43	39	38.2	
6	"		"		34	38	38	40	40	38	38.3	
7	"		"		34	38	34.5	41	39	33	36.9	
8	"		"		35	35	37	37	38	33	35.7	
9	Long Island				35	34	36	37	36	33	34.8	
10	Adelaide Bay				33	34	38	39	34	33	35.2	
11	...		...		33	36	39	39	36	41	37.0	
12	...		...		38	39	40.5	38	39.5	40	39.0	
13	...		...		38	37	38.6	38.8	41	41	39.0	
14	...		...		41	41	40	38	38.5	42	41.1	
15	Off Fury Beach				39	38	37	35	34.5	31	35.7	
16	Off Elwin Bay				31	35.5	36	33	33	31	33.1	
17	...		...		..	..	..	..	..	..	..	+34°.0
18	72°	55'	67°	10'	33	35	36	34	35	36	35.0	
19	71	58	70	45	33	31	31	33	33	31	32.3	
20	73	12	76	40	33	31	35	36	30	31	32.8	
21	73	43	78	4	33	31	35	31.8	34	34	33.1	
22	73	51	67	17	35	34	34	31	32	31	32.8	
23	73	19	60	15	35	34	36	36	38	30	34.9	
24	72	7	59	6	38	38	36	37	37	37	37.2	
25	70	40	65	57	38	37	39	35	38	38	38.3	
26	69	35	58	50	35	35	37	37	38	37	36.9	
27	Godhavn				33	34	35	35	35	36	35.8	
28			"		31	36	38	40	36	36	34.9	
29			"		37	38	40	42	47	33	39.5	
30			"		33	39	47	44	40	38	40.0	
31			"		36	38	44	42	38	37	39.3	
Mean	71.9		70.6		+34.85	+36.37	+37.97	+37.63	+37.10	+35.35	+36.64	

The correction to refer mean of 6 to mean of 24 observations [illegible].

TEMPERATURE OF THE AIR IN SHADE OBSERVED ON BOARD THE YACHT FOX.
(Expressed in degrees of Fahrenheit's scale.)

September, 1859.

Day of the month.	Latitude north.	Longitude west of Greenwich.	4^h	8^h	Noon.	4^h	8^h	Midn't.	Mean.
1	67° 43'	64° 09'	37°	37°	41°	42°	40°	41°	+37.3
2	67 38	67 22	36	39	37	40	37	35	37.7
3	66 11	57 06	33	34	36	37	37	34	35.0
4	63 47	54 42	34	39	40	40	40	39	38.7
5	62 38	54 20	41	43	43	42	42	39	41.2
6	62 33	54 54	38	40	39	42	38	38	39.2
7	61 22	53 47	37	38	38	38	37	36	37.3
8	60 30	52 31	38	40	41	40	39	37	39.5
9	58 41	48 31	37	39	41	42	39	39	39.5
10	58 19	44 51	39	43	47	44	43	45	43.3
11	57 37	40 13	43	43	44	45	46	43	43.7
12	58 16	34 19	45	42	48	48	47	44	45.3
13	58 34	31 04	44	52	54	54	54	54	52.7
14	58 25	26 01	56	56	57	54	52	50	53.4
15	58 23	22 36	55	57	59	57	56	53	56.1
16	59 25	18 11	54	58	64	53	56	58	56.5
17	61 18	16 23	54	59	63	61	60	58	58.0
18	60 30	12 35	56	56	59	58	59	60	58.6
Mean	60.9	41.9	+43.6	+45.7	+47.4	+47.3	+45.6	+45.0	+45.79

Correction to refer mean of 6 to mean of 24 readings — zero.

Notes to the preceding Abstract of the Temperature Record.

July, 1857. The column headed "mean" contains the mean daily temperature derived from six equidistant observations; the figures in the next column of "deduced mean" were obtained as follows: Suppose the mean temperature of July 3d be required from the observations at 8 A. M. and 8 P. M., the observations at each of these hours in the *full* series were compared with their respective mean, as given in the preceding column; thus, from 23 values, we find the correction to the 8 A. M. reading, to obtain the mean reading of the day, +0°.8, and in a similar manner, for the 8 P. M. reading, +0°.2. Applying these corrections to 67°.0 and 67°.5 respectively, and taking the mean, we find for July 3d the mean temperature 67°.7. The following table contains these corrections to each observing hour in the month of July, in order to produce the mean of six readings a day, viz:—

For 4 A. M.	+0°.5	For 4 P. M.	—1°.5
" 8 A. M.	+0.8	" 8 P. M.	+0.2
" noon	—0.8	" midnight	+1.0

The means require a further small correction to refer them to what they would be if hourly observations had been made. For this purpose, I have made use of the tables of hourly corrections for periodic variations for Boothia Felix and Drontheim, as given in the Smithsonian collection of meteorological and physical tables by A. Guyot, and also of a similar table given in the discussion of Dr. Kane's meteorological observations for Van Rensselaer Harbor, in Vol. XI. of the Smithsonian Contributions to Knowledge. For these localities, to which has been added Leith, we have, for the month of July, the correction to the mean of six observations at 4h, 8h, 12h, A. M. and P. M., to obtain the daily mean from twenty-four observations:—

	Latitude.	Longitude.	Fahrenheit.
Boothia Felix	69° 59′	92° 1′	0°.00
Drontheim	63 26	—10 25	—0.09
Van Rensselaer	78 37	70 53	—0.06
Leith	55 59	— 3 10	+0.04
Adopted correction			—0.03

The resulting mean temperature for the month of July, in latitude 62° N. and longitude 39°.1 W. is, therefore, +45°.56 —0°.03 = +45°.53, as given in the general table of results. The means for the hours 4, 8, and 12, are derived from the observations between the 6th and the 31st, omitting those on the 10th, and taking 53° for the interpolated value at 4h A. M. on the 6th.[1] For the sake of uniformity, the quantity +1°.26 has been added to each of these hourly means, so that the mean of all may again produce 45°.56.

The correction to refer the mean from the observations at certain hours of the day to the mean derived from twenty-four readings a day, for the remaining months, has been deduced from the observations at Van Rensselaer Harbor and Boothia Felix. The following table contains these corrections:—

Month.	Year.	Observed Hours.	Correction Derived. Van Rensselaer Harbor.	Correction Derived. Boothia Felix.	Correction Derived. Mean.
August	1857, 1858, 1859	4, 8, 12, A. M. and P. M.	—0°.01	0°.00	0°.00
September	"	2, 4, 6, 8, 10, 12, A. M. and P. M.	—0.01	—0.07	—0.04
October	"	" " "	+0.04	0.00	+0.02
November	" 1858	" " "	+0.02	+0.22	+0.12
December	" "	" " "	0.00	+0.01	0.00
January	1858, 1859	" " "	—0.05	—0.01	—0.03
February	" "	" " "	—0.05	—0.01	—0.03
March	" "	" " "	+0.04	0.00	+0.02
April	"	" " "	+0.03	+0.01	+0.02
May	"	4, 8, 12, A. M. and P. M.	—0.13	—0.01	—0.07
June	"	" "	—0.14	+0.01	—0.07
July	"	" "	—0.05	0.00	—0.03
September	"	" "	+0.04	—0.01	0.00
October	"	" "	+0.10	0.00	+0.05
April	1859	4, 8, 12, A. M.; 4, 8, 11, P. M.	—0.24	—0.13*	—0.17
May	"	" " "	—0.43	—0.34*	—0.39
June	"	" " "	—0.44	—0.39*	—0.41

* Indicates that the weight 2 has been given to the correction derived from the Boothia Felix station, as being the nearer one.

August, 1857. The two omissions on the 6th were supplied by 42° and 43°.

September, 1857. The values for the 21st were interpolated as follows: 2 A. M. 12°.0, 6 A. M. 15°.2, and 10 A. M. 21°.2. From the observations between the 21st and 30th, we find that the mean of twelve observations a day is 0°.15 smaller than that derived from six observations a day; the second column of means between the 1st and 21st, therefore, is derived from the preceding column by subtracting

[1] The interpolated value for 8 P. M. on the 21st is 38°.8.

0°.1 and 0°.2 alternately from the successive daily means. The monthly mean temperature at the hours 4, 8, noon, 4, 8, midnight, was first made out (if diminished by the above constant 0°.15, their mean would exactly give 19°.55). To obtain the intermediate values for 2, 6, 10, A. M. and P. M., the observations between the 21st and 30th were used as follows:—

Mean temp. at midnight for last 10 days . .	12°.30	Same for 30 days, 17°.38
" 2 A. M. " " . .	11.85	
Difference . . .	—0.45	

which, applied to 17°.38, gives 16°.93; in the same way, we obtain from the following hour, 4 A. M., the value 17°.38. The mean, or 17°.15, has consequently been adopted as the mean monthly temperature at 2 A. M. The remaining values were derived in a similar manner.

February, 1858. On the 11th and some following days, there are occasionally pencil figures inserted between the lines. These are neither used nor explained.

April, 1858. The daily mean from six observations differs from the daily mean from twice this number of observations by 0°.13, as found from the values between the 1st and 17th; a correction of —0°.13 has, therefore, been applied to the deduced means on and after the 18th, in order to refer the same to the result produced by twelve observations. The hourly means at the bottom of the page were obtained in the manner explained in the note to the hourly means of the month of September, 1857, viz: through a comparison of the hourly means of the *full series*, and applying the correction (the mean found from the preceding and following column) to the monthly mean at the hours 4, 8, 12, etc.

May, 1858. The temperature at 8 A. M. on the 2d was assumed to be 30°.5.

March, 1859. The correction to refer the mean from six observations on each of the last four days of the month to the daily mean as resulting from twelve observations, was found by comparison of the respective means on the twelve days preceding; it was found —0°.10. The mean hourly temperature for the hours 2, 6, 8, 10, was obtained by the process applied on two former occasions.

April, 1859. The bar in the column for 4^h and in the column for midnight, indicates that the observations were taken one hour later and one hour earlier, or at 5^h and 11^h respectively. This practice was discontinued on the 5th of July following.

July, 1859. For the temperatures of the 5th, at the hours 2, 4, 6, 10, A. M., I have adopted the interpolated values 36°, 36°.5, 39°, 43°, respectively. The correction to refer the mean of six observations (hours 5, 8, noon, 4, 8, 11) to the mean of twelve observations (hours 4, 8, 12, A. M. and P. M.), was derived from the tables constructed for Van Rensselaer and Boothia Felix; the latter value having the weight 2, it was found = —0°.21, which quantity was applied in the first column of means, July 1st to July 4th inclusive. To obtain the correct hourly means for the month, the numbers in the column for 5^h (first four days) were first referred to the reading at 4^h by subtracting 0.5. The same correction was applied to refer the readings from 11 P. M. to midnight. The monthly means for the hours 4, 8, 12, A. M. and P. M., being known, the means for the intermediate hours were found by comparison of the respective readings on the last twenty-seven days of the month, as has been explained in similar cases.

August, 1859. The value 34°.0 for the mean temperature on the 17th was interpolated, which required a corresponding diminution of 0°.06 for each of the hourly means, in order to produce the same monthly temperature of +36°.58.

September, 1859. The means of this month are of little value, the month being incomplete, and the change in latitude (and longitude) very considerable.

The two following tables contain a recapitulation of the results of the preceding abstracts. Table I exhibits the mean monthly temperature at the locality indicated by its latitude and longitude, also the *relative* maxima and minima, and relative monthly extreme range, as observed in either the bi-hourly or the four-hourly series. The absolute maxima and minima were not recorded. Table II contains the mean monthly temperatures for each observing hour, and is intended to serve as the basis for the discussion of the diurnal variation, while the first table furnishes the means for the discussion of the annual variation of the temperature. The column headed "mean," in Table II, differs from the corresponding column in Table I, for this reason: that, in Table II, no correction has been applied to refer the mean of six or twelve observations in a day (as the case may be) to the reading of twenty-four observations.

TABLE I.—RECAPITULATION OF RESULTS OF MONTHLY MEAN TEMPERATURES OF THE AIR IN SHADE OBSERVED ON BOARD THE YACHT FOX.

(Expressed in degrees of Fahrenheit's scale.)

Year.	Month.	Latitude north.	Longitude west.	Mean temperature.	Relative maxima.	Relative minima.	Relative range.	Correction for index error [illegible]
1857	July	[illegible]	[illegible]	[illegible]	[illegible]	[illegible]	[illegible]	
"	August	[illegible]	[illegible]	[illegible]	[illegible]	[illegible]	[illegible]	
"	September	[illegible]	[illegible]	[illegible]	[illegible]	[illegible]	[illegible]	
"	October	[illegible]	[illegible]	[illegible]	[illegible]	[illegible]	[illegible]	[illegible]
"	November	[illegible]	[illegible]	[illegible]	[illegible]	[illegible]	[illegible]	[illegible]
"	December	[illegible]	[illegible]	[illegible]	[illegible]	[illegible]	[illegible]	[illegible]
1858	January	[illegible]	[illegible]	[illegible]	[illegible]	[illegible]	[illegible]	[illegible]
"	February	[illegible]	[illegible]	[illegible]	[illegible]	[illegible]	[illegible]	[illegible]
"	March	[illegible]	[illegible]	[illegible]	[illegible]	[illegible]	[illegible]	[illegible]
"	April	[illegible]	[illegible]	[illegible]	[illegible]	[illegible]	[illegible]	[illegible]
"	May	[illegible]	[illegible]	[illegible]	[illegible]	[illegible]	[illegible]	
"	June	[illegible]	[illegible]	[illegible]	[illegible]	[illegible]	[illegible]	
"	July	[illegible]	[illegible]	[illegible]	[illegible]	[illegible]	[illegible]	
"	August	[illegible]	[illegible]	[illegible]	[illegible]	[illegible]	[illegible]	
"	September	[illegible]	[illegible]	[illegible]	[illegible]	[illegible]	[illegible]	
"	October	[illegible]	[illegible]	[illegible]	[illegible]	[illegible]	[illegible]	[illegible]
"	November	[illegible]	[illegible]	[illegible]	[illegible]	[illegible]	[illegible]	[illegible]
"	December	[illegible]	[illegible]	[illegible]	[illegible]	[illegible]	[illegible]	[illegible]
1859	January	[illegible]	[illegible]	[illegible]	[illegible]	[illegible]	[illegible]	[illegible]
"	February	[illegible]	[illegible]	[illegible]	[illegible]	[illegible]	[illegible]	[illegible]
"	March	[illegible]	[illegible]	[illegible]	[illegible]	[illegible]	[illegible]	[illegible]
"	April	[illegible]	[illegible]	[illegible]	[illegible]	[illegible]	[illegible]	[illegible]
"	May	[illegible]	[illegible]	[illegible]	[illegible]	[illegible]	[illegible]	
"	June	[illegible]	[illegible]	[illegible]	[illegible]	[illegible]	[illegible]	
"	July	[illegible]	[illegible]	[illegible]	[illegible]	[illegible]	[illegible]	
"	August	[illegible]	[illegible]	[illegible]	[illegible]	[illegible]	[illegible]	
"	September	[illegible]	[illegible]	[illegible]	From [illegible] days' observations			

3

Table II.—Diurnal Variation of the Temperature of the Air in Shade:

Recapitulation of the preceding mean hourly values for each month, and of their monthly mean temperatures.

Year.	Month.	Lat. North.	Long. West.	2h	4h	6h	8h	10h	Noon.	2h	4h	6h	8h	10h	Midn't.	Mean.
1857	July	[illegible]	[illegible]	. .	[illegible]	. .	[illegible]	. .	[illegible]	. .	[illegible]	. .	[illegible]	. .	[illegible]	[illegible]
"	Aug.	[illegible]	[illegible]	. .	[illegible]	. .	[illegible]	. .	[illegible]	. .	[illegible]	. .	[illegible]	. .	[illegible]	[illegible]
"	Sept.	[illegible]	[illegible]	[illegible]	[illegible]	[illegible]	[illegible]	[illegible]	[illegible]	[illegible]	[illegible]	[illegible]	[illegible]	[illegible]	[illegible]	[illegible]
"	Oct.	[illegible]	[illegible]	[illegible]	[illegible]	[illegible]	[illegible]	[illegible]	[illegible]	[illegible]	[illegible]	[illegible]	[illegible]	[illegible]	[illegible]	[illegible]
"	Nov.	[illegible]	[illegible]	[illegible]	[illegible]	[illegible]	[illegible]	[illegible]	[illegible]	[illegible]	[illegible]	[illegible]	[illegible]	[illegible]	[illegible]	[illegible]
"	Dec.	[illegible]	[illegible]	[illegible]	[illegible]	[illegible]	[illegible]	[illegible]	[illegible]	[illegible]	[illegible]	[illegible]	[illegible]	[illegible]	[illegible]	[illegible]
1858	Jan.	[illegible]	[illegible]	[illegible]	[illegible]	[illegible]	[illegible]	[illegible]	[illegible]	[illegible]	[illegible]	[illegible]	[illegible]	[illegible]	[illegible]	[illegible]
"	Feb.	[illegible]	[illegible]	[illegible]	[illegible]	[illegible]	[illegible]	[illegible]	[illegible]	[illegible]	[illegible]	[illegible]	[illegible]	[illegible]	[illegible]	[illegible]
"	March	[illegible]	[illegible]	[illegible]	[illegible]	[illegible]	[illegible]	[illegible]	[illegible]	[illegible]	[illegible]	[illegible]	[illegible]	[illegible]	[illegible]	[illegible]
"	April	[illegible]	[illegible]	[illegible]	[illegible]	[illegible]	[illegible]	[illegible]	[illegible]	[illegible]	[illegible]	[illegible]	[illegible]	[illegible]	[illegible]	[illegible]
"	May	[illegible]	[illegible]	. .	[illegible]	. .	[illegible]	. .	[illegible]	. .	[illegible]	. .	[illegible]	. .	[illegible]	[illegible]
"	June	[illegible]	[illegible]	. .	[illegible]	. .	[illegible]	. .	[illegible]	. .	[illegible]	. .	[illegible]	. .	[illegible]	[illegible]
"	July	[illegible]	[illegible]	. .	[illegible]	. .	[illegible]	. .	[illegible]	. .	[illegible]	. .	[illegible]	. .	[illegible]	[illegible]
"	Aug.	[illegible]	[illegible]	. .	[illegible]	. .	[illegible]	. .	[illegible]	. .	[illegible]	. .	[illegible]	. .	[illegible]	[illegible]
"	Sept.	[illegible]	[illegible]	. .	[illegible]	. .	[illegible]	. .	[illegible]	. .	[illegible]	. .	[illegible]	. .	[illegible]	[illegible]
"	Oct.	[illegible]	[illegible]	. .	[illegible]	. .	[illegible]	. .	[illegible]	. .	[illegible]	. .	[illegible]	. .	[illegible]	[illegible]
"	Nov.	[illegible]	[illegible]	[illegible]	[illegible]	[illegible]	[illegible]	[illegible]	[illegible]	[illegible]	[illegible]	[illegible]	[illegible]	[illegible]	[illegible]	[illegible]
"	Dec.	[illegible]	[illegible]	[illegible]	[illegible]	[illegible]	[illegible]	[illegible]	[illegible]	[illegible]	[illegible]	[illegible]	[illegible]	[illegible]	[illegible]	[illegible]
1859	Jan.	[illegible]	[illegible]	[illegible]	[illegible]	[illegible]	[illegible]	[illegible]	[illegible]	[illegible]	[illegible]	[illegible]	[illegible]	[illegible]	[illegible]	[illegible]
"	Feb.	[illegible]	[illegible]	[illegible]	[illegible]	[illegible]	[illegible]	[illegible]	[illegible]	[illegible]	[illegible]	[illegible]	[illegible]	[illegible]	[illegible]	[illegible]
"	March	[illegible]	[illegible]	[illegible]	[illegible]	[illegible]	[illegible]	[illegible]	[illegible]	[illegible]	[illegible]	[illegible]	[illegible]	[illegible]	[illegible]	[illegible]
"	April	[illegible]	[illegible]	. .	[illegible]	. .	[illegible]	. .	[illegible]	. .	[illegible]	. .	[illegible]	. .	[illegible]	[illegible]
"	May	[illegible]	[illegible]	. .	[illegible]	. .	[illegible]	. .	[illegible]	. .	[illegible]	. .	[illegible]	. .	[illegible]	[illegible]
"	June	[illegible]	[illegible]	. .	[illegible]	. .	[illegible]	. .	[illegible]	. .	[illegible]	. .	[illegible]	. .	[illegible]	[illegible]
"	July	[illegible]	[illegible]	[illegible]	[illegible]	[illegible]	[illegible]	[illegible]	[illegible]	[illegible]	[illegible]	[illegible]	[illegible]	[illegible]	[illegible]	[illegible]
"	Aug.	[illegible]	[illegible]	. .	[illegible]	. .	[illegible]	. .	[illegible]	. .	[illegible]	. .	[illegible]	. .	[illegible]	[illegible]
"	Sept.	[illegible]	[illegible]	. .	[illegible]	. .	[illegible]	. .	[illegible]	. .	[illegible]	. .	[illegible]	. .	[illegible]	[illegible]

Discussion of the Annual Variation and of the Temperature at Different Seasons of the Year.

The monthly means brought out in Table I refer to different localities and years, and require to be combined with reference to these changes. The "Fox" remained stationary at the winter quarters for nearly a whole year—between August, 1858, and August, 1859—and we will, therefore, first examine the annual variation, the mean temperature of the seasons and of the whole year, for Port Kennedy, in north latitude 72° 01′, west longitude 94° 14′, near the eastern entrance to Bellot Straits, which separates North Somerset from Boothia Felix. Our monthly means for August, 1858 and 1859, require to be corrected for difference of position. For this purpose, I have projected on a suitable chart the two isothermal lines for the month of August, constructed by me on the basis of Dove's investigation, and published in the 2d volume, Appendix No. XIII, of Dr. Kane's Narrative of his Arctic Expedition (north of Smith Straits), in the years 1853–'54–'55. By means of these curves, we find that the positions of August, 1858 (viz., latitude 73°.1, longitude 88°.5), and of August, 1859 (viz., latitude 71°.9, longitude 79°.3), can be assumed as lying nearly on the same isotherm, with a temperature of 1°.4 Fahr. relatively colder than the isotherm passing through Port Kennedy in that month; the normal distance between the isotherms differing 4°.5 in temperature being nearly 6° of arc. In the following table, the temperature for the month of August is derived from the mean of the respective observations of 1858 and 1859 increased by 1°.4, in order to refer the value to the locality of Port Kennedy.

TABLE III.—MEAN MONTHLY TEMPERATURE OF THE AIR IN SHADE OBSERVED AT PORT KENNEDY, IN LATITUDE 72° 01′ N., AND LONGITUDE 94° 14′ W.; IN THE YEARS 1858 AND 1859.

1858–9	August	+36°.93	1859	February	−36°.06
1858	September	+25.41	"	March	−17.74
"	October	+ 7.53	"	April	− 2.62
"	November	−11.17	"	May	+13.04
"	December	−32.97	"	June	+35.11
1859	January	−33.17	"	July	+40.19

To express the above and other periodic results in an analytical form, Bessel's formula of interpolation for periodic functions, and depending on the method of least squares,[1] will be made use of throughout the discussion; a practice which has now become almost universal in meteorological and many other physical investigations.

The above numbers will be found represented by the formula—

$$T = +2^\circ.17 + 36^\circ.10 \sin(\theta + 265^\circ 4') + 0^\circ.68 \sin(2\theta + 179^\circ 57') + 1^\circ.16 \sin(3\theta + 275^\circ 53')$$

T representing the monthly values of the annual variation, and the angle θ counting from January 1st at the rate of 30° a month. According to this expression, the mean annual temperature at Port Kennedy is +2°.17 Fahr.

The strict application of Bessel's formula requires the intervals between the successive observations or means to be of equal length, and a small correction, therefore, becomes necessary on account of the unequal length of the months. This correction, generally too small to be noticed in low latitudes, is of sufficient magnitude in very high latitudes not to be neglectable. The following numbers show the quantity, in days and fractions of a day, by which the middle of each actual month differs from the mean of each month of average duration (30.4 days for a common, and 30.5 days for a leap, year), and for which interval a correction, —depending, also, on the magnitude of the variation of the temperature—is to be applied. A positive sign indicates that the middle of the actual month occurs earlier than the middle of the normal month; a negative sign indicates the reverse. Commencing with January, and proceeding in regular order, these intervals are as follows:—[2]

−0d.3	+0.6	+1.5	+1.5	+1.4	+1.0	+1.2	+0.7	+0.2	+0.5	+0.4	+0d.3
−0.8	+0.2	+0.3	+0.8	+0.8	+0.3	+0.6	+0.1	+0.3	+0.2	+0.9	+0.2

The upper line is for a common year, the lower line for a leap year. These numbers suppose the angle θ to be zero for the commencement of the civil year, and that the daily mean temperature, so far as the annual fluctuation is concerned, refers to the middle of the day. The corrections become greatest for the spring and autumn months, when the annual variation is most rapid. To obtain an ap-

[1] Explained at length by Sir J. Herschel in the article "Meteorology," Vol. XIV, 8th edition of the *Encyclopædia Britannica*.

[2] These numbers were given in my discussion of the meteorological observations of the second Grinnell Expedition, under command of Dr. E. K. Kane. See Vol. XI of the Smithsonian Contributions to Knowledge. 1859.

proximate value for the diurnal change for the middle of each month, the above formula was used, the increase in the value of θ for one day being 59′.2. Multiplying the daily change into the above intervals, we obtain the following mean monthly temperatures corrected for unequal duration, to which numbers the correction for index error has been added, as given in the third column of the table.

PORT KENNEDY. MEAN TEMPERATURE OF THE AIR IN SHADE IN EACH NORMAL MONTH.

Month.	Mean temp.	Corr'd for index.	Month.	Mean temp.	Corr'd for index.
January	−31°.41	−31°.48	July	+37°.94	+37°.98
February	−36.87	−36.93	August	+36.76	+36.76
March	−16.98	−17.41	September	+25.13	+25.13
April	− 1.88	− 1.95	October	+ 7.27	+ 7.13
May	+15.81	+15.87	November	−11.41	−11.86
June	+33.42	+33.87	December	−33.03	−33.73

The maximum corrections for inequality in the length of the month were +0°.04, in April, and —0°.32, in October. The above monthly means, as corrected for index error, will be found represented by the expression (II)—

$$T = +2°.02 + 33°.20 \sin(\theta + 249° 5') + 0°.80 \sin(2\theta + 256° 56') + 1°.06 \sin(3\theta + 274° 43').$$

The numerical coefficients differ but slightly from the corresponding values in the first expression. The observations are represented as follows (the hundredths have been omitted as having no real value):—

Month.	Mean corrected for index error.	Mean corrected for index and inequality.	Same by Form. II.	Difference.	Month.	Mean corrected for index error.	Mean corrected for index and inequality.	Same by Form. II.	Difference.
January	−31°.40	−31°.44	−33°.47	+2°.0	July	+41°.11	+39°.96	+40°.92	−0°.9
February	−37.04	−36.79	−33.13	−3.6	August	+36.95	+36.26	+34.91	0.0
March	−16.23	−17.44	−19.74	+2.3	September	+25.41	+25.13	+24.96	+0.2
April	− 1.93	− 1.98	− 2.07	+0.1	October	+ 7.44	+ 7.13	+ 7.63	−0.5
May	+15.06	+15.87	+17.32	−1.5	November	−11.40	−11.86	−13.12	+1.3
June	+35.11	+35.61	+34.01	+1.7	December	−33.63	−33.76	−31.18	−2.6
					Mean	+ 1.85	+ 2.02	+ 2.05	0.0

The differences between the observed and computed mean monthly temperatures are greatest in winter, which is due to the greater fluctuations of the temperature in that season. The same result was found from my reduction of the Van Rensselaer Harbor temperatures, as observed by Dr. Kane. The average probable error of representation of the mean temperature of any one month is accordingly ±2°.1, and of the result for the mean annual temperature ±0°.6.

The following table contains the temperature of the several seasons at Port Kennedy; December, January, and February being reckoned as winter months (and so on for the other seasons), in accordance with meteorological usage. The results by Formula II refer to the corrected normal months; the results headed "by observation," are corrected for index error.

Mean Temperatures of the Seasons.

At Port Kennedy, Lat. 72° 1', Long. 94° 14'. Seasons.	By observation.	By Form. II.		At Van Rensselaer Harbor, Lat. 78° 37', Long. 70° 53'. Seasons.	By observation.	By Form. II.	
Winter	−35°.04	−34°.23		Winter	−28°.59	−29°.1	
Spring	− 2.04	− 1.83		Spring	−10.89	− 9.9	
Summer	+37.40	+37.73		Summer	+33.19	+33.8	
Autumn	+ 7.49	+ 6.48		Autumn	− 4.13	− 4.6	
Year	+ 1.38	+ 2.03	±0°.4	Year	− 2.44	− 2.26	±0°.7

The corresponding values at Van Rensselaer Harbor have been inserted for comparison, and show a remarkable difference in the temperatures of spring and autumn, at which seasons it was much colder at Van Rensselaer Harbor than at Port Kennedy, whereas the mean winter temperature was lowest at Port Kennedy. The observations give the range between the summer and winter mean at Port Kennedy 72°.4, and at Van Rensselaer Harbor 62°.0. According to Formula II, we find, as a close approximation, the warmest day July 20th, with $T = +41°.0$, and the coldest day January 19th, with $T = -38°.4$; hence, the range of the annual fluctuation 79°.4. The mean temperature of the year is reached on April 23d and October 22d.

The annual fluctuation of the temperature, or the observed and computed monthly (normal) means (corrected for index error), are represented in the annexed diagram (A). The curve shows the computed, and the dots the observed, temperature.

(A.) Annual Fluctuation of the Temperature of the Air at Port Kennedy.

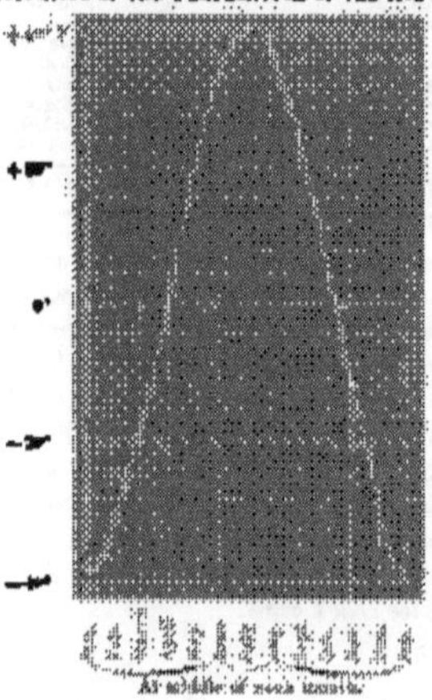

By means of Table I, we can make the following combinations of mean temperatures of the seasons of the year at different localities, which tabular numbers and combinations may be useful in future investigations of the course of the monthly isothermal lines, and of the isotherms of the several seasons.

Year.	Season.	North latitude.	West longitude.	Mean temperature.	Corrected for index error.
1857	Autumn	72°.1	67°.3	+ 6°.52	+ 6°.74
1857-8	Winter	73.0	64.0	−29.59	−29.79
1858	Spring	68.0	66.8	+11.23	+11.47
1858	Summer	74.0	78.0	+35.70	+35.79

The last three (but one) columns of Table I, exhibit the observed monthly maxima and minima of the temperature, and the extreme monthly range. These numbers are only relative, since the absolute extremes were not found recorded.

The highest temperature observed near Port Kennedy was +55°.0, on July 29th, 1859, and the lowest, —49°.8 (the index correction having been applied), on January 21st, 1859, and February 15th and 16th, 1859. Extreme range recorded at the winter quarters of the "Fox," 104°.8 of Fahrenheit's scale. To compare with the above numbers, Dr. Kane recorded at Van Rensselaer Harbor a maximum temperature of +51°.0, on July 23d, 1854, and a minimum temperature of —66°.4, on February 5th, 1854, and of —66°.5, on January 8th, 1855; observed absolute range 117°.4 Fahr., exceeding the Port Kennedy range by 12°.6.

The monthly range is greatest in March and April and in October and November; its value may be set down as 52° at Port Kennedy. This range is least in December and January and in July and August, when it does not exceed 27°. The extreme monthly range occurred in April, 1858 (viz., 64°), and in August, 1859 (viz., 17°).

Diurnal Variation of the Temperature.

The material collected in Table II furnishes the basis for the discussion of the diurnal fluctuation of the temperature. The hourly means (at certain observing hours) recorded there do not present the true daily fluctuation of the temperature in each month, on account of the disturbing effect of the annual change during the interval of a day, an effect which cannot be neglected in a locality where the annual fluctuation amounts to the excessive quantity of 79°.4. The tabular numbers, therefore, must first be cleared of this disturbing effect. This is best done by computing, by means of our expression for T, the change of the annual variation in a day for the middle of each month, and by correcting the means for the hours 0 A. M. and 12 P. M. by one half of this change, with opposite signs. There is no correction for noon, and a proportional one for the intermediate hours between morning and noon, and between noon and midnight; the signs in the second interval being the reverse from those in the first. The diurnal fluctuation during the long arctic night is so small as to be almost effaced by the overpowering effect of the annual fluctuation during a day.

Confining our attention for the present to the diurnal variation of the temperature in each month at Port Kennedy, we find an anomaly in the table of results in April, May, and June, 1859, when the symmetry of the observing hours is interrupted by observations being taken at 5 A. M. and 11 P. M. To remedy this defect, I have first established an approximate equation of the diurnal variation, and, by means of it, computed the difference between the mean at 4^h and 5^h, and also between 11^h and 12^h. These differences were applied respectively to the mean for 5^h and to the mean for 11^h, which gave the deduced means for 4^h and 12^h.

The maximum corrections for diurnal effect of the annual change occur at midnight, and are as follows:—

In January . .	0°.00	In July	0°.00
February . .	−0.15	August	+0.14
March . .	−0.26	September	+0.25
April . .	−0.32	October .	+0.34
May . .	−0.30	November .	+0.32
June . .	−0.22	December . .	+0.20

At 0^h A. M., the corrections are the same with the sign reversed; at noon, they are zero; at intermediate hours, proportional values were applied. The monthly mean is left unchanged (or very nearly so).

For August, I have combined the means of August, 1858 and 1859.

Accordingly, we have the following table of the diurnal variation of the temperature for each month of the year:—

TABLE IV.—DIURNAL VARIATION OF THE TEMPERATURE AT PORT KENNEDY.

	2^h	4^h	6^h	8^h	10^h	Noon.	2^h	4^h	6^h	8^h	10^h	Mid't.
	°	°	°	°	°	°	°	°	°	°	°	°
January	[illegible]	[illegible]	[illegible]	[illegible]	[illegible]	[illegible]	[illegible]	[illegible]	[illegible]	[illegible]	[illegible]	[illegible]
February	[illegible]	[illegible]	[illegible]	[illegible]	[illegible]	[illegible]	[illegible]	[illegible]	[illegible]	[illegible]	[illegible]	[illegible]
March	[illegible]	[illegible]	[illegible]	[illegible]	[illegible]	[illegible]	[illegible]	[illegible]	[illegible]	[illegible]	[illegible]	[illegible]
April	..	−4.42	..	[illegible]	..	[illegible]	..	[illegible]	..	[illegible]	..	[illegible]
May	..	[illegible]	..	[illegible]	..	[illegible]	..	[illegible]	..	[illegible]	..	[illegible]
June	..	[illegible]	..	[illegible]	..	[illegible]	..	[illegible]	..	[illegible]	..	[illegible]
July	[illegible]	[illegible]	[illegible]	[illegible]	[illegible]	[illegible]	[illegible]	[illegible]	+41.07	[illegible]	[illegible]	[illegible]
August	..	[illegible]	..	[illegible]	..	[illegible]	..	[illegible]	..	[illegible]	..	[illegible]
September	..	[illegible]	..	[illegible]	..	[illegible]	..	[illegible]	..	[illegible]	..	[illegible]
October	..	[illegible]	..	+ 7.22	..	[illegible]	..	+ 7.48	..	+ 7.47	..	[illegible]
November	[illegible]	[illegible]	[illegible]	[illegible]	[illegible]	[illegible]	[illegible]	[illegible]	[illegible]	[illegible]	[illegible]	[illegible]
December	[illegible]	[illegible]	[illegible]	[illegible]	[illegible]	[illegible]	[illegible]	−33.12	−33.17	[illegible]	−33.23	[illegible]

For the purpose of making full use of all the bi-hourly observations, it was thought advisable to express the values for the months of April, May, June, and August, September, October, analytically, and to supply by interpolation values for the hours 2, 6, 10, A. M. and P. M. The values thus computed were derived from the following expressions, in which the angle θ counts from midnight, and is reckoned at the rate of 15° an hour:—

For April, $t = -8°.54 + 8°.67 \sin(\theta + 255°) + 0°.70 \sin(2\theta + 37°)$
" May, $t = +13.16 + 1.09 \sin(\theta + 255) + 0.24 \sin(2\theta + 251)$
" June, $t = +33.17 + 4.65 \sin(\theta + 267) + 0.00 \sin(2\theta + 191)$

For August, $t = +35°.51 + 1°.32 \sin(\theta + 228°) + 0°.18 \sin(2\theta + 142°)$
" September, $t = +25.47 + 1.30 \sin(\theta + 213) + 0.31 \sin(2\theta + 65)$
" October, $t = +7.59 + 0.17 \sin(\theta + 258) + 0.35 \sin(2\theta +$ [illegible]$)$

The following table (IV, *b*) contains the interpolated values, by the insertion of which Table IV will be rendered complete:—

TABLE IV (*b*).—ADDITIONAL HOURLY VALUES OF THE DIURNAL FLUCTUATION AT PORT KENNEDY.

	2 A.M.	6 A.M.	10 A.M.	2 P.M.	6 P.M.	10 P.M.	Mean.
April	[illegible]	[illegible]	[illegible]	[illegible]	[illegible]	[illegible]	[illegible]
May	[illegible]	[illegible]	[illegible]	[illegible]	[illegible]	[illegible]	[illegible]
June	[illegible]	[illegible]	[illegible]	[illegible]	[illegible]	[illegible]	[illegible]
August	[illegible]	[illegible]	[illegible]	[illegible]	[illegible]	[illegible]	[illegible]
September	[illegible]	[illegible]	[illegible]	[illegible]	[illegible]	[illegible]	[illegible]
October	[illegible]	[illegible]	[illegible]	[illegible]	[illegible]	[illegible]	[illegible]

The two preceding tables furnish the following values for the amplitude of the diurnal fluctuation in each month of the year, also in each season, and for the whole year, together with the hours of maximum and minimum temperature, and the hours when the mean temperature is reached, for each of the periods.

TABLE V.—DAILY EXTREMES, RANGE, HOURS OF MAXIMA AND MINIMA, AND CRITICAL INTERVAL, FOR EACH MONTH OF THE YEAR.

Month.	Maximum.	Minimum.	Range.	Hour of max.	Hour of min.	Critical int.
January	[illegible]	[illegible]	1°.01	6 P.M.	4 A.M.	1
February	[illegible]	[illegible]	1.17	Noon	Midn't	12
March	−11.69	[illegible]	[illegible]	Noon	6 A.M.	8
April	+ 1.72	[illegible]	7.42	2 P.M.	Midn't	14
May	[illegible]	+11.03	7.24	2 P.M.	2 A.M.	12
June	[illegible]	[illegible]	[illegible]	10 A.M.	2 A.M.	8
July	[illegible]	[illegible]	6.97	Noon	2 A.M.	10
August	[illegible]	+34.16	[illegible]	2 P.M.	4 A.M.	10
September	[illegible]	[illegible]	[illegible]	2 P.M.	6 A.M.	8
October	[illegible]	[illegible]	[illegible]	Noon	Midn't	12
November	[illegible]	[illegible]	[illegible]	10 A.M.	Midn't	10
December	[illegible]	[illegible]	[illegible]	4 A.M.	8 A.M.	—4

The annexed diagram (B) exhibits the monthly values of the diurnal range:—

(B.) DIURNAL AMPLITUDE.

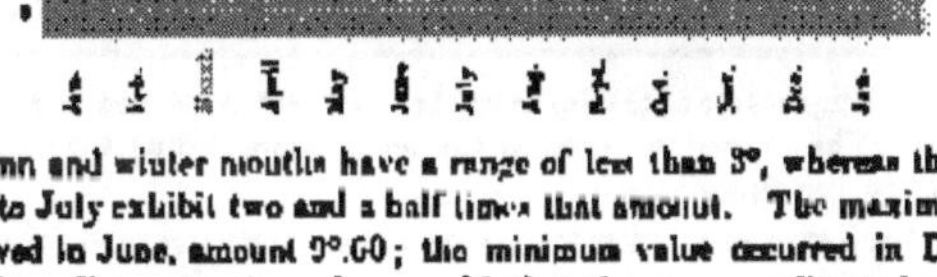

The autumn and winter months have a range of less than 3°, whereas the months of March to July exhibit two and a half times that amount. The maximum value was observed in June, amount 9°.60; the minimum value occurred in December, value 0°.14. For comparison, I may add that the corresponding values at Van

Rensselaer Harbor occurred in April, amount 9°.09, and in November, amount 1°.00; showing a correspondence in amount but not in time. The diurnal variation never disappears altogether, and even during the long arctic night there appears to be a daily propagation or existence of a thermal wave producing a range of about 1°. The amount of the amplitude changes tolerably regular from month to month; the high value in March, however, either presents a distinct feature or is due to some anomaly. Altogether, the curve indicates no secondary maximum, such as was found in September at Van Rensselaer Harbor.

On the average, the maximum temperature is reached between noon and 1 P. M., and the minimum between 2 and 3 A. M.; whereas, at Van Rensselaer Harbor, these hours were respectively 2 P. M. and 1 A. M.

The following table contains the hourly values of the diurnal variation for each season and the whole year:—

TABLE VI.—DIURNAL VARIATION IN EACH SEASON.

Season.	2h	4h	6h	8h	10h	Noon.	2h	4h	6h	8h	10h	Midn't.	Mean.
	°	°	°	°	°	°	°	°	°	°	°	°	°
Winter	−34.33	−34.34	−34.11	−34.43	−34.04	−33.79	−33.94	−34.06	−34.18	−34.16	−34.14	−34.64	−34.10
Spring	− 5.07	− 4.43	− 3.84	− 1.65	+ 0.34	+ 2.72	+ 2.57	+ 1.59	− 1.34	− 3.80	− 4.83	− 6.19	− 1.72
Summer	+33.64	+34.85	+34.27	+35.86	+36.63	+39.18	+38.33	+39.49	+37.61	+36.47	+35.31	+34.06	+35.96
Autumn	+ 6.60	+ 6.64	+ 6.61	+ 7.10	+ 7.01	+ 6.33	+ 9.17	+ 7.10	+ 7.34	+ 7.10	+ 6.84	+ 6.23	+ 7.[illegible]
Year	+0.21	+0.96	+1.78	+2.53	+3.10	+4.53	+4.10	+3.42	+2.37	+1.34	+0.86	+0.21	+2.0[illegible]
Same by formula	+0.10	+0.63	+1.30	+2.43	+3.13	+4.83	+4.09	+3.25	+2.42	+1.73	+0.66	+0.37	+2.0[illegible]
Differ'ce	+0.11	+0.03	−0.03	−0.09	−0.03	0.00	+0.02	+0.17	+0.05	+0.16	0.00	+0.06	

The computed diurnal variation for the whole year is derived from the expression given below. Comparing the means as stated above with corresponding values derived in the preceding discussion of the mean temperature of the seasons, we may add to each horizontal line the following corrections: to values for winter, −0°.05; for spring, +0°.30; for summer, +0°.29; for autumn, −0°.78; for the year, −0°.06. These differences arise from changes in the observing hours, and consequent necessity of interpolation.

TABLE V (b).

Season.	Maximum.	Minimum.	Range.	Hour of max.	Hour of min.	Critical int.
Winter	−33°.79	−34°.64	0°.75	Noon	Midn't	12h
Spring	+ 2.07	− 6.19	8.09	2 P. M.	Midn't	10
Summer	+39.49	+33.64	6.33	Noon	2 A. M.	14
Autumn	+ 9.28	+ 6.53	1.64	Noon	Midn't	12
Year	+ 4.53	+ 0.21	4.12	Noon	1 A. M.	13
By formula	+ 4.33	+ 0.09	4.24	0h 22m P. M.	1h 30m A. M.	13h 10m

The mean temperature of the day is reached at 7h 21m A. M. and at 6h 56m P. M., by formula. The diurnal variation of the temperature during the whole year is represented by the formula:—

$$t = +2^{\circ}.06 + 2^{\circ}.02 \sin (x + 258^{\circ}\ 57') + 0^{\circ}.33 \sin (2x + 117^{\circ}) + 0^{\circ}.09 \sin (3x + 261^{\circ}).$$

If we supply the constant term, and change the epoch from noon to midnight, as in the above expression, the diurnal variation at Van Rensselaer Harbor has been represented by

$$t = -2^{\circ}.21 + 1^{\circ}.85 \sin(\theta + 244^{\circ}\ 55') + 0^{\circ}.08 \sin(2\theta + 97^{\circ}) + 0^{\circ}.03 \sin(3\theta + 308^{\circ}),$$

which is here added for comparison.

In either expression, the constant term might be omitted, as not essential in the inquiry of the diurnal fluctuation; or the values +2°.02 and −2°.20, which are the true mean annual temperatures respectively, might be substituted in their place.

The maximum and minimum value is given by the formula:—

$$o = +2^{\circ}.02 \cos(\theta + 253^{\circ}\ 57') + 0^{\circ}.51 \cos(2\theta + 117^{\circ}) + 0^{\circ}.25 \cos(3\theta + 251^{\circ}).$$

The following diagram (C) exhibits the diurnal variation during the whole year:—

(C.) Diurnal Variation.

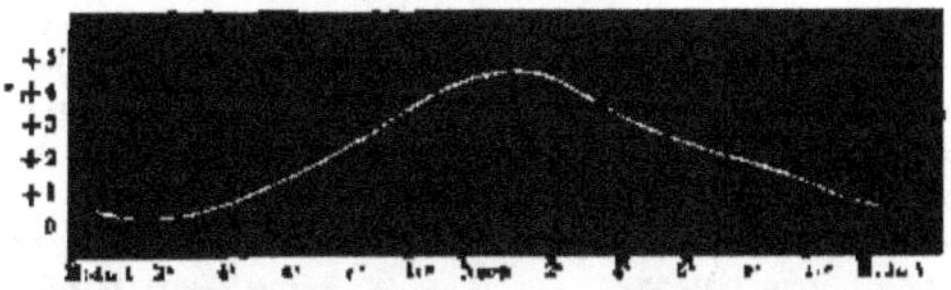

Hourly Corrections for Periodic Variations.—Under this head, a number of tables have been given by Prof. Guyot in his meteorological and physical tables, prepared for the Smithsonian Institution. These tables furnish the means of correcting other incomplete material at stations in the vicinity. A similar table was prepared by me for Van Rensselaer Harbor. The following table for Port Kennedy is directly derived from the values in Table II, in connection with Tables IV and IV (*b*). For those hours requiring interpolation in the latter case, the small corrections for the effect of the annual change during a day has again been deducted.

Arctic America.—Port Kennedy, Lat. 72° 01′ N., Long. 94° 14′ W. of Greenwich.

Corrections to be applied to any Bi-hourly or set of Bi-hourly Observations to obtain the Mean Temperature of the Day.

Degrees of Fahrenheit's scale.

Hour	Jan.	Feb.	March	April	May	June	July	Aug.	Sept.	Oct.	Nov.	Dec.	Year
	°	°	°	°	°	°	°	°	°	°	°	°	°
2 A.M.	+0.24	+0.41	+3.29	+3.14	+4.11	+3.12	+3.03	+1.23	+0.74	+0.22	+0.24	−0.43	+1.87
4	+0.72	+0.29	+3.22	+2.07	+3.03	+3.97	+2.55	+1.31	+1.21	+[illegible]	−0.[illegible]	−0.56	+1.65
6	+0.61	+0.22	+3.79	+1.45	+1.91	+0.56	+0.88	+0.91	+1.28	+0.31	−[illegible]	−0.37	+0.60
8	+0.43	−0.12	+1.57	−0.24	−1.11	−2.16	−1.16	+0.16	+0.78	+0.30	−0.98	+0.35	−0.25
10	−0.02	−0.23	−2.99	−2.15	−2.13	−4.41	−2.77	−0.61	−0.09	−0.77	−1.29	−0.10	−1.51
Noon	−0.23	−0.72	−3.13	−3.16	−3.67	−4.43	−3.33	−1.17	−0.99	−1.46	−0.51	−0.16	−2.25
2 P.M.	+0.01	−0.78	−4.12	−4.58	−3.13	−3.35	−2.29	−1.31	−1.42	−0.75	−0.27	−0.25	−2.03
4	−0.25	−0.21	−4.01	−2.11	−2.93	−1.73	−1.61	−1.03	−1.37	+0.02	+0.28	+0.21	−1.31
6	−0.62	+0.25	+0.63	−0.77	−1.18	−0.34	−0.94	−0.71	−0.80	+0.33	+0.18	+0.30	−0.50
8	−0.64	+0.04	+1.44	+1.59	+0.93	+1.76	+0.11	−0.77	−0.37	+0.31	+0.48	+0.38	+0.50
10	−0.41	−0.07	+1.74	+2.75	+2.35	+2.48	+1.97	+0.35	+0.39	+0.71	+0.94	+0.13	+1.13
Midn't	+0.24	+0.56	+2.88	+2.87	+3.46	+4.42	+3.15	+1.02	+0.73	+1.04	+1.28	+0.32	+1.67
8, 8	−0.13	+0.27	+2.22	+0.34	−0.29	0.00	−0.02	+0.10	+0.24	+0.32	−0.06	−0.00	+0.25
6, 6	0.00	−0.06	+1.38	+0.66	−0.26	−0.50	−0.52	−0.05	+0.31	+0.25	−0.01	+0.17	+0.17
10, 10	−0.21	−0.15	−0.62	+0.30	0.00	−0.81	−0.60	−0.13	+0.06	−0.07	−0.16	+0.12	−0.18
6, 2, 10	0.00	−0.19	−0.07	−0.03	−0.16	−0.02	+0.04	+0.02	−0.01	+0.03	+0.03	−0.14	−0.04

Owing to the fact that the observations extend over one year only, the table, in some instances, must necessarily contain some small irregularities. The closest results are obtained from the hours 0, 2, 10, which was also the case at Van Rensselaer Harbor.

Connection of the Lunar Phases with Low Winter Temperature.

The apparent connection of the lunar phases with the observed temperature of the air during the Arctic winter, the thermometer being below the zero of Fahrenheit's scale, was long ago noticed by Arctic explorers, and was again independently observed by Dr. Kane, in the discussion of whose observations I have attempted an explanation of the phenomenon. In that paper, the connection of the lunar phases with the serenity of the sky and the fall of snow was also discussed; for the observations now on hand, the numerical relations alone will be represented.

Dividing the daily means of the temperature into penthemera (or periods of five days), a table was formed showing the time of full and new moon and the mean temperatures; and, by means of differences of the alternate means at these periods, the amount by which the mean temperature is lower at full moon than at new moon is exhibited in column headed Δ.

FIRST WINTER, 1857–'58.
BAFFIN BAY.
Between lat. 76°.0, long. 68°.0 and lat. 63°.5, long. 62°.2.

Pentheme.	Moon's phase.	Temp.	Alt. means.	Δ
Nov. 23–27		−7°.8		
28–32	1st ○	−27.0	. . .	(−4°.1)
Dec. 3–7		−28.1		
8–12		−23.4		
13–17	10th ●	−29.3	−25.7	−6.6
18–22		−19.9		
23–27		−15.5		
28–32	30th ○	−34.4	−21.2	−3.8
Jan. 2–6		−19.9		
7–11		−17.6		
12–16	16th ●	−32.0	−25.1	−7.6
17–21		−23.2		
22–26		−25.0		
27–31	29th ○	−36.5	−16.1	−10.7
Feb. 1–5		−21.8		
6–10		−26.1		
11–15	13th ●	−10.8	−19.2	−9.0
16–20		− 6.1		
21–25		−13.7		
26–30	27th ○	− 3.6	. . .	(+8.7)

Omitting the first and last (incomplete) values of Δ, we find its average value = −7°.5.

SECOND WINTER, 1858–'59.
PORT KENNEDY, BELLOT STRAIT.
Lat. 72°.0, long. 94°.2.

Pentheme.	Moon's phase.	Temp.	Alt. means.	Δ
Nov. 2–6	6th ●	−7°.5		
7–11		−12.0		
12–16		−17.0		
17–21	20th ○	+ 4.7	−19.0	+23.7
22–26		−23.9		
27–31		−19.6		
Dec. 2–6	6th ●	−30.0	−13.1	+17.2
7–11		−20.3		
12–16		−28.5		
17–21	20th ○	−30.9	−33.9	+ 3.0
22–26		−30.0		
27–31		−34.5		
Jan. 1–5	4th ●	−37.1	−33.7	+ 4.4
6–10		−34.4		
11–15		−31.0		
16–20	19th ○	−34.4	−33.5	− 1.3
21–25		−36.9		
26–30		−39.9		
31–35	3d ●	−39.6	−37.5	− 9.3
Feb. 5–9		−39.8		
10–14		−34.1		
15–19	17th ○	−41.3	−26.7	−14.6
20–24		−35.8		
25–29		−34.3		
March 2–6	4th ●	−23.9	−23.0	− 0.7
7–11		−14.3		
12–16		−21.4		
17–21	18th ○	−36.8	−13.0	−13.7
22–26		− 4.9		
27–31		−11.7		
April 1–5	3d ●	− 1.1	. . .	(−25.1)
6–10		−12.6		

The temperature between Nov. 17–21 is anomalous, and affects also the following value (17.2) of Δ; these values, as well as that of April 1–5, have been omitted in the mean. For the period Nov. 17–21, the wind was S. E.; weather misty, with occasional snow, and variable.

Average Δ, winter 1858–'59 = −4°.7.

The average fall of the temperature for the period from new moon to full moon, from the above comparisons, is 7½°. The separate results may, perhaps, not appear as conclusive as those obtained at Van Rensselaer Harbor (lat. 78°.6); still, the general deduction is confirmed. The following account of the weather for each day, the day preceding and the day following, of the full and new moon, is copied from the record and refers to noon. Beaufort's signification of letters is used.

Full Moon.				New Moon.			
1857 Dec. 1	b. v.	b. v.	b. v.	1857 Dec. 16	b. v.	b.	b. m.
Dec. 30	m. c.	b. v.	b. c.	1858 Jan. 15	b. c.	m.	m. c.
1858 Jan. 29	b.	b. c.	b, c.	Feb. 13	b. c.	b. c.	b. c.
Feb. 27	b. m. s.	b. c.	b. c.				
1858 Nov. 20	c. m.	m. c. s.	c. m.	1858 Nov. 5	b. m. s.	b. m.	b. c. m.
Dec. 20	b. c, m.	c, m. s.	b., m. s.	Dec. 5	b. o.	m.	b. c.
1859 Jan. 18	m. s	c.	b. m.	1859 Jan. 4	b. c.	b. c. s.	b. m. c.
Feb. 17	b. m.	m. c.	b. m.	Feb. 3	m.	b. c.	b. c. s.
Mar. 18	b. c. s.	b. c.	b. m.	March 4	m.	b.	b. c.
				April 3	b.	b. c.	c. s.

b stands for blue sky. c stands for clouds, detached. m stands for misty, hazy.
o " overcast. s " snow. v " visibility, transparency.
d " snow drift.

In the first winter, the weather appears to have been finer and clearer at full moon; whereas, in the second winter, there is little or no difference, a misty weather and snow drifts characterizing the locality; under these circumstances, the lunar effect could hardly be expected to show itself as distinctly as brought out above. Captain McClintock makes the following remark (page 1x of the 4th number of meteorological papers published by the Board of Trade): "The dense and continued mist over Bellot Strait, caused by considerably warmer water than the air above it, and the strong local winds, perhaps partly caused by this speedy evaporation and condensation, are special features."

No recurrence of cold was noticed, either in 1858 or in 1859, about May 11th—the period Dove has called attention to.

Temperature of the Winds.—To ascertain the elevating or depressing influence of the various winds on the temperature, the following method of investigation was adopted:—

The normal temperature of each day was made out by taking the mean of the temperature of that day, the two preceding and the two following days. The observed temperature at the hours 6 A. M. and 6 P. M., and at noon and midnight, were then compared with the respective normal temperature (the mean of five days); the differences thus obtained were tabulated according to one of the eight winds (or calm) N., N. E., E., S. E., etc., blowing at the respective hours. The mean difference for each wind, and for a period extending over a season, very nearly indicates the elevating or depressing influence of each wind, and at each season, on the temperature of the air. The + sign indicate warmer, the — sign colder, than the average. The diurnal variation being generally small, and in the absence of any regularity of a certain wind blowing regularly at certain hours, the effect of this variation will disappear in the resulting average values. In the exceptional case when no observations are recorded at 6 A. M. and P. M., the mean of observations at 4 and 8 A. M. and P. M. were substituted. For notes referring to the observations of the winds, see the record or Part II of this discussion. The directions of the wind are "true." This method of investigation is less laborious than that followed by me in a similar discussion of the temperature of the various winds at Van Rensselaer Harbor.

All results in Baffin Bay have been united, and a second group has been formed from the observations at Port Kennedy.

The seasons and localities for Baffin Bay, for which results were deduced, are as follows:—

Season. Months.	Between latitudes		Between longitudes	
Autumn—Sept., Oct., Nov., 1858 . . .	75°.8 and	74°.6	65°.0 and	68°.1
Winter—Dec., 1858, Jan., Feb., 1859 . .	74.3	71.5	61.4	60.9
Spring—March, April, May, 1859 . .	68.4	68.7	59.1	63.7
Summer—June, July, August, 1859 . .	74.6	73.1	66.1	65.5
Mean	72°.5 N.		63°.6 W.	

This average position is nearly in the middle of Baffin Bay.

ELEVATING OR DEPRESSING EFFECTS OF THE WINDS ON THE TEMPERATURE OF THE AIR.

+ warmer, — colder, than the mean temperature.

	Calm.	N.	N. E.	E.	S. E.	S.	S. W.	W.	N. W.	Mean.
Autumn 1858	−5°.0	−0°.2	+3°.1	+1°.0	+0°.1	+0°.7	−3°.6	−1°.8	+0°.3	
Winter 1858–9	−1.6	−0.1	−0.3	−1.0	+0.8	−0.4	−2.4	−0.2	+1.2	
Spring 1859	+0.7	−1.5	+1.0	+1.5	+5.8	+2.8	−0.7	−0.3	−2.0	
Summer 1859	+0.8	0.0	+0.5	−0.5	−0.5	+0.5	0.0	+0.0	−0.5	
Mean	−1.0	−0.5	+1.1	+0.4	+3.3	+0.8	−1.4	−0.4	−0.5	+0°.2
Result for year	−1.2	−0.7	+0.9	+0.2	+3.1	+0.6	−1.6	−0.6	−0.7	

The results in the last line, obtained after deducting 0°.2 from the preceding line, show that the S. E. winds are the warmest, and the S. W. winds the coldest; also, that during calms the temperature is lower. At Van Rensselaer Harbor, the depressing effect of the calms amounted to 3°.4.

The following table shows the results for Port Kennedy:—

	Calm.	N.	N. E.	E.	S. E.	S.	S. W.	W.	N. W.	Mean.
Autumn 1858	+5°.4	+0°.0	+1°.3	+3°.7	+3°.4	+0°.3	+1°.0	−1°.1	−1°.5	
Winter 1858–9	−0.5	+2.0	−0.8	+2.3	. . .	. . .	+2.8	+0.7	−0.6	
Spring 1859	−0.4	+0.4	+0.3	+0.5	. . .	. . .	. . .	−0.6	−1.8	
Summer 1859	−0.8	−0.4	−0.3	+0.1	−1.8	−1.3	+0.3	+0.6	−0.3	
Mean	+0.1	+0.7	+0.2	+1.5	+0.8	+1.5	+1.8	−0.4	−1.0	+0°.5
Result for year	−0.5	+0.1	−0.3	+1.2	+0.4	+1.0	+1.5	−0.6	−1.5	

The results for winds from the S. E., S., and S. W. are not very reliable, on account of the scarcity of wind from these directions. At Port Kennedy, the E. winds are the warmest and the N. W. the coldest; during calms, the mean temperature is depressed 0°.6. The local configuration of the land, and the peculiar situation of the port, may possibly affect the results deduced.

The following recapitulation of results shows a tolerably fair agreement between the localities—middle of Baffin Bay, Van Rensselaer Harbor,[1] and Port Kennedy.

True direction of wind.	Baffin Bay. Lat. [illegible] N. Long. 65°.6 W.	Van Rensselaer Harbor. Lat. 78°.6 N. Long. [illegible]°.9 W.	Port Kennedy. Lat. 72°.0 N. Long. 94°.2 W.
N.	—0°.8	—1°.4	+0°.1
N. E.	+0.7	0.0	—0.4
E.	+0.1	—0.1	+1.2
S. E.	+3.0	+0.8	+0.1
S.	+0.4	+0.6	+1.0
S. W.	—1.7	+0.4	+0.5
W.	—0.9	+0.1	—1.0
N. W.	—0.8	—1.4	—1.5

(The positive and negative values have been made to balance, after omitting the value for the calms.)

Counting θ from the north (or belonging to a true north wind), in the direction east, south, etc., to 360°, the above tabular numbers can be expressed by the formulæ—

	Lat.	Long.	
Middle of Baffin Bay,	72°.5	65°.6	$T = +1°.5 \sin(\theta + 308°) + 0°.6 \sin(2\theta + 178°)$
Van Rensselaer Harbor,	78.6	70.9	$T = +1.0 \sin(\theta + 286) + 0.3 \sin(2\theta + 335)$
Port Kennedy,	72.0	94.2	$T = +0.9 \sin(\theta + 370) + 0.4 \sin(2\theta + 86)$

The second terms are of subordinate value; the first, or significant terms, correspond upon the whole very close, considering the peculiarity of each station, in reference to free exposure to the various winds.

From the 4th number of the meteorological papers published by the Board of Trade in 1860, I extract the following remark of Captain McClintock's: "The Danish settlers at Upernavik, in Northwest Greenland, are at times startled by a sudden rise of temperature during the depth of winter, when all nature has been long frozen; rain sometimes falls in torrents. It is called the warm southeast wind." In reference to a warm northwest wind in Upper Baffin Bay, alluded to in the same paper (p. iv), the above table for that locality shows that, although this wind is warm in winter, it is considerably colder in spring, and also colder, on the average, for the whole year.

Temperature of the Soil.—The following is copied from p. 309 of the record: "On 14th September, 1858, as soon as it appeared probable that we should winter at Port Kennedy, I sunk a brass tube two feet two inches vertically in the ground, and inserted a padded thermometer. The ground, at time of sinking the tube, was frozen from six inches below the surface, and it was with great difficulty I could get the tube sufficiently far down. The surface soil was similar to that

[1] See results given on page 111 of my discussion of Dr. Kane's meteorological observations, Vol. XI of the Smithsonian Contributions to Knowledge. As explained elsewhere (and confirmed by Mr. Sonntag and Dr. Hayes), the true direction of the wind was actually observed at Van Rensselaer Harbor; hence, the results given in the paper cited above required a corresponding change.

strewn over the land, but from below six inches it was of a yellowish mud. The thermometer used was one of very small bore, with a long stem finely graduated (it had been prepared for taking temperatures of trees). From 18th to 29th September, 1858, no register was made, as the ship was not in port; also from 18th to 28th March, 1859, as I was absent from the ship travelling. The minimum temperature registered was +0°.6, on March 10th, 1859; the lowest may be assumed as at zero, on March 16th. The register was continued until June 16th, when water entered the tube, and the thermometer was frozen to the side so that it could not be detached. Column No. 1 gives the register of this thermometer. Column No. 2 gives the depth of overlaying snow, which was always greater than the average on the land. On 17th January, 1859, a tube was placed one foot one inch deep in a mixture of shingle and earth; in this a thermometer was placed. The position of the ground was such that scarcely any snow lay upon it, the strong wind constantly blowing removing it almost as soon as deposited. Column No. 3 is the register of this thermometer. February 12th, 1859, a tube was placed horizontally on the surface of the ground, beneath the snow lying on the ground, where thermometer No. 1 was sunk. The temperature as shown by this thermometer (Column No. 4) was registered until the snow all disappeared. Column No. 5 gives the mean temperature of the air for the day on which the registers of the different thermometers were taken. Column No. 6 gives the mean temperature of the air for the number of days or hours intervening between the registers of the thermometers. All the temperatures of the different thermometers are corrected so as to reduce them to the standard of the air thermometer, comparisons having previously been made as opportunity offered."

(Signed) DAVID WALKER.

Date.	No. 1.	No. 2.	No. 3.	No. 4.	No. 5.	No. 6.
1858		inches				
Sept. 30	30°.4	..	..	..	+24°.2	
Oct. 1	30.0	..	..	..	+23.4	Between Sept. 30 and Oct. 1 = +24°.3
" 4	29.5	3	..	..	+22.3	" Oct. 1 " 4 +23.7
" 7	27.9	5	..	..	+13.6	" " 4 " 7 +22.3
" 9	24.5	6	..	..	− 1.3	" " 7 " 9 + 8.1
" 13	24.1	7	..	..	− 0.7	" " 9 " 13 + 7.0
" 16	22.4	7½	..	..	+10.5	" " 13 " 16 0.0
" 19	22.2	9	..	..	+ 8.1	" " 16 " 19 + 9.2
" 23	20.3	15	..	..	− 8.8	" " 19 " 23 + 2.2
" 26	19.4	19	..	..	− 2.0	" " 23 " 26 − 0.6
Nov. 6	17.9	43	..	..	− 9.6	" " 26 Nov. 6 − 2.6
" 13	14.8	42	..	..	− 9.2	" Nov. 6 " 13 −10.7
" 20	14.0	66	..	..	−13.4	" " 13 " 20 − 7.6
" 27	14.1	67	..	..	−23.4	" " 20 " 27 −16.3
Dec. 4	13.8	69	..	..	−28.6	" " 27 Dec. 4 −16.6
" 11	12.9	72	..	..	−32.0	" Dec. 4 " 11 −28.6
" 16	10.9	61	..	..	−33.6	" " 11 " 16 −26.7
1859						
Jan. 1	4.3	69	..	..	−30.3	" " 16 Jan. 1 −34.9
" 8	0.9	69	..	..	−34.7	" Jan. 1 " 8 −38.8
" 14	0.4	64	−18°.7	..	−29.3	" " 8 " 14 −29.2
" 21	..	..	−22.7	..	−42.0	" " 14 " 21 −33.4
" 27	4.4	71	−22.2	..	−35.8	" " 21 " 27 −37.8
Feb. 1	..	..	−24.7	..	−32.3	" " 27 Feb. 1 −32.1
" 13	2.9	73	−23.7	..	−27.7	" Feb. 1 " 13 −34.1
" 17	..	..	−23.1	..	−34.0	" " 13 " 17 −36.0
" 26	1.9	69	−25.7	− 3°.0	−34.3	" " 17 " 26 −27.4
March 4	..	..	−23.7	..	−22.2	" " 26 Mar. 4 −32.1
" 10	0.0	73	−14.4	− 3.9	−23.4	" March 4 " 10 −17.0
" 26	0.0	70	−10.9	− 2.7	−15.4	" " 10 " 26 −17.6
April 2	..	..	−12.4	..	+ 2.9	" " 26 April 2 −10.9
" 7	1.1	70	−10.0	− 2.3	−10.4	" April 2 " 7 − 3.1
" 12	..	..	−12.8	..	−16.3	" " 7 " 12 −12.3
" 16	1.4	77	−11.9	+ 0.9	− 1.1	" " 12 " 16 −16.1
" 23	1.0	79	− 9.9	+ 1.3	− 0.9	" " 16 " 23 + 2.0
" 28	..	..	− 6.0	..	− 1.3	" " 23 " 28 − 3.7
" 30	2.3	84	− 3.0	+ 2.3	+14.4	" " 28 " 30 + 6.9
May 7	2.8	93	− 2.0	+ 2.7	+ 4.3	" " 30 May 7 + 6.0
" 10	..	..	+ 2.0	..	+11.0	" May 7 " 10 + 7.0
" 14	2.1	73	+ 8.0	+ 4.0	+20.4	" " 10 " 14 +14.6
" 21	3.0	74	+11.1	+ 6.0	+17.0	" " 14 " 21 +19.1
" 25	..	..	+14.0	..	+16.7	" " 21 " 25 +17.1
" 29	4.3	71	+14.9	+ 8.6	+25.4	" " 25 " 29 +22.7
June 4	4.9	70	+18.0	+ 7.7	+34.1	" " 29 June 4 +26.9
" 11	10.1	84	+23.1	+21.8	+35.5	" June 4 " 11 +23.7
" 16	..	.	+31.5	..	+36.2	" " 11 " 16 +27.6
" 19	frozen	36	+33.6	+32.3	+36.9	" " 16 " 19 +40.1
" 24	frozen	14	+30.3	+33.7	+34.8	" " 19 " 24 +34.6
July 1	thawed	0	+32.6	+34.9	+40.6	" " 24 July 1 +36.8

The thermometer sunk two feet two inches, and the ground above covered with snow, gave its lowest indication on March 10th, when it reached +0°.5, and may be assumed as having reached zero about March 10th. The temperature of the air was lowest about January 10th ($T = -38°.4$); hence, the greatest cold of the soil at that depth occurred 57 days later. The thermometer sunk one foot one inch, and the ground free of snow, reached its lowest indication already on February 20th ($T = -25°.7$); hence, 38 days later than the time of the lowest atmospheric temperature.

Temperature of the Surface of the Sea.—Frequent observations (at irregular hours of the day) were made for temperature of the surface of the sea, between July 2d, 1857, and September 12th, 1857. It suffices, however, to give an abstract of these observations, and the following record contains the maximum, minimum, and mean temperature observed each day. The observations were resumed April

18th, 1858, and continued till September 11th, 1858. They were again resumed August 21st, 1859. Some other observations will be given below. For the latitude and longitude, see preceding abstract.

Temperature of the Surface of the Sea.

July, 1857.				August, 1857.				September, 1857.			
Date.	Max.	Min.	Mean.	Date.	Max.	Min.	Mean.	Date.	Max.	Min.	Mean.
1	..	..	..	1	48°	39°	44°.8	1	30°	28°	29°.4
2	..	..	34°	2	44	41	43.2	2	31	29	30
3	..	..	35.2	3	44	42	42.3	3	30	29	29.2
4	..	..	36	4	48	38	42.9	4	32.0	28	29.7
5	..	..	36	5	41	34	36.7	5	30.5	28	29.2
6	38°	33°	35.4	6	43	37	39.3	6	30	27	28.6
7	41	34	37	7	38	31	34	7	30	28	29.0
8	50	50	47.4	8	37	36	35.7	8	30	29	29.9
9	35	33	34	9	38	31	33	9	32	29	30.7
10	44	33	33.1	10	38	30	32.2	10	32	30	31
11	53	41	38	11	38	33	33.3	11	31	29.5	30.4
12	61	42.5	48.4	12	35	32	32.7	12	30	28	29.2
13	47	40	44.3	13	34	32	33	13	..	..	..
14	44	33	38	14	38	33	35.3	14	..	..	..
15	43	42	42.2	15	37	33	33.7	15	..	..	..
16	43	39	41.3	16	36	30	32.7	16	..	..	..
17	38	33	36.4	17	40	32	37	17	..	..	..
18	35	36	34.5	18	36	30	30.7	18	..	..	..
19	..	..	38	19	34	30	30.2	19	..	..	..
20	..	..	..	20	33	32	32.7	20	..	..	..
21	..	..	36	21	32	33	33	21	..	..	..
22	38	36	37.1	22	32	30	31	22	..	..	..
23	34	37	..	23	33	30	32	23	..	..	..
24	40	31	39	24	32	30	32.3	24	..	..	..
25	41	31	38.2	25	34	30	31	25	..	..	..
26	40	37	38.7	26	33	30	30.5	26	..	..	..
27	38	37	36.2	27	33	30	31.3	27	..	..	..
28	40	37	38.1	28	33	31	31.7	28	..	..	..
29	41	38	39.1	29	32	30	31	29	..	..	..
30	43	38	41.5	30	30	29	30.1	30	..	..	..
31	40	42	40.6	31	33	30	30.3				

Notes.—July, 1857.

14th. Pack ice in sight.
17th. Sailing through the ice.
18th. Bergs and pack ice.
21st. In [illegible].
28th. Surface temp. 50°, and at 120 fathoms depth 31°.5.
29th–30th. Icebergs in sight.

Notes.—August, 1857.

2d and 3d. Many icebergs in sight.
11th. Fast to a berg.
13th. At 1 P. M., temp. in shade, thermometer freely suspended, 40°; against iceberg, receiving its reflected rays, 53°; against iceberg in the sun, 45°; another 4 black surface in the sun, 72°.
14th. Deep sea thermometer:—
At 114 fathoms, 30°
" 50 " 29.5
" 20 " 31.5
" surface 31
Fresh water on berg, 32.2.
16th. Temp. 3 feet in the iceberg, 29°.15; its surface, 32°.1; temp. of the air 41°.6, at 9 A. M.
16th and 17th. Fast to a floe.

Notes.—September, 1857.

4th. At 10 A. M.—
120 fathoms, temp. 29°.5
50 " 29.0
25 " 29.0
Surface, 30.3.
13th. 24 icebergs in sight from aloft.
24th. Temp. of sea at surface, 29°.

NOTES.

1857
Nov. 9th. Temp. of sea surface, 28°.9
1858.
Feb. 3d. Temp. of sea surface, 28.5
" 22d. " " 29.3
Temp. at 4 fath's 29.6
" 120 " 31.5
March 1st. " 120 " 31.3
" 4 " 29.4

1858
Mar. 19th. Temp. at 120 fath's 30°.2
" 100 " 30.0
" 4 " 29.4
Mar. 28th. " 64 " 30.0
" 4 " 29.5
Mar. 30th. " 120 " 30.9
" 4 " 29.9
April 7th " 110 " 30.8

1858
April 7th. Temp. at 4 fath's 29°
April 10th. " 120 " 34
" 4 " 30
April 14th. " 110 " 33
" 4 " 29.1
April 21st. " 100 " 31.2
" 4 " 29.3

Temperature of the Surface of the Sea.

April, 1858.

Date.	Max.	Min.	Mean.
16	..	..	29°.0
19	..	..	29.0
20	27°	27°.9	27.7
21	29	28	27.0
22	..	..	..
23	..	..	29.1
24	..	..	..
25	..	..	29.1
26	33	30	30.4
27	33	29.5	30.3
28	33	30	30.0

May, 1858.

Date.	Max.	Min.	Mean.
6	..	..	27.0
9	..	..	29.0
10	..	..	28.0
11	..	..	29.0
29	40°	34°	34.8
30	34	31	32.0
31	33	31	31.1

June, 1858.

Date.	Max.	Min.	Mean.
1	35°	32°	33°.5
2	35	33	33.7
3	32	31	31.7
4	32	32	32.3
5	33.5	31	32.3
6	33	31.5	32.0
7	33	31	32.5
8	33	32	32.7
9	33	31.5	32.3
10	32	31	31.4
11	33	32	32.3
12	33	30	31.3
13	31.8	30	30.5
14	32	30	31.0
15	32	31	31.7
16	32	30	31.0
17	32	31	32.3
18	32	30	31.3
19	33	31	31.0
20	33	31	31.7
21	31	31	31.0
22	33	30	30.5
23	32	30	30.3
24	32	30.5	31.0
25	33	31	32.3
26	33	31	31.8
27	31	31	31.7
28	32.5	32	32.1
29	33	32	32.8
30	33	31	31.7

July, 1858.

Date.	Max.	Min.	Mean.
1	34°	31°	32°.0
2	32	31	31.8
3	32	31	31.3
4	32.8	31.3	32.3
5	32	31	31.7
6	32	30.5	31.8
7	32	31	31.7
8	31	32	32.0
9	34	31	32.7
10	32.8	31	31.8
11	33	32	32.3
12	32	31	31.7
13	32	31	31.7
14	32	31	31.3
15	32	31	31.9
16	32.7	31	31.3
17	32.3	31	32.1
18	32.8	30	31.3
19	32.8	31	31.3
20	35	32	32.9
21	33	32	32.3
22	33	31	32.0
23	34	32	32.6
24	37	32	33.9
25	41	32	33.0
26	36	32	34.0
27	35	32	33.8
28	33	32.3	33.8
29	33	33	33.8
30	34	31	32.8
31	34	33	33.0

August, 1858.

Date	Max	Min	Mean
1	35°	33°	33°.0
2	33	33	34.0
3	34	33	33.8
4	37	32	33.7
5	35	31	33.3
6	34	33	33.3
7	34	31	32.4
8	..	..	32.0
9	..	..	29.3
10	32.5	32	32.1
11	32	32	32.7
12	..	..	34.0
13	..	..	..
14	..	..	..
15	..	..	..
16	..	..	32.5
17	32	31	31.3
18	32	30	31.2
19	31	31	31.0
20	31	31	31.0
21	33	30	30.8
22	33	30	31.3
23	31	30	30.3
24	31	30	30.3
25	32	30	30.1
26	30	30	30.0
27	32	30	30.7
28	30	30	30.1
29	32	30	30.7
30	32	29	30.1
31	33	29	29.0

September, 1858.

Date	Max.	Min.	Mean.
1	29°	29°	29°.0
2	32	28	29.0
3	30	28	29.2
4	29	26	27.0
5	29	28	28.0
6	30	28	29.5
7	32	30	30.3
8	31	29	29.7
9	30	29	29.5
10	30.5	28	29.6
11	..	..	29.2

Sept. 27th. Temp. at 75 fathoms, 31°; surface temp., 29°.

September, 1859.

Date	6 A.M.	6 P.M.	Mean.
2	..	37° 0	37°.0
3	38°.8	39.8	39.3
4	40.0	41.2	40.6
5	41.0	41.0	41.0
6	41.5	42.0	41.7
7	38.5	40.5	39.5
8	42.5	44.0	43.2
9	43.0	44.3	43.7
10	43.0	44.3	43.7
11	47.5	48.0	47.7
12	..	51.0	51.0
13	50.0	52.5	51.2
14	..	54.0	54.0
15	..	56.0	56.0
16	..	56.5	56.5
17	..	56.0	56.0

August, 1859.

Date.	6 A.M.	6 P.M.	Mean.
21	..	30°.0	30°.0
22	29°.5	30.0	29.8
23	30.0	30.5	30.2
24	32.0	33.2	32.1
25	34.2	34.5	34.3
26	30.5	33.8	32.1

TABLE OF MEAN RESULTS FOR TEMPERATURE OF THE SURFACE OF THE SEA.

Date.	Locality.		Temp. of Sea.	REMARKS.
	Between N. lat.	Between W. long.		
1857.				
July 2—15	[illegible]	[illegible]	31°.7	Aberdeen to off Cape Farewell.
" 16—31	[illegible]	[illegible]	34.3	Off Cape Farewell to Lievely.
Aug. 1—15	[illegible]	[illegible]	33.9	Lievely to near Melville Bay.
" 16—31	[illegible]	[illegible]	30.6	" "
Sept. 1—12	[illegible]	[illegible]	31.6	" "
" 24	74.1	65.3	29.0	" "
Nov. 9	74.4	60.5	28.0	" "
1858.				
Feb. 1—28	[illegible]	[illegible]	29.8	Baffin Bay.
March 1—29	[illegible]	[illegible]	29.8	Near Davis Strait, at 4½ fathoms depth.
April 7—11	[illegible]	[illegible]	30.9	Davis strait 4 fathoms.
" 19—24	[illegible]	[illegible]	29.8	Davis Strait.
May 1—11	[illegible]	[illegible]	29.5	Holsteinborg to Whalefish Islands.
" 20—31	[illegible]	[illegible]	33.5	Omenak Fiord to off Upernavik.
June 1—16	[illegible]	[illegible]	30.6	Off Upernavik to south of Melville Bay.
" 16—30	[illegible]	[illegible]	30.4	Melville Bay.
July 1—15	[illegible]	[illegible]	31.7	Upper Baffin Bay.
" 16—31	[illegible]	[illegible]	30.4	Baffin Bay.
Aug. 1—12	[illegible]	[illegible]	30.8	Near Lancaster Sound and Barrow Strait.
" 13—31	[illegible]	[illegible]	30.3	Prince Regent Inlet, Port Kennedy.
Sept. 1—11	72.0	94.0	29.3	Near Port Kennedy.
" 27	72.0	94.0	28.0	" "
1859.				
Aug. 21—31	[illegible]	[illegible]	30.5	Lower Baffin Bay.
Sept. 2—9	[illegible]	[illegible]	41.0	Off South Greenland.
" 10—17	[illegible]	[illegible]	53.5	"

The lowest temperatures of the surface of the sea were observed in November, 1857, near Melville Bay, and in September, 1858, at Port Kennedy (viz., 28°.0); the highest temperature, north of Davis Strait, in May, 1858, off Swarte Hook Peninsula (viz., 33°.5).

The following table of monthly mean temperatures of the air (in shade), expressed in degrees of Fahrenheit's scale, has been prepared by Captain McClintock, and is here appended as forming part of the most valuable material for the construction of the isothermal lines, and for the investigation of the climatic relations of this portion of the Arctic regions. I have added two columns, containing the results from the Second American Grinnell Expedition, under command of Dr. E. K. Kane, from my discussion of the observations, as published by the Smithsonian Institution, and the results for Port Kennedy as made out by me in the preceding discussion. This last column may be substituted for that given by Captain McClintock in his general table.

Table of Mean Monthly Temperatures Registered by Modern Expeditions to the American Arctic Regions.

Month.	[illegible]	[illegible]	[illegible]	[illegible]	[illegible]	[illegible]	[illegible]	[illegible]	[illegible]	[illegible]	[illegible]	[illegible]	[illegible]	[illegible]
	°	°	°	°	°	°	°	°	°	°	°	°	°	°
January	−33.13	−28.38	−30.13	−27.75	−27.2	−30.4	−14.19	−24.2	−13.3	−18.20	−19.45	−33.5	−28.6	−31.8
February	−34.41	−24.96	−15.58	−30.73	−29.9	−32.5	−21.90	−17.8	−27.7	[illegible]	−21.08	−37.1	−27.3	−31.3
March	−18.26	−28.96	−18.03	−12.86	−29.9	−34.3	−29.60	−12.3	−13.0	[illegible]	−17.06	−28.6	−25.4	−18.4
April	+ 0.33	− 3.62	− 0.85	− 0.85	+ 1.6	− 8.4	− 0.80	+ 5.6	+ 2.4	+10.12	− 2.63	− 4.9	− 6.5	−[illegible]
May	+24.41	+17.68	+25.14	+15.05	+15.3	+19.0	+32.30	+15.5	+20.9	[illegible]	+15.41	+18.5	+17.8	+16.4
June	+35.16	+27.36	+32.16	+36.75	+25.8	+31.5	+32.37	+34.7	[illegible]	[illegible]	[illegible]	+34.1	+34.1	+34.7
July	+38.98	+41.86	+39.80	+42.08	+44.6	+32.8	. .	+38.2	+34.4	+41.82	+41.14	+37.6	+37.2	+39.0
August	+35.24	+36.32	+28.08	+36.83	+40.4	+36.8	. .	+43.8	+37.0	+33.63	+37.36	+36.8	+36.6	+34.2
September	+21.98	+26.37	+25.10	+27.92	+29.6	+32.4	. .	+29.9	+24.8	+26.10	+26.45	+30.2	+25.2	+28.8
October	+12.26	+12.86	+13.73	+ 3.55	− 7.3	+11.6	+ 0.56	+ 4.1	− 0.5	+ 7.56	+ 7.45	+ 0.8	+10.6	+10.8
November	+ 7.88	+ 8.46	−20.68	− 7.17	− 8.6	−13.4	− 6.43	− 8.2	− 7.7	− 8.31	−11.24	−16.6	− 6.6	−12.8
December	−16.82	−13.17	−29.35	−31.87	−23.1	−29.2	−29.84	− 5.4	−21.0	−17.40	−32.36	−23.4	−19.6	−30.5
Mean annual temp.	+ 0.88	+ 3.86	+ 0.37	+ 2.86	+6.87	+3.46	. .	Both years +7.24		+ 8.67	+ 3.58	+6.90	+4.83	+1.88
	Taken from Parry's voyage.	[illegible]	Parry's voyage.	[illegible]	[illegible]	[illegible]				[illegible]	[illegible]	[illegible]	Parry's voyage.	

Month.	[illegible]	[illegible]	[illegible]	[illegible]	[illegible]	[illegible]	[illegible]	[illegible]	[illegible]	[illegible]	[illegible]	The following columns are additions to preceding table.	[illegible]	[illegible]
	°	°	°	°	°	°	°	°	°	°	°		°	°
January	−27.3	−41.4	−31.80	−29.6	−31.4	−36.73	−32.4	−40.13	−37.4	−36.07	−40.60		−29.98	−34.48
February	−25.8	−28.8	−33.69	−14.0	−34.8	−41.12	−34.9	−40.83	−31.2	−31.09	−33.30		−28.83	−33.83
March	−20.4	−31.4	−28.70	−13.0	−23.0	−31.34	−19.5	−13.16	−30.8	−12.47	−27.71		−33.34	−17.44
April	− 1.4	− 4.6	− 1.08	− 1.8	+ 0.3	− 7.19	− 4.9	− 2.87	− 4.8	+ 3.74	− 4.30		− 0.40	− 1.96
May	+10.2	+11.9	+ 0.34	+14.9	+18.6	. .	+10.7	+14.90	− 0.8	+23.42	+14.79		+14.29	+12.87
June	+32.8	. .	+32.67	+34.8	+30.6	. .	+30.2	+35.24	+27.9	+34.58	+29.86		+33.58	+35.67
July	+36.1	. .	+34.98	+39.4	+37.6	. .	+42.4	+38.42	+36.1	+40.55	+35.80		+38.38	+39.29
August	+35.5	+23.8	+33.77	+34.8	+34.8	. .	+32.7	+33.10	+36.2	+37.47	+33.60		+31.89	+36.78
September	+20.6	+20.1	+20.36	+25.4	+18.5	+17.58	+23.5	+24.20	+27.0	+20.10	+24.63		+25.12	+25.19
October	+ 8.5	− 5.8	− 0.30	+ 3.8	+ 8.6	+ 4.60	− 4.9	− 6.06	+ 3.8	+12.32	− 1.85		− 4.53	+ 7.18
November	−18.2	−18.5	+ 4.56	− 6.32	−15.8	−21.37	−21.0	−12.70	−16.6	−18.66	− 8.64		−21.36	−11.46
December	−20.6	−26.3	−22.36	−24.7	−28.1	−31.95	−22.0	−25.85	−30.0	−27.58	−28.50		−31.40	−25.74
Mean annual temp.	+3.16	. .	+ 0.47	Both years +3.06		. .	+0.41	+ 2.86	−3.60	+ 4.23	− 5.38		− 3.30	+ 2.98
	[illegible]	[illegible]		[illegible]	[illegible]		Parry's voyage.		[illegible]		[illegible]		[illegible]	[illegible]

PART II.

WINDS.

RECORD AND DISCUSSION OF THE DIRECTION AND FORCE OF THE WIND.

The direction and force of the wind was recorded at the same hours as those given in the preceding record of the observations for temperature, and are the same at which all other meteorological observations were made.

In the preface to the journal containing the original record, Captain McClintock states—"The true direction of the wind is given throughout;" and "the force of the wind is indicated according to the Beaufort scale of notation, 0 to 12, see Admiralty's Manual." Comparing the direction of the wind given in the fourth number of Meteorological Papers published by authority of the Board of Trade, 1860, I find that for a part of the cruise the magnetic direction is given, which in Captain McClintock's record is already converted into "true," the magnetic variation having been applied; I have, therefore, added to the record of the wind the observed variation of the needle to show the amount allowed for in the conversion of the directions. The proper reduction of the winds requires a knowledge of the velocity of the air corresponding to each number expressing the force according to Beaufort's scale; this I have derived from the following table:—

Denomination of wind.	Estimated number of force.	Pressure in pounds per square foot.	Velocity in miles per hour.
Calm	0	0.000	0
Light air	1	0.005	1
Gentle breeze	2	0.08	4
Moderate breeze	3	0.7	12
Fresh breeze	4	2.4	22
Strong breeze	5	5.1	32
Fresh gale	6	7.9	40
Strong gale	7	12.0	50
Storm	8	18.0	60
Tempest	9	31.0	80
Hurricane	10	49.0	100

The relation of the tabular numbers of pressure and velocity is in accordance with Smeaton's table, and also agrees with that following from Dr. Bernoulli's formula. By simple proportion, or by means of a diagram, we obtain the following velocity number corresponding to Beaufort's scale, or to a graduation from 0 to 12.

Force according to Beaufort's notation.	Corresponding adopted velocity in miles per hour.	Force according to Beaufort's notation.	Corresponding adopted velocity in miles per hour
0	0	7	40
1	1	8	48
2	4	9	56
3	10	10	67
4	17	11	82
5	24	12	100
6	32		

The force of the wind being obtained by estimation, a moderate accuracy in the velocity numbers suffices.

Record of the Observations for Direction and force of the Wind.

This record may be divided in two parts; the first part comprising the period from September, 1857, to August, 1858, when the ship was in Baffin's Bay, and the second part between September, 1858, and August, 1859, when she was at Port Kennedy. These two periods will be discussed separately. The daily and mean monthly positions of the Fox are given in the record of the temperatures; those for the several seasons are as follows:—

	Between north lat's—		and	Mean long's—	
Autumn—Sept., Oct., Nov., 1857 . .	75°.3 and	74°.8 N.		65°.0 and	69°.1 W. of Gr.
Winter—Dec., Jan., Feb., 1857–8 . .	74.8	71.5		67.4	60.9
Spring—March, April, May, 1858 . .	69.4	68.7		58.1	53.7
Summer—June, July, Aug., 1858 . .	74.6	78.1		60.1	58.5
Whole year—average position, Baffin's Bay	72°.5 N.		and	63°.5 W. of Gr.	
Second year—at Port Kennedy . . .	72.0			94.3	

Remarks relating to winds are given in notes.

Direction (true) and Force of the Wind observed on board the yacht Fox.

July, 1857.—Mean position: Lat. 69° N.; long. 39°.1 W. of Greenwich.

Date.	4h.	8h.	Noon.	4h.	8h.	Midn't.	Variation allow'd.	Remarks.
1	....	....	....	....	....	....		
2	4 S. S. W.	2 W. S. W.	4 S. W.	4 S. by W.	4 S. W. by W.	4 S. S. W.		This variation applied for the 3d, 4th, 5th, and 6th is not given.
3	6 S.	4 S.	5 N. S. W.	1 N. W.	Calm	4 N. E. by N.		
4	5 N. E. by N.	6 N. N. by N.	5 N. E. by N.	6 N. E. by N.	6 N. by E.	7 N. by E.		
5	5 N.	2 N.	4 N.	2 W. N. W.	2 W. N. W.	2 N. W. by W.	W.	
6	3 N. W. by W.	1 N. W.	1 N. W.	4 W. N. W.	1 W. N. W.	1 N. W.	33°	
7	1 N.	Calm	1 N.	1 N.	4 N. E. N.	4 E. N. E.	[illegible]	
8	5 N. S. E.	4 N. S. E.	4 E. S. E.	7 E. by S.	7 E. by S.	7 E. by S.	42	
9	7 E. by S.	7 E. by S.	6 E.	5 E.	3 E.	1 E'ly	47	
10	3 E.	4 E. N. E.	6 E. N. E.	5 E. by N.	1 E. by S.	1 var.	51	
11	1 N. N. E.	4 E. N. E.	5 N. N. E.	5 N. N. E.	5 N. N. E.	7 N. N. E.	52	
12	7 N. N. E.	6 N.	4 N. by W.	4 N. N. E.	4 N. N. E.	3 N.	55	
13	3 N. W.	1 N. W.	1 W. N. W.	1 W. N. W.	1 N'ly	1 N'ly	55	
14	Calm	1 E'ly	2 N. E.	2 N'ly	4 E'ly	4 N. by E.	55	
15	Calm	1 S. E.	4 N. W.	4 W. by N.	5 N. N. W.	1 N. N. W.	54	15th. Current S. S. W. 1 m.
16	1 W. by N.	1 N. W.	1 N. W. by N.	1 N. W.	1 N. W.	5 N. N. W.	55	
17	4 N. W.	4 N. W.	5 N. W.	4 N. W.	4 N. W. by N.	3 N. W. by N.	58	
18	3 N. W. by W.	3 N. W. by N.	5 N. W., E.	2 N. N. W.	2 N. W. by N.	2 N. W. by N.	58	
19	2 N.	....	....	4 N. W.	3 N. W.	3 N. N. W.		19th. Current S. W. 10'; variation applied; between the 19th & 25th estimated.
20	6 S.	4 S.	3 N. by E.	4 N. W.	3 N. W.	4 N. W.		
21	4 N. W.	3 N. W.	2 N. W.	3 N. W. by W.	3 N. W. by W.	3 W.		
22	3 N. W. by N.	1 N. W. by N.	3 N. W. by N.	5 N. W. by N.	3 N. W. by N.	3 N. W. by N.		
23	4 N. W. by N.	4 N. W. by N.	5 N. W. by N.	4 N. W. by N.	6 N. W. by N.	3 N. W. by N.		
24	Calm	4 N. W.	4 S. E. by S.	2 S. W. by S.	1 N. W.	1 N. W.		
25	6 N.	3 N.	1 N. N. W.	2 N. N. W.	1 N.	1 N.		
26	1 N.	1 N.	2 N.	2 N.	2 N.	2 N.		
27	5 N.	1 N.	3 N. by W.	3 N. by W.	3 N. N. W.	4 N. N. W.	62	
28	3 N. N. W.	1 N. N. W.	2 S. S. E.	4 N. N. E.	4 E. S. E.	7 N. N. E.	64	
29	7 N. N. E.	4 N.	4 N.	2 N. N. E.	2 N.	1 N.	70	
30	3 W. N. W.	4 N. W. by N.	6 N. W. by N.	7 N. W. by N.	7 N. W. by N.	3 N. W. by W.	75	
31	2 N. by E.	2 N. N. E.	Calm	Calm	Calm	Calm		

August, 1857.—Mean position: Lat. 74° N.; long. 58°.8 W.

Date.	4h.	8h.	Noon.	4h.	8h.	Midn't.	Variation allow'd.	Remarks.
1	Calm	Calm	Calm	3 N'ly	4 N. E. N.	4 N. E. by N.	W.	
2	4 N. E. by E.	3 N. E.	1 E'ly	1 E'ly	Calm	Calm	72°	
3	1 E'ly	Calm	Calm	4 E. by S.	4 S. E. by S.	4 S. E. by S.		
4	3 S. E. by S.	2 S. E. by S.	5 S. E. by S.	4 S. W. by W.	4 S. W. by W.	4 W. S. W.		4th. Sailing closely with strong gusts.
5	5 W.	5 W.	4 W.	5 W. by S.	5 W. by S.	5 W. by S.	78	
6	4 S'ly	4 S'ly	5 S. S. E.	6 S. S. E.	3 S. S. E.	3 S. S. E.		
7	1 S. E. by S.	3 W. N. W.	3 N. N. W.	3 N'ly	1 N'ly	3 N'ly	80	
8	3 N. E. by E.	3 N. E. by E.	2 N. E. by E.	4 E. by N.	4 E'ly	5 E'ly		
9	3 S. E.	4 S.	5 S. S. E.	3 S. S. E.	3 S.	3 S. E.	82	
10	3 S. S. E.	3 S. S. E.	3 S. S. E.	1 W. N. W.	2 W'ly	2 N. W.	87	
11	4 N. W.	4 W. N. W.	4 N. W.	3 N. W.	3 N. W.	3 N. W.	90	
12	1 N. W.	1 N. W.	3 N. E.	3 N. E.	Calm	Calm	96	
13	Calm	Calm	Calm	Calm	1 W'ly	1 N. E. by N.	99	
14	Calm	Calm	Calm	Calm	Calm	Calm		
15	Calm	Calm	Calm	3 N. W.	3 N. W.	6 N. W.	97	Var'n observed.
16	1 W'ly	Calm	3 S. S. E.	3 S. S. E.	3 S. S. E.	5 S. S. E.	99	
17	3 N. E.	4 N. E.	3 N. E.	4 N. N. E.	4 N. E.	3 N. E.	99	
18	3 N. E.	4 N. N. E.	3 N. N. E.	2 N. E.	1 N. E.	1 N. E.	99	
19	1 N. N. E.	1 N. N. E.	1 N. N. E.	2 N.	3 S. S. E.	5 E'ly	98	
20	3 S. E.	3 S.	3 N. N. E. by N.	3 N. E. by N.	2 S. E. by S.	2 N. E.	102	
21	1 N. E.	3 S. S. E.	2 N. W. by W.	1 N. W. by N.	1 N. W. by N.	Calm	103	
22	1 N. W.	Calm	Calm	1 S. E.	3 S. E.	1 N. N. E.	103	
23	1 E.	3 E.	4 N. N. E.	3 E.	3 N. N. E.	1 N. N. E.	103	
24	1 N. E.	3 N. by E.	5 N. W. by N.	3 N. W. by N.	5 N. W. by N.	3 N.	93 30'	Var'n observed.
25	3 N.	4 E. by N.	3 N.	4 N. by N.	5 N. by N.	3 N. by N.		
26	3 S. by S.	3 N. by E.	5 N. N. E.	3 N.	3 N. by N.	5 N. by N.	103 30	Var'n observed.
27	3 N.	4 N. N. E.	4 N. N. E.	3 N. E. by N.	3 N. N. E.	2 N. by N.	93 30	
28	Calm	2 N. by S.	1 N. N. E.	1 N. N. E.	4 N. N. E.	3 N. N. E.		
29	1 N. E.	1 N. E.	2 N. N. E.	1 N. W. by W.	4 W. N. W.	4 W. N. W.	102 30	Mean Variation, the mean of the Azimuths and Amplitudes S. E. & S. W.
30	3 N.	3 N.	6 N. E.	7 N.	7 N. N. E.	6 N. N. E.		
31	4 S. S. E.	5 S. E.	3 N. N. E.	3 N. N. W.	4 N. W. by W.	4 N. W. by W.	94 23	

6

Direction (true) and Force of the Wind observed on board the yacht Fox.

September, 1857.—Mean position: Lat. 75° 5 N.; long. 45° W.

Date.	4h.	8h.	Noon.	4h.	8h.	Midn't.	Variation observed.
1	2 N. W.	1 E.	2 S. W.	1 W. N. W.	3 S. S. W.	2 S. E.	
2	1 N. E.	3 S. by E.	1 E.	Calm	Calm	1 N. W.	
3	1 N. W. by W.	1 N. W. by W.	1 N. W. by W.	1 N. N. W.	1 N. N. W.	1 N. W. by W.	
4	3 S. S. W.	3 S.	3 S. E. by S.	4 S. E.	5 E. S. E.	6 E. by S.	
5	1 N. E.	2 S. E.	3 E. by N.	3 E.	Calm	3 S. E.	W.
6	3 E. S. E.	3 S. E. by E.	5 E.	3 E. N. E.	3 N.	1 N. N. W.	84° [illegible]
7	1 N. N. W.	1 W. by S.	3 W. S. W.	3 E.	4 N. E.	6 E. S. E.	
8	8 W. S. W.	7 S. S. W.	6 N. E.	7 S. E.	6 S. by W.	4 S. E. by S.	
9	5 S. by E.	6 S. E. by S.	6 S. by E.	6 S. by E.	7 S. by E.	6 S. by E.	
10	1 S. E. by S.	2 E. by N.	3 E. by E.	1 S. by E.	1 W. N. W.	1 W. by S.	
11	2 E. by S.	4 E. by N.	5 S. E.	7 S. E.	6 S. E.	6 N. N. W.	
12	4 W. by S.	3 W. by N.	3 W.	3 W. by N.	1 W. by N.	1 W. by N.	
13	4 W. by N.	3 W. N. W.	1 W. by N.	3 N. W.	5 S. S. E.	4 E. by N.	84 4
14	8 E.	4 N. E. by E.	4 S. S. E.	6 S. by E.	6 W. by S.	3 W.	
15	1 W. by S.	3 S. by E.	2 N. N. W.	1 S. E. by S.	1 E. by S.	2 E. N. E.	
16	4 S. by E.	3 E. by S.	4 E. by S.	3 S. by E.	4 E. S. E.	8 E. by N.	
17	2 S. E.	1 N. by W.	1 N. W. by N.	1 N. N. W.	1 N. W.	8 W.	85 16
18	2 N. by E.	8 N. N. W.	2 N. W.	4 N. W.	5 W. N. W.	5 W. N. W.	
19	6 N. E.	5 N. N. W.	1 N.	2 N. E. by W.	8 N. E. by N.	2 N. E.	
20	8 N. W. by N.	2 N. by E.	2 N. E.	2 N. W.	4 N. W. by W.	4 N. W. by W.	
21	6 N. W. by W.	4 N. W. by W.	5 N. W. by W.	4 N. W. by W.	4 N. W.	2 N. N. W.	
22	4 W.	4 N. W. by W.	6 W. N. W.	4 W. N. W.	6 W. by S.	7 W. N. W.	
23	2 W. N. W.	3 N. W.	2 N. N. W.	1 W. N. W.	Calm	Calm	84 14
24	3 E. by S.	5 N. N. E.	6 N. N. E.	3 N. W.	3 N. W.	4 N. W.	
25	4 N. W.	4 N. W.	2 N. W.	2 N. W. by N.	1 N. E.	1 N. E.	
26	1 N. N. E.	2 W. by S.	3 N. W. by W.	3 N. W. by W.	3 N. W. by W.	3 W. N. W.	
27	2 N. W. by W.	8 N. N. W.	4 E. N. E.	4 N. E.	2 E. N. E.	5 N. E. by N.	
28	1 N. N. E.	Calm	2 E.	2 N. N. E.	Calm	Calm	
29	2 N. W. by W.	3 W. N. W.	1 W. N. W.	Calm	1 W. N. W.	3 W. N. W.	
30	Calm	1 N. W. by W.	4 N. N. W.	5 N. W. by W.	5 N. W. by W.	8 W. N. W.	
	2h.	6h.	10h.	2h.	6h.	10h.	
30	Calm	1 N. W.	3 N. W. by W.	4 N. W. by W.	4 N. W. by W.	3 W. N. W.	

Remarks.

1st. Ice driving to S. W., and afterwards to N. W.
2d. " " N. and N. W.
3d. " " S. E. and N. W.
4th. " " E., S. W., and W.
5th. Ice drift to westward.
6th. Var'n observed. Ice drift to E., N. W., & S. W.
7th. Ice drift to S. E. and N. W.
8th. " N. W. and N.
9th. " westward.
10th. " S. W., N. E. and E.
11th. " westward and N. W.
12th. " eastward and westward.
13th. " N. E. and N. W.
14th. " westward.
15th. " northward.
16th. Ice drift to S. W.
17th. " S. W.
18th. " S. W. and N. E.
19th. " N. and S. E.
20th. " S. E.
21st. " S. E.
22d. " S. E.
23d. " S. E., N. E., and S. W.
24th. " S. E.
25th. " S. E. and S.
26th. " S. E.
27th. " S. E. and S. W.
28th. " S. E. and S. W.
29th. " S. E.
30th. " S. E.

DIRECTION (TRUE) AND FORCE OF THE WIND OBSERVED ON BOARD THE YACHT FOX.

October, 1857.—Mean position: Lat. 75°.2 N.; long. 67°.5 W.

DAYS.	2h.	4h.	6h.	8h.	10h.	Noon.
1	1 W. N. W.	1 W. N. W.	Calm	2 E. by S.	2 E. N. E.	2 E. N. E.
2	2 E. S. E.	1 E. S. E.	Calm	Calm	1 W.	2 S. W.
3	2 W. N. W.	2 W. N. W.	2 W. N. W.	3 N. W. by W.	2 N. W. by W.	2 N. W. by W.
4	4 N. W. by W.	4 N. W.	3 N. W.	3 N. W. by W.	2 W. N. W.	2 W. N. W.
5	2 N. N. W.	1 N. W.	3 N. W.	3 N. W.	3 N. W.	2 N. W. by W.
6	3 N. W.	2 N. W.	2 N. by E.	1 N. by E.	1 N. by W.	1 N. by W.
7	Calm	Calm	1 E. by N.	1 E. by N.	1 S. by E.	1 S. S. W.
8	2 W. S. W.	1 W. S. W.	2 N. N. E.	2 N. E. by E.	1 E. by S.	1 E. by S.
9	1 E. by S.	1 E. by S.	1 N. W. by N.	2 N.	2 N. E.	2 N. E.
10	4 W. N. W.	4 W. N. W.	2 W. N. W.	2 W. N. W.	2 W. N. W.	1 W. N. W.
11	3 N. W. by W.	2 N. W. by W.	2 W. N. W.	2 W. N. W.	2 W. N. W.	2 W. N. W.
12	4 W. N. W.	4 W. N. W.	4 W. N. W.	4 N. W.	2 W. by N.	2 W. by N.
13	2 W. by N.	1 W. by N.	1 W.	1 W.	1 N. N. E.	3 E. N. E.
14	2 E. N. E.	3 E. N. E.	3 E. N. E.	3 E. N. E.	3 E. N. E.	2 E. S. E.
15	7 E. S. E.	3 E. S. E.	4 S. E. by E.	4 S. E. by E.	7 S. E.	7 S. E.
16	4 E. S. E.	4 E. S. E.	4 E. N. E.	2 N. E.	3 S. E.	3 E. by S.
17	3 S. S. E.	4 E. S. E.	4 E. by N.	3 E.	4 N. E.	4 N. E.
18	3 E. by S.	1 E. by S.	3 W.	3 W.	3 W. N. W.	3 N. by W.
19	3 N. W.	4 N. W.	4 N. W.	4 N. W.	4 W. N. W.	4 W. N. W.
20	4 E. N. E.	4 E. S. E.	3 E. N. E.	3 S. W. by S.	3 S. W. by S.	2 S. W. by S.
21	3 S. by E.	4 E. by S.	5 S. E. by E.	5 S. E. by E.	4 S. E. by S.	4 S. E.
22	2 N. E. by E.	4 N. E. by E.	4 N. W. by W.	4 N. W. by W.	4 W. by N.	2 W. by N.
23	4 S. W.	4 S. W.	3 S. W.	3 S. W.	3 S. W.	2 S. W.
24	4 W. by N.	4 N. W.	4 N. W.	4 W. N. W.	4 W. N. W.	3 W. N. W.
25	Calm	Calm	1 W.	1 W.	1 E. by N.	1 N. N. W.
26	2 S. W. by W.	2 S. W. by W.	1 W. by S.	1 W. by S.	1 S. W. by W.	1 S. W. by W.
27	3 S. E. by E.	1 S. E. by E.	1 S. E. by E.	2 S. W.	1 W.	3 S. W.
28	3 S. W.	2 S. W.	1 S. W.	3 S. W.	3 S. W.	3 S. W.
29	1 S. by W.	2 S. by W.	1 S. by W.	1 S. W. by W.	1 N. W. by W.	1 N. W. by W.
30	3 N. W.	3 N. W.	3 N. W.	1 N. E. by E.	3 N. N. E.	3 E. N. E.
31	2 N. E. by N.	3 N. E. by N.	4 N. E. by N.	2 N. by E.	3 N. by E.	3 N. by E.

DAYS.	2h.	4h.	6h.	8h.	10h.	Midn't.
1	2 S. E. by E.	1 S. E. by E.	4 S. E.	4 E.	4 E. S. E.	4 E. S. E.
2	1 E. by S.	1 S. S. E.	1 W.	1 W.	Calm	2 W.
3	2 N. W.	2 N. W. by N.	2 N. W. by N.	2 N. W. by N.	2 N. W. by W.	3 N. W. by W.
4	2 W. N. W.	3 W. N. W.	3 W. N. W.	1 W. N. W.	3 W. by N.	2 W. by N.
5	3 W. N. W.	3 W. N. W.	2 W. N. W.	3 W. N. W.	2 N. W.	2 N. N. W.
6	1 S. by W.	2 S. W.	3 N. W.	2 W.	2 W.	Calm
7	1 S. W.	1 S. W.	1 S. W.	Calm	Calm	1 S. W.
8	1 E. by S.	1 E. by S.	1 E. by S.	1 E. by S.	Calm	1 E. by S.
9	4 N. E.	4 N. E.	3 N. N. E.	4 N. N. E.	4 N. N. E.	4 N. N. E.
10	2 W. N. W.	2 W.	1 W.	2 W.	2 W.	2 W.
11	3 W. N. W.	3 W. N. W.	3 W. N. W.	2 W. N. W.	3 W. N. W.	2 W. N. W.
12	2 W. by N.	2 W. by N.	1 W. by N.	2 W. by N.	2 W. by N.	2 W. by N.
13	4 E. N. E.	3 E. N. E.	4 E. N. E.	4 E. N. E.	4 E. N. E.	7 E. N. E.
14	7 E. S. E.	6 S. by E.	4 E. by S.	3 S. E. by E.	4 S. E.	7 S. E. by S.
15	8 S. S. E.	3 S. E. by S.	2 S. S. E.	Calm	Calm	Calm
16	3 E. by S.	4 E. by S.	4 E. by S.	4 E.	2 E. by S.	4 S. S. E.
17	3 E. by N.	3 E. by N.	4 E. by N.	3 E. by N.	3 E. by N.	3 E. by S.
18	3 S. S. W.	1 S. by W.	1 S. by W.	Calm	Calm	1 W. S. W.
19	4 W. by N.	3 W. by N.	3 W. by N.	3 W. by N.	2 E. N. E.	2 E. N. E.
20	3 S. E.	5 S. E.	3 E. S. E.	3 S. E. by E.	7 S. by E.	7 S. by E.
21	3 S. E. by E.	3 S. E. by E.	2 N. by W.	4 E. by S.	5 N. E. by E.	4 N. E. by E.
22	3 W. by N.	3 W. by N.	3 W. by N.	2 W.	4 S. W. by W.	3 S. W. by W.
23	3 S. W.	3 S. W.	3 S. W. by W.	3 S. W. by W.	3 S. W. by W.	3 W. by S.
24	1 W.	Calm	1 W. by S.	1 E. by S.	1 E. by S.	1 E. by S.
25	1 S. by E.	Calm	1 W. by S.	1 W. by S.	2 W. by S.	3 S. W. by W.
26	1 S. S. W.	2 S. S. W.	2 S. S. W.	Calm	Calm	Calm
27	3 S. W. by W.	4 S. W. by W.	2 N. W. by W.	2 N. W. by W.	3 N. W. by W.	4 N. W. by W.
28	3 N. W. by W.	2 E.	1 E.	Calm	2 N. E. by N.	1 N. W. by W.
29	2 N. W. by W.	2 S. W. by W.	3 N. W. by W.	4 N. W. by W.	6 N. W. by W.	4 N. W. by W.
30	2 E. N. E.	2 E. by S.	1 E. by S.	2 E. by W.	3 E. by N.	2 E. by N.
31	6 N.	4 N.	5 N.	3 N.	4 E. N. E.	4 E. N. E.

* Variation 83° W.

Direction (true) and Force of the Wind observed on board the yacht Fox.

November, 1857.—Mean position; Lat. 74°.8 N.; long. 69°.1 W.

Date.	2h.	4h.	6h.	8h.	10h.	Noon.
1	4 E. by N.	4 E. by N.	5 E. by N.	3 E. by N.	4 E. by N.	3 E. by N.
2	4 N. W. by W.	3 N. W. by W.	Calm	Calm	Calm	3 E. S. E.
3	2 E. N. E.	3 E. N. E.	3 E. N. E.	1 S. W. by S.	2 S. W. by S.	3 S. W. by S.
4	2 E. N. E.	3 E. N. E.	4 E. N. E.	2 E. N. E.	3 E. by S.	3 E. by S.
5	3 N. W.	2 N. W.	3 N. W.	2 N. W.	1 N. N. W.	1 N. N. W.
6	3 W. N. W.	3 W. N. W.	3 W. N. W.	3 W. N. W.	3 W. N. W.	3 W. N. W.
7	3 N. W.	3 N. W.	3 N. W.	3 N. W.	3 N. W.	4 N. W.
8	3 W. N. W.	4 W. N. W.	4 W. N. W.	3 W. N. W.	3 W. N. W.	4 W. N. W.
9	5 N. W. by W.	3 N. W. by W.	5 N. W. by W.	6 N. W. by W.	5 N. W. by W.	4 N. W. by W.
10	6 W. by N.	5 W. N. W.	5 N. W. by W.	3 N. N. W.	3 N. by W.	3 N. by W.
11	1 N. E. by N.	2 N. E. by N.	1 W.	2 W. S. W.	3 N. W.	3 N. W.
12	2 N. W. by W.	1 N. W. by W.	5 W. N. W.	4 W. N. W.	3 W.	3 W.
13	Calm	3 W.	2 W.	Calm	3 W. by N.	2 W. by N.
14	4 E.	4 E.	6 E.	7 E. S. E.	7 E. S. E.	7 E. S. E.
15	5 S.	3 S.	4 S.	5 S.	6 E. by N.	5 E. by N.
16	7 E. N. E.	7 E. N. E.	6 E. N. E.	3 E. N. E.	1 E. N. E.	1 E. N. E.
17	5 N.	4 N.	4 W. N. W.	4 W. N. W.	5 N. N. E.	4 N. N. E.
18	Calm	Calm	Calm	3 W.	1 W. N. W.	3 W. N. W.
19	1 W. N. W.	1 W. N. W.	Calm	2 W. N. W.	1 W. N. W.	3 W. N. W.
20	2 N. by W.	1 N. by W.	1 N. by W.	1 N. by W.	1 N. by W.	1 N. by W.
21	4 N. E.	3 N. E.	3 N. E.	3 N. E.	2 N. E. by E.	4 E.
22	3 N. E. by E.	6 N. E. by E.	5 N. E. by E.	5 N. E. by E.	2 N. E. by E.	3 N. E. by E.
23	4 S. S. W.	4 S. S. W.	5 S. S. W.	7 S. S. W.	6 S. S. W.	4 S. S. W.
24	2 N. W.	2 N. W.	1 N. W.	1 N. W.	1 N. W.	Calm
25	3 N. N. E.	4 N. N. E.	5 N. E. by E.	4 N. E. by E.	1 N. E.	1 N. E.
26	2 W.	5 W. N. W.	5 W. N. W.	4 W. N. W.	3 W. N. W.	4 W. N. W.
27	4 N. W.	3 N. W.	4 N. W.	4 N. W.	4 N. W.	4 N. W.
28	3 W. N. W.	4 W. N. W.	5 W. N. W.	4 W. N. W.	5 W. N. W.	5 W. by N.
29	4 W.	5 W.	5 W.	2 W.	2 N. W.	3 N. W.
30	3 W. by N.	2 W. by N.	2 W. by N.	2 N. W.	1 N. W.	3 N. W.

Date.	2h.	4h.	6h.	8h.	10h.	Midn't.
1	2 E. N. E.	3 E. N. E.	3 E. N. E.	3 N. W.	2 N. W.	4 N. W.
2	1 E. S. E.	2 E. S. E.	1 E. S. E.	1 E. S. E.	2 E. S. E.	Calm
3	2 S. W.	2 S. W.	2 S. W.	1 S. W.	2 N. W. by W.	3 N. W. by W.
4	3 E.	2 E.	2 E.	1 E.	1 E.	1 N. W.
5	2 N. W.	1 N. W.	1 N. W.	Calm	Calm	5 N. W. by W.
6	3 N. W.	2 N. W.	6 N. W.	7 N. W.	7 N. W.	6 N. W.
7	3 N. W. by N.	3 N. W. by N.	3 N. W. by N.	2 N. W. by N.	4 N. W.	4 N. W.
8	4 W. N. W.	2 W. N. W.	4 W. N. W.	5 W. N. W.	2 W. N. W.	1 W. N. W.
9	3 N. W. by W.	4 W.	7 W.	7 W.	7 W.	5 W.
10	5 S. S. W.	3 S. S. W.	2 S. S. W.	1 S.	1 N. E.	1 N. E.
11	2 N. W.	2 N. W.	4 S. W.	2 N. W.	9 N. W.	7 N. W.
12	3 W.	3 W. by N.	3 W. by N.	4 W. by N.	4 W. by N.	1 W. by N.
13	1 S. W.	1 S. W.	2 N. E.	3 S. E.	2 E. by N.	3 E. by N.
14	7 E. N. E.	6 E. N. E.	5 E. N. E.	3 E. N. E.	3 E. N. E.	1 E. N. E.
15	4 E. by N.	3 E. by N.	5 N. E. by E.	5 N. E. by E.	3 N. E. by E.	4 N. E. by E.
16	3 S. W. by S.	2 S. W. by S.	1 S. W. by S.	3 S. W. by S.	4 S. W. by S.	5 S. W. by S.
17	5 E. N. E.	3 E. S. E.	6 E. S. E.	5 E. S. E.	3 E. S. E.	1 E. N. E.
18	3 W. N. W.	2 W. N. W.	2 W. N. W.	3 W. N. W.	2 W. N. W.	2 W. N. W.
19	2 W. by N.	3 W. by N.	1 W. by N.	Calm	Calm	Calm
20	Calm	Calm	1 N. E.	1 N. E.	3 N. E.	1 N. E.
21	3 S. E.	3 S. E. by E.	4 S. E. by E.	7 N. E. by E.	3 N. E. by E.	3 N. E. by E.
22	3 S. E. by S.	2 S. E. S.	3 E. S. E.	2 E. S. E.	3 E. S. E.	4 E. S. E.
23	4 S. by W.	4 S. by W.	3 S. W. by S.	3 S. W. by S.	4 S. W. by S.	3 S. W. by S.
24	Calm	Calm	Calm	3 S.	3 S.	2 S. S. E.
25	3 N. W. by W.	3 N. W. by W.	5 N. W. by W.	4 N. W. by W.	2 W. S. W.	4 W. by N.
26	2 W. by N.	3 W. by N.	2 W. by N.	5 W. by N.	4 W. by N.	4 W. by N.
27	3 W. by N.	4 W. by N.	3 W. by N.	4 W. by N.	3 W. by N.	3 W. by N.
28	3 W. by N.	4 W. by N.	4 W. by N.	4 W. by N.	3 W. by N.	4 W. by N.
29	3 N. W.	5 N. W.	6 W. by N.	5 W. by N.	2 W. by N.	1 W. by N.
30	1 N. W.	1 N. W.	1 N. W.	1 N. W.	1 N. W.	1 N. W.

Direction (true) and Force of the Wind observed on board the yacht Fox.

December, 1857.—Mean position: Lat. 14°.3 N.; long. 61°.4 W.

Date.	2h.	4h.	6h.	8h.	10h.	Noon.	Variation.
1	1 N.W. by W.	2 N.W. by W.	3 N.W. by W.	2 N.W. by W.	3 N.W. by W.	1 N.W. by W.	
2	1 N.W.	1 N.W.	1 N.W.	1 N.W.	1 N.W.	1 N.W.	
3	1 N.W. by N.	3 N.W. by N.	2 N.W. by N.	1 N.W. by N.	1 N.W. by N.	2 W.N.W.	
4	3 S. by W.	4 S. by W.	3 S. by W.	3 S. by W.	3 S. by W.	3 S. by W.	
5	3 S. by E.	2 S. by E.	4 W. by N.	4 W. by N.	6 W. by N.	6 W. by N.	
6	7 N.W. by W.	2 N.W. by W.	3 N.W. by W.	7 N.W. by W.	2 S.S.E.	3 S.S.E.	
7	5 S.S.E.	1 S.S.E.	3 S.S.W.	1 S.S.W.	2 S.S.W.	1 S.S.E.	
8	2 N.E.	2 N.E.	Calm	Calm	1 N.W.	1 N.W.	
9	3 N.W. by W.	3 N.W. by W.	1 N.W. by W.	1 S.S.E.	1 S.E.	1 S.E.	
10	1 N.W.	1 N.W.	1 N.W.	1 N.W.	2 N.N.E.	2 N.N.E.	
11	1 N.W. by N.	2 N.W. by N.	1 N.W. by N.	5 N.W. by N.	3 N.W. by N.	3 N.W. by N.	
12	4 N.E. by E.	5 N.N.W.	8 N.W. by N.	8 N.W. by N.	8 N.W.	6 N.W.	
13	7 W.N.W.	7 W.N.W.	7 N.W. by W.	7 N.W. by N.	7 N.W. by W.	7 N.W. by W.	
14	3 N.W.	8 N.W.	5 W.S.W.	2 W.S.W.	3 W.S.W.	1 S.W.	
15	Calm	Calm	Calm	Calm	Calm	1 W.N.W.	
16	1 W.	1 W.	1 N.E.	1 W.N.W.	1 W.N.W.	1 W.N.W.	
17	2 N.E.	2 N.E.	2 N.	6 N.N.W.	2 N.W.	2 N.W.	
18	2 W.	3 W.	3 W.	2 W.	2 W.	1 W.	
19	Calm	2 S.	2 S.	2 S.	4 W.N.W.	4 W.N.W.	
20	3 N.E.	4 E. by N.	4 W.S.W.	4 S. by W.	4 S. by E.	4 E. by N.	
21	4 N.W.	5 N.W.	3 N.W.	1 N.W.	2 W.N.W.	5 W.N.W.	
22	1 N.W.	3 S. by E.	4 S. by E.	5 S. by E.	4 S. by E.	4 E. by E.	87° W.
23	5 E.S.E.	5 S.S.E.	5 E.S.E.	4 S.S.E.	4 S.S.E.	4 E.S.E.	(about)
24	1 S.E.	1 S.E.	1 N.E.	3 N.N.E.	1 N.N.E.	1 N.N.W.	
25	3 N.N.E.	3 N.N.E.	4 N.N.E.	4 E. by N.	4 S. by E.	4 N. by E.	
26	2 N. by E.	2 N. by E.	3 N. by E.	3 N. by W.	1 N. by W.	1 N. by W.	
27	4 N. by W.	5 N. by W.	4 N.W.	6 N.W.	6 N.W.	4 N.W.	
28	4 W.N.W.	4 N.N.W.	4 N.N.W.	5 N. by W.	4 N. by W.	3 N.W. by N.	
29	6 S.E. by S.	1 S.E. by S.	1 S.E. by S.	5 N.E.	4 E. by N.	2 E. by S.	
30	3 S. by W.	3 S. by W.	3 W. by N.	1 W. by N.	3 N.E.	3 N.E.	84° W.
31	3 W.N.W.	3 W.N.W.	3 W.N.W.	3 N.W. by W.	2 W. by S.	2 W. by S.	(Calcul.)

Date.	2h.	4h.	6h.	8h.	10h.	Midn't.
1	1 N.W. by W.	2 N.W. by W.	3 N.W. by W.	1 N.W. by W.	3 N.W. by W.	1 N.W. by W.
2	1 N.W. by N.	1 N.W. by N.	1 N.W. by N.	1 N.W. by N.	1 N.W. by N.	1 N.W. by N.
3	3 W.S.W.	3 W.S.W.	2 S.W. by S.	2 S.W. by S.	1 S.W. by S.	3 S.W. by S.
4	4 S.	2 S.	4 S.	2 S.	3 S.	3 S.
5	2 W. by N.	4 W. by N.	2 W. by N.	6 W. by N.	3 N.W.	2 S.W.
6	3 S.E.	4 S.E.	3 S.E.	2 S.E. by E.	2 S.E.	4 S.S.E.
7	5 S.S.E.	4 S.S.E.	4 S.S.E.	1 S.S.E.	1 S.S.E.	1 S.E.
8	1 N.W.	1 N.W.	1 N.W.	1 N.W.	1 N.W.	2 N.W.
9	1 S.E.	1 S.E.	1 S.E.	1 S.E.	1 N.W.	1 N.W.
10	1 N.N.W.	1 W.N.W.	2 N.E.	2 N.E.	2 N.E.	1 N.E.
11	3 N.N.W.	3 N.	3 N.	3 N.	3 N.	4 N.N.E.
12	4 W.N.W.	5 W.N.W.	5 W.N.W.	5 W.N.W.	4 W.N.W.	6 W.N.W.
13	6 N.W. by W.	6 N.W. by W.	6 N.W. by W.	4 N.W. by W.	4 N.W. by W.	8 N.W. by W.
14	3 S.W.	1 S.W.	Calm	Calm	Calm	Calm
15	1 W.S.W.	1 W.S.W.	1 W.S.W.	1 W.S.W.	1 W.S.W.	1 W.N.W.
16	2 W.	1 W.	2 N.	5 N.E.	1 N.E.	1 N.E.
17	1 W. by N.	1 W. by N.	2 W. by N.	3 W. by N.	2 W. by N.	2 W.
18	1 N.W.	1 N.W.	1 N.W.	1 N.W.	1 W. by S.	1 W. by S.
19	2 W.	Calm	1 N.E.	1 N.E.	1 N.E.	3 N.E.
20	3 W.S.W.	3 W.S.W.	2 W.S.W.	2 W.S.W.	Calm	Calm
21	4 W.N.W.	4 W.N.W.	4 W.N.W.	1 W.N.W.	1 N.W.	1 S.W.
22	4 S.S.E.	4 S.S.E.	6 S.S.E.	5 S.S.E.	5 S.S.E.	6 S.S.E.
23	6 S. by E.	4 S. by E.	8 S. by E.	3 S. by E.	2 E. by S.	3 E. by N.
24	1 N. by E.	1 N. by E.	3 N.	1 N.	3 N.	3 N.
25	8 N. by E.	3 N. by E.	3 N. by E.	2 N. by E.	4 N. by E.	4 N. by E.
26	1 N. by W.	3 N. by W.	3 N. by W.	1 N. by W.	2 N.	3 N. by W.
27	6 N.W. by N.	4 N.W. by N.	1 N.N.W.	1 N.N.W.	7 N.N.W.	5 N.N.W.
28*	4 N.N.W.	5 N.N.W.	6 N.N.W.	4 N.	5 S.E. by S.	6 S.E. by S.
29	4 E.	2 E.	3 E.	3 E.	3 S. by W.	3 E. by W.
30	3 N.W.	2 N.W.	2 W. by N.	2 W. by N.	3 W. by N.	8 W.
31	2 W. by S.	2 W.N.W.	2 W.N.W.	1 W.N.W.	1 W.N.W.	1 W.N.W.

* At 8h. the wind veered from N. by E. to S.E. by E.

Direction (true) and Force of the Wind observed on board the yacht Fox.
January, 1858.—Mean position: Lat. 13°.2 N.; long. 42°.7 W.

Date.	2h.	4h.	6h.	8h.	10h.	Noon.	Variation.
1	3 W. by N.	1 W. by N.	1 N. W.	1 N. W.	1 W. N. W.	1 W. N. W.	21° W. (about)
2	3 W. by N.	4 W. by N.	4 W. by N.	4 W. by N.	4 W. N. W.	3 W. N. W.	
3	4 N. N. W.	4 N. N. W.	4 N. N. W.	4 N. N. W.	5 N. N. W.	4 N. N. W.	
4	4 N. by W.	3 N. by W.	3 N. by E.	2 N. by E.	1 N. by W.	1 N. by W.	
5	4 N. by E.	3 N. N. E.	4 N. by W.	4 N. by W.	4 N. by W.	1 N. by W.	
6	3 N. by W.	4 N. by W.	4 N. by W.	3 N. N. W.	2 N. N. W.	4 N. N. W.	
7	6 N. W.	4 N. W.	7 N. W.	3 N. W.	7 N. W.	7 N. W.	
8	7 N. W.	7 N. W.	7 N. W.	8 N. W.	5 W. by N.	5 W. by N.	
9	7 W.	8 W.	8 W. N. W.	8 W. N. W.	7 W. N. W.	6 W. N. W.	
10	4 N. N. W.	4 N. N. W.	4 N. N. W.	6 N. N. W.	6 N. N. W.	3 N. N. W.	40
11	5 W. N. W.	3 W. N. W.	Calm	Calm	1 N. N. W.	1 N. N. W.	
12	1 N. by E.	1 N. by E.	Calm	Calm	Calm	1 N. E.	
13	4 N. N. W.	4 N. N. W.	2 N. N. W.	6 N. N. W.	3 N. W.	3 N. W.	42
14	6 S. S. W.	1 S. S. W.	3 S. S. E.	3 S. S. E.	2 S. E.	2 S. S. E.	
15	4 N. E.	3 N. E.	3 N. E.	3 N. E. by E.	3 N. E. by N.	3 N. E. by N.	
16	6 N. N. W.	5 N. N. W.	4 N. N. W.	4 N. N. W.	6 N. N. W.	6 N. W.	40
17	4 N. N. W.	4 N. N. W.	4 N. N. W.	4 N. N. W.	6 N. W.	6 N. W.	
18	2 W. by S.	2 W. by S.	1 W.	Calm	1 W.	1 N. N. W.	45
19	1 N. by E.	2 N. by E.	2 N. by E.	1 E. N. E.	1 N. N. W.	1 N. E. by N.	
20	4 E. S. E.	3 E. S. E.	6 E.	2 E.	2 E. by N.	6 E. N. E.	
21	7 N. N. W.	4 N. N. W.	4 N. N. W.	4 N. N. W.	7 N. W.	7 N. W.	44
22	1 N. by W.	2 N. by W.	1 N. by E.	1 N. by E.	1 N. N. E.	1 N. N. E.	47
23	6 N. N. W.	6 N. N. W.	2 W. N. W.	2 W. N. W.	6 W.	6 W.	47
24	Calm	Calm	1 S. W.	1 S. W.	1 S. W.	1 N. N. E.	
25	4 N. by W.	4 N. by W.	2 E. N. E.	2 N. N. E.	1 N. N. E.	1 N. N. E.	
26	6 W. N. W.	6 W. N. W.	4 W. by N.	6 W.	6 W. by N.	6 W. by N.	47
27	6 W.	7 W.	5 W.	4 W. by N.	6 W. N. W.	6 N. W. by W.	
28	1 N. E. by N.	6 N. E. by E.	1 N. E. by E.	1 N. E. by E.	1 N. E. by E.	1 N. E. by E.	
29	1 N. N. E.	Calm	1 W. N. W.	1 E. N. E.	1 E. by N.	1 E. by N.	
30	1 E.	1 E.	2 E. by S.	2 E. by S.	3 E. N. E.	1 E. S. E.	
31	1 S. E.	3 S. E.	1 E. N. E.	1 E. N. E.	5 N. by W.	4 N. by W.	46

Date.	2h.	4h.	6h.	8h.	10h.	Midnight.
1	1 W. N. W.	2 W. N. W.	6 W. N. W.	6 N. W.	2 N. W.	2 N. W.
2	6 W. N. W.	1 W. N. W.	4 N. by E.	2 N. N. W.	4 N. N. W.	3 N. N. W.
3	4 N. N. W.	6 N. W.	3 N. W.	3 N. W.	2 N. W.	2 N. by W.
4	2 N. N. W.	2 N. W.	1 N. by W.	1 N. by W.	1 N. by W.	1 N. by W.
5	1 N. by W.	2 N. by E.	4 N. by E.	3 N. by E.	2 N. by E.	4 N. by E.
6	5 N. W.	6 N. W.	6 N. W.	6 N. W.	7 N. W.	7 N. W.
7	7 N. W.	7 N. W.	6 N. W.	8 N. W.	6 N. W.	6 N. W.
8	6 W.	8 W.	5 W.	4 W.	5 W.	5 W.
9	4 W. N. W.	4 W. N. W.	4 N. W. by N.	6 N. N. W.	4 N. N. W.	4 N. N. W.
10	3 N. N. W.	4 W. N. W.	4 W. N. W.	4 W. N. W.	4 W. N. W.	4 W. N. W.
11	1 E.	1 E.	1 E.	1 E. by N.	1 N. by E.	1 N. by E.
12	1 N. E. by N.	1 N. N. E.	1 N. by E.	1 N. by E.	3 N. by W.	3 N. by W.
13	4 N. W.	4 W. by S.	4 S. S. W.	4 S. S. W.	2 S. S. W.	2 S. S. W.
14	2 E.	3 E.	2 E.	6 E.	2 S. E.	4 N. E.
15	6 N. W. by N.	3 N. E. by N.	5 N. E. by E.	5 N. by W.	5 N. by W.	5 N. N. W.
16	6 N. N. W.	4 N. W. by N.	6 N. W. by N.	4 W. N. W.	4 W. N. W.	4 W. by N.
17	6 N. W.	4 N. W.	4 W.	4 W.	4 W.	5 W.
18	1 N. N. W.	1 N. N. W.	1 N. by E.	1 N. by E.	1 N. by E.	1 N. by E.
19	1 N. N. E.	2 N. E. by E.	3 E. by N.	4 E.	4 E. by S.	4 E. S. E.
20	1 N. N. E.	1 N. N. E.	2 N. N. E.	2 N. N. E.	1 N.	1 N.
21	3 N. W.	3 N. W.	3 W. by N.	4 N. W. by W.	2 N. W. by N.	2 N. W. by N.
22	1 N. N. W.	4 N. N. W.	2 N. N. W.	4 N. N. W.	6 N. N. W.	4 N. N. W.
23	4 W. by N.	3 W. by N.	6 W. by N.	1 W. by N.	1 W. N. W.	2 W. by N.
24	3 N. by W.	1 N. by E.	5 N. by E.	2 N. W.	2 N. W.	3 N. W.
25	1 N. N. E.	1 N. N. E.	1 N.	3 N.	5 N. N. W.	3 N. N. W.
26	6 W. by N.	6 W. by N.	6 W. by N.	6 W.	6 W.	5 W.
27	3 N. by E.	3 N. by E.	6 N. N. E.	2 N. N. E.	2 N. N. E.	1 N. E. by N.
28	1 N. E. by E.	3 N. N. E.	2 N. N. E.	1 N. N. E.	1 N. N. E.	1 N. N. E.
29	1 E. by S.	1 E. by S.	1 E. by S.	1 E. by S.	1 E. by S.	1 E. by S.
30	2 E. S. E.	1 E. S. E.	1 E. N. E.	1 E. S. E.	1 E. S. E.	1 E. S. E.
31	3 N. by W.	4 N. by W.	7 N. by W.	7 N. by W.	7 N.	1 N.

Direction (true) and Force of the Wind observed on board the yacht Fox.
February, 1858.—Mean position: Lat. 11°.5 N.; long. 59°.5 W.

Date.	2h.	4h.	6h.	8h.	10h.	Noon.	Variation.
1	4 N. N. W.	6 N. N. W.	5 N. N. W.	5 N. N. W.	5 N. N. W.	4 N. N. W.	55° W.
2	4 N. W.	4 N. W.	4 N. W.	4 N. W.	4 N. W.	4 N. W.	55
3	2 N. W.	2 N. W.	2 N. W.	2 N. W.	2 N. W.	1 N. W.	55
4	2 N. N. W.	2 N. N. W.	2 N. N. W.	2 N. N. W.	2 N. by W.	2 N. by E.	53
5	Calm	Calm	1 N.	1 N.	Calm	Calm	55
6	Calm	Calm	1 N. by E.	1 N. N. W.	1 N. N. W.	1 N. N. W.	
7	3 W. by N.	2 W. by N.	3 N. N. W.	3 W.	2 W.	1 W.	54
8	Calm	Calm	Calm	Calm	3 N. by W.	2 N.	55
9	3 N. N. E.	3 N. N. E.	3 N. by W.	3 N. by W.	4 N. by W.	4 N. by W.	55
10	2 N. N. W.	2 N. N. W.	5 N. N. W.	5 N. N. W.	5 N. N. W.	3 N. W. by N.	53
11	1 N. by E.	4 N. E. by N.	6 E. by N.	6 N. N. E.	6 N. N. E.	4 N. N. E.	
12	7 N. W. by N.	6 N. W. by N.	6 N. W. by N.	4 N. W. by N.	3 W. by N.	3 W. by S.	
13	4 N. N. W.	4 N. by W.	4 N. by W.	3 N. by W.	3 N. by W.	3 N. by W.	54
14	7 N. by W.	7 N. by W.	7 N. by W.	7 N. by W.	5 N. by W.	4 N. by W.	
15	6 N.	6 N.	7 N.	4 N. by W.	5 N. by W.	4 N. by W.	53
16	5 N. by W.	6 N. by W.	6 N. by W.	5 N. by W.	5 N. by W.	4 N. by W.	
17	4 N. by W.	4 N. by W.	6 N. by W.	2 N.	4 N.	4 N.	52
18	4 N. N. W.	5 N. N. W.	6 N. by W.	6 N. by W.	6 N. by W.	5 N.	
19	6 N. W.	3 N. W.	6 N. W.	7 N. W.	5 N. W. by N.	4 N. W. by N.	53
20	1 N. W. by N.	2 W. N. W.	2 W. N. W.	3 W. N. W.	4 N. N. W.	6 N. N. W.	
21	6 N. W. by W.	5 N. W. by W.	4 N. W. by W.	4 N. W. by W.	4 N. W. by W.	5 N. W. by W.	
22	1 S. W.	1 W. by S.	Calm	1 N. W. by W.	1 N. by W.	1 N. E. by N.	
23	7 N. N. E.	7 N. N. E.	2 N.	7 N.	7 N. by W.	7 N. by W.	51
24	7 N. by W.	7 N. W. by N.	8 N. W. by N.	8 N. W. by N.	6 N. N. W.	6 N. W. by N.	
25	10 N. W. by N.	10 N. W. by N.	10 N. W. by W.	9 N. W. by W.	6 N. W. by W.	6 N. W. by W.	
26	4 N. W. by W.	6 N. W. by W.	5 N. W. by W.	3 N. W. by W.	1 W. N. W.	1 W. N. W.	
27	3 S. by E.	3 S. by E.	3 S. by E.	3 S. by E.	3 S. by E.	3 S. by E.	
28	1 S. E. by S.	5 S. E. by S.	5 S. E. by S.	5 S. E. by S.	4 S. S. E.	4 S. S. E.	18 ab't

Date.	2h.	4h.	6h.	8h.	10h.	Midn't.
1	4 N. N. W.	4 N. N. W.	4 N. N. W.	3 N. N. W.	3 N. N. W.	3 N. N. W.
2	4 N. W.	4 N. W.	4 N. W.	4 N. W.	5 N. W.	4 N. W.
3	1 N. W.	2 N. W.	2 N. W.	2 N. W.	1 N. W.	2 W. N. W.
4	2 N. by E.	2 N. by E.	1 N. by E.	1 N. by E.	1 N. by W.	Calm
5	1 N. by E.	1 N. by E.	1 N. by E.	1 N. by E.	1 N. by E.	Calm
6	1 W.	2 W.	4 W. by N.	3 W. by N.	4 W. by N.	3 W. by N.
7	1 W.	2 W.	1 W.	Calm	Calm	Calm
8	2 N. E.	1 N. E.	1 N.	1 N. N. E.	3 N. N. E.	3 N. N. E.
9	6 N. by W.	4 N. by W.	6 N. by W.	5 N. W.	6 N. N. W.	6 N. N. W.
10	8 N. W. by N.	4 N. W. by N.	6 N. W. by N.	1 N. N. W.	3 N. by W.	3 N. by W.
11	2 N. by E.	1 N. by E.	Calm	4 N. by W.	5 N. by W.	7 N. by W.
12	1 W. by S.	3 W. by S.	3 N. W.	2 N. W.	3 N. N. W.	4 N. N. W.
13	2 N. by W.	3 N. by W.	5 N. by W.	4 N. by W.	6 N. by W.	6 N. by W.
14	7 N. by W.	6 N. by W.	4 N.	6 N.	4 N.	6 N.
15	4 N. by W.	4 N. by W.	6 N. by W.	6 N. by W.	4 N. by W.	6 N. by W.
16	6 N. by E.	6 N. by E.	6 N. by E.	6 N.	5 N.	7 N. N. W.
17	6 N.	6 N. by W.	5 N. by W.	3 N. by W.	5 N. by W.	6 N. by E.
18	5 N.	5 N.	6 N.	6 N.	4 N. N. W.	7 N. W. by W.
19	3 N. W. by N.	3 W. N. W.	3 W.	4 W.	3 N. W. by N.	1 N. W. by N.
20	7 N. N. W.	7 N. N. W.	4 N. N. W.	5 N. W. by W.	5 N. W. by W.	6 N. W. by W.
21	3 N. W. by W.	3 W. N. W.	3 N. W. by W.	Calm	Calm	Calm
22	1 N. E. by N.	3 N. E. by N.	5 N. by W.	4 N. N. E.	6 N. N. E.	7 N. N. E.
23	5 N. by W.	5 N. by W.	4 N. W. by N.	4 N. W. by N.	6 N. by W.	7 N. by W.
24	8 N. N. W.	8 N. W. by N.	8 N. W. by N.	10 N. N. W.	10 N. N. W.	10 N. N. W.
25	7 N. W. by W.	8 N. W. by W.	7 N. W. by W.	6 N. W. by W.	7 N. W. by W.	7 N. W. by W.
26	Calm	1 S. E. by E.	1 S. E. by E.	2 S. by W.	2 S. by E.	3 S. by E.
27	3 S. S. E.	3 S. E. by E.	4 S. S. E.	4 S. by W.	4 S. by E.	3 S. E. by S.
28	3 S. E. by S.	1 S. by W.	1 S. E. by E.	1 S. E. by S.	1 S. E. by S.	1 S. E. by S.

Direction (true) and Force of the Wind observed on board the yacht Fox.

March, 1858.—Mean position: Lat. 69°.4 N.; long. 59°.1 W.

Date.	2a.	4a.	6a.	8a.	10a.	Noon.	Variation.
1	9 N. E. by E.	6 N. E. by E.	2 N. E. by E.	1 N. E. by E.	3 N. E. by N.	1 N. E. by E.	
2	7 E. by N.	7 E. by N.	6 E. by N.	3 S. W. by S.	3 S. by W.	1 S. W. by S.	
3	1 W. by N.	1 W. by N.	1 N. W. by W.	1 N. W.	1 N. by W.	1 N. by W.	
4	10 S. S. W.	9 S. S. W.	9 S. by W.	6 S. by W.	6 S. W. by S.	7 S. W. by S.	
5	1 S.	9 S.	1 S. W. by W.	1 S. W. by W.	1 S. W. by W.	1 S. W. by W.	78° W.
6	1 S. W. by W.	8 W. S. W.	6 N. W. by N.	3 N. W.	3 N. W.	3 N. W.	
7	1 N. W. by N.	1 N. W. by N.	5 N. N. W.	4 N. by W.	4 N.	6 N.	76
8	6 N. by W.	6 N. by W.	6 N. by W.	6 N. by W.	4 N. by W.	4 N. by W.	
9	2 N.	8 N. N. E.	3 N. N. E.	1 N. E. by E.	1 E. S. E.	3 E. by S.	
10	9 N. E. by N.	4 N. E. by N.	5 S. E. by S.	5 S. E. by S.	6 E. S. E.	5 E. S. E.	
11	5 S. E. by E.	3 S. E. by E.	6 S. E. by E.	6 S. E. by E.	6 S. E. by E.	9 S. E. by E.	
12	4 S. S. E.	6 S. S. E.	2 E. by S.	2 S. by E.	2 E. by S.	2 S. by W.	
13	2 E. by S.	6 S. by E.	5 S. S. E.	4 S. S. E.	5 S. S. W.	3 S.	
14	3 W.	5 W.	3 W. by N.	4 W. N. W.	3 W. N. W.	3 N. W. by N.	77 30'
15	4 N. W. by N.	4 N. W. by N.	4 N. W. by N.	5 N. W. by N.	5 N. W. by N.	7 N. W. by N.	
16	7 N. W. by N.	6 N. W. by W.	6 N. W. by W.	4 N. W. by W.	4 N. W. by W.	3 W. by N.	
17	6 N. W. by W.	4 N. W. by W.	4 N. N. W.	4 N. N. W.	5 N. N. W.	4 N. N. W.	
18	2 N. by W.	2 N. by W.	3 N. by W.	3 N.	3 N.	3 N.	
19	6 N.	7 N. by W.	6 N. W. by N.	6 N. W. by N.	5 N. W. by N.	4 N. W. by N.	
20	3 N. N. W.	3 N. by E.	1 N. E. by E.	1 E. S. E.	1 N. E. by E.	1 N. E. by E.	75
21	2 N. W. by N.	3 N. W. by N.	1 N.	1 N. E. by E.	1 N. E. by E.	1 N. E. by E.	(about)
22	1 N. E. by E.	1 N. E. by E.	1 E. by S.	3 S. E. by S.	3 E. by S.	3 E. by S.	
23	10 S. E. by E.	10 S. E. by E.	7 S. E. by S.	6 S.	6 S. W. by W.	1 S. by W.	
24	6 N. W. by N.	6 N. W. by N.	6 N.	6 N. by E.	4 N. by E.	4 N. by E.	
25	6 N. by W.	6 N. by W.	9 N. by W.	7 N.	6 N.	8 N.	75
26	9 N. W. by N.	8 N. W. by N.	9 N. N. W.	8 N. W. by N.	9 N. W. by N.	9 N. W. by N.	(about)
27	8 N. N. W.	8 N. N. W.	8 N. N. W.	7 N. N. W.	7 N. N. W.	7 N. N. W.	
28	6 N. N. W.	4 N. N. W.	6 N. N. W.	6 N. N. W.	6 N. N. W.	3 N. N. W.	
29	4 N. N. W.	4 N. N. W.	6 N. N. W.	6 N. N. W.	4 N. W. by N.	6 N. W. by N.	71
30	8 N. E. by E.	3 N. E. by E.	2 E. by N.	3 E.	3 E.	8 S. E. by E.	(about)
31	7 N. by W.	7 N. W. by N.	6 N. W. by N.	6 N. W. by N.	6 N. N. W.	6 W. N. W.	

Date.	2p.	4p.	6p.	8p.	10p.	Midn't.
1	8 E. by N.	6 E. by N.	6 E. by N.	6 S. E. by S.	4 S. by E.	6 S. by E.
2	1 N. W. by W.	1 N. W. by W.	5 N. W. by N.	4 N. W. by N.	3 W. by S.	3 W. by S.
3	7 N. E. by E.	3 N. E. by N.	4 N. E. by N.	7 N. E. by N.	9 N. E. by N.	9 N. E. by E.
4	6 S. W.	8 S. W. by S.	8 S. W. by S.	3 S. W. by S.	Calm	1 S. by E.
5	2 S. W. by W.	4 S. W. by W.	4 S. W. by W.	3 S. W. by W.	1 W. N. W.	1 N. W. by W.
6	3 N. W. by N.	3 N. W. by N.	3 N. W. by N.	3 N. W. by N.	2 N. W. by N.	1 N. W. by N.
7	4 N.	5 N.	4 N.	4 N. by W.	5 N. by W.	5 N. by W.
8	4 N. by W.	4 N. by W.	8 N. N. W.	1 N. N. W.	5 N.	3 N.
9	2 N. E. by E.	3 N. N. E.	8 N. N. E.	3 N. N. E.	8 N. N. E.	1 N. N. E.
10	8 E. S. E.	4 E. by N.	5 E. by N.	3 E. by N.	3 E. by N.	3 E.
11	6 S. E. by S.	3 S. E. by S.	3 S. E. by S.	4 S. E. by E.	4 S. E. by E.	4 S. S. E.
12	2 S. by E.	6 S. by E.	3 S. W. by W.	3 S. W. by W.	5 S. W.	8 S. S. W.
13	5 S.	3 S.	3 S.	3 W. by N.	3 W. by N.	3 W. by N.
14	4 N. W. by N.	3 N. W. by N.	4 N. W. by N.	3 N. W. by N.	8 N. W. by N.	3 N. W. by N.
15	7 N. W. by N.	7 N. W. by N.	7 N. W. by N.	7 N. W. by N.	7 N. W. by N.	7 N. W. by W.
16	3 W. by N.	3 W. by N.	3 N. W. by N.	3 N. W. by N.	6 N. W. by W.	4 N. W. by W.
17	4 N. N. W.	3 N. N. W.	4 N. by W.	3 N. by W.	8 N. by W.	3 N. by W.
18	4 N.	4 N.	6 N.	4 N.	6 N.	5 N.
19	4 N. W. by N.	4 N. W. by N.	3 N. W. by N.	6 N. W. by N.	3 N. W. by N.	1 N. W. by N.
20	1 N. E. by E.	1 N. by E.	2 N. N. E.	2 N. N. E.	2 N. N. E.	2 N. N. E.
21	1 N. E. by E.	1 S. E. by S.	1 N. E. by E.	1 E. by N.	Calm	1 E.
22	5 S. S. E.	5 S. E. by E.	8 E. by S.	7 E. by S.	9 S. E. by E.	9 S. E. by E.
23	5 N. W. by W.	3 N. W. by W.	5 W. by N.	4 W. by N.	4 W. N. W.	4 W. N. W.
24	6 N. by W.	5 N.	6 N. by W.	6 N. by W.	5 N. by W.	4 N. by W.
25	9 N.	9 N.	9 N. W. by N.	9 N. W. by N.	9 N. W. by N.	8 N. W. by N.
26	6 N. W. by N.	9 N. N. W.	6 N. N. W.	6 N. N. W.	6 N. N. W.	5 N. N. W.
27	7 N. N. W.	7 N. N. W.	7 N. N. W.	7 N. N. W.	7 N. N. W.	6 N. N. W.
28	6 N. N. W.	5 N. N. W.	3 N. N. W.	4 N. N. W.	4 N. N. W.	4 N. N. W.
29	2 N. W. by N.	2 N. W. by N.	2 N. W. by N.	2 N.	2 N.	8 N. E. by N.
30	2 S. E. by E.	8 N. N. E.	2 N.	6 N. by W.	7 N. by W.	6 N. by W.
31	5 W. N. W.	6 W. by N.	8 W. N. W.	3 W. N. W.	3 W. N. W.	2 W. by N.

March 4th. Wind shifted from N. E. by E. through E. to S. S. W. between midnight and 1 A. M.

Direction (true) and Force of the Wind observed on board the yacht Fox.
April, 1858.—Mean position: Lat. [illegible]° N.; long. 57°.1 W.

Date.	2a.	4a.	6a.	8a.	10a.	Noon.	Variation.
1	2 W. by N.	3 W. by N.	4 S. W. by W.	2 S. W. by W.	1 S. W. by W.	1 S. W. by W.	74° W.*
2	3 N. E. by E.	2 N. E. by N.	1 N. E. by E.	2 N. N. E.	3 N. N. E.	2 N. N. E.	73 31'
3	6 N.	6 N.	6 N.	7 N.	7 N.	5 N.	
4	10 N. by W.	10 N. by W.	10 N. by W.	10 N. by W.	10 N. by W.	10 N. by W.	
5	10 N. by W.	8 N. by W.	6 N. by W.	3 N. W. by N.	3 N. W. by N.	7 N. W. by N.	
6	7 N. W. by W.	3 N. W. by W.	5 N. W. by W.	4 W. N. W.	3 W. by N.	6 W. by N.	72
7	5 N. W. by N.	3 N. E. by E.	2 N.	4 N.	3 N.	4 N.	
8	6 N. N. W.	6 N. N. W.	7 N. W. by W.	5 N. W. by N.	6 N. W. by N.	4 N. W. by N.	
9	8 N. N. W.	1 N. N. W.	1 N. N. W.	3 N. N. W.	4 N. N. W.	4 N. N. W.	70 03
10	4 N. N. W.	4 N. N. W.	4 N. N. W.	2 N. N. W.	2 N. N. W.	2 N. N. W.	
11	3 N.	3 N.	5 N.	2 N.	2 N. by E.	2 N. N. W.	
12	4 N. N. W.	6 N. N. W.	6 N. N. W.	2 N.	4 N.	4 N.	75 34
13	3 N. N. E.	2 N. N. E.	6 N. N. E.	6 N. N. E.	3 N. N. E.	3 N. N. E.	
14	3 N. by E.	3 N. E.	3 N. E.	4 N. E.	4 N. E.	4 N. E. by E.	
15	2 N.	3 N.	4 N.	4 N. by E.	2 N. by W.	6 N. by W.	
16	7 N. by W.	7 N. by W.	7 N. by W.	7 N. by W.	3 N. by W.	6 N. by W.	69
17	3 N. by E.	3 N. by E.	3 N. by E.	3 N. by E.	3 N. by E.	2 N. by E.	
18	....	7 N. E.	....	7 N.	....	6 N.	
19	....	7 N.	....	5 N.	....	6 N.	
20	....	5 N. N. W.	....	3 N. N. W.	....	6 N. W.	64
21	....	4 N. N. W.	....	3 N. N. W.	....	6 N. N. W.	
22†	....	6 N. N. W.	....	4 N. N. W.	....	3 N. N. W.	
23	....	3 N. N. W.	....	3 N. W. by W.	....	3 N. W.	63
24	....	2 N. N. E.	....	6 S. S. E.	....	5 E. N. E.	
25	....	6 N. N. W.	....	Calm	....	5 N. N. W.	
26	....	5 W. N. W.	....	4 N. by W.	....	5 N. by W.	
27	....	6 W. N. W.	....	3 W.	....	6 W. N. W.	59
28	....	6 W. S. W.	....	2 S. S. E.	....	4 S. S. E.	60
29	....	3 E. N. E.	....	1 E. N. E.	....	Calm	
30	....	3 E. N. E.	....	2 S. S. W.	....	2 E. N. E.	

Date.	2p.	4p.	6p.	8p.	10p.	Midn't.
1	2 W. by S.	2 W. by N.	3 W. by N.	1 W. by S.	Calm	2 N. E. by N.
2	3 N. N. E.	4 N. N. E.	3 N. N. E.	4 N. by E.	6 N. by E.	4 N. by E.
3	7 N. by W.	7 N. by W.	6 N. by W.	8 N. by W.	2 N. by W.	10 N. by W.
4	10 N. by W.	10 N. by W.	10 N. by W.	10 N. by W.	10 N. by W.	10 N. by W.
5	7 N. W. by N.	8 N. W. by N.	7 N. W. by N.	2 N. W. by W.	7 N. W. by W.	8 N. W. by W.
6	2 W. by N.	Calm	Calm	Calm	Calm	1 N. E. by N.
7	4 N.	6 N. by W.	5 N. by W.	5 N. by W.	2 N. by W.	6 N. N. W.
8	5 N. W. by N.	7 N. W. by N.	3 N. W. by N.	3 N. W. by N.	3 N. W. by N.	3 N. W. by N.
9	4 N. by W.	4 N. by W.	4 N. by W.	4 N. by W.	4 N. N. W.	6 N. N. W.
10	4 N. by W.	3 N. N. W.	3 N.	3 N.	3 N.	3 N.
11	1 N. W. by W.	1 N. W. by W.	1 N. W. by W.	3 W. N. W.	2 N. W.	4 N. N. W.
12	2 N.	2 N.	3 N.	3 N.	3 N. by W.	2 N. by W.
13	3 N. N. E.	1 N. E. by N.	1 N. by E.	1 N. by E.	1 N. by E.	1 N. by E.
14	6 N. by E.	4 N. by E.	3 N. by E.	3 N. E. by E.	4 N. E. by E.	3 N. by W.
15	2 N. by W.	7 N. by W.	6 N. by W.	3 N. by W.	6 N. by W.	7 N. by W.
16	3 N.	7 N.	3 N. by E.	3 N. by E.	6 N. by E.	6 N. by E.
17	6 N.	6 N.	3 N. by E.	2 N. by E.	7 N. by E.	3 N. by E.
18	....	6 N.	....	5 N.	....	7 N.
19	....	6 N. W. by N.	....	6 N. by E.	....	6 N. by E.
20	....	5 N. W.	....	3 N. W.	....	6 N. W.
21	....	6 N. N. W.	....	1 N. N. W.	....	3 N. N. W.
22	....	3 N. W. by N.	....	3 N. N. W.	....	3 N. N. W.
23	....	3 N. W.	....	3 N. N. W.	....	Calm
24	....	6 E. S. E.	....	3 S. S. E.	....	6 E. S. E.
25	....	4 N. W.	....	4 W. S. W.	....	4 W. S. W.
26	....	4 S. by W.	....	3 W. S. W.	....	5 W. S. W.
27	....	2 W. S. W.	....	2 W. S. W.	....	5 W. S. W.
28	....	3 var.	....	3 W.	....	4 E. N. E.
29	....	3 E. N. E.	....	4 E. N. E.	....	3 E. N. E.
30	....	2 E. N. E.	....	4 E. by N.	....	3 S. E.

* Azim. † Experienced a S. W. current.

3

Direction (true) and Force of the Wind observed on board the yacht Fox.

May, 1858.—Mean position: Lat. 65°.7 N.; Long. 55°.7 W.

Date.	4h	8h	Noon.	4h	8h	Midn't.	Variation.
1	7 S.	3 S.	4 S. S. E.	4 S. S. W.	4 W. S. W.	4 W. S. W.	
2	3 E. N. E.	Calm	3 S. S. W.	4 N. E.	4 E. N. E.	5 N. by E.	
3	3 E. N. E.	4 E. N. E.	4 N. E.	3 N. E.	8 E. N. E.	3 E. N. E.	
4	4 E. N. E.	6 S. S. E.	8 S. S. E.	6 S. S. E.	5 S. S. E.	7 S. by E.	
5	6 S. by E.	6 N. N. W.	6 N. W. by W.	5 N. W.	6 N. W.	5 N. W.	
6	6 N. N. W.	4 N. N. W.	3 N. N. W.	4 N. N. W.	4 N. N. W.	3 N. N. E.	
7	4 N.	2 N. E.	3 N. E.	4 N. N. W.	4 N. N. W.	4 E.	
8	2 S. S. W.	8 E.	6 N.	4 N. N. W.	8 N.	3 N'ly	
9	3 E'ly	4 E'ly	8 N. N. W.	2 Variable	8 E. S. E.	6 Variable	79° W.
10	8 to 1 E. N. E.	6 E.	6 E. by S.	7 E.	7 E.	6 E. S. E.	73
11	4 S. E. by E.	5 S. E.	6 E. N. E.	6 E'ly	5 E. S. E.	6 E. E.	(about)
12	8 E. N. E.	3 N. N. W.	4 S. S. E.	4 S. S. E.	4 S. by W.	4 S. by W.	
13	6 N.	5 N. E. by E.	3 N. E. by N.	5 N. E.	3 S. E.	Calm	
14	8 S.	Calm	8 W. N. W.	2 N. by E.	Calm	2 S. by W.	
15	2 E. S. E.	8 E. N. E.	Calm	Calm	Calm	1 W. S. W.	
16	3 N. N. W.	8 N. E.	1 W. by N.	6 W. N. W.	4 W. N. W.	6 W. S. W.	
17	2 E.	2 E. S. E.	4 N. N. W.	2 W. S. W.	Calm	6 E. S. E.	
18	3 S. S. E.	1 W. N. W.	1 W. N. W.	2 W. N. W.	1 W. N. W.	Calm	
19	5 S. S. E.	2 S. S. E.	Calm	3 W. S. W.	3 W. S. W.	Calm	
20	Calms and	light variable	winds			Calm	
21	Calm	3 E. N. E.	2 E. N. E.	3 W. S. W.	2 W. S. W.	1 W. S. W.	
22	6 E. N. E.	6 E.	5 E.	4 E. N. E.	1 E. S. E.	Calm	
23	Calm	5 E. N. E.	4 E. N. E.	2 W. S. W.	1 W. S. W.	1 W. S. W.	
24	1 E'ly	4 S. S. E.	3 S. S. E.	Calm	Calm	Calm	
25	Calm	2 S. W.	Calm	2 S. E.	2 S. E.	2 S. E.	
26	4 S. E.	4 S. E.	8 E. S. E.	3 S. S. E.	Calm	1 N. N. W.	
27	2 S. S. E.	2 S. E.	Calm	4 N. N. W.	Calm	Calm	73 (ab't)
28	1 W. S. W.	3 S. E.	4 Variable	Calm	Calm	1 E. S. E.	74 30'
29	2 E. N. E.	2 S. S. E.	1 S. S. E.	1 S. S. E.	Calm	1 N. W.	79
30	1 N. W. by W.	Calm	Calm	1 N. W.	3 S'ly	2 S'ly	
31	4 S. S. E.	4 S. S. E.	5 E.	2 S. S. W.	2 N. E.	Calm	

June, 1858.—Mean position: Lat. 74°.6 N.; Long. 60°.1 W.

Date.	4h	8h	Noon.	4h	8h	Midn't.	Variation.
1	1 N. W.	1 N. W.	2 N. N. W.	1 N. N. W.	1 N. N. E.	1 E. N. E.	
2	2 E. N. E.	2 N. W.	1 N. E.	1 N. E.	Calm	2 S. W. by S.	
3	4 S. by E.	6 S. by E.	4 S. by W.	1 S. W. by S.	Calm	1 N. W. by N.	
4	1 N. W. by N.	3 N. W. by N.	4 N. W. by W.	Calm	2 S. E. by S.	2 S. E. by S.	
5	5 S. E. by S.	4 S. E. by S.	3 S. E. by S.	Calm	4 N.	1 N.	82° W.
6	4 N. N. E.	3 N. W. by N.	3 N. W. by S.	3 N. E.	8 N. E.	Calm	
7	2 N. W. by N.	1 S. E. by S.	Calm	8 S. E. by S.	Calm	Calm	84
8	Calm	1 S. E. by E.	1 N. W. by N.	1 N. W. by N.	Calm	3 N. N. E.	86
9	Calm	Calm	Calm	1 S. E.	Calm	1 S.	
10	1 S. W.	Calm	1 S. W.	Calm	1 S. W.	1 S. W.	
11	1 S. E.	1 N.	1 S. E.	Calm	Calm	1 W.	86
12	Calm	3 W. by S.	5 W.	2 N. by W.	4 N. by W.	5 N. N. W.	(about)
13	5 N. N. W.	6 N. W. by N.	4 N. by W.	4 N. by W.	4 N. W. by N.	4 N. W. by N.	
14	8 N. W.	3 N. N. W.	5 N. N. W.	1 N.	5 N. by E.	8 N. by E.	
15	3 N'ly	1 N'ly	3 N. W.	4 W.	4 W. N. W.	1 W. N. W.	
16	4 W. N. W.	4 N. W.	4 N. W.	5 W. by N.	8 N. W.	3 S. E.	89
17	8 S. E.	4 E. S. E.	2 E. N. E.	8 S. E.	3 E. by S.	1 E. by S.	91
18	1 E. by S.	1 N. N.	2 W. N. W.	8 Variable	Calm	Calm	80 (ab't)
19	8 N. W. by W.	2 N. W.	3 N. W.	3 N. W.	2 W. S. W.	1 S. W.	83
20	8 N. by E.	8 N. W.	4 W. N. W.	2 W. N. W.	1 N. W.	1 E.	(about)
21	Calm	2 N. W.	6 N. by W.	6 W. N. W.	3 N. N. W.	3 N. N. W.	
22	8 N. N. W.	3 N. W. by N.	3 W. N. W.	1 S. E.	Calm	1 N. by E.	85
23	1 N. E.	4 N. E.	3 S. E.	3 E.	4 E. by N.	8 E.	(about)
24	5 N. E.	4 E.	8 E. by N.	8 N. by E.	2 N. by E.	2 N. by E.	94
25	2 N. N. W.	8 N. N. W.	8 N. E.	5 E. by S.	8 E. N. E.	1 E. by S.	
26	Calm	8 N. by W.	1 N. N. W.	2 N. W.	3 N. W.	3 N. E.	94
27	5 E'ly	8 E'ly	6 E. by S.	6 E. by S.	6 E. by S.	6 S. E.	(about)
28	4 E. S. E.	8 S. E.	3 N. E.	2 N. E.	1 S. E.	3 S. E.	
29	1 S. E.	1 N. E.	3 S. E.	3 E. by N.	5 E. by S.	6 E. by N.	
30	5 E. by S.	3 S. by E.	7 S. E. by E.	1 S. E. by E.	8 N. W. by W.	2 N. W. by W.	85

Direction (true) and Force of the Wind observed on board the yacht Fox.

July, 1858.—Mean position: Lat. 74°.4 N.; long. 78°.4 W.

Date.	4h.	8h.	Noon.	4h.	8h.	Midn't.	Variation.	Remarks.
1	1 N.W. by W.	Calm	1 S. E.	3 S. by E.	4 W. S. W.	6 W. S. W.	95° W.	
2	4 S. S. W.	3 W. S. W.	Calm	3 S. E.	4 S. E.	6 S. E'ly		
3	1 S. E.	1 N. W.	2 N. W.	Calm	1 W.	3 S. W.	99	[illegible]
4	Calm	Calm	3 N.W. by W.	2 N.	2 N.	2 N. E.		
5	4 N. E. by N.	4 E. N. E.	4 N.	4 S. E. by E.	1 N. E.	4 N. E.		
6	6 E.	6 E. by S.	4 E. S. E.	4 N.E. by N.	4 N. E. by E.	3 N. by E.	100	
7	4 N. by E.	4 N. N. W.	3 N.	3 N.	4 N.	3 N. N. W.		
8	4 N.W. by W.	4 N.W. by W.	3 N.W. by W.	3 N.W. by W.	4 N.W. by W.	3 N. W.	102	
9	3 N.W. by W.	3 N.W. by W.	3 N.W. by W.	4 N.W. by W.	4 N.W. by N.	3 N.W. by W.		
10	3 N. W.	4 N.W. by N.	4 N. W.	4 N. W.	3 N.W. by W.	3 N.W. by W.		
11	3 N. N. W.	3 N. N. W.	3 N.W. by N.	1 W'ly	3 W'ly	3 S. E.	101	
12	1 W. S. W.	Calm	1 S. E'ly	6 N. E.	4 N. E.	7 N. E. by N.		
13	3 N. E. by E.	6 N. E. by E.	7 N. E. by N.	5 S. W'ly	6 W. S. W.	4 E. N. E.		At 2 P.M. wind suddenly became light and fell to calm(?)
14	1 E. N. E.	2 W.	3 W.	2 W.	4 W.	4 S. W.		
15	Calm	1 S. W.	2 E'ly	4 E'ly	6 E. N. E.	4 S. E. by E.	104	
16	4 S. E. by E.	3 S. S. E.	1 E'ly	1 W'ly	Calm	1 S. E.	102	
17	Calm	1 E.	1 Variable	2 N. E'ly	2 N. N. E.	2 N. N. E.		
18	Calm	1 N. E'ly	3 E'ly	4 E'ly	3 E'ly	2 E'ly	100	A strong current(?) [illegible]; the ship drifting with it.
19	2 E. by N.	2 E. by S.	2 E. by E.	3 S. E. by E.	1 S. E. by E.	1 S. E. by E.	99	
20	Calm	1 E'ly	Calm	1 W. by N.	Calm	Calm		
21	1 S. W.	1 S. W.	1 N. W.	3 N. W. by E.	3 S. W. by S.	6 W. S. W.	103½	
22	5 S.W. by W.	2 W. by S.	2 W. by N.	3 W.	3 W. N. W.	3 W. by S.	114	
23	2 W. S. W.	1 N. W.	2 W.	1 W. S. W.	1 W. S. W.	1 W. S. W.		
24	5-3 W. S. W.	3 W.	4 W.	1 S. W.	1 S. S. W.	1 S.		
25	Calm	Calm	Calm	Calm	Calm	3 S. S. E.	111?	
26	3 S. S. E.	2 S. by W.	1 S. S. W.	1 S. W. by S.	3 S. E. by E.	3 S. E. by E.	107	A swell(?) set to the southward.
27	3 E. by S.	Calm	3 N. by W.	Calm	Calm	2 E. by N.	106	
28	1 S. E. by E.	Calm	1 W. by S.	4 N. E. by N.	1 S. E. by E.	1 E. by E.		
29	3 N. E. by N.	1 N. E. by N.	2 N.	Calm	1 E. N. E.	1 E. S. E.		
30	Calm	1 N. W.	7 N. N. W.	6 N.	1 N. E. by E.	5 W. N. W.		
31	7 N.W. by W.	4 W.	4 W. S. W.	4 S. W.	6 S. W.	6 S.		

August, 1858.—Mean position: Lat. 73°.1 N.; long. 88°.5 W.

Date.	4h.	8h.	Noon.	4h.	8h.	Midn't.	Variation.	Remarks.
1	3 W.	4 S. W.	5 S. W. by W.	6 S.W. by W.	5 W. by S.	3 W. by S.	140° W.	
2	7 W. by S.	4 W. by S.	6 W. S. W.	5 W. by S.	2 S. E. by E.	Calm		
3	1 N. E'ly	Calm	Calm	1 E'ly	2 E'ly	Calm		
4	Calm	Calm	Calm	3 S. E.	3 S. S. E.	1 E. S. E.		
5	Calm	Calm	1 E'ly	1 E'ly	Calm	Calm		
6	Calm	Calm	Calm	Calm	1 S. E. by E.	3 S. E. by E.		
7	3 S. E. by S.	4 S. E. by E.	5 S. E. by E.	7 S. E. by S.	7 S. E. by E.	7 S. E. by E.	108	[illegible]
8	10 E. S. E.	10 E. S. E.	10 E. S. E.	6 E.	6 E.	6 E.	110	A heavy gale.
9	8 E.	7 E.	3 E.	1 E. S. E.	1 E. S. E.	1 E. N. E.		
10	1 E. N. E.	2 E. N. E.	3 E. N. E.	Calm	Calm	1 Variable	115	
11	1 Variable	2 N. W.	Calm	Calm	Calm	Calm	120	[illegible]
12	Calm	Calm	2 N'ly	4 N. E.	4 E.	4 S. E.		
13	3 E.	4 E.	4 E. S. E.	3 E.	2 E.	3 E.		
14	3 N. N. E.	4 N.	5 N.	4 N. N. W.	5 N.	5 N.		
15	6 N. N. E.	6 N. N. E.	6 N. N. E.	6 N'ly	6 N. N. W.	6 N. N. W.		
16	6 N. N. W.	4 W. N. W.	4 W. N. W.	6 N. W.	6 S. W.	6 N. W.		
17	4 W. S. W.	6 W. by N.	6 W. by N.	6 W.	4 W.	4 N. W.	140	
18	6 S. W.	4 W.	5 W.	5 W'ly	8 S. S. W.	4 W'ly		
19	3 S. S. W.	5 W.	4 W.	5 W.	4 W. S. W.	3 W. S. W.		
20	4 W.	4 W. S. W.	3 W.	6 N. N. W.	7 N. W.	4 W.		
21	5 N. W.	6 N. W.	4 W.	6 W.	6 W.	4 W.		
22	4 W. S. W.	3 W. S. W.	3 E'ly	3 S. S. E.	3 S. S. E.	3 S. S. E.		
23	Calm	3 S. W.	4 W.	6 W.	6 W.	6 W.		
24	6 W.	5 W.	4 W.	3 N. E.	6 N. N. E.	7 N. N. E.		
25	6 N. N. E.	6 N. N. W.	6 N. N. W.	4 N. N. W.	6 W. N. W.	6 W. N. W.		
26	6 N. N. W.	6 N. N. W.	5 N. N. W.	5 N. W.	6 W. N. W.	6 W. N. W.		
27	1 Variable	Calm	5 W. N. W.	6 N. W.	5 N. W.	7 N. W.		
28	4 N. N. W.	6 N. W.	5 N. W.	4 Variable	4 Variable	3 N. E.		
29	3 E. S. E.	3 E. S. E.	5 N. E.	3 E. N. E.	2 E. N. E.	2 N'ly		
30	4 N. E.	3 N. N. W.	3 S.	2 S.	2 S. E.	Calm		
31	3 S. E.	3 S. E.	5 N. E.	5 N. W.	6 W.	3 W.		

Direction (true) and Force of the Wind observed on board the yacht Fox.

September, 1858.—Mean position: Lat. 72° N.; long. 94°.5 W.

Days.	4h.	8h.	Noon.	4h.	8h.	Midn't.
1	3 N. W.	4 N. N. W.	2 S. W.	2 W.	4 W. N. W.	4 W. N. W.
2	5 N. N. W.	4 W. N. W.	4 S. by W.	4 S. E.	6 W. N. W.	4 W. N. W.
3	3 W. by N.	4 W. by N.	3 W. by N.	4 W. by S.	4 W. by N.	5 W. by S.
4	5 W. by N.	6 W. by N.	3 W. by N.	7 W.	6 W. by N.	5 W. by N.
5	4 W.	6 W.	7 W.	4 W.	4 W.	4 W.
6	4 W.	4 W. S. W.	3 S. W.	4 S. by W.	4 S'ly	4 S'ly
7	3 E'ly	3 E'ly	3 S'ly	4 S. S. E.	4 S. E.	4 S. E.
8	4 S. E.	4 S. E.	4 S. S. E.	4 S. S. E.	4 S. S. E.	4 W. by S.
9	4 S. W.	3 W. by S.	5 W.	6 W.	4 W.	3 W.
10	3 N. W.	2 S. S. W.	2 S. S. W.	Calm	1 N. W.	2 N. W.
11	3 S. S. E.	3 S. S. E.	4 E.	3 N. E.	3 N. E.	3 N. E.
12	3 N. E.	3 N. E.	4 N. E.	4 N. E.	4 N. E.	4 N. E.
13	3 N. N. W.	Calm	3 S'ly	3 S. S. W.	3 W.	Calm
14	3 N. E.	4 N. E.	3 N. W'ly	3 E'ly	3 N. E.	2 N. by E.
15	3 N. by E.	4 N. by E.	3 N. N. E.	3 N. N. E.	4 N'ly	3 N'ly
16	4 N'ly	3 N'ly	3 N. N. W.	5 N. N. W.	3 N. N. W.	4 N. N. W.
17	4 N. N. W.	6 N. N. W.	3 N. N. W.	4 N. N. E.	4 N. N. E.	4 N. N. E.
18	4 N. N. E.	4 N. N. E.	3 N. N. E.	3 N. W.	3 N. W.	3 N. W.
19	3 N. W.	4 N. N. W.	4 W.	4 W.	4 N. W.	5 S. W.
20	4 N. N. W.	4 N. N. W.	4 S. W.	6 W.	6 S. W.	3 S. W.
21	3 N. N. W.	4 S. W.	4 S. S. W.	4 S. W.	3 S. W.	6 N. W.
22	3 N. W.	4 W. by N.	5 W. by N.	3 W. S. W.	4 W. N. W.	7 N. W.
23	4 W. N. W.	3 W.	3 W.	1 W.	7 to 8 N. W.	1 N. W.
24	3 N. W.	4 W.	5 W.	6 W.	3 W.	3 W. N. W.
25	7 W. N. W.	4 W.	5 W.	6 W.	5 W. by S.	4 W. by S.
26	4 W. N. W.	5 W. N. W.	5 W. N. W.	4 N. W.	2 N. W.	2 N. W.
27*	Calm	3 S. W'ly	3 S. E'ly	3 S. S. E.	3 S. S. E.	3 S. E.
28	3 S. E.	4 S. E.	4 S. S. E.	4 S. S. E.	3 S. S. E.	4 S'ly
29	2 S. W.	3 S. W.	3 S. W.	3 W.	2 S.	3 S'ly
30	2 N.	3 S. E.	4 N. E.	2 N. E.	4 N. E.	3 N. E.

October, 1858.—At winter quarters; Lat. 72° N.; long. 94°.2 W.

Days.	4h.	8h.	Noon.	4h.	8h.	Midn't.
1	3 N. E.	3 N. E.	5 N. E.	6 N. E.	5 N. E.	5 N. E.
2	7 N. E. by E.	7 N. E. by E.	7 N. E. by E.	7 N. E.	7 N. E.	7 N. E.
3	7 N. E.	7 N. E.	8 N. N. E.	7 N. E.	9 N. E.	6 N. E.
4	7 N. E.	6 E. N. E.	6 E. N. E.	5 N. E. by E.	5 N. E.	5 N. E.
5	4 E'ly	3 S. E.	2 S. E.	3 E. N. E.	3 S. E.	3 S. E.
6	3 E. N. E.	3 E. N. E.	1 S. S. E.	2 S.	4 S. W.	3 S. W.
7	4 S. S. W.	2 S. W.	2 W.	3 S. W.	10 S. W.	Calm
8	Calm	Calm	3 W. N. W.	1 W.	1 W. N. W.	1 W. N. W.
9	3 W.	3 W.	3 W.	1 N. E.	5 N. E.	1 E. by N.
10	Calm	4 N. E.	6 E.	7 N. E.	4 N. N. E.	3 E. N. E.
11	4 E. N. E.	3 S. E.	4 N. E. by E.	5 N. E. by E.	3 N. E. by E.	4 N. E.
12	6 N. E.	7 N. N. E.	3 N. E.	2 N. E.	3 N. E.	1 N. E.
13	3 N. E.	6 N. E. by E.	2 N. E.	3 N. E.	5 N. W.	5 W.
14	7 W. N. W.	5 W. N. W.	5 W. N. W.	2 W. N. W.	5 N. W.	3 N. W.
15	3 N. W.	3 N. W.	3 N. W.	3 N. W.	3 N. by W.	4 N. N. E.
16	4 N. W.	6 N. W.	6 N. W.	6 N. W.	5 W. N. W.	6 W. N. W.
17	6 W. N. W.	5 W. N. W.	5 W. N. W.	5 N. W.	3 N. W.	5 N. W.
18	5 N. W.	7 N. W.	7 W. N. W.	4 N. W.	3 N. W.	3 N. W.
19	3 E. N. E.	3 E. N. E.	3 E. N. E.	4 E. N. E.	3 E. N. E.	5 E. N. E.
20	4 N. W.	3 S. S. E.	3 E. N. E.	3 E. N. E.	2 N. E.	3 N. by W.
21	6 N. by E.	5 N. W.	6 N. N. W.	6 N. N. W.	7 N. N. W.	8 N. N. W.
22	3 N. W.	5 N. W.	3 N. W.	3 W. N. W.	3 N. W.	5 N. W.
23	3 N. W.	3 S. E. by E.	3 N. E.	2 E. N. E.	4 E. N. E.	1 N. E.
24	1 N. E.	3 S.	3 S.	3 N. N. E.	3 N. N. E.	3 W. by N.
25	2 N. W.	3 N. E.	2 N. E.	5 N. E. by E.	4 N. E. by N.	4 N. N. E.
26	10 W. N. W.	6 W. N. W.	7 W. N. W.	8 N. W.	8 N. W.	10 N. W.
27	10 N. W.	10 N. W.	5 N. W.	7 N. W.	7 N. W.	4 N. W.
28	Calm	3 N. W.	1 N. W.	1 N. E.	3 N. E.	Calm
29	Calm	2 N. W.	1 N. W.	1 N. W.	6 N. W.	3 N. W.
30	2 N. W.	7 N. W.	7 N. W.	5 N. W.	4 N. W.	2 N. W.
31	3 N. W.	4 N. N. W.	4 N. N. W.	4 N. W.	4 N. W.	2 N. W.

* Went into winter quarters, Port Kennedy.

Direction (true) and Force of the Wind observed on board the yacht Fox.

November, 1858.—At winter quarters.

Date.	2h.	4h.	6h.	8h.	10h.	Noon.
1	2 N.W.	1 N.W.	1 W.N.W.	Calm	Calm	Calm
2	Calm	3 N.W.	2 N.W.	8 N.W.	3 N.W.	3 N.W.
3	9 N.W.	6 N.W.	6 W.N.W.	6 W.N.W.	5 W.N.W.	7 W.N.W.
4	8 W.N.W.	6 W.N.W.	6 W.N.W.	6 W.N.W.	5 W.N.W.	10 W.N.W.
5	6 N.W.	6 N.W.	3 N.W.	6 N.W.	6 N.W.	7 N.W.
6	8 N.W.	5 N.W.	6 N.W.	1 N.W.	4 N. by E.	3 N. by E.
7	7 N.W.	7 N.W.	5 N.W.	6 N.W.	4 N.W.	6 N.W.
8	4 N.W.	8 N.W.	6 N.W.	6 N.W.	4 N.W.	4 N.W.
9	3 N.W.	8 N.W.	8 N.W.	1 N.W.	1 N.W.	1 N.W.
10	8 N.W.	8 N.W.	4 N.W.	4 N.W.	8 N.W.	3 N.W.
11	6 N.W.	5 N.W.	5 N.W.	4 N.W.	4 N.W.	6 N.W.
12	1 N.W.	Calm	Calm	1 N.W.	6 N.W.	3 N.W.
13	1 E.N.E.	3 E.	Calm	3 E.N.E.	1 E.N.E.	8 E.N.E.
14	1 E.N.E.	8 E.N.E.	1 E.N.E.	Calm	1 N.W.	8 N.W.
15	4 N.W.	1 N.W.	8 N.W.	6 N.W.	8 N.W.	6 N.W.
16	Calm	Calm	8 N.E.	8 N.E.	8 N.E.	3 N.E.
17	6 N.E.	4 N.E.	4 E.S.E.	1 E.N.E.	8 E.N.E.	5 E.N.E.
18	3 E.N.E.	4 E.N.E.	6 E.N.E.	3 E.N.E.	Calm	Calm
19	Calm	Calm	8 N.E.	8 N.E.	2 E.N.E.	2 E.N.E.
20	2 N.E.	6 N.N.W.	4 N.N.W.	9 N.N.W.	4 N.E. by E.	6 N.E. by E.
21	3 E.N.E.	3 E.N.E.	1 E.N.E.	1 E.N.E.	1 N.E.	Calm
22	3 N.W.	3 N.W.	8 N.W.	4 N.W.	2 N.W.	6 N.W.
23	8 N.W.	2 N.W.	8 N.W.	3 N.W.	5 N.W.	3 N.W.
24	4 N.W.	2 N.W.	8 N.W.	3 N.W.	1 N.W.	1 N.W.
25	8 N.W.	4 N.W.	8 N.W.	4 N.W.	6 N.W.	5 N.W.
26	6 N.W.	8 N.W.	6 N.W.	6 W.N.W.	6 W.N.W.	6 W.N.W.
27	4 W.N.W.	4 W.N.W.	Calm	Calm	Calm	3 N.E.
28	6 N.E.	6 N.N.E.	5 N.N.W.	8 N.N.W.	6 N.N.W.	5 N.E.
29	9 N.E.	6 N.E.	9 N.E.	5 N.E.	6 N.E.	4 N.E.
30	10 N.E.	10 N.E.	6 N.E.	9 N.E.	6 E.N.E.	6 E.N.E.

Date.	2h.	4h.	6h.	8h.	10h.	Midn't.
1	Calm	Calm	Calm	1 N.E.	Calm	Calm
2	4 N.W.	8 N.W.	5 N.W.	4 N.W.	6 N.W.	6 N.W.
3	7 W.N.W.	7 W.N.W.	6 W.N.W.	4 W.N.W.	4 W.N.W.	6 W.N.W.
4	5 W.N.W.	6 W.N.W.	6 W.N.W.	6 W.N.W.	7 W.N.W.	4 W.N.W.
5	7 N.W.	7 N.W.	7 N.W.	7 N.W.	7 N.W.	4 N.W.
6	6 N.W.	5 N.W.	4 N.W.	6 N.W.	8 N.W.	4 N.W.
7	3 N.W.	5 N.W.	4 N.W.	4 N.N.W.	4 N.N.W.	6 N.N.W.
8	8 N.W.	6 N.W.	9 N.W.	1 N.W.	1 N.W.	1 N.W.
9	Calm	Calm	Calm	Calm	Calm	Calm
10	8 W.	9 W.	9 N.W.	6 N.W.	3 N.W.	4 N.W.
11	6 N.W.	5 N.W.	4 N.W.	9 N.W.	8 N.W.	8 N.W.
12	8 N.W.	8 N.W.	1 N.W.	1 N.W.	1 N.W.	1 E.N.E.
13	3 E.N.E.	4 E.N.E.	9 E.N.E.	3 E.N.E.	3 E.N.E.	1 E.N.E.
14	6 N.W.	4 N.W.	6 N.W.	6 N.W.	6 N.W.	5 N.W.
15	6 N.W.	6 N.W.	3 N.W.	8 N.W.	3 N.W.	6 N.W.
16	4 N.E.	6 N.E.	4 N.E.	6 N.E.	6 N.E.	6 N.E.
17	1 E.N.E.	3 E.N.E.	6 E.N.E.	4 E.N.E.	6 E.N.E.	9 E.N.E.
18	Calm	Calm	8 N.W.	1 N.W.	1 N.W.	Calm
19	3 E.N.E.	8 E.N.E.	9 N.E.	8 N.E.	8 N.E.	8 N.E.
20	3 E.N.E.	3 E.N.E.	8 E.N.E.	Calm	Calm	1 N.E.
21	1 N.E.	1 N.E.	1 E.N.E.	1 E.N.E.	1 E.N.E.	3 N.W.
22	3 N.W.	3 N.W.	8 N.W.	3 N.W.	6 N.W.	3 N.W.
23	3 N.W.	8 N.W.	3 N.W.	3 N.W.	5 N.W.	8 N.W.
24	3 N.W.	3 N.E.	Calm	Calm	Calm	Calm
25	6 N.W.	7 N.W.	6 N.W.	5 N.W.	6 N.W.	6 N.W.
26	6 W.N.W.	6 W.N.W.	6 W'ly	8 W'ly	4 W'ly	4 W'ly
27	3 N.E.	8 N.E.	8 N.E.	3 N.E.	8 N.E.	6 N.E.
28	7 N.E.	6 N.E.	9 N.E.	6 N.E.	6 N.E.	6 N.E.
29	10 N.E.	10 N.E.	10 N.E.	10 N.E.	10 N.E.	10 N.E.
30	5 E.N.E.	6 E.N.E.	6 E.N.E.	4 E.N.E.	6 N.E.	Calm

DIRECTION (TRUE) AND FORCE OF THE WIND OBSERVED ON BOARD THE YACHT FOX.

December, 1858.—At winter quarters.

Days.	2h.	4h.	6h.	8h.	10h.	Noon.
1	Calm	1 S. W.	1 N. W.	3 N. W.	2 N. N. W.	2 N. W.
2	3 N. W.	3 N. W.	1 N. W.	4 N. W.	4 N. W.	4 N. W.
3	4 N. W.	4 N. W.	4 N. W.	4 N. W.	3 N. W.	4 N. W.
4	4 N. W.	3 N. W.	3 N. W.	3 N. W.	7 N. W.	4 N. W.
5	4 N. N. W.	3 N. N. W.	2 N. N. W.	3 N. W.	4 N. W.	3 N. W.
6	2 N. W.	4 N. W.	2 N. W.	5 N. W.	4 N. W.	4 N. W.
7	3 N. W.	4 N. W.	5 N. W.	3 N. W.	2 N. W.	2 N. W.
8	1 N. W.	1 N. W.	2 N. W.	3 N. W.	3 N. W.	2 Variable
9	3 N. E.	2 N. E.	Calm	3 N. W.	1 N. W.	1 N. W.
10	4 N. W.	4 N. W.	4 N. W.	2 N. W.	3 N. W.	3 N. W.
11	3 N. W.	3 N. W.	4 N. W.	3 N. W.	1 Variable	Calm
12	Calm	1 N. E.	2 N. E.	2 N. E.	3 N. N. E.	3 N. N. E.
13	1 N. N. E.	1 N. N. E.	1 N. N. E.	Calm	2 N. E.	2 N. E.
14	4 N. N. E.	3 N. N. E.	3 N. N. E.	3 N. E.	Variable	Variable
15	3 N. W.	3 N. W.	7 W. N. W.	7 N. W.	6 N. W.	4 N. W.
16	4 N. W.	4 N. W.	6 N. W.	4 N. W.	4 N. W.	2 N. W.
17	3 N. W.	3 N. W.	4 N. W.	7 N. W.	4 N. W.	4 N. W.
18	3 N. E.	3 N. E.	3 N. E.	4 N. E.	4 N. N. E.	4 N. N. E.
19	4 N. N. E.	4 N. N. E.	4 N. N. E.	4 N. N. E.	3 N. N. E.	2 N. N. E.
20	1 N. N. E.	4 N. E.	3 N. E.	3 N. E.	3 N. N. E.	7 N. N. E.
21	3 N. N. W.	4 N. W.	2 N. W.	3 N. W.	3 N. W.	3 N. W.
22	Calm	2 N. W.	1 N. W.	3 N. E.	2 W. by N.	1 N. W.
23	3 N. W.	Calm	1 N. W.	Calm	Calm	Calm
24	Calm	1 N. W.	2 N. W.	4 N. W.	3 N. W.	4 N. W.
25	4 N. W.	4 N. W.	3 N. W.	3 N. W.	3 N. W.	3 W. by N.
26	7 W.	3 W.	3 W.	4 W.	4 W.	3 N. W.
27	3 N. W.	3 N. W.	4 N. W.	3 N. W.	3 N. W.	7 W. N. W.
28	7 W.	4 W.	4 W.	4 W.	4 W.	4 W.
29	3 N. W.	Calm	Calm	Calm	Calm	Calm
30	Calm	Calm	Calm	Calm	1 N. W.	1 N. N. W.
31	Calm	3 N. W.	4 N. W.	4 N. W.	3 N. W.	2 N. W.

Days.	2h.	4h.	6h.	8h.	10h.	Midn't.
1	3 N. W.	3 N. W.	4 N. W.	4 N. W.	4 N. W.	3 N. W.
2	3 N. W.	3 N. W.	3 N. W.	4 N. W.	3 N. W.	Calm
3	4 N. W.	5 N. W.	3 N. W.	7 N. W.	7 N. W.	7 N. W.
4	4 N. W.	4 N. W.	3 N. W.	3 N. W.	4 N. W.	4 N. N. W.
5	3 N. W.	4 N. W.	3 N. W.	4 N. W.	3 N. W.	3 N. W.
6	3 N. W.	3 N. W.	7 N. W.	7 N. W.	4 N. W.	4 N. W.
7	3 N. W.	Calm	Calm	Calm	Calm	Calm
8	3 N. E.	4 N. E.	3 N. E.	4 N. E.	4 N. E.	4 N. E.
9	3 N. W.	3 N. W.	3 N. E.	3 N. W.	3 N. W.	3 N. W.
10	7 N. W.	3 N. W.	4 N. W.	4 N. W.	3 N. W.	3 N. W.
11	Calm	Calm	Calm	Calm	Calm	Calm
12	3 N. E.	3 N. E.	3 N. E.	4 N. E.	4 N. N. E.	1 N. N. E.
13	3 N. E.	4 N. N. E.	4 N. N. E.	3 E. N. E.	3 E. N. E.	4 E. N. E.
14	Calm	Calm	Calm	3 N. W.	3 N. W. by W.	4 N. W. by W.
15	7 N. N. W.	3 N. N. W.	3 N. N. W.	1 N. W.	1 N. W.	2 N. W.
16	6 N. W.	3 N. W.	4 N. W.	4 N. W.	3 N. W.	3 N. W.
17	2 N. W.	1 N. W.	Calm	1 N. N. E.	1 N. N. E.	1 N. N. E.
18	3 E. N. E.	4 N. N. E.	3 N. N. E.	Calm	1 N. N. E.	3 N. N. E.
19	3 N. N. E.	3 N. N. E.	3 N. N. E.	Calm	1 N. E.	3 N. E.
20	3 N. N. E.	3 N. N. E.	4 N. N. E.	1 N. N. E.	3 N. by W.	3 N. N. W.
21	4 N. W.	3 N. W.	4 N. W.	2 N. W.	1 N. W.	Calm
22	3 N. W.	3 N. W.	2 N. W.	1 N. W.	2 N. W.	3 N. W.
23	Calm	1 N. E.	1 N. E.	Calm	Calm	Calm
24	4 N. W.	3 N. W.	4 N. W.	4 N. W.	4 N. W.	3 N. W.
25	3 W. by N.	3 W. N. W.	4 W. N. W.	4 W. N. W.	7 W.	7 W.
26	7 W.	7 W.	3 W.	7 N. W.	6 N. W.	6 N. W.
27	1 W. N. W.	7 W. N. W.	6 N. W.	4 N. W.	7 W.	4 W.
28	4 W.	4 W.	4 W.	6 W.	7 W.	3 W.
29	Calm	Calm	Calm	1 N. E.	Calm	Calm
30	3 N. W.	3 N. W.	Calm	Calm	Calm	Calm
31	4 N. W.	3 W.	3 W.	3 W.	4 N. W.	3 N. W.

Direction (true) and Force of the Wind observed on board the yacht Fox.

January, 1859.—At winter quarters.

Date.	2h.	4h.	6h.	8h.	10h.	Noon.
1	5 N.W.	4 N.W.	6 N.W.	4 N.W.	3 N.W.	3 N.W.
2	4 N.W.	3 N.W.	4 N.W.	4 N.N.E.	3 N.N.E.	3 N.N.E.
3	4 N.N.W.	4 N.	4 N.	4 N.	3 N.	3 N.
4	3 N.	3 N.	3 N.	4 N.W.	4 N.W.	3 N.W.
5	4 N.W.	3 N.W.	3 N.W.	5 N.	4 N.	4 N.
6	3 N.W.	3 N.W.	3 N.W.	4 N.W.	4 W.	4 W.
7	4 N.W.	4 N.W.	4 N.W.	2 N.W.	3 N.W.	3 N.W.
8	6 N.W.	4 N.W.	4 N.W.	5 N.W.	7 N.W.	4 N.W.
9	Calm	Calm	Calm	3 N.W.	3 N.W.	4 N.W.
10	Calm	1 N.W.	Calm	and variable	air.	1 N.E.
11	1 N.E.	3 N.E.	2 N.E.	3 N.E.	2 N.E.	4 N.E.
12	4 N.N.E.	4 N.N.E.	4 N.N.E.	3 N.N.E.	2 N.E.	1 Variable
13	1 N.N.E.	Calm	1 N.E.	1 N.E.	Calm	Calm
14	3 W.N.W.	4 W.N.W.	2 W.N.W.	Calm	3 N.W.	3 N.W.
15	3 N.W.	4 N.W.	4 N.W.	5 N.W.	7 N.W.	1 N.W.
16	5 N.W.	4 N.W.	4 N.W.	3 N.W.	4 N.W.	4 N.W.
17	4 W.N.W.	3 W.N.W.	2 N.W.	4 N.W.	4 N.W.	3 W.N.W.
18	3 N.W.	3 N.W.	3 N.W.	Calm	Calm	1 N.E.
19	2 N.E.	Calm	Calm	1 N.W.	2 N.W.	1 N.W.
20	4 N.W.	7 N.W.	7 N.W.	5 N.W.	3 N.W.	3 N.W.
21	1 N.E.	Calm	1 W. by N.	2 N.W.	1 N.W.	1 N.W.
22	4 N.W.	4 N.W.	4 N.W.	3 N.W.	4 N.W.	3 N.W.
23	3 N.W.	4 N.W.	3 N.W.	2 N.W.	2 N.W.	1 N.W.
24	4 W.N.W.	2 W.N.W.	4 W.N.W.	6 W.N.W.	2 W.N.W.	2 W.N.W.
25	5 N.W.	4 N.W.	7 N.W.	5 N.W.	6 N.W.	4 N.W.
26	4 N.W.	4 N.W.	3 N.W.	2 N.W.	4 N.W.	1 Variable
27	1 N.W.	Calm	Calm	2 N.E.	Calm	Calm
28	6 N.W.	3 N.W.	4 N.W.	3 N.W.	3 N.W.	4 N.W.
29	4 N.W.	2 N.W.	3 N.W.	4 N.W.	2 N.W.	5 N.W.
30	1 N.W.	2 N.W.	4 N.W.	3 N.W.	3 N.W.	1 N.W.
31	3 N.E.	3 N.E.	1 N.E.	1 N.E.	1 N.E.	1 N.E.

Date.	2h.	4h.	6h.	8h.	10h.	Midn't.
1	4 N.W.	3 N.W.	4 N.W.	4 N.W.	6 N.W.	5 N.W.
2	3 N.E.	6 N.	4 N.	3 N.	3 N.	3 N.
3	6 N.	4 N.	4 N.	4 N.	4 N.	4 N.
4	7 N.W.	6 N.W.	6 N.W.	7 N.W.	4 N.W.	4 N.W.
5	Calm	Calm	1 W.	Calm	3 N.W.	3 N.W.
6	1 W.	2 W.	3 W.	4 W.	4 W.	6 W.
7	4 N.W.	5 N.W.	4 N.W.	4 N.W.	7 N.W.	6 N.W.
8	4 N.W.	4 N.W.	Calm	Calm	Calm	Calm
9	3 N.W.	4 N.W.	3 N.W.	2 W.	3 N.N.W.	3 N.W.
10	1 N.E.	Calm	Calm	Calm	4 N.E.	2 N.E.
11	4 N.E.	4 N.E.	4 N.E.	3 N.E.	2 N.E.	2 N.E.
12	2 N.E.	3 N.E.	6 N.E.	2 N.N.E.	3 N.N.E.	1 N.N.E.
13	Calm	Calm	Calm	3 W.N.W.	4 W.N.W.	3 W.N.W.
14	5 N.W.	4 N.W.	4 N.W.	4 N.W.	4 N.W.	3 N.W.
15	6 N.W.	7 N.W.	7 N.W.	4 N.W.	3 N.W.	3 N.W.
16	4 N.W.	4 N.W.	5 N.W.	3 N.W.	4 N.W.	4 N.W.
17	4 W.N.W.	4 W.N.W.	4 W.N.W.	4 N.W.	6 N.W.	7 N.W.
18	2 N.E.	3 N.E.	3 N.E.	3 N.E.	6 N.E.	5 N.E.
19	4 N.W.	6 N.W.	4 N.W.	3 N.W.	1 N.W.	3 N.W.
20	1 N.W.	Calm	Calm	1 N.E.	Calm	1 N.E.
21	3 N.W.	5 N.W.	3 W.N.W.	4 W.N.W.	5 N.W.	6 N.W.
22	5 N.W.	6 N.W.	3 N.W.	3 N.W.	4 N.W.	4 N.W.
23	6 N.W.	3 N.W.	3 N.W.	3 N.W.	4 N.W.	3 W.N.W.
24	4 W.N.W.	5 N.W.	6 N.W.	4 N.W.	5 N.W.	7 N.W.
25	5 N.W.	6 N.W.	5 N.W.	3 N.W.	6 N.W.	5 N.W.
26	1 N.E.	1 N.E.	1 N.E.	Calm	Calm	Calm
27	3 N.W.	3 N.W.	4 N.W.	3 N.W.	4 N.W.	4 N.W.
28	5 N.W.	4 N.W.	3 N.W.	4 N.W.	6 N.W.	4 N.W.
29	4 N.W.	4 N.W.	3 N.W.	3 N.W.	2 N.W.	1 N.E.
30	1 N.W.	2 N.W.	Calm	Calm	2 N.E.	3 N.E.
31	2 N.E.	1 N.E.	1 N.E.	Calm	Calm	Calm

Direction (true) and Force of the Wind observed on board the Yacht Fox.

February, 1859.—At winter quarters.

Date.	2h.	4h.	6h.	8h.	10h.	Noon.
1	Calm	Calm	Calm	Calm	Calm	Calm
2	4 W. by N.	6 W. N. W.	6 W. N. W.	4 N. W.	1 N. W.	1 N. W.
3	1 E. N. E.	1 E. N. E.	1 E. N. E.	1 E. N. E.	1 E. N. E.	1 E. N. E.
4	1 E. S.	Calm	Calm	2 N. W.	2 N. W.	3 N. W.
5	3 N. W.	3 N. W.	3 N. W.	1 N. W.	3 N. W.	3 N. W.
6	3 N. W.	4 N. W.	4 N. W.	6 N. W.	6 N. W.	5 N. W.
7	6 N. W.	6 N. W.	5 N. W.	3 N. W.	3 N. W.	3 N. W.
8	3 N. W.	Calm	Calm	4 N. W.	5 N. W.	3 N. W.
9	3 N. W.	4 N. W.	3 N. W.	Calm	1 W. N. W.	1 W. N. W.
10	1 N. E.	Calm	Calm	Calm	Calm	3 N. W.
11	4 N. W.	4 N. W.	6 N. W.	7 N. W.	2 N. W.	5 N. W.
12	1 N. W.	6 N. W.	1 N. W.	1 N. W.	1 W.	2 W.
13	4 W. N. W.	3 W. N. W.	2 W. N. W.	4 W. N. W.	3 W. N. W.	3 W. N. W.
14	6 W. N. W.	6 W. N. W.	6 N. W.	4 N. W.	4 N. W.	4 N. W.
15	7 N. W.	7 N. W.	7 N. W.	5 W. N. W.	2 W. N. W.	6 W. N. W.
16	4 W.	6 W.	8 W.	6 W.	4 W.	4 W.
17	3 N. W.	1 N. W.	Calm	1 N. E.	Calm	Calm
18	3 W.	4 W.	5 W.	5 W.	6 W.	1 W.
19	2 W.	6 W.	6 W.	3 W.	4 W.	2 W.
20	Calm	Calm	2 N. E.	3 N. E.	3 N. E.	4 N. E.
21	Calm	Calm	Calm	Calm	Calm	Calm
22	5 N. E.	4 N. E.	6 N. E.	5 N. E.	4 N. E.	4 N. E.
23	3 N. E.	1 N. E.	Calm	Calm	3 W.	3 W.
24	3 N. W.	6 N. W.	3 N. W.	1 W.	2 W.	2 W.
25	6 N. W.	7 N. W.	1 N. W.	1 N. W.	4 W.	4 W.
26	4 N. W.	6 N. W.	4 N. W.	2 N. W.	2 N. W.	1 N. W.
27	3 W.	3 W.	3 W.	4 W.	4 W.	5 W.
28	6 W.	5 W.	3 W.	6 N. W.	2 N. W.	7 N. W.

Date.	2h.	4h.	6h.	8h.	10h.	Midn't.
1	Calm	3 E.	3 N. W.	3 N. W.	3 W. by N.	8 W. by N.
2	1 N. W.	3 S. E.	1 E. N. E.	2 N. E.	2 E. N. E.	2 E. N. E.
3	1 E. N. E.	3 E. N. E.	1 E. N. E.	1 E. N. E.	1 E. N. E.	1 E. N. E.
4	6 N. W.	3 N. W.	6 N. W.	2 N. W.	3 N. W.	4 N. W.
5	3 N. W.	1 N. W.	3 N. W.	3 N. W.	3 N. W.	4 N. W.
6	4 N. W.	4 N. W.	4 N. W.	3 N. W.	4 N. W.	3 N. W.
7	4 W. N. W.	1 W. N. W.	6 W. N. W.	2 N. W.	1 N. W.	1 N. W.
8	7 N. W.	3 N. W.	4 N. W.	4 N. W.	4 N. W.	4 N. W.
9	1 W. N. W.	Calm	1 N. W.	Calm	Calm	1 N. E.
10	1 N. W.	3 N. W.	3 N. W.	1 N. W.	4 N. W.	4 N. W.
11	4 N. W.	4 N. W.	7 N. W.	4 N. W.	7 N. W.	7 N. W.
12	3 W.	4 W.	4 N. W.	5 W. N. W.	4 W. N. W.	4 W. N. W.
13	3 W. N. W.	3 W. N. W.	4 W. N. W.	5 W. N. W.	3 W. N. W.	3 W. N. W.
14	6 N. W.	4 N. W.	4 N. W.	5 N. W.	5 N. W.	6 N. W.
15	5 W. N. W.	4 W. N. W.	5 W. N. W.	5 W. N. W.	4 W. N. W.	3 W. N. W.
16	5 W.	4 W.	4 N. W.	4 N. W.	4 N. W.	4 N. W.
17	2 W.	2 W.	2 W.	4 W.	5 W.	4 W.
18	2 W.	3 W.	3 W.	3 W.	1 W. N. W.	2 W.
19	2 W.	1 W.	Calm	Calm	Calm	Calm
20	3 N. E.	2 N. E.	2 N. E.	3 N. E.	Calm	Calm
21	Calm	Calm	3 N. E.	3 N. E.	3 N. E.	1 N. E.
22	4 N. E.	4 N. E.	4 N. E.	3 N. E.	3 N. E.	4 N. E.
23	1 W.	1 W.	2 W.	1 W.	Calm	1 N. W.
24	2 W.	2 W.	3 W.	3 N. W.	3 N. W.	4 N. W.
25	4 W.	4 N. W.	4 N. W.	4 N. W.	4 N. W.	4 N. W.
26	1 N. W.	1 N. W.	1 N. W.	1 N. W.	Calm	Calm
27	5 N. W.	5 N. W.	1 W.	5 W.	3 W.	1 W.
28	3 W.	9 N. W.	4 N. W.	6 N. W.	5 N. W.	6 N. W.

Direction (true) and Force of the Wind observed on board the yacht Fox.

March, 1859.—At winter quarters.

Date.	2h.	4h.	6h.	8h.	10h.	Noon.
1	3 N. W.	3 N. W.	7 N. W.	3 W.	7 W.	3 W.
2	3 W.	3 W.	Calm	Calm	Calm	Calm
3	2 N. E.	3 N. E.	3 N. E.	4 N. E.	4 N. E.	4 N. E.
4	3 N. E.	1 N. E.	3 N. E.	3 N. E.	Calm	Calm
5	Calm	Calm	Calm	Calm	Calm	Calm
6	Calm	Calm	Calm	Calm	Calm	Calm
7	2 N. E.	4 N. E.	4 N. E.	4 N. E.	6 N. E.	6 N. E.
8	3 E. N. E.	3 E. N. E.	3 E. N. E.	3 E. N. E.	3 E. N. E.	3 E. N. E.
9	2 E. N. E.	1 E. N. E.	5 E. N. E.	2 E. N. E.	3 E. N. E.	4 E. N. E.
10	1 N. E.	2 N. E.	Calm	2 N. E.	1 N. W.	1 N. W.
11	3 W. N. W.	7 W. N. W.	7 W. N. W.	7 W. N. W.	7 W. N. W.	7 N. W.
12	2 W. N. W.	2 W. N. W.	6 W. N. W.	7 W. N. W.	3 N. W.	6 N. W.
13	4 N. W.	3 N. W.	3 N. W.	4 N. W.	3 N. W.	2 N. W.
14	4 N. W.	3 N. W.	Calm	Calm	Calm	Calm
15	Calm	2 N. E.	5 N. E.	2 N. E.	5 N. E.	7 N. E.
16	2 N. E.	4 N. E.	5 N. E.	4 N. E.	4 N. E.	6 N. E.
17	2 N. W.	6 N. W.	7 N. W.	7 N. W.	3 N. W.	3 N. W.
18	2 W.	4 W.	5 W.	5 N. W.	5 N. W.	4 N. W.
19	3 N. W.	4 N. W.	3 N. W.	3 N. W.	3 N. W.	3 N. W.
20	Calm	Calm	Calm	Calm	Calm	Calm
21	Calm	Calm	Calm	Calm	Calm	Calm
22	1 N. W.	Calm	Calm	Calm	3 N. E.	1 N. E.
23	3 N. E.	4 N. E.	4 N. E.	2 N. E.	3 N. E.	5 N. E.
24	Calm	Calm	Calm	Calm	1 W.	3 W.
25	1 N. W.	Calm	Calm	1 N. W.	2 N. W.	1 N. W.
26	4 N. E.	3 N. E.	3 N. E.	3 N. E.	5 N. E.	4 N. E.
27	3 N. E.	5 N. E.	4 N. E.	3 N. E.	3 N. E.	Calm
28	....	1 N. E.	....	Calm	....	Calm
29	....	Calm	....	Calm	....	2 N. W.
30	....	2 N. E.	....	1 N. E.	....	1 N. E.
31	....	Calm	....	Calm	....	Calm

Date.	2h.	4h.	6h.	8h.	10h.	Midn't.
1	5 W.	3 W.	2 W.	2 W.	2 W.	3 W.
2	Calm	Calm	3 N. E.	3 N. E.	4 N. E.	4 N. E.
3	2 N. E.	3 N. E.	1 N. E.	3 N. E.	3 N. E.	3 N. E.
4	Calm	Calm	Calm	Calm	Calm	Calm
5	Calm	Calm	Calm	Calm	Calm	Calm
6	1 N. E.	2 N. E.	2 N. E.	3 N. E.	2 N. E.	3 N. E.
7	3 N. E.	3 N. E.	4 E. N. E.	4 E. N. E.	4 E. N. E.	3 E. N. E.
8	3 E. N. E.	2 E. N. E.	3 E. N. E.	3 E. N. E.	2 E. N. E.	3 E. N. E.
9	1 E. N. E.	3 N. W.	4 N. W.	3 N. W.	2 N. W.	Calm
10	Calm	Calm	1 N. E.	3 N. W.	3 N. W.	4 W. N. W.
11	3 N. W.	2 N. W.	3 N. W.	6 N. W.	2 N. W.	3 W. N. W.
12	7 N. W.	2 N. W.	7 N. W.	7 N. W.	4 N. W.	2 W.
13	3 N. W.	5 N. W.	5 N. W.	4 N. W.	3 N. W.	4 N. W.
14	Calm	Calm	Calm	2 N. E.	Calm	Calm
15	2 N. E.	2 N. E.	4 N. E.	4 N. E.	4 N. E.	4 N. E.
16	3 N. E.	3 N. E.	1 N. E.	1 N. E.	Calm	Calm
17	2 N. W.	2 N. W.	3 N. W.	5 N. W.	2 W.	3 W.
18	3 N. W.	3 N. W.	3 N. W.	4 N. W.	4 N. W.	5 N. W.
19	3 N. W.	2 N. W.	1 N. W.	1 N. W.	1 N. W.	Calm
20	Calm	Calm	Calm	Calm	Calm	Calm
21	Calm	Calm	Calm	1 N. E.	1 N. W.	1 N. W.
22	3 N. E.	3 N. E.	2 N. E.	1 N. E.	2 N. E.	4 N. E.
23	2 N. E.	1 N. E.	Calm	Calm	Calm	3 N. W.
24	3 N. W.	2 N. W.	2 N. W.	3 N. W.	1 N. W.	1 N. W.
25	1 N. W.	1 N. E.	2 N. E.	3 N. E.	4 N. E.	4 N. E.
26	3 N. E.	4 N. E.	3 N. E.	2 N. E.	2 N. E.	3 N. E.
27	3 N. E.	3 N. E.	1 N. E.	Calm	3 N. E.	3 N. E.
28	....	Calm	....	Calm	....	Calm
29	....	2 N. W.	....	2 N. W.	....	Calm
30	....	1 N. E.	....	1 N. E.	....	Calm
31	....	Calm	....	Calm	....	2 N. W.

Direction (true) and Force of the Wind observed on board the yacht Fox.

April, 1859.—At winter quarters.

Days.	4h.	8h.	Noon.	4h.	8h.	12h.
1	4 N. W.	6 N. W.	7 N. W.	6–7 W. S. W.	6 W. S. W.	7–8 W. S. W.
2	9 W. S. W.	2 W. S. W.	4 W.	1 W.	2 W.	3 W.
3	6 W.	2 W.	3 W.	1 W.	Calm	1 N. E.
4	5 E. N. E.	3 N. N. E.	4 N. E.	4 N. E.	2 N.	1 N.
5	4 W'ly	5 W'ly	4 W. N. W.	6 W. N. W.	6 W. N. W.	6 W. N. W.
6	6 W.	1 W. S. W.	1 W. S. W.	4 W.	4 N. W.	3 N. W.
7	3 N.	2 N.	1 N. N. W.	1 N.	Calm	Calm
8	Calm	Calm	2 N. N. E.	2 N. N. E.	3 N. N. E.	2 N. N. E.
9	6 E. N. E.	4 E. N. E.	4 E. N. E.	1 E. N. E.	Calm	Calm
10	Calm	Calm	4 W.	4 W.	2 W.	1 W.
11	Calm	Calm	Calm	Calm	Calm	Calm
12	3 N. W.	3 N. W.	4 W. N. W.	6 W. N. W.	7 W. N. W.	3 W. N. W.
13	Calm	1 Variable	Calm	Calm	2 N. N. E.	3 N. N. E.
14	2 E.	2 E.	4 N. E.	3 N. E.	3 N. E.	4 N. E.
15	1 N. E.	Calm	Calm	Calm	5 E. N. E.	4 E. N. E.
16	4 E. N. E.	4 E. N. E.	5 E. N. E.	4 N. E.	6 N. E.	6 N. E.
17	6 N. E.	6 N. E.	6 N. E.	6 N. E.	6 E. N. E.	6 E. N. E.
18	7 E. N. E.	7 N. E.	4 N. E.	7 N. E.	6 N. E.	1 N. E.
19	3 E. N. E.	4 E. S. E.	1 E. S. E.	7 E. S. E.	3 E. N. E.	8 E. N. E.
20	4 E. N. E.	2 E. N. E.	3 N. E.	6 N. E.	5 N.	4 E. N. E.
21	5 N. N. E.	3 N. N. E.	5 N. N. E.	2 N.	4 N.	6 N.
22	4 N.	1 N.	4 W. N. W.	8 W. N. W.	4 N. N. W.	2 N.
23	3 E. by N.	3 E. by N.	4 N. E.	6 N. E.	4 N. E.	9 N. E.
24	5 E. N. E.	6 E. N. E.	6 E. N. E.	3 E. N. E.	5 E. N. E.	5 N. E. by E.
25	7 E. N. E.	6 E. N. E.	2 E. N. E.	8 N. E. by E.	Calm	Calm
26	Calm	Calm	1 E. N. E.	8 E. N. E.	9 N. E.	4 N. E.
27	4 E. N. E.	4 E. N. E.	4 E. N. E.	5 E. N. E.	2 E. N. E.	2 N. E. by E.
28	Calm	1 N. E.	1 N. E.	Calm	1 N. E.	3 N. E.
29	2 N. E.	2 N. E.	3 N. E.	9 N. E.	4 N. E.	4 N. E.
30	1 N. E.	3 N. E.	Calm	5 W.	6 W.	9 W.

May, 1859.—At winter quarters.

Days.	4h.	8h.	Noon.	4h.	8h.	12h.
1	9 W.	9 W.	9 W.	7 W.	4 W.	4 W.
2	9 W.	5 W.	6 W.	8 W.	8 W.	7–8 W.
3	7 W.	4 W.	5 W.	6–8 W.	4–6 W.	6 W.
4	6 W. N. W.	2 W. N. W.	3 W. N. W.	1 W. N. W.	4 W. N. W.	6 W.
5	4 W.	3 W.	1 W.	3 W.	5 W.	4 W.
6	3 W.	1 W.	3 W.	3 W.	6 W. N. W.	4 W. N. W.
7	3 W.	3 W.	4 W.	6 W.	6 W.	6–8 W.
8	4 W.	3 W.	6 W.	5 W.	3 W.	Calm
9	7 N. E.	7 N. E.	6 N. E.	3 N. E.	6 N. N. E.	Calm
10	3 N. W.	6 N. W.	4 N. W.	Calm	Calm	5 W.
11	3 W. by N.	1 W. by N.	5 W. by N.	2 N. E.	3 N. N. W.	3 N. N. W.
12	Calm	Calm	4 N. N. W.	3 N. N. W.	4 N. N. W.	5 N. N. W.
13	6 N. N. W.	5 N. N. W.	3 N. W.	8 N. W.	8 N. W.	Calm
14	Calm	Calm	1 E. N. E.	4 N. N. E.	5 N. N. E.	3 N. N. E.
15	3 N. N. E.	2 N. N. E.	2 N. N. E.	1 N. N. E.	1 N. N. E.	3 N. N. E.
16	Calm	Calm	4 N. W.	7 N. W.	6–7 N. W.	5 N. W.
17	4 N. W.	1 N. W.	8 N. W.	5 N. W.	4 N. W.	6 N. N. W.
18	Calm	Calm	Calm	1 N. N. W.	Calm	Calm
19	2 N. E.	Calm	Calm	Calm	1 N. E.	2 E. by N.
20	3 N.	2 N.	6 N. W.	7–9 N. W.	6 N. W.	5 W. N. W.
21	6 W. N. W.	1 W. N. W.	Calm	Calm	Calm	2 N. N. E.
22	3 E. N. E.	8 E. N. E.	1 E. N. E.	3 E. N. E.	1 E. N. E.	8 E. N. E.
23	3 E. N. E.	8 E. N. E.	3 E. N. E.	3 E. N. E.	1 E. N. E.	Calm
24	1 E. N. E.	3 N. by E.	8 N. N. W.	3 N. W.	1 N. W.	2 N. W.
25	6 W. by N.	4–6 W. by N.	3–5 N. W.	3 W. by N.	5 W. by N.	3 N. by E.
26	6 N. E.	3 N. E.	4–5 N. W.	3 N. W.	6 W.	6 W.
27	6 W.	5 W.	5 W.	5 W.	1 W.	3 N. E.
28	1 N. E.	Calm	Calm	1 N.	1 N.	1 N.
29	Calm	Calm	Calm	Calm	Calm	1 N.
30	Calm	Calm	6 N. W.	4–6 N. W.	4 N. N. W.	8 N. N. W.
31	4 N. N. W.	5 N. N. W.	4 N. N. W.	3 N. N. W.	3 N. N. W.	5 N. N. W.

DIRECTION (TRUE) AND FORCE OF THE WIND OBSERVED ON BOARD THE YACHT FOX.

June, 1859.—At winter quarters.

Date.	4h.	8h.	Noon.	4h.	8h.	11h.
1	4 N. W.	3 N. W.	5-7 N. W.	5-6 N. W.	3 N. N. W.	10 N. N. W.
2	7 N. W.	6 N. W.	6 N. W.	7 N. W.	6 N. W.	7 N. W.
3	4 N. N. W.	1 N.	6 N.	1 N. N. W.	2 N. E.	3 N. E.
4	4 N. E.	4 N. E.	1 N. E.	Calm	2 N. E.	Calm
5	7 N. E.	2 N. E.	Calm	4 N. W.	1 N.	3 N.
6	5 N. E.	3 E. N. E.	2 E. N. E.	Calm	6 N. E.	5 N. E.
7	Calm	6 N. E.	6 N. E. by E.	4 N. E. by E.	6 N. E. by E.	8 N. E. by E.
8	8 N.	4 N.	4 N. W.	7-8 N. W.	7-8 W. by S.	5-7 N. W.
9	3 N.	5 N.	Calm	2 N. E.	1 N. E.	3 N. E.
10	4 N. E.	4 N. E.	4 N. E.	4 N. E.	5 N. E.	Calm
11	4 W. N. W.	4 W.	5 W.	5 N. W.	8-9 N. N. W.	3-5 N. N. W.
12	3 W. by N.	4 W. by N.	9 N. N. E.	5 N. N. E.	4 N. N. E.	3 N. N. E.
13	5 N. E.	9 N. E.	Calm	1 N. W.	3 N. W.	5 N. W.
14	5 N. W.	5 N. W.	5 N. W.	Calm	1 N. W.	1 N. by W.
15	2 W.	2 W.	Calm	Calm	4 N. W.	9 N. W.
16	3 E. N. E.	9 E. N. E.	1 N. E.	1 N. E.	1 N. E.	Calm
17	Calm	Calm	Calm	Calm	Calm	1 N. E.
18	3 E.	1 E.	Calm	5 W.	4 N. W.	5-6 N. N. W.
19	5 W.	9 W.	4 N. E.	4 N. E.	6 N. W.	5 N. W.
20	3 N. W.	9 N. W.	1 N. W.	Calm	3 E.	Calm
21	Calm	1 S. E.	Calm	1 S. S. W.	5 W. N. W.	7 N. W.
22	9 W.	7 W.	5 N. W.	5 N. W.	9 N. W.	5 N. W.
23	6 N. W.	8 N. W.	6 N. W.	9 N. W.	6 N. W.	3-6 N. W.
24	7 N. W.	9 N. W.	7-8 N. W.	5 N. W.	1 N. W.	6 N. W.
25	6 N. W.	5 N. W.	6 N. W.	5 N. W.	7 N. W.	6 N. W.
26	6 N. W.	8 N. W.	6 N. W.	3 N. W.	6 N. W.	Calm
27	1 E. N. E.	1 E. N. E.	3 E. N. E.	3 E. N. E.	1 E. N. E.	6 E. N. E.
28	4 E. N. E.	4 E. N. E.	3 E. N. E.	3 E. N. E.	3 E. N. E.	2 N. E.
29	3 N. E.	1 W.	4 W. N. W.	9 W. N. W.	Calm	1 N. N. W.
30	Calm	3 N. W.	5 N. W.	7 N. W.	7 N. W.	3 N. W.

Direction (true) and Force of the Wind observed on board the yacht Fox.

July, 1858.—At winter quarters.

Days.	2h.	4h.	6h.	8h.	9h.	10h.	Noon.
1	....	....	2 N. W.	....	7 N. W.	....	5 N. W.
2	....	....	3 N. W.	....	4 N. W.	....	3 N. W.
3	....	....	1 E. N. E.	....	1 E. by N.	....	2 E. N. E.
4	....	....	3 E. N. E.	....	3 E. N. E.	....	3 E. by N.
5	....	....	3 E. N. E.	....	6 E. N. E.	....	3 E. N. E.
6	Calm	Calm	....	3 N. W.	4 N. W.	3 W. N. W.	6 W. N. W.
7	6 W. N. W.	4 W. N. W.	....	3 W. N. W.	2 W. N. W.	3 W. N. W.	1 W. N. W.
8	3 E. N. E.	3 E.	....	2 N.	3 W. N. W.	3 W. N. W.	4 W. N. W.
9	4 N. N. W.	3 N. N. W.	....	5 N. N. W.	2 N. N. W.	Calm	2 W. N. W.
10	6 W. by N.	3 W. by N.	....	3 W. by N.	6 W. by N.	8 W. by N.	4 N. N. W.
11	7 N. E. by N.	6 N. E. by N.	....	3 N. E. by N.	7 N. E. by N.	1 N. E. by N.	7 N. E. by N.
12	5 N. N. W.	3 W. N. W.	....	4 W. N. W.	3 W. N. W.	4 W. N. W.	4 W. N. W.
13	5 W. N. W.	4 W. N. W.	....	6 W. N. W.	6 W. N. W.	8 W. N. W.	5 W. N. W.
14	Calm	Calm	....	4 N. E.	4 N. E.	3 N. W.	3 N. E.
15	4 N. W.	4 N. W.	....	3 N. W.	4 N. W.	4 N. W.	3 N. W.
16	4 N. W.	4 N. W.	....	4 N. W.	4 N. W.	6 N. W.	5 N. W.
17	Calm	Calm	....	3 N. W.	3 N. W.	4 N. W.	3 N. W.
18	5 N. W.	4 W. by N.	....	4 N. W.	4 N. W.	6 N. W.	6 N. W.
19	7 N. W.	7 N. W.	....	3 N. E.	3 N. E.	4 N. E.	4 N. E.
20	4 N. E.	4 N. E.	....	3 N. E.	3 N. N. W.	3 N. W.	3 N. N. W.
21	5 N. E.	4 N. E.	....	4 N. E.	5 N. E.	2 N. E.	6 N. E.
22	5 N. E.	4 N. E.	....	4 N. E.	5 N. E.	3 N. E.	5 N. E.
23	4 N. E.	3 N. E.	....	3 N. E.	3 N. E.	4 E. by N.	3 E. by N.
24	Calm	Calm	....	Calm	Calm	Calm	1 N. W.
25	5 N. W.	5 N. W.	....	6 N. W.	6 N. W.	4 W. S. W.	6 W. S. W.
26	4 W. S. W.	5 W. S. W.	....	5 W. S. W.	4 W. S. W.	1 W. S. W.	1 W. S. W.
27	3 E. by N.	3 E. by N.	....	3 E. by N.	4 E. by N.	4 E. by N.	1 N. E.
28	Calm	Calm	....	Calm	Calm	Calm	Calm
29	1 W. by N.	2 W. by N.	....	2 N. N. E.	3 W. S. W.	2 W. S. W.	2 W. S. W.
30	3 N. W.	3 N. W.	....	3 N. W.	3 N. W.	3 N. W.	3 N. W.
31	3 N. W.	3 N. W.	....	3 S. W.	3 S. W.	3 S. W.	3 W.

Days.	2h.	4h.	6h.	8h.	10h.	11h.	Midn't.
1	....	3 W. S. W.	....	4 N. W.	....	4 N. W.	....
2	....	3 N. W.	....	3 N. E.	....	5 N. E.	....
3	....	2 E. N. E.	....	1 N. E.	....	1 N. E. by E.	....
4	....	1 E. N. E.	....	1 E. N. E.	....	3 E. N. E.	....
5	2 E. N. E.	3 E.	2 E.	3 E. N. E.	1 E. N. E.	....	2 N. W.
6	6 W. N. W.	6 W. N. W.	6 W. N. W.	6 W. N. W.	6 W. N. W.	....	5 W. N. W.
7	3 W. N. W.	3 W. N. W.	3 W. N. W.	Calm	3 N. N. E.	....	3 E. N. E.
8	4 W. N. W.	6 W. N. W.	4 W. N. W.	5 W. N. W.	3 W. N. W.	....	6 S. S. W.
9	3 W. N. W.	3 W. N. W.	4 W. N. W.	3 W. by N.	3 W. by N.	....	4 W. by N.
10	7 N. N. W.	7 N. N. W.	7 N. N. W.	7 N. N. W.	7 N. E. by N.	....	4 N. E. by N.
11	4 N. E. by N.	3 N. E. by N.	Calm	Calm	Calm	....	Calm
12	4 W. N. W.	4 W. N. W.	4 W. N. W.	4 W. N. W.	4 W. N. W.	....	4 W. N. W.
13	4 N. N. W.	Calm	2 N. W.	3 N. W.	3 W. N. W.	....	Calm
14	3 N. E.	3 N. E.	4 N. by W.	4 N. by W.	3 N. W.	....	4 N. W.
15	4 N. W.	4 N. W.	4 N. W.	4 N. W.	3 N. W.	....	3 N. W.
16	4 N. W.	4 N. W.	3 N. W.	3 N. W.	4 N. W.	....	4 N. W.
17	4 N. W.	4 N. W.	4 N. W.	4 N. W.	5 N. W.	....	4 N. W.
18	4 N. W.	6 N. W.	3 N. W.	5 N. W.	6 N. W.	....	4 N. W.
19	6 N. E.	7 N. E.	4 N. E.	4 N. E.	7 N. E.	....	7 N. E.
20	3 E. by N.	3 E. by N.	4 E. N. E.	5 N. E.	4 N. E.	....	4 N. E.
21	4 N. E. by N.	6 N. E. by N.	6 N. E. by N.	5 N. E. by N.	4 N. E.	....	4 N. E.
22	3 E. N. E.	2 E.	1 E.	Calm	Calm	....	Calm
23	Calm	1 N. W.	1 N. W.	Calm	Calm	....	Calm
24	4 N. W.	4 N. W.	4 N. W.	4 N. W.	4 N. W.	....	4 N. W.
25	4 W. S. W.	4 W. S. W.	6 W. S. W.	6 W. S. W.	6 W. S. W.	....	4 W. S. W.
26	Calm	1 E.	Calm	Calm	1 E.	....	1 E.
27	7 N. W.	2 N. W.	Calm	Calm	4 N. E.	....	Calm
28	Calm	1 N. W.	4 N. W.	Calm	Light	....	Variable
29	1 N. W.	3 W. N. W.	4 W. N. W.	4 N. W.	3 N. W.	....	3 N. W.
30	3 N. W.	3 N. W.	3 N. W.	3 N. E.	3 N. W.	....	3 N. W.
31	5 W. N. W.	3 W. N. W.	5 W. N. W.	3 W. N. W.	3 W. N. W.	....	3 W.

DIRECTION (TRUE) AND FORCE OF THE WIND OBSERVED ON BOARD THE YACHT FOX.

August, 1859.—Mean position: Lat. 71°.9 N.; long. 79°.8 W.

DATE.	4h.	8h.	Noon.	4h.	8h.	Midn't.	Variation.
1	3 W.	2 W.	1 W.	1 W.	Calm	1 E. by N.	
2	3 E.	2 E.	1 E. by N.	4 E. N. E.	3 N. E.	3 N. E.	
3	8 N. E.	6 N. E.	6 N. E.	6 N. E.	6 N. E.	6 E. N. E.	
4	6 N. E.	7 N. E.	7 N. E. by E.	6 N. E. by E.	6 N. E. by E.	Calm	
5	Calm	2 N. W.	3 W.	4 W.	2 W.	2 W.	
6	Calm	Calm	2 E. W.	3 N. W.	3 N. W.	3 N. W.	
7	1 W.	3 W.	5 N. W. by W.	4 N. W.	4 N. W.	4 N. W.	
8	6 W.	4 W. N. W.	3 W.	4 W.	4 W.	6 W.	
9*	6 W.	4 W. by S.	6 W. by S.	6 N. N. W.	3 W. N. W.	1 E. E.	
10	C'lm, light var	2 S. E.	1 E.	Calm	Calm	3 E.	
11	3 E. by S.	3 E. by S.	4 E. by S.	6 E. S. E.	6 N. E.	6 N. N. E.	
12	6 E. N. E.	4 E. by S.	6 E. by N.	7 E. by S.	7 E. by S.	7 E. by S.	
13	7 E. by S.	7 E. by S.	6 E. by S.	8 E. by S.	6 E. by S.	7 E. by S.	
14	6 E. by S.	6 E. by S.	5 E. by S.	4 E. by S.	5 E. by S.	6 E. by S.	
15	6 E. by S.	6 W. S. W.	5 N. W.	5 W. N. W.	6 N. W. by W.	6 W. by N.	
16	2–6 N. W. by N.	8 W.	4 S. W.	6 S. by E.	3 S. by E.	5 S.	
17	Calm	2 N. by W.	8 N. E.	8 N. E.	3 Variable	3 N. N. E.	
18	1 N. E.	5 N. W.	3 W. N. W.	4 W. S. W.	4 W.	6 W.	
19	6 W. by S.	5 W. N. W.	6 N. W.	4 W.	6 W.	4 W.	
20	2 W.	Calm	1 N. E.	1 N.	6 N.	6 N. N. E.	
21	6 N. W.	3 S.	6 S. E.	3 E.	3 S. E. by E.	3 E.	
22	1 W.	6 W.	6 W.	4 W.	6 S. S. E.	5 S. E.	80° W.
23	3 S. E.	6 E. S. E.	8 S. E.	3 E. S. E.	3 E. S. E.	1 E. N. E.	80
24	6 N. N. W.	6 N. N. W.	6 N. W. by N.	7 N. N. W.	6 N. N. W.	6 N. N. W.	82
25	4 N. N. W.	Calm	1 N.	1 S.	3 S. W. & var.	3 S. W. & var.	79
26	3 Variable, S.	3 E.	2 E.	5 N. W.	5 N. W.	1 E.	73
27	2 E.	3 E. N. E.	4 E. N. E.	6 E. N. E.	3 E. N. E.	3 E. N. E.	
28	1 E. N. E.	3 E. N. E.	8 E. S. E.	3 N. N. E.	2 E. N. E.	8 E. N. E.	
29	9 E. N. E.	1 E. N. E.	Calm	4 N. N. E.	2 N. E.	Calm	
30	Calm	Calm	6 N. N. W.	2 N. N. W.	Calm	Calm	
31	2 E. N. E.	2 E. N. E.	8 N. E.	1 N. W.	Calm	Calm	

September, 1859.—Mean position: Lat. 58°.9 N.; long. 40°.9 W.

DATE.	4h.	8h.	Noon.	4h.	8h.	Midn't.	Variation.
1	2 E. N. E.	4 E. N. E.	2 N. N. E.	2 N.	3 N. W.	5 N. W.	72° W.
2	5 N. N. W.	7 N. N. W.	7 N. W.	6 N. N. W.	4 N. N. W.	7 N. N. W.	72
3	6 N. N. W.	6 N. N. W.	6 N. N. W.	3 N. W.	8 S. S. E.	8 S. W.	66
4	4 S. S. W.	4 S. W.	4 S. W. by E.	1 S. S. W.	4 S.	6 S. by W.	62
5	8 S. E. by S.	7 S. E. by S.	7 S. S. W.	7 S.	8 W. S. W.	8 W. S. W.	60
6	1 S. W. by S.	1 S. W. by S.	6 S. W. by S.	4 S. S. W.	4 S. S. W.	4 S. W. by W.	60
7	3 W.	3 W.	5 W. by N.	5 W.	3 W.	8 W. N. W.	62
8	Calm	3 N. E.	3 N. E.	4 N. E.	8 N. N. E.	1 N.	54
9	1 N. by W.	8 N. N. W.	5 N. W.	6 W. N. W.	6 W. N. W.	4 W. N. W.	52
10	4 W. S. W.	4 W. S. W.	4 W. N. W.	6 W. N. W.	6 W. N. W.	8 W. N. W.	58
11	7 W. N. W.	7 W.	7 W. N. W.	7 W. N. W.	7 W. N. W.	7 W. N. W.	60
12	7 W. S. W.	7 S. W.	4 S. S. W.	6 S. W.	6 W. S. W.	8 W. S. W.	60
13	8 S. S. W.	3 S.	4 S. W.	4 S. W.	4 S. W.	7 S. W.	66
14	7 S. S. W.	6 S. W.	6–7 W. S. W.	7 W.	7 W. N. W.	7 W. N. W.	62
15	7 W. N. W.	6 N. W.	6 N. W.	8 N. W.	6 N. W.	6 N. W.	60
16	7 N. W. by N.	6 N. N. W.	8 N. N. W.	6 N. N. E.	9 N. E.	1 N. E.	55
17	6 S. S. W.	6 S. S. W.	4 S. S. W.	4 S. S. W.	4 S. S. W.	6 S. S. W.	35
18	4 S. S. W.	6 S. W.	3 W.	6 S. W. by S.	5 S. W. by S.	6 W.	

* Steamed out of Port Kennedy.

Method of Reduction.—The method of reduction used is the same as that employed in the discussion of Kane's observations—it is by Lambert's improved formula, so as to include the velocity of the wind, and not the relative frequency alone. It is given in its outline in the article "Meteorology," in the 8th edition of the Encyclopædia Britannica.

Let θ_1 θ_2 θ_3 . . . . . be the angles which the directions of the wind make with the meridian (true), reckoned round the horizon, according to astronomical usage, from the south, westward to 360°, a direction corresponding to that of the rotation of the winds in the northern hemisphere; and v_1 v_2 v_3 . . . . . its respective velocities, which may be supposed expressed in miles per hour; and let the observations be made at equal intervals (for instance, hourly). Adding up all velocity-numbers referring to the same wind during a given period (say one month), and representing these quantities by s_1 s_2 s_3 . . . . ., the number of miles of air transferred bodily over the place of observation by winds *from* the southward is expressed by the formula

$$R_s = s_1 \cos \theta_1 + s_2 \cos \theta_2 + s_3 \cos \theta_3 + \ldots\ldots$$

And for winds *from* the westward

$$R_w = s_1 \sin \theta_1 + s_2 \sin \theta_2 + s_3 \sin \theta_3 + \ldots\ldots$$

The resulting quantity R, and the angle ϕ it forms with the meridian, is found by the expressions

$$R = \sqrt{R_s^2 + R_w^2}, \text{ and } \tan \phi = \frac{R_w}{R_s}$$

The general formulæ, in the case of eight principal directions θ, assume the following convenient form:—

$$R_s = (S-N) + (SW-NE)\sqrt{\tfrac{1}{2}} - (NW-SE)\sqrt{\tfrac{1}{2}}$$
$$R_w = (W-E) + (SW-NE)\sqrt{\tfrac{1}{2}} + (NW-SE)\sqrt{\tfrac{1}{2}}$$

Where the letters S, SW, W, etc., represent the sum of all velocities during the given period, or the quantity of air moved in the directions S, SW, W, etc., respectively; R_s represents the total quantity of air transported *to the northward*, and R_w the same transferred *to the eastward*. These formulæ, for practical working, may be put in the following shape:—

Put $S-N=a$ $\qquad$ $SW-NE=c$
$\qquad W-E=b$ $\qquad$ $NW-SE=d$

Then

$$R_s = R\cos\phi = a + 0.707\,(c-d)$$
$$R_w = R\sin\phi = b + 0.707\,(c+d).$$

Since R_s R_w R, represents the quantity of air passed over during the given period in the direction 0°, 90°, ϕ°, respectively, we must, in order to find the mean velocity for any resulting direction, divide by n, or by the number of observations during that period; we then have

$$V_s = \frac{R_s}{n}, \quad V_w = \frac{R_w}{n}, \text{ and } V = \frac{R}{n}.$$

A particle of air which has left the place of observation at the commencement of the period—of a day, for instance—will be found at its close in a direction 180 + ϕ, and at a distance of R miles, equal to a movement with an average velocity of

$\frac{R}{n}$; this supposes an equal and parallel motion of all particles passing over; the length of the path described by each can be found by the summation of all the v's (for each hour) during the period.

The great variability in the direction and force of the atmospheric motion renders the taking of resulting values for short intervals unnecessary, and a subdivision of the reduction into monthly periods has been found convenient.

To include more than eight directions into the discussion would not only render it very tedious, but would give no materially increased accuracy. Observed directions, intermediate of the eight directions, are referred to the nearest principal direction; and if midway, and occurring more than once, they are referred to the nearest preceding and following direction alternately.

The winds observed during July and August, 1857, and in September, 1859, cannot well be combined with the body of the observations, and have, therefore, not been reduced.

To illustrate the process of reduction, the working up of the observations for direction and force of the wind in the month of September, 1857, is here given as an example.

ABSTRACT OF THE QUANTITY OF WIND REFERRED TO THE EIGHT PRINCIPAL DIRECTIONS AND OBSERVED IN THE MONTH OF SEPTEMBER, 1857, BETWEEN LATITUDES 16°.5 AND 75° N., AND LONGITUDES 64°.1 AND 66° W.

Observations at 4, 8, 12, A. M. and P. M.

(The few intermediate observations on the last day of the month were not taken into account.)

True direct'n	1st.	2d.	3d.	4th.	5th.	6th.	7th.	8th.	9th.	10th.	11th.	12th.	13th.	14th.	15th.
N.	—	16	—	50	—	—	—	72	153	15	26	—	19	46	4
S.	—	—	2	—	—	10	24	—	—	—	—	—	—	—	—
W.	—	—	5	—	—	—	34	64	—	2	—	33	29	48	1
E.	4	1	—	56	6	14	19	—	—	—	17	—	17	24	3
S. W.	6	—	—	—	—	—	—	—	—	—	—	—	—	—	—
N. E.	—	—	—	—	1	10	17	—	—	—	—	—	—	—	4
N. W.	5	3	1	—	—	10	—	—	—	—	—	—	4	—	4
S. E.	10	19	—	37	8	10	43	104	24	24	90	—	—	—	1
Sum	27	23	6	143	17	34	117	234	178	42	143	31	69	122	15

True direct'n.	16th.	17th.	18th.	19th.	20th.	21st.	22d.	23d.	24th.	25th.	26th.	27th.	28th.	29th.	30th.	Sums
N.	—	—	—	—	—	—	—	—	—	—	—	—	—	—	—	365
S.	—	2	8	8	8	4	—	—	—	—	4	10	8	—	—	[illegible]
W.	—	6	29	—	—	80	48	—	—	—	6	—	—	—	—	354
E.	75	—	—	—	—	—	—	—	10	—	—	17	6	—	—	[illegible]
S. W.	—	—	—	—	—	—	—	—	—	—	—	—	—	—	—	9
N. E.	—	6	—	29	4	—	—	—	16	2	—	27	—	—	—	153
N. W.	—	3	27	10	44	17	122	33	81	67	40	14	—	11	79	443
S. E.	—	—	—	—	—	—	—	—	—	—	—	—	—	—	—	350
Sum	75	12	63	67	14	151	170	33	97	69	[illegible]	6	8	11	79	2049

By preceding formulæ we find—

$c = -145$ | $0.7\,(c-d) = -190$ | $R_s = +109$

$d = +126$ | $0.7\,(c+d) = -\ 13$ | $R_w = +\ 83$

$c-d = -271$ | $a = +239$ | $R = +137$

$c+d = -\ 19$ | $b = +\ 96$ | $\phi = 37°$

equivalent to a resulting direction of the wind S. W. ¼ S.

The following table shows the velocity-numbers for each of the principal eight winds, as well as the resulting direction of the wind, for each month between Sept. 1857, and Aug. 1859, as deduced by application of the preceding formulæ.

1857–'58. True direction.	September. Mean Lat. [illegible] Long. [illegible] 6 obs. a day.	October. Mean Lat. [illegible] Long. [illegible] 12 obs. a day.	November. Mean Lat. [illegible] Long. [illegible] 12 obs. a day.	December. Mean Lat. [illegible] Long. [illegible] 12 obs. a day.	January. Mean Lat. [illegible] Long. [illegible] 12 obs. a day.	February. Mean Lat. [illegible] Long. [illegible] 12 obs. a day.
S.	365	846	230	449	145	184
N.	66	178	0	331	533	2361
W.	354	476	1121	345	770	161
E.	258	977	447	23	139	1
S. W.	6	318	700	135	20	67
N. E.	153	648	417	174	169	223
N. W.	473	1307	1546	2056	2305	3473
S. E.	356	948	1024	660	152	869
φ	37°	176°	96°	134°	171°	156°

1858. True direction.	March. Mean Lat. [illegible] Long. [illegible] 12 obs. a day.	April. Mean Lat. [illegible], Long. [illegible]. From 1st–17th 12 obs. a day.	From 18th–30th 6 obs. a day.	May. Mean Lat. [illegible] Long. [illegible] 6 obs. a day.	June. Mean Lat. [illegible] Long. [illegible] 4 obs. a day.	July. Mean Lat. [illegible] Long. [illegible] 6 obs. a day.	August. Mean Lat. [illegible] Long. [illegible] 6 obs. a day.
S.	386	0	106	271	63	17	32
N.	1446	3354	418	138	158	139	138
W.	137	91	39	1	48	136	769
E.	279	53	0	351	311	156	231
S. W.	341	23	236	133	35	506	401
N. E.	394	386	67	454	82	449	301
N. W.	3112	1136	478	457	437	246	914
S. E.	764	0	216	603	294	165	477
φ	149°	105°		254°	224°	175°	314°

Port Kennedy. 1858–'59. True direction.	September. 6 obs. a day.	October. 6 obs. a day.	November. 12 obs. a day.	December. 12 obs. a day.	January. 12 obs. a day.	February. 12 obs. a day.
S.	134	45	0	0	0	1
N.	167	68	31	90	369	0
W.	1671	69	106	773	380	1164
E.	37	26	4	0	0	0
S. W.	663	67	0	166	0	66
N. E.	416	3519	2392	740	469	644
N. W.	799	2132	4916	3723	4074	2336
S. E.	349	90	17	10	0	2
φ	99°	169°	160°	130°	167°	163°

Port Kennedy. 1859. True direction.	March. 12 obs. a day. The numbers for the last 4 days were doubled.	April. 8 obs. a day. The two odd hours were treated like even hours.	May. 6 obs. a day. Odd and even hours treated alike.	June. 4 obs. a day. Odd and even hours treated alike.	July. 12 obs. a day. Numbers for the first 4½ days were doubled.	August. 6 obs. a day.
S.	0	0	0	0	1	63
N.	0	172	33	80	49	39
W.	294	349	2245	376	125	609
E.	0	34	0	0	136	486
S. W.	4	319	0	1	163	60
N. E.	1234	1361	373	847	1439	878
N. W.	2158	313	859	1268	2027	718
S. E.	0	88	0	1	14	220
φ	155°	196°	117°	146°	201°	187°

The above results for the resulting direction of the wind in each month, when expressed to the nearest half point, are contained in the following table:—

RESULTING DIRECTION OF THE WIND.

First year.			Second year.		
1857	September	S. W. ½ S.	1858	September	W. ½ N.
	October	N. ½ W.		October	N. by W.
	November	W. ½ N.		November	N. N. W. ½ N.
	December	N. W. by W.		December	N. W.
1858	January	N. W. ½ W.	1859	January	N. W. ½ N.
	February	N. N. W. ½ W.		February	N. W. ½ W.
	March	N. N. W. ½ W.		March	N. N. W.
	April	N. N. W. ½ N.		April	N. N. E. ½ N.
	May	E. ½ N.		May	W. N. W. ½ N.
	June	N. E.		June	N. W. by N.
	July	N. ½ W.		July	N. N. W. ½ W.
	August	W. N. W.		August	N. N. E. ½ N.

For the combination of the monthly results to quarterly, half-yearly, and yearly results, we have to double the numbers for R_s and R_w for all months in which but 6 observations a day were taken, in order to make them correspond to the numbers for the other months in which 12 observations a day were recorded; the latter number of observations having been adopted as standard. The numbers in the second column for April, 1858, were doubled and added to the corresponding numbers in column one, before the formula was applied.

The following table contains the resulting values for R_s and R_w as they resulted (or in part were referred to) from bi-hourly observations:—

Month.		R_s	R_w	Month.		R_s	R_w
1857	September	+ 238	+ 166	1858	September	− 404	+ 2003
	October	− 432	+ 51		October	− 4746	+ 832
	November	− 142	+ 1891		November	− 473	+ 1766
	December	− 178	+ 1309		December	− 3614	+ 2806
1858	January	− 2513	+ 2283	1859	January	− 3774	+ 2582
	February	− 4916	+ 1978		February	− 2428	+ 3236
	March	− 1834	+ 1793		March	− 2867	+ 685
	April	− 2843	+ 1344		April	− 3134	− 870
	May	− 69	− 1568		May	− 1844	+ 2221
	June	− 524	− 316		June	− 3518	+ 1472
	July	− 614	+ 190		July	− 3709	+ 1671
	August	− 544	+ 1423		August	− 1034	− 142

Resulting Direction of the Wind in the different Seasons of the Year.							
Season.		ΣR_w	ΣR_n	φ	Direction.	Mean lat.	Mean long.
1857	Autumn	− 871	+ 1656	109° =	W. by N. ½ N.	74°.1 N.	67°.3 W.
1857–58	Winter	− 7927	+ 6214	143	N. W. ¾ N.	73.0	66.0
1858	Spring	− 1529	+ 1911	167	N. by W.	64.0	66.4
"	Summer	− 1714	+ 2160	146	N. W. by N.	74.0	73.0
Winter half,	November–April	−15417	+15430	147° =	N. W. by N.	71.6	67.0
Summer half,	May–October	− 2024	+ 307	172	N. ½ W.	73.4	66.4
1857–58	Year	−17441	+16707	140° =	N. N. W. ½ W.	72.5	66.4
1858	Autumn	− 7909	+ 3696	151° =	N. N. W. ½ W.	Port Kennedy,	
1858–59	Winter	− 8304	+ 8152	136	N. W.	Lat. 72°.0 N.,	
1859	Spring	− 6818	+ 3601	150	N. N. W. ½ W.	Long. 94°.2 W.	
"	Summer	− 7625	+ 3235	164	N. N. W.		
Winter half,	November–April	−16734	+11277	145° =	N. N. W. ½ W.		
Summer half,	May–October	−14507	+10661	144	N. W. by N.		
1858–59	Year	−33331	+21804	147° =	N. W. by N.		

At Port Kennedy, the resulting direction of the wind is remarkably constant for the several seasons, and the differences with the corresponding values for Baffin Bay are also small, the final direction for the two localities being practically identical.

For further comparison, I add a table showing the resulting (true) direction of the wind for Baffin Bay (lat. 72°.5 N., long. 65°.8 W.), Van Rensselaer Harbor[*] (lat. 78°.0 N., long. 70°.9 W.), and Port Kennedy (lat. 72°.0 N., long. 94°.2 W.)

Season.	Baffin Bay.	Van Rensselaer Harbor.	Port Kennedy.
Autumn	106°	96°	151°
Winter	143	351	136
Spring	167	81	150
Summer	146	78	154
Year	149	19	147

These numbers show that the wind at Van Rensselaer Harbor is rather anomalous in its direction when compared with either of the two more southern stations, the resulting directions being S. by W. ¼ W., whereas at Baffin Bay and Port Kennedy, it is N. W. by N. ¼ N.

Average Velocity of the Resulting Wind.—We find the average velocity of the resulting wind by dividing the quantity *R* by the actual number of observations (exclusive of calms). This velocity, on account of the neutralization of the opposing winds, is necessarily smaller than the average velocity of the winds.

[*] See my discussion of the winds in the Smithsonian Contributions to Knowledge, Vol. XI. Meteorological Observations in the Arctic Seas, by E. K. Kane, U. S. N., p. 17. It is to be remarked that, according to Mr. Sonntag and Dr. Hayes, the *true* direction, and not the magnetic direction, was observed at Van Rensselaer Harbor—a statement otherwise confirmed in the discussion of the winds at that station; a corresponding change of the results is therefore to be made. [S.]

Thus, for September, 1857, we found $R = 137$, and n = number of observations (minus calms) = 170, hence $V = 0.8$. The following table contains the quantities for each month, season, and the whole year. The numbers for April, 1858, were changed so as to refer to 12 daily observations throughout. A similar remark applies to March, 1859, and to July, 1859.

MEAN VELOCITY, IN MILES PER HOUR, OF THE RESULTING WIND.									
		R	n	V			R	n	V
1857	September . . .	137	170	0.8	1858	September . . .	1464	178	8.2
	October . . .	532	349	1.5		October . . .	2434	174	13.9
	November . . .	1217	338	3.6		November . . .	3063	202	15.2
	December . . .	1466	333	4.4		December . . .	4187	220	19.0
1858	January . . .	3646	363	10.0	1859	January . . .	4794	333	14.4
	February . . .	3199	315	10.1		February . . .	3145	221	14.2
	March . . .	2347	279	8.4		March . . .	2346	240	9.8
	April . . .	3546	348	10.0		April . . .	1135	152	7.5
	May . . .	321	153	2.1		May . . .	1847	154	12.0
	June . . .	363	158	2.3		June . . .	2133	158	13.5
	July . . .	346	161	2.2		July . . .	2164	232	9.3
	August . . .	728	160	4.5		August . . .	794	187	4.2

	Baffin Bay.	Port Kennedy.
V in Autumn	1.9	12.5
" Winter	10.2	12.9
" Spring	7.0	9.8
" Summer	2.9	9.2
V for the year	6.0	11.4

At Van Rensselaer, the annual mean was $V = 4.5$.

Average Velocity of the Winds.—The average velocity with which each of the eight principal winds passes over the place of observation in each month, season, and whole year, is found by dividing the sum of the velocity-numbers of each wind by the number of entries in the period; thus, for the month of September, 1857, we have—

True direction of the wind.	Sum of velocities.	Number of entries.	Mean velocity.
S.	285	20	14.2
S. W.	6	1	6.0
W.	451	35	12.9
N. W.	423	41	10.3
N.	48	10	4.8
N. E.	153	14	10.9
E.	258	22	11.7
S. E.	356	18	19.8
Sum . . .	2030	170	12.2

The following table shows the mean velocity of the winds, expressed in miles per hour, for each month of observation:—

Year.	True direction.	January.	February.	March.	April.	May.	June.	July.	August.	September.	October.	November.	December.	Year.
1857–1858	S.	5.6	8.5	16.0	26.2	18.4	16.6	2.2	5.5	19.2	16.4	11.3	11.0	12.5
	S. W.	6.6	2.0	12.9	18.3	4.8	3.3	11.9	17.4	4.0	7.1	14.7	4.5	10.8
	W.	18.6	4.9	6.7	9.1	3.0	9.6	6.7	25.1	12.3	9.9	30.0	10.0	13.9
	N. W.	21.3	32.0	21.6	20.9	16.6	9.3	12.0	29.5	18.3	21.5	18.0	14.2	18.8
	N.	11.8	21.1	21.5	33.3	17.3	6.3	13.6	19.3	4.7	7.7	..	8.5	20.9
	N. E.	4.0	13.6	7.2	9.4	13.5	4.7	19.3	19.7	11.0	18.3	12.8	8.6	11.0
	E.	3.4	1.0	10.9	13.0	22.8	13.5	8.6	23.7	31.7	9.7	10.6	10.5	13.0
	S. E.	4.1	24.3	22.8	19.5	16.4	10.3	6.0	18.4	39.8	24.3	25.8	16.1	16.6
	Mean	14.1	22.0	18.3	22.0	14.8	9.2	11.2	20.0	12.3	12.5	17.7	11.7	16.0
1858–1859	S.	..	1.8	..	..	..	..	1.0	11.0	13.6	23.2	..	..	13.2
	S. W.	..	24.5	4.0	30.5	..	1.0	15.1	11.0	18.2	12.4	..	11.7	16.9
	W.	19.1	18.9	15.3	14.2	22.4	21.3	17.9	16.4	23.4	9.6	17.7	23.7	19.8
	N. W.	17.2	19.2	22.3	14.4	15.4	24.6	18.7	31.6	23.4	29.0	22.7	19.2	20.4
	N.	16.8	..	..	6.6	3.6	7.5	12.0	7.5	16.7	14.7	18.5	19.0	11.9
	N. E.	18.5	8.9	9.1	14.4	9.1	10.3	18.1	14.8	16.7	22.5	20.3	16.8	16.3
	E.	..	..	..	8.5	..	3.0	8.3	21.4	13.5	12.5	4.0	..	13.3
	S. E.	..	1.0	..	6.5	..	1.0	1.7	15.1	18.4	4.9	17.9	18.0	12.8
	Mean	18.5	17.1	16.6	18.4	15.7	16.0	17.1	15.6	20.0	21.5	21.7	17.2	17.8

In the first year, while in Baffin Bay, the velocity of the wind was greatest in the months of February and March, and least in the months of June and July; in the second year, at Port Kennedy, it was greatest in October and November, and least in March and April. In Baffin Bay, during 1857, '58, the N. W. and N. winds blew with the greatest strength, and the S. W. and N. E. with the least; whereas, in the following year, at Port Kennedy, it was the W. and N. W. wind which blew strongest, and the N. and S. E. which blew with the least force. The mean velocity of each of the eight winds is shown in the annexed diagram, which contains also, for comparison, the velocity of the winds as observed at Van Rensselaer Harbor.

Fig. 1.

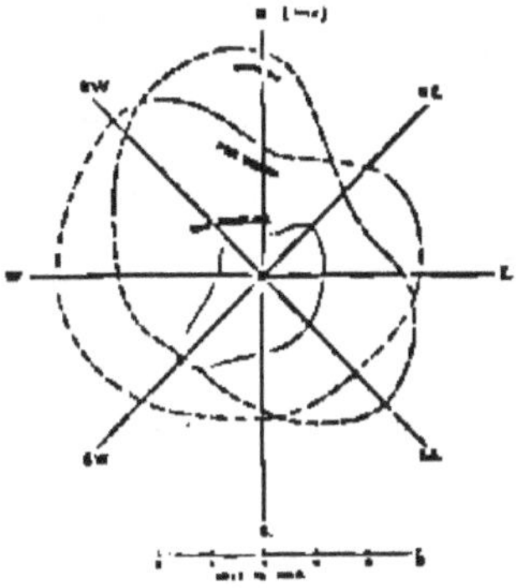

The velocity of the wind being only estimated at each place, the apparently small velocities at Van Rensselaer Harbor may, in a measure, be due to a different scale of estimating, although the great number of calms seems to point to their reality.

We have next to consider the relative frequency of each wind; for this purpose it is only necessary to refer the number of entries, n, of each wind, as used in the preceding computation for the velocity, to an equal number of hours of observation for each month. This has been done by simple proportion, and the numbers were all referred to twelve observations a day; thus, the numbers' of entries, for all months of six observations a day, have all been doubled. The following table contains the relative frequency of each wind:—

	True direction.	January.	February.	March.	April.	May.	June.	July.	August.	September.	October.	November.	December.	Total.
1857-1858 Baffin Bay.	S.	33	19	23	8	24	30	16	8	40	15	19	41	243
	S. W.	14	9	28	29	38	22	62	38	6	30	42	20	245
	W.	51	22	20	13	3	10	14	40	18	44	18	39	428
	N. W.	190	125	131	103	14	77	54	63	74	116	115	136	1233
	N.	45	100	65	123	16	41	60	14	56	14	0	49	580
	N. E.	32	30	41	46	64	38	65	41	77	37	33	31	454
	E.	23	1	23	4	23	49	72	31	44	43	35	2	299
	S. E.	37	16	35	32	73	54	60	50	36	46	40	41	603
	Calm	9	21	8	31	70	46	60	63	20	22	21	15	341
Sum and check		373	330	373	318	342	3[illegible]	370	368	360	372	360	373	4.466
1858-1859 Port Kennedy.	S.	0	1	0	0	0	0	1	14	20	5	0	0	41
	S. W.	0	2	0	16	0	2	78	10	13	16	0	17	154
	W.	11	48	12	3	110	36	13	62	89	14	4	20	428
	N. W.	254	174	188	38	110	152	117	66	14	152	273	194	1670
	N.	22	0	0	25	18	16	4	8	29	0	8	1	181
	N. E.	37	45	160	172	70	108	48	92	50	134	168	78	1104
	E.	0	0	0	0	0	6	22	64	4	1	1	0	108
	S. E.	0	3	0	0	0	3	3	26	47	28	1	3	116
	Calm	44	67	112	54	64	80	43	36	0	14	39	33	581
Sum and check		370	334	371	354	372	360	372	370	360	373	360	348	4363

In the above table a few variable winds have not been counted in.

In both localities the N. W. is the most frequent next to this, in Baffin Bay the N. wind, and at Port Kennedy the N. E.; the least frequent wind in both seasons is from the S. and E. The results at Port Kennedy are remarkable for the scarcity of winds from the S., E., and S. E. This is most probably due to the configuration of the surrounding land; the same cause may also explain the scarcity of winds from the north, midway between the most frequent N. W. and N. E. winds. The following diagram exhibits the relative frequency of each wind for the two localities, to which has been added the result obtained at Van Rensselaer Harbor (the numbers for that harbor refer to twenty-four observations a day, and were therefore halfed in order to make them comparable with the numbers deduced above.)

RELATIVE FREQUENCY OF THE WINDS.

True direction.	Baffin Bay.	Van Rensselaer Harbor.	Port Kennedy.
S.	243	110	41
S. W.	245	154	159
W.	428	118	428
N. W.	1232	230	1670
N.	580	144	181
N. E.	454	77	1104
E.	299	56	108
S. E.	543	411	114
Calm	341	1533	581

In Baffin Bay the calms occur less frequently than any of the eight winds; at Port Kennedy they are more frequent; the frequency of the calms at Van Rensselaer exceeds that at Baffin Bay and Port Kennedy in the ratio of nearly 7 and 5 respectively.

Fig. 2.

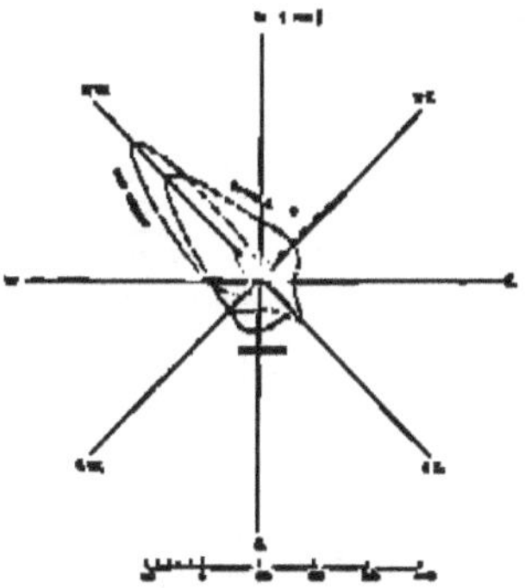

The preponderance of the N. W. and N. E. winds at Port Kennedy is very striking on the diagram.

The quantity of air which has been transferred over the place of observation in a given period, is directly proportional to the velocity-numbers, or the number of miles travelled over by a particle of air in any direction during the period. The observations not having all been made at regular and equal intervals of two hours, the numbers indicating the relative quantity of air in April, 1858, March and July, 1859, were referred by simple proportion to twelve observations a day, to which all other numbers refer; the number for all months of six observations a day have been doubled.

RELATIVE QUANTITY OF AIR PASSED OVER THE PLACE OF OBSERVATION.
Referring to 12 observations a day.

Year.	True direction.	January.	February.	March.	April.	May.	June.	July.	August.	September.	October.	November.	December.	Sum.
1857–1859 Baffin Bay.	S.	143	134	395	310	612	160	23	44	770	246	220	440	[illegible]
	S. W.	93	37	261	833	862	79	735	862	16	912	760	138	[illegible]
	W.	972	161	137	137	2	86	236	1370	700	474	1111	[illegible]	[illegible]
	N. W.	2074	3039	3111	2133	174	916	766	1429	964	1327	1046	2704	[illegible]
	N.	851	2371	1615	4179	778	251	372	270	173	188	0	331	10284
	N. E.	198	853	394	360	448	164	930	616	369	864	417	176	5168
	E.	116	1	239	63	602	622	598	642	616	377	917	22	4375
	S. E.	151	348	744	439	1148	698	339	864	713	868	1048	880	6101
	Sum	6187	6946	6777	8443	4692	2880	3803	6392	6164	4368	6016	4184	[illegible]
1858–1859 Port Kennedy.	S.	0	1	0	0	0	0	1	144	[illegible]	170	0	0	[illegible]
	S. W.	0	48	4	434	0	1	683	118	1128	176	0	198	2140
	W.	300	1148	240	616	2400	482	330	1018	2143	118	170	173	9795
	N. W.	4606	3236	2132	636	2718	3770	3037	1430	1602	4264	6410	5731	[illegible]
	N.	365	0	8	240	65	114	60	60	274	14	22	10	1296
	N. E.	640	645	1254	2092	164	1094	1430	1216	932	3024	2203	240	[illegible]
	E.	0	0	0	64	0	18	152	1370	14	40	4	0	1722
	S. E.	0	7	0	63	0	2	14	478	738	160	17	10	1468
	Sum.	5426	5081	3670	4474	4239	5480	5093	5448	7064	[illegible]	6981	5423	63108

The following table contains the comparative values at Van Rensselaer Harbor with the above, the result at Van R. having first been halfed to refer to twelve observations a day.

True direction.	Baffin Bay.	Van Rensselaer Harbor.	Port Kennedy.
S.	5223	3040	606
S. W.	2891	4009	2658
W.	6067	481	2765
N. W.	22234	1612	31658
N.	19254	500	1808
N. E.	6150	169	15961
E.	4105	236	1122
S. E.	3161	2600	1485
Sum . .	67793	13750	63163

These results of the relative quantity of air moved over each place are also shown in the annexed diagram.

Fig. 2.

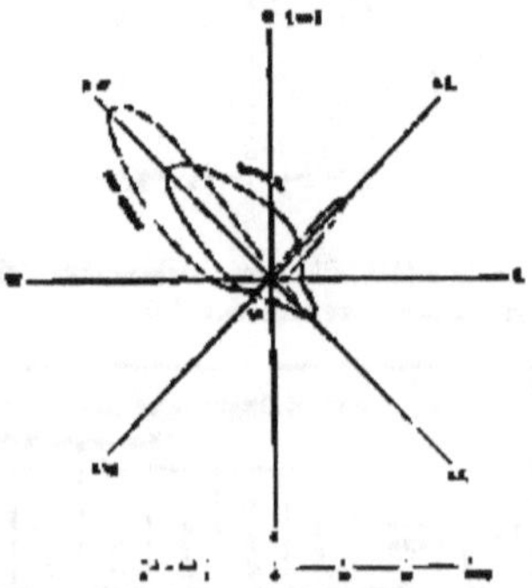

Owing to the small differences in the velocity of the several winds, the above diagram of the quantity of wind resembles that of the frequency of the winds, at least, in all its characteristics.

It cannot be expected that the relations of the wind within the Arctic Circle should come out with any degree of certainty from but a single year of observation, or even from several years; and before we can arrive at their true characteristics, we must combine results at different stations as well as in different years.

Rotation of the Wind.—For the purpose of ascertaining the law of the rotation of the wind, the observations were examined in reference to the number of times the wind arrived at each of the eight principal directions, the motion each time not being less than 45°; and also in reference to the sum total of angular motion, in a direct and retrograde sense. The direction in which the hands of a watch (face up) turn, and which corresponds to the direction of the rotation of the wind, according to Dove, has been assumed as direct, and is indicated by a + sign; the opposite direction is indicated by a — sign.

The following table exhibits the number of changes of the wind, or the number of times it arrived at any one of the principal directions during a given period, and also the amount it shifted, or its angular motion expressed in units of 45°. In making out these numbers for each wind, not only the four-hourly series of observations, but also the intermediate observations in certain months were used. After each calm the counting was commenced anew, and also in cases where the wind shifted suddenly 180°.

Baffin Bay: Mean Lat. 72°.5 N.; Mean Long. 65°.8 W.

Changes in	Autumn, 1857. Direction +	Direction −	Amount +	Amount −	Winter, 1857-8. Direction +	Direction −	Amount +	Amount −	Spring, 1858. Direction +	Direction −	Amount +	Amount −	Summer, 1858. Direction +	Direction −	Amount +	Amount −	Year, 1857-8. Direction +	Direction −	Amount +	Amount −
N.	3	1	3	2	5	3	16	5	3	4	1	12	5	4	8	8	21	13	34	27
N. E.	4	11	11	20	11	8	34	13	6	8	25	11	9	9	19	23	31	[illegible]	91	64
E.	11	18	30	19	0	1	19	8	8	6	17	11	3	6	5	[illegible]	20	24	53	[illegible]
S. E.	12	7	[illegible]	15	2	5	4	16	13	3	43	6	12	6	30	25	30	21	[illegible]	[illegible]
S.	4	5	12	11	3	4	10	9	8	6	4	10	3	4	9	9	13	21	25	[illegible]
S. W.	7	4	17	15	6	4	15	15	10	8	31	16	5	14	9	[illegible]	27	29	73	72
W.	3	17	11	35	1	16	3	42	1	4	1	8	9	5	10	17	14	30	25	[illegible]
N. W.	11	7	31	19	6	[illegible]	15	17	6	10	26	26	6	10	14	19	23	35	79	81
Sum	45	64	130	133	34	43	97	117	40	45	153	99	51	56	104	136	243	[illegible]	444	[illegible]
Excess	...	1	...	3	...	9	...	20	5	...	64	...	...	5	...	32	...	6	...	1

From the above it appears that the direction of the wind is shifting in spring only direct, in the other seasons it is retrograde; the total amount of angular motion, however, is balanced (within 45°) in the whole year.

Port Kennedy: Lat. 72°.0 N.; Long. 94°.2 W.

Changes in	Autumn, 1858. Direction +	Direction −	Amount +	Amount −	Winter, 1858-9. Direction +	Direction −	Amount +	Amount −	Spring, 1859. Direction +	Direction −	Amount +	Amount −	Summer, 1859. Direction +	Direction −	Amount +	Amount −	Year, 1858-9. Direction +	Direction −	Amount +	Amount −
N.	3	1	3	5	1	0	1	0	1	1	5	1	3	1	4	1	7	3	10	7
N. E.	10	4	24	13	3	1	6	3	4	2	11	3	11	5	24	8	28	12	45	85
E.	3	0	6	0	1	0	1	0	5	0	7	0	7	2	11	5	16	2	25	5
S. E.	2	4	4	11	0	1	0	1	1	0	2	0	3	3	11	3	6	7	17	11
S.	1	1	3	3	0	0	0	0	0	0	0	0	1	3	1	9	2	4	4	12
S. W.	0	9	0	17	0	0	0	0	0	2	0	4	0	6	0	21	0	23	0	36
W.	5	5	14	8	1	14	3	14	1	0	1	15	0	13	0	16	7	41	18	65
N. W.	9	17	37	28	22	3	28	4	7	6	7	16	13	8	16	26	50	28	89	73
Sum	37	34	72	85	28	23	39	31	16	20	51	57	37	40	67	89	116	119	279	262
Excess	...	4	...	13	5	...	8	...	...	1	...	6	...	3	...	23	...	3	...	30

As might have been expected from the peculiar situation of Port Kennedy, and the results as given on Figs. 2 and 3, the rotation of the wind seems to be greatly affected in this locality; the resulting direction is retrograde, and the amount equals four circumferences.

The following table contains,[1] for comparison, the results of a similar investigation of the rotation of the winds at Van Rensselaer Harbor, from Dr. Kane's observations in 1853, '54, '55. Seventeen months of observations (hourly) were discussed, and the results, by the same months in different years, were united into one mean: the results for September, October, November, December, and January, have double weight, for this reason, when compared with the remaining months.

[1] These results are here published for the first time.

Van Rensselaer Harbor: Lat. 78°.6 N.; Long. 70°.9 W.																				
Changes to	Autumn, 1853-4.				Winter, 1853, '4, '5.				Spring, 1854.				Summer, 1854.				Year, 1853, '4, '5.			
	Direction.		Amount.		Direction.		Amount.		Direction.		Amount.		Direction.		Amount.		Direction.		Amount.	
	+	−	+	−	+	−	+	−	+	−	+	−	+	−	+	−	+	−	+	−
N.	10	1	11	2	8	5	5	19	4	0	5	6	11	5	13	0	38	17	35	33
N. E.	3	1	2	3	0	2	0	4	0	1	0	3	4	0	6	0	6	4	6	10
E.	1	6	2	11	1	10	2	22	0	5	0	18	0	3	0	0	2	24	2	40
S. E.	3	14	4	27	10	17	12	33	2	11	3	27	3	4	6	5	20	36	27	62
S.	14	16	10	23	14	20	24	29	15	13	20	17	7	3	8	2	52	56	70	79
S. W.	20	1	27	4	25	6	41	7	12	4	17	14	3	0	4	0	64	16	91	27
W.	6	4	11	8	11	1	24	1	2	1	2	2	2	25	4	24	21	32	43	33
N. W.	4	9	6	13	4	5	6	5	5	5	33	1	10	5	22	6	25	25	66	29
Sum	60	59	65	99	74	44	120	112	44	45	79	93	50	64	66	52	229	215	343	335
Excess	1	—	—	3	30	...	4	...	—	1	—	13	4	—	14	...	114	—	7	—

The result is in favor of the direct motion of not quite a circumference. The result deduced for Baffin Bay agrees with this within the limit of uncertainty of the final value itself, and both indicate that the law of rotation probably does not hold good for these high latitudes.

Occurrence and Duration of Storms.—The following table contains the date, duration, and direction (true), of all storms experienced between the dates of the record. In each case the intensity rises to 8 (of the scale) or beyond it, and there are at least two consecutive entries of this or a higher number; in other words, gusts of wind blowing for less than three hours are not noted.

Date.	Duration.	Direction and changes.
1857, Aug. 30, 31.	12h	E. S. E. to S. S. E. and S. E.
Oct. 10,	12	E. N. E. to S. S. E.
" 23,	14	N. W. to W.
" 27, 28,	8	N. W.
Nov. 6, 7,	18	N. W.
" 17,	16	S. to S. W., S. E., and S. S. E.
*" 21, 22, 23,	68	N. E. to S. E., S., S. W., and S. S. W.
Dec. 6, 8,	18	W. to N. W.
" 18,	18	N. W. to W. N. W.
1858, Jan. 7,	4	N. W.
" 21,	8	N. N. W.
" 22,	8	N. N. W. to W. N. W.
Feb. 1,	6	N. N. W.
" 8,	24	N. W. to N. N. W. and N. W.
" 15,	4	N.
" 24,	32	N. W. to N. N. W. and N. W.
" 28,	6	S. E.
*March 3, 4,	14	N. E. to S. S. W., S., and S. W.
" 22, 23,	6	S. E.
" 25, 26, 27,	46	N. to N. W. and N. N. W.
April 3, 4, 5,	54	N. to N. W.
" 8,	8	N. W.
" 16, 17, 18,	58	N.
*May 4,	36	S. S. E. to S., N. N. W. and N. W.
July 13,	12	N. E.
Aug. 3,	20	E. S. E. to E.

* Indicates storms in which the direction of the wind is completely reversed; they belong to the rotatory storms or cyclones. Two of these turn from the N. E. to the S. W., and the third from the S. E. to the N. W.

In the year 1857–8 (Baffin Bay), there were 26 storms of an average duration of 19 hours, and from the prevailing quarters, almost to the exclusion of all others, from the N. W. and S. E. (true); at Van Rensselaer Harbor, the prevailing storm quarters were S. W. and S. E. (true), and the average duration was 7 hours; 13 storms were recorded during 17 months.

Storms Recorded at Port Kennedy in 1858–59.

Date	Duration.	Direction and changes.
1858, Sept. 4,	8h	W.
Oct. 3,	9	N. E.
" 16, 17,	24	W. N. W. to N. W.
" 25, 26, 27,	48	N. E. to N. N. E., N. N. W., and N. W.
Nov. 2, 3,	16	N. W. to N. N. W.
" 4,	20	W. N. W.
" 5,	4	N. W.
" 14,	6	N. W.
" 28,	54	N. N. E. to N. N. W. and N. E.
Dec. 4,	8	N. W.
" 26,	1	N. W.
" 27,	4	N. W.
1859, Jan. 6,	1	N. W.
" 24, 25,	10	N. W.
Feb. 14,	4	W. N. W.
Feb. 28, and March 1,	24	W. N. W.
March 11,	26	N. W. to W. N. W. and N. W.
" 17,	4	N. W.
April 28,	19	N. E.
April 30, and May 1,	20	W.
June 1, 2,	23	N. N. W. to N. W.
July 11,	4	N. E.

There were 22 storms in the second year, almost all from the N. W., with a few from the N. E., but not a single one from either S. W. or S. E.

As in Baffin Bay, storms are more frequent in the winter and autumn than in summer.

Five of the storms were accompanied by sudden falls of the barometer; they are the more remarkable ones, and have been illustrated by diagrams, showing the hour, direction, and force of wind, and reading of the aneroid barometer. Of these five, the storms of January 21, and March 3, 4, 1858, are perhaps the most interesting; in each case the barometer fell over one inch. During the storm of May 4, 1858, the barometer was not much affected.

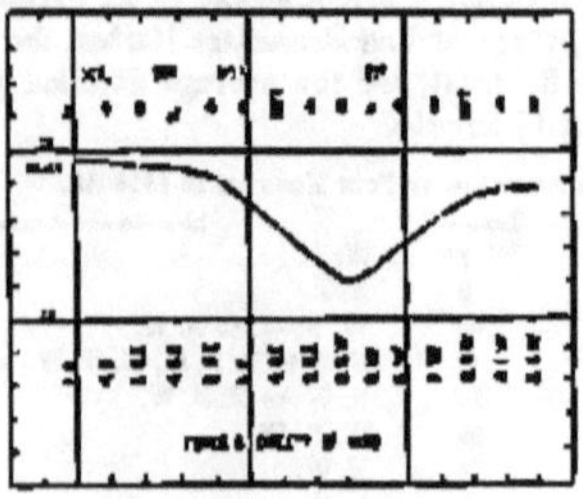

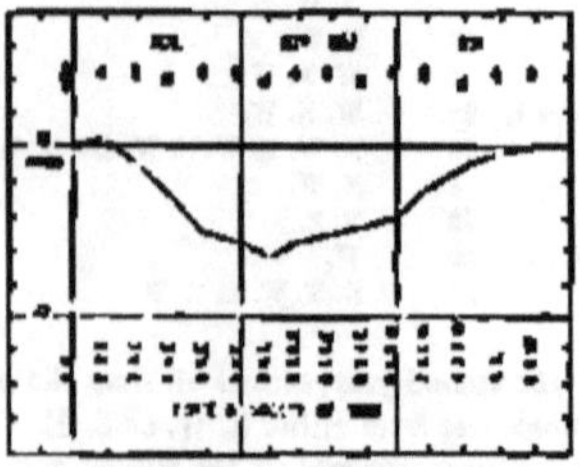

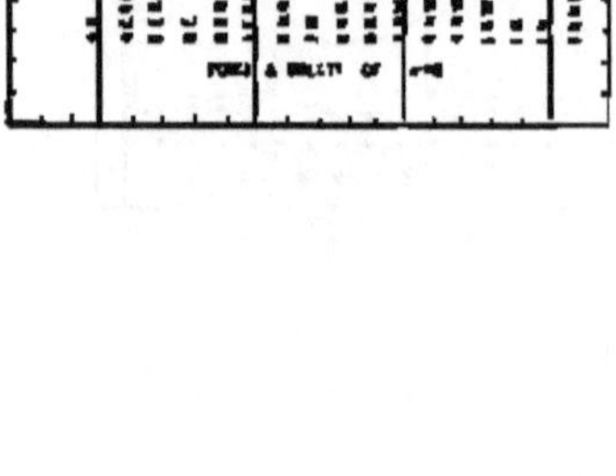

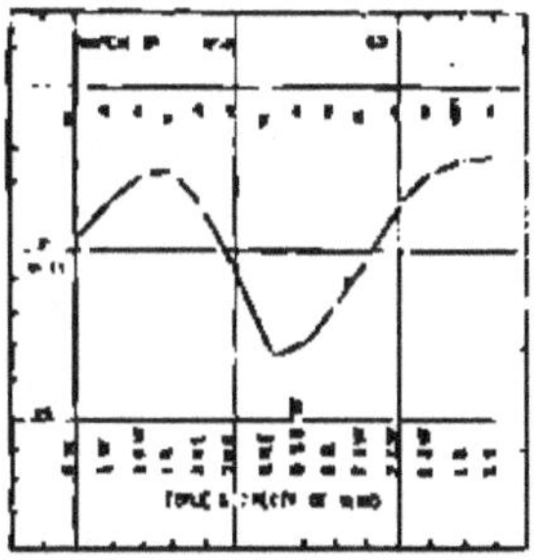

The relation of the different winds to the atmospheric temperatures has already been investigated in the preceding paper; other relations, as those with the atmospheric pressure, will be given on subsequent pages.

PART III.

ATMOSPHERIC PRESSURE.

RECORD AND REDUCTION OF THE OBSERVATIONS FOR ATMOSPHERIC PRESSURE.

INTRODUCTORY REMARKS.

The observing hours are the same as those for the other meteorological observations, that is, in part at equal intervals of two hours, and in part at intervals of four hours. There are two records, one of the aneroid readings, the other of the readings of the mercurial barometer.

The series of observations by the aneroid is continued throughout the cruise; the mercurial barometer was used only between September 20, 1857, and April 10, 1858. The readings in the month of July and August, 1857, and of September, 1859, are given in the record, but are not further introduced in the discussion, since the ship was then rapidly changing her position, not permitting a combination of the daily observations.

The mercurial marine barometer, Adie No. 208, was compared with a standard instrument at Kew both at departure and after return. The comparisons for index correction are as follows (communicated in a letter from Captain McClintock, dated London, December 12th, 1860):—

Corrections to be applied to Barometer by Adie No. 208 (or No. 107, private mark of the maker.)

Before Embarkation in the Fox.		Subsequent to its Return.	
At inches.	Correction.	At inches.	Correction.
30.5	+0.006	30.5	+0.006
30.0	+0.006	30.0	+0.006
29.5	+0.007	29.5	+0.007
29.0	+0.007	29.0	+0.006
28.5	+0.007	28.5	+0.005
28.0	+0.008	28.0	+0.005

This mercurial barometer had been used by Professor Piazzi Smyth at Teneriffe, and is highly thought of by Admiral Fitzroy, in whose office it is now in use.

It is specially stated in the reduction whenever the above correction was applied. Comparisons of the readings of the mercurial and aneroid barometers will be found in the discussion.

The cistern of the mercurial barometer was four feet above the level of the sea (in reference to the position of the aneroid, no statement is given). The barometric readings recorded give the combined pressure of the dry air and aqueous vapor; the latter, however, is very small: no hygrometric observations were found recorded.

The following tables commence with the aneroid readings, and conclude with the readings of the mercurial barometer and its corresponding temperature. A few occasional omissions in the record were supplied by interpolation; such figures are distinguished by being placed between brackets. The mean position of the "Fox" is given for each month (the daily position is already given in the preceding temperature paper).

RECORD OF THE OBSERVATIONS OF THE ATMOSPHERIC PRESSURE MADE ON BOARD THE YACHT "FOX," UNDER COMMAND OF F. L. McCLINTOCK, R. N., IN THE ARCTIC SEAS, IN 1857, '58, '59.

READINGS OF ANEROID BAROMETER 1170 ON BOARD THE YACHT FOX.

July, 1857. 29 Inches +. Mean Lat. 65°.0 N., Long. 29°.1 W. of Greenwich.

DAY.	6h.	9h.	Noon.	3h.	9h.	Midn't.	Mean.
1	....	....	....	....	....	....	Inches.
2	(1.10)	1.10	1.05	1.15	.99	(.92)	1.25
3	(.91)	.95	(.97)	(.99)	.93	(.91)	0.94
4	(.91)	.91	(.94)	(.98)	1.01	(1.05)	0.99
5	(1.05)	1.11	(1.11)	(1.12)	1.13	(1.12)	1.11
6	(1.12)	1.12	1.13	1.07	1.19	1.30	1.10
7	1.20	1.22	1.23	1.22	1.23	1.22	1.23
8	1.18	1.14	1.19	1.01	1.02	.88	1.09
9	.72	.90	.86	.65	.62	.60	0.66
10	.78	.60	.57	.52	.52	.61	0.58
11	.48	.46	.44	.40	.40	.44	0.44
12	.49	.50	.54	.61	.70	.74	0.60
13	.82	.85	.92	.92	.96	.90	0.91
14	.94	.94	.92	.97	.90	.92	0.93
15	.95	.92	.94	.95	.97	.91	0.94
16	.90	.69	.86	.82	.69	.92	0.80
17	.94	.92	.94	.83	.90	.97	0.93
18	.73	.94	.94	.72	.52	.44	0.80
19	.66	(.74)	(.74)	(.74)	(.72)	.72	0.71
20	.76	.74	.74	.74	.74	.80	0.75
21	.82	.82	.84	.82	.88	.87	0.84
22	.85	.81	.80	.92	.84	.84	0.83
23	.84	.78	.76	.65	.74	.71	0.80
24	.74	.74	.73	.79	.88	.80	0.80
25	.96	(.95)	.91	.84	.80	.95	0.83
26	.98	.80	.50	.60	.90	.54	0.80
27	.54	.50	.41	.60	.50	.46	0.47
28	.53	.55	.46	.72	.60	.64	0.50
29	.79	.85	.78	.86	.72	.73	0.80
30	.70	.60	.66	.65	.64	.96	0.68
31	.75	.80	.74	.90	.92	.84	0.83
Mean	29.819	29.841	29.841	29.834	29.834	29.844	29.842

August, 1857. 29 Inches +. Mean Lat. 74°.0 N., Long. 59°.6 W.

DAY.	6h.	9h.	Noon.	3h.	9h.	Midn't.	Mean.
1	.84	.90	.75	.98	.94	.94	0.90
2	.89	.87	.88	.96	.79	.96	0.94
3	.88	.86	(.94)	(.90)	(.90)	(.93)	0.91
4	.76	.76	.70	.72	.74	.83	0.79
5	1.02	1.13	1.15	1.24	1.26	1.23	1.17
6	1.18	1.08	1.00	.98	.80	.96	1.03
7	.79	1.10	1.10	1.15	1.13	1.15	1.09
8	1.18	1.18	1.02	.84	.88	.80	0.99
9	.78	.78	.91	.88	.98	.95	0.83
10	.92	.93	.94	1.00	1.76	1.06	0.98
11	1.10	1.10	.97	.84	.73	.69	0.88
12	.74	.87	.69	.93	.96	.90	0.91
13	1.00	1.24	1.06	1.02	1.03	1.02	1.03
14	.86	.80	.88	.87	.82	.80	0.84
15	.60	.81	.70	(.73)	(.67)	(.80)	0.74
16	.41	.63	.65	.60	.63	.82	0.60
17	.47	.64	.66	.51	.55	.80	0.58
18	.64	.64	.72	.77	.79	.80	0.73
19	.83	.85	.80	.94	.85	.96	0.81
20	.92	1.06	1.13	1.06	1.08	1.10	1.05
21	1.08	1.10	1.03	1.03	1.09	.98	1.03
22	.84	.86	.91	.90	.94	.84	0.90
23	.85	.82	.80	.80	.84	.74	0.80
24	.74	.71	.98	.86	.84	.86	0.83
25	.84	.63	.82	.91	.93	.84	0.80
26	.83	.84	.84	.95	.87	.82	0.93
27	.83	.65	.93	.62	.68	.98	0.84
28	.76	.82	.92	1.09	1.04	1.10	0.94
29	1.04	1.20	1.30	1.06	.80	.80	1.03
30	.65	.84	.94	.54	.64	.78	0.97
31	.84	.97	.88	.75	.80	.64	0.79
Mean	29.870	29.920	29.856	29.860	29.952	29.842	29.884

READINGS OF ANEROID BAROMETER 17701 ON BOARD THE YACHT FOX.

September, 1857. 29 Inches +. Mean Lat. 73°.5 N., Long. 65°.5 W.

Day.	2h.	4h.	6h.	8h.	10h.	Noon.	2h.	4h.	6h.	8h.	10h.	Midn't.	Mean.
1	(0.41)	.41	(0.47)	.44	(.45)	.42	(.40)	.37	(.41)	.40	(.44)	.42	0.41
2	(0.86)	.70	(0.73)	.75	(.80)	.81	(.80)	.83	(.83)	.88	(.53)	.81	0.78
3	(0.83)	.83	(0.94)	.85	(.47)	.89	(.82)	.86	(.97)	1.01	(1.08)	1.04	0.87
4	(1.03)	1.03	(1.09)	1.19	(1.13)	1.12	(1.30)	1.22	(1.24)	1.14	(1.16)	1.14	1.11
5	(1.21)	1.01	(1.07)	1.06	(1.03)	.86	(.84)	.94	(.83)	.81	(.81)	.82	0.98
6	(0.93)	.94	(1.02)	.93	(.90)	.90	(.93)	.84	(.83)	.84	(.77)	.76	0.90
7	(0.81)	.82	(0.80)	.45	(.44)	.48	(.40)	.49	(.45)	.42	(.36)	.34	0.47
8	(0.40)	.40	(0.51)	.32	(.73)	.34	(.71)	.66	(.71)	.72	(.78)	.78	0.59
9	(0.77)	.77	(0.70)	.74	(.81)	.86	(.87)	.80	(.80)	.69	(.82)	.83	0.84
10	(0.84)	.76	(0.72)	.38	(.73)	.73	(.70)	.68	(.70)	.73	(.30)	.88	0.78
11	(0.88)	.84	(1.00)	1.02	(1.06)	1.02	(1.10)	.68	(.86)	.84	(.86)	.98	0.94
12	(1.08)	1.07	(1.16)	1.12	(1.14)	1.12	(1.21)	1.16	(1.30)	1.30	(1.32)	1.24	1.19
13	(1.30)	1.37	(1.41)	1.46	(1.51)	1.26	(1.28)	1.36	(1.21)	1.46	(1.42)	1.34	1.46
14	(1.42)	1.30	(1.41)	1.46	(1.41)	1.39	(1.30)	1.46	(1.31)	1.31	(1.20)	1.28	1.30
15	(1.31)	1.41	(1.40)	1.18	(1.12)	1.16	(1.21)	1.28	(1.20)	1.28	(1.40)	1.43	1.21
16	(1.30)	1.31	(1.32)	1.20	(1.31)	1.32	(1.31)	1.31	(1.33)	1.28	(1.30)	1.38	1.30
17	(1.36)	1.30	(1.29)	1.12	(1.13)	1.10	(1.20)	1.20	(1.26)	1.32	(1.24)	1.28	1.24
18	(1.22)	1.20	(1.12)	1.04	(1.00)	1.06	(.90)	.80	(.60)	.60	(.76)	.77	0.88
19	(0.16)	.70	(0.96)	.90	(0.80)	.87	(1.00)	1.06	(1.20)	1.10	(1.10)	1.21	1.00
20	(1.32)	1.31	(1.34)	1.30	(1.27)	1.30	(2.21)	1.30	(1.15)	1.10	(1.06)	.96	1.18
21	(0.88)	.78	(0.71)	.64	(.62)	.60	.82	.65	.54	.70	.70	.70	0.68
22	.64	.60	.88	.63	.69	.72	.76	.66	.66	.60	.66	.80	0.74
23	.86	.60	.80	.80	.88	1.00	1.06	1.00	1.12	1.14	1.10	1.20	1.02
24	1.12	1.17	1.17	1.12	1.00	1.04	1.12	1.06	1.03	.98	.92	.88	1.08
25	.78	.74	.70	.69	.76	.74	.76	.58	.68	.67	.68	.66	0.70
26	.66	.60	.54	.60	.56	.47	.64	.54	.54	.64	.60	.54	0.60
27	.56	.60	.60	.28	.53	.64	.44	.44	.44	.44	.46	.48	0.48
28	.40	.50	.60	.40	.48	.44	.48	.50	.50	.43	.44	.48	0.48
29	.14	.38	.50	.50	.32	.48	.34	.44	.53	.48	.42	.30	0.42
30	.44	.52	.24	.18	.23	.32	.30	.48	.04	.08	.06	.00	0.32
Mean	0.898	0.905	0.929	0.831	0.848	0.840	0.900	0.851	0.862	0.863	0.894	0.889	29.843

October, 1857. 29 Inches +. Mean Lat. 75°.2 N., Long. 67°.8 W.

Day.	2h.	4h.	6h.	8h.	10h.	Noon.	2h.	4h.	6h.	8h.	10h.	Midn't.	Mean.
1	.50	.92	.90	.62	.71	.74	.76	.78	.61	.64	.84	.94	0.73
2	.60	.33	.72	.84	1.00	1.02	1.02	1.01	1.06	1.00	1.20	1.12	1.02
3	1.13	1.12	1.10	1.10	1.14	1.14	1.14	1.16	1.06	1.12	1.18	1.18	1.19
4	1.14	1.12	1.16	1.06	1.09	1.07	1.04	1.04	1.00	1.06	1.00	.89	1.07
5	.96	.80	.90	.88	.84	.88	.79	.16	.74	.78	.70	.69	0.87
6	.77	.61	.81	.76	.80	.87	.81	.67	.81	.80	.80	.96	0.86
7	.68	.30	.46	.86	.81	.92	.88	.54	.88	.96	.80	.87	0.82
8	.98	.94	.92	1.00	1.08	1.04	1.04	1.04	1.06	1.09	1.20	1.13	1.03
9	1.12	1.16	1.10	1.10	1.00	1.11	1.11	1.30	1.00	1.30	1.32	1.22	1.12
10	1.27	1.22	1.30	1.18	1.18	1.12	1.10	1.12	1.13	1.12	1.14	1.16	1.18
11	1.14	1.06	1.00	1.04	1.10	1.10	1.14	1.02	1.06	1.01	.98	.94	1.03
12	.88	.84	.80	.78	.82	.81	.85	.86	.82	.84	.59	.64	0.82
13	.79	.61	.61	.80	.80	.86	.78	.74	.64	.62	.65	.66	0.71
14	.46	.40	.30	.34	.30	.06	.45	.43	.60	.81	.88	.84	0.49
15	.81	.38	.80	.52	.80	.80	.64	.70	.74	.75	.76	.78	0.68
16	.72	.71	.26	.71	.74	.78	.78	.82	.80	.84	.80	.94	0.80
17	1.06	1.10	1.10	1.14	1.12	1.06	1.06	1.02	1.06	1.09	1.06	1.06	1.09
18	1.02	1.04	1.03	1.06	1.06	1.06	1.04	1.02	.98	.88	.80	.80	1.00
19	.78	.78	.61	.69	.70	.64	.63	.74	.74	.78	.74	.78	0.71
20	.74	.74	.74	.61	.48	.48	.30	.60	.61	.84	.94	.88	0.56
21	.89	.84	.80	.84	.02	.02	.97	.61	.76	.03	.30	.31	0.52
22	.43	.34	.28	.30	.34	.28	.87	.40	.83	.50	.64	.76	0.41
23	.72	.74	.74	.77	.84	.68	.84	.63	.90	.78	.74	.74	0.76
24	.78	.77	.62	.82	.98	1.07	1.13	1.20	1.20	1.33	1.34	1.38	1.06
25	1.30	1.38	1.38	1.42	1.40	1.46	1.40	1.52	1.54	1.60	1.60	1.62	1.49
26	1.62	1.60	1.63	1.64	1.70	1.70	1.66	1.70	1.74	1.71	1.76	1.70	1.68
27	1.40	1.36	1.40	1.40	1.44	1.08	1.30	1.38	1.30	1.24	1.18	1.14	1.32
28	1.16	1.30	1.47	1.43	1.13	1.14	1.12	1.18	1.13	1.24	1.23	1.20	1.15
29	1.16	1.16	1.12	1.18	1.22	1.30	1.14	1.18	1.40	1.08	1.00	.88	1.14
30	.84	.63	.79	.78	.60	.62	.68	.66	.65	.96	.69	.66	0.84
31	.46	.52	.40	.61	.46	.44	.49	.46	.40	.32	.32	.30	0.67
Mean	0.944	0.930	0.915	0.936	0.968	0.954	0.961	0.978	0.965	0.990	0.985	0.871	29.960

READINGS OF ANEROID BAROMETER 17701 ON BOARD THE YACHT FOX.

November, 1857. 29 inches +. Mean Lat. 74°.3 N., Long. 67°.1 W.

Day.	2h.	4h.	6h.	8h.	10h.	Noon.	2h.	4h.	6h.	8h.	10h.	Midn't.	Mean.
1	.88	.86	.86	.88	.84	.84	.94	.84	.86	.84	.88	.90	0.89
2	.84	.84	.83	.80	.87	.81	.88	.90	.84	.86	.86	.88	0.85
3	.89	.83	.81	.81	.88	.86	.84	.94	1.01	1.04	1.04	1.06	0.93
4	1.10	1.07	1.09	1.09	1.11	1.20	1.23	1.25	1.25	1.20	1.29	1.28	1.19
5	1.33	1.34	1.35	1.34	1.29	1.31	1.37	1.34	1.36	1.37	1.34	1.34	1.30
6	1.28	1.25	1.09	1.23	1.24	1.22	1.20	1.26	1.23	1.25	1.13	1.04	1.23
7	.88	.89	.86	.92	.90	.88	.94	.84	.93	.89	.99	.96	0.93
8	.98	.86	.96	.97	1.00	1.03	1.06	1.13	1.16	1.23	1.28	1.20	1.10
9	1.30	1.20	1.24	1.20	1.26	1.19	1.15	1.10	1.06	1.04	1.03	1.04	1.14
10	1.07	1.10	1.18	1.15	1.20	1.22	1.23	1.23	1.24	1.23	1.24	1.25	1.19
11	1.17	1.08	1.03	.99	.88	.83	.83	.81	.70	.73	.70	.71	0.88
12	.71	.70	.75	.77	.68	.48	.66	.61	.63	.53	.61	.61	0.64
13	.64	.91	.74	.73	.73	.72	.68	.65	.63	.66	.67	.67	0.72
14	.67	.62	.80	.79	.79	.74	.73	.75	.60	.61	.60	.61	0.73
15	.61	.50	.50	.74	.74	.61	.60	.53	.50	.43	.40	.38	0.51
16	.30	.30	.27	.34	.24	.16	.10	.10	.04	.03	.09	.16	0.16
17	.38	.56	.60	.43	.44	.47	.50	.58	.60	.66	.64	.73	0.51
18	.75	.90	.87	.93	1.10	1.04	1.06	1.16	1.27	1.24	1.26	1.28	1.05
19	1.30	1.23	1.10	1.10	1.17	1.10	1.14	1.17	1.20	1.20	1.19	1.17	1.16
20	1.18	1.10	1.36	1.13	1.17	1.17	1.19	1.19	1.14	1.16	1.10	1.06	1.18
21	1.05	1.04	.84	.84	1.00	1.00	1.00	1.01	1.08	.67	.76	.69	0.88
22	.50	.50	.61	.48	.47	.50	.47	.48	.44	.40	.40	.53	0.47
23	.54	.50	.50	.70	.58	.67	.91	.84	.80	.07	.97	.97	0.83
24	.97	.91	.80	.80	.86	.90	.80	1.00	1.06	1.13	1.10	1.05	0.99
25	1.06	.63	.56	.65	.60	.97	.20	.17	.13	.13	.14	.16	0.43
26	.10	.18	.10	.12	.12	.30	.30	.13	.33	.23	.33	.37	0.18
27	.40	.30	.30	.34	.30	.30	.44	.67	.51	.35	.50	.60	0.41
28	.60	.61	.63	.63	.70	.70	.73	.73	.75	.76	.80	.76	0.70
29	.83	.76	.80	.86	1.01	1.04	1.10	1.10	1.10	1.24	1.33	1.33	1.05
30	1.33	1.33	1.34	1.36	1.30	1.33	1.33	1.36	1.39	1.40	1.40	1.41	1.33
Mean	0.887	0.883	0.880	0.885	0.889	0.881	0.846	0.875	0.888	0.880	0.893	0.897	29.885

December, 1857. 29 inches +. Mean Lat. 74°.5 N., Long. 61°.4 W.

Day.	2h.	4h.	6h.	8h.	10h.	Noon.	2h.	4h.	6h.	8h.	10h.	Midn't.	Mean.
1	1.41	1.39	1.39	1.39	1.40	1.36	1.38	1.39	1.38	1.32	1.31	1.32	1.36
2	1.20	1.23	1.18	1.15	1.16	1.13	1.11	1.10	1.07	1.07	1.04	1.09	1.13
3	1.06	.86	.83	.80	.86	.90	.83	.85	.80	.77	.75	.73	0.85
4	.73	.70	.70	.60	.56	.56	.67	.56	.70	.60	.67	.64	0.60
5	.53	.60	.53	.54	.53	.47	.43	.42	.41	.38	.30	.39	0.40
6	.38	.30	.33	.31	.33	.38	.34	.35	.41	.44	.40	.58	0.34
7	.59	.63	.57	.74	.83	.86	.90	.93	.94	1.70	1.03	1.06	0.88
8	1.04	1.03	1.03	1.03	1.10	1.08	1.10	1.13	1.16	1.20	1.34	1.29	1.11
9	1.33	1.19	1.23	1.24	1.30	1.30	1.35	1.30	1.30	1.30	1.39	1.35	1.27
10	1.37	1.33	1.33	1.31	1.35	1.34	1.32	1.30	1.29	1.31	1.31	1.32	1.37
11	1.36	1.39	1.33	1.33	1.30	1.30	1.35	1.37	1.34	1.31	1.36	1.19	1.33
12	1.06	.84	.75	.64	.64	.61	.60	.55	.55	.52	.45	.44	0.66
13	.64	.52	.37	.33	.33	.33	.30	.33	.34	.38	.33	.43	0.53
14	.44	.68	.48	.49	.93	.59	.60	.62	.65	.60	.66	.97	0.57
15	.60	.60	.64	.60	.70	.73	.74	.79	.74	.77	.75	.76	0.73
16	.75	.74	.74	.76	.79	.74	.79	.78	.79	.75	.77	.75	0.74
17	.77	.76	.77	.74	.70	.76	.80	.83	.83	.84	.84	.84	0.80
18	.74	.84	.83	.65	.84	.80	.86	.84	.85	.85	.86	.73	0.84
19	.83	.80	.75	.80	.85	.80	1.00	1.06	1.04	1.03	.80	.90	0.93
20	.90	.90	.76	.77	.74	.73	.75	.79	.76	.78	.76	.74	0.77
21	.80	.80	.67	.70	.80	.83	.83	.80	.73	.83	.86	1.01	0.83
22	1.00	1.00	.90	1.06	1.76	1.04	1.03	1.04	1.01	.95	.90	.90	1.01
23	.93	.91	.84	.87	.60	.50	.80	.83	.84	.97	.99	1.01	0.93
24	1.06	1.03	1.03	1.06	1.12	1.20	1.10	1.13	1.11	1.10	1.06	1.03	1.07
25	.83	.80	.80	.79	.75	.73	.73	.70	.71	.70	.70	.60	0.78
26	.65	.56	.11	.04	.54	.54	.56	.54	.66	.51	.49	.43	0.37
27	.30	.30	.34	.30	.15	.19	.15	.13	.03	.00	.00	.95	0.17
28	.10	.30	.00	.04	.00	.04	.03	.00	.00	*.96	*.98	*.96	0.03
29	*.80	*.84	*.86	*.92	.03	.00	.15	.33	.31	.30	.43	.48	0.16
30	.91	.83	.34	.55	.63	.80	.73	.74	.70	.79	.47	.83	0.60
31	.83	.83	.45	.57	.63	.84	.87	.50	.80	.90	.63	.90	0.63
Mean	0.760	0.760	0.760	0.763	0.760	0.775	0.779	0.791	0.780	0.780	0.764	0.796	29.777

* Refers to 28 inches.

Readings of Aneroid Barometer 1761 on board the Yacht Fox.

January, 1858. 29 Inches +. Mean Lat. 73°.2 N., Long. 63°.7 W.

Day.	2h	4h	6h	8h	10h	Noon.	2h	4h	6h	8h	10h	Midn't.	Mean.
1	.64	.67	.79	.84	.89	.92	.78	.73	.73	.73	.64	.80	0.76
2	.64	.63	.60	.60	.16	.34	.64	.63	.34	.51	.43	.11	0.43
3	.35	.28	.39	.12	.18	.01	*.96	*.93	*.82	*.69	*.91	*.83	0.06
4	*.93	*.92	*.92	*.94	*.93	*.90	*.98	.08	.04	.11	.13	.20	0.01
5	.23	.24	.24	.23	.21	.32	.20	.20	.23	.24	.26	.23	0.23
6	.19	.15	.14	.11	.13	.18	.13	.16	.12	.12	.10	.09	0.13
7	.09	.07	.07	.09	.14	.17	.19	.23	.24	.29	.30	.31	0.17
8	.31	.23	.27	.28	.28	.26	.28	.27	.24	.28	.28	.34	0.28
9	.28	.31	.31	.33	.35	.33	.30	.31	.33	.39	.37	.37	0.33
10	.33	.38	.38	.40	.43	.46	.61	.64	.58	.49	.43	.54	0.48
11	.57	.59	.67	.67	.71	.73	.75	.80	.82	.83	.83	.85	0.73
12	.74	.86	.81	.90	.86	.74	.76	.85	.84	.83	.91	.77	0.82
13	.73	.71	.97	.98	.73	.80	.80	.99	1.10	1.22	1.33	1.41	0.98
14	1.40	1.35	1.36	1.53	1.69	1.45	1.63	1.37	1.40	1.36	1.33	1.28	1.43
15	1.10	1.13	1.06	1.05	1.09	1.01	1.00	.99	1.00	.94	.90	.96	1.03
16	.93	.90	.83	.83	.81	.79	.74	.77	.80	.63	.64	.66	0.73
17	.94	.90	.99	.90	.91	.81	.90	.80	.89	1.04	1.13	1.21	0.97
18	1.22	1.23	1.35	1.25	1.24	1.30	1.35	1.25	1.34	1.23	1.35	1.30	1.28
19	1.10	1.17	1.16	1.17	1.23	1.36	1.34	1.29	1.29	1.27	1.26	1.31	1.22
20	1.19	1.10	.99	.93	.91	.80	.70	.75	.64	.60	.40	.40	0.80
21	.32	.39	.16	.16	.25	.33	.40	.31	.65	.74	.83	.90	0.45
22	.97	.84	.84	.97	1.02	1.08	.96	.93	.98	.76	.67	.56	0.86
23	.47	.60	.43	.81	.64	.72	.80	.50	.92	.94	.91	.90	0.71
24	.24	.10	.76	.67	.67	.61	.65	.46	.35	.34	.35	.35	0.53
25	.24	.34	.23	.20	.23	.19	.15	.14	.11	.10	.05	.06	0.19
26	.06	.05	.34	.17	.24	.26	.31	.32	.32	.34	.30	.36	0.23
27	.33	.23	.34	.26	.86	.64	.50	.60	.95	.76	.92	.85	0.50
28	.93	.95	.96	1.03	1.00	1.10	1.12	1.14	1.17	1.19	1.21	1.22	1.09
29	1.38	1.20	1.30	1.38	1.45	1.60	1.53	1.59	1.60	1.70	1.73	1.60	1.51
30	1.83	1.44	1.70	1.94	2.01	2.14	2.10	2.14	2.14	2.14	2.14	2.14	2.03
31	2.06	2.05	1.86	1.81	1.96	1.92	1.70	1.62	1.50	1.40	1.33	1.27	1.71
Mean	0.725	0.713	0.707	0.704	0.739	0.745	0.71.	0.756	0.764	0.763	0.750	0.753	29.730

February, 1858. 29 Inches +. Mean Lat. 71°.5 N., Long. 60°.9 W.

Day.	2h	4h	6h	8h	10h	Noon.	2h	4h	6h	8h	10h	Midn't.	Mean.
1	1.22	1.17	1.16	1.14	1.15	1.19	1.15	1.15	1.12	1.09	1.07	1.00	1.14
2	.92	.80	.66	.96	.86	.84	.81	.81	.81	.80	.61	.60	0.76
3	.75	.76	.75	.78	.75	.72	.76	.75	.73	.72	.70	.70	0.73
4	.64	.64	.64	.68	.69	.69	.66	.71	.73	.75	.79	.60	0.70
5	.80	.79	.74	.76	.78	.79	.76	.74	.72	.70	.69	.66	0.76
6	.55	.63	.61	.49	.49	.41	.47	.47	.47	.46	.40	.51	0.48
7	.51	.63	.66	.69	.84	.85	.73	.78	.91	.93	.94	.99	0.70
8	.95	.96	.91	.93	1.00	1.05	1.06	1.08	1.11	1.11	1.11	1.12	1.03
9	1.17	1.08	1.03	1.02	1.03	1.03	.97	.93	.86	.76	.73	.68	0.94
10	.58	.53	.44	.46	.45	.43	.46	.45	.46	.56	.56	.66	0.49
11	.65	.74	.74	.92	1.10	1.12	1.20	1.23	1.22	1.30	1.09	.94	1.02
12	.95	.90	.90	1.06	1.15	1.22	1.36	1.29	1.35	1.40	1.34	1.34	1.19
13	1.34	1.34	1.41	1.40	1.45	1.48	1.50	1.53	1.50	1.48	1.47	1.44	1.44
14	1.37	1.31	1.38	1.30	1.31	1.29	1.30	1.30	1.39	1.32	1.29	1.26	1.31
15	1.23	1.23	1.21	1.20	1.20	1.20	1.20	1.16	1.14	1.14	1.12	1.06	1.17
16	1.04	1.00	.96	.98	.90	.91	.86	.86	.86	.94	.83	.83	0.91
17	.42	.80	.84	.85	.84	.84	.84	.85	.88	.80	.84	.80	0.76
18	.79	.74	.73	.79	.76	.73	.69	.62	.55	.53	.44	.35	0.63
19	.33	.32	.33	.33	.37	.26	.34	.47	.56	.44	.70	.73	0.43
20	.59	.53	.43	.48	.56	.55	.61	.64	.68	.40	.40	.63	0.55
21	.83	.54	.83	.45	.73	.77	.73	.76	.80	.94	.90	.99	0.75
22	1.02	1.02	1.05	1.09	1.10	1.10	1.06	1.06	1.10	.90	.90	.96	1.02
23	.78	.75	.73	.74	.75	.76	.77	.75	.80	.91	.80	.80	0.77
24	.76	.70	.73	.66	.60	.64	.63	.63	.62	.59	.69	.40	0.65
25	.40	.42	.43	.44	.53	.59	.54	.57	.88	.64	.64	.64	0.57
26	.66	.60	.70	.72	.90	.74	.80	.91	.94	.96	1.01	1.02	0.84
27	1.01	1.01	1.03	1.05	1.10	1.16	1.10	1.11	1.10	1.13	1.16	1.17	1.09
28	1.10	1.06	1.07	1.11	1.19	1.16	1.16	1.16	1.19	1.18	1.10	1.10	1.14
Mean	0.863	0.859	0.837	0.833	0.866	0.871	0.874	0.899	0.899	0.866	0.877	0.861	29.862

* Refers to 28 inches.

Readings of Aneroid Barometer 1716 on board the Yacht Fox.

March, 1858. 29 Inches +. Mean Lat. 68°.4 N., Long. 57°.1 W.

Day.	2h.	4h.	6h.	8h.	10h.	Noon.	2h.	4h.	6h.	8h.	10h.	Midn't.	Mean.
1	1.04	1.16	.99	.94	.95	.91	.81	.81	.89	.85	.88	.94	0.93
2	1.10	1.13	1.16	1.44	1.17	1.40	.96	.91	.94	.87	1.04	2.11	1.12
3	1.22	1.22	1.16	1.40	1.46	1.48	1.30	1.32	1.69	.68	.80	.89	1.14
4	.61	.46	.54	.63	.65	.97	1.12	1.30	1.40	1.48	1.29	1.34	1.02
5	1.34	1.31	1.02	1.40	1.70	1.74	1.31	1.71	1.40	1.40	1.74	2.04	1.55
6	1.46	1.40	1.44	1.10	1.76	1.79	1.44	1.60	1.44	1.50	1.46	1.19	1.41
7	1.09	1.26	1.13	1.14	1.36	1.40	1.41	1.50	1.53	1.76	1.74	1.07	1.37
8	1.03	1.16	1.30	1.10	1.14	1.53	1.37	1.30	1.52	1.56	1.42	1.28	1.17
9	1.31	1.30	1.45	1.06	1.40	1.40	1.30	1.36	1.28	1.50	1.48	1.04	1.26
10	.10	.76	.80	.90	.42	.72	.80	.91	.29	.20	.03	*.57	0.51
11	*.02	*.81	*.86	*.90	*.71	*.94	*.80	*.28	*.04	*.92	.40	.10	*0.12
12	.02	.15	.04	.06	.13	.11	.16	.30	.31	.44	.40	.34	0.23
13	.48	.36	.39	.51	.34	.54	.44	.53	.46	.36	.51	.46	0.53
14	.06	.27	.68	.60	.30	.56	.70	.79	.40	.65	.56	.08	0.71
15	.06	.94	.69	.49	.65	.82	.36	.98	1.03	1.09	1.04	1.19	0.92
16	1.10	1.18	1.26	1.16	1.30	1.26	1.31	1.23	1.32	1.30	1.30	1.25	1.18
17	1.20	1.35	1.22	1.14	1.24	1.26	1.24	1.16	1.29	1.16	1.20	1.17	1.23
18	1.24	1.46	1.16	1.03	1.03	.96	.92	.90	.86	.80	.64	.48	0.97
19	.00	.76	.79	.77	.60	.60	.67	.37	.44	.61	.51	.39	0.56
20	.56	.40	.58	.58	.36	.66	.51	.42	.79	.36	.20	.71	0.13
21	.58	.46	.46	.70	.74	.22	.33	.20	.54	.06	.61	.32	0.06
22	.56	.56	.56	.50	.50	.34	.51	.08	.84	.84	.51	.68	0.53
23	.86	.42	.80	.49	.20	.86	.96	1.30	1.14	1.34	1.30	1.36	0.99
24	1.40	1.31	1.44	1.44	1.36	1.35	1.38	1.31	1.34	1.36	1.50	1.68	1.41
25	1.38	1.40	1.43	1.42	1.46	1.48	1.44	1.63	1.42	1.47	1.30	1.54	1.40
26	1.55	1.56	1.54	1.56	1.40	1.65	1.40	1.40	1.44	1.54	1.66	1.60	1.57
27	1.64	1.63	1.90	1.66	1.34	1.43	1.57	1.90	1.80	1.85	1.64	1.44	1.61
28	1.69	1.52	1.62	1.58	1.58	1.34	1.49	1.43	1.43	1.48	1.46	1.47	1.50
29	1.62	1.46	1.46	1.41	1.46	1.42	1.40	1.34	1.51	1.50	1.36	1.36	1.44
30	1.60	1.44	1.36	1.27	1.10	1.31	1.29	1.28	1.36	1.25	1.30	1.28	1.31
31	1.27	1.34	1.24	1.34	1.36	1.44	1.35	1.16	1.19	1.20	1.20	1.34	1.32
Mean	1.090	1.052	1.072	1.049	1.120	1.108	1.149	1.134	1.119	1.144	1.134	1.101	29.103

April, 1858. 29 Inches +. Mean Lat. 68°.6 N., Long. 57°.2 W.

Day.	2h.	4h.	6h.	8h.	10h.	Noon.	2h.	4h.	6h.	8h.	10h.	Midn't.	Mean.
1	1.30	1.26	1.15	1.22	1.22	1.21	1.25	1.28	1.28	1.20	1.32	1.22	1.23
2	1.15	1.12	1.12	1.19	1.10	1.16	1.06	1.05	1.07	1.07	1.06	1.03	1.09
3	1.03	.90	.86	.90	.86	.94	.84	.92	.91	.92	.92	.92	0.91
4	.80	.80	.82	.84	.84	.82	.81	.81	.88	.86	.86	.84	0.84
5	.71	.70	.73	.70	.72	.71	.76	.73	.79	.62	.64	.63	0.70
6	.82	.96	.97	1.00	1.10	1.20	1.30	1.30	1.39	1.13	1.33	1.33	1.11
7	1.32	1.25	1.36	1.20	1.35	1.36	1.36	1.30	1.52	1.66	1.54	1.66	1.37
8	1.14	1.14	1.11	1.40	1.66	1.36	1.52	1.41	1.54	1.64	1.72	1.74	1.56
9	1.74	1.77	1.76	1.74	1.73	1.70	2.02	1.64	1.68	1.62	1.62	1.61	1.69
10	1.86	1.62	1.69	1.28	1.94	1.84	2.04	1.83	1.90	2.00	1.77	1.58	1.76
11	1.60	1.64	1.92	1.58	1.80	1.55	2.24	1.52	1.62	1.82	1.54	1.50	1.16
12	1.62	1.16	1.72	1.79	1.68	1.60	2.47	1.64	2.43	1.56	1.40	1.44	1.61
13	1.74	1.22	1.52	1.47	1.03	1.54	2.32	1.40	2.44	1.42	1.36	1.38	1.35
14	1.30	1.32	1.29	1.10	1.20	1.12	1.83	1.10	2.06	1.01	1.10	1.07	1.25
15	1.01	.07	.63	.93	.06	.64	.00	.44	.54	.84	.63	.85	0.9
16	.00	.00	.06	.64	.00	.82	.00	.00	.52	.64	.35	.50	0.81
17	.10	.52	.16	.77	.78	.75	.60	.74	.72	.71	.54	.48	0.74
18	(.06)	.88	(.60)	.64	(.63)	.72	(.79)	.70	(.74)	.74	(.30)	.77	0.71
19	(.72)	.85	(.72)	.74	(.60)	.62	(.64)	.70	(.59)	.62	(.52)	.62	0.64
20	(.52)	.61	(.53)	.40	(.53)	.60	(.06)	.34	(.31)	.64	(.31)	.94	0.56
21	(.06)	.00	(.55)	.52	(.56)	.62	(.61)	.56	(.53)	.84	(.06)	.83	0.83
22	(.96)	.10	(1.05)	1.30	(1.12)	1.15	(1.17)	1.30	(1.22)	1.25	(1.36)	1.23	1.24
23	(1.22)	1.30	(1.20)	1.26	(1.19)	1.10	(1.13)	1.10	(1.10)	1.12	(1.00)	1.00	1.13
24	(1.00)	.87	(.85)	.86	(.80)	.77	(.74)	(.71)	(.64)	(.60)	(.62)	(.63)	0.77
25	(.60)	.53	(.53)	.56	(.60)	.64	(.60)	.43	(.53)	.63	(.84)	.93	0.58
26	(.86)	.76	(1.00)	1.20	(1.11)	1.16	(1.22)	1.26	(1.35)	1.44	(1.32)	1.44	1.21
27	(1.40)	1.40	(1.20)	1.14	(1.55)	1.40	(1.58)	1.54	(1.59)	1.61	(1.40)	1.61	1.36
28	(1.52)	1.63	(1.12)	1.40	(1.44)	1.64	(1.62)	1.64	(1.65)	1.66	(1.56)	1.61	1.63
29	(1.46)	1.60	(1.40)	1.46	(1.19)	1.15	(1.45)	1.30	(1.35)	1.23	(1.31)	1.04	1.47
30	(1.20)	1.27	(1.05)	.96	(.94)	.96	(.94)	.93	(.94)	.96	(.83)	.98	1.10
Mean	1.140	1.138	1.132	1.140	1.153	1.141	1.143	1.144	1.134	1.149	1.138	1.148	29.153

* Refers to 28 inches.

Readings of Aneroid Barometer 1778 on board the Yacht Fox.

May, 1858. 29 inches +. Mean Lat. [illegible]°.7 N., Long. [illegible]°.7 W.

Day.	4h.	8h.	Noon.	4h.	8h.	Midn't.	Mean.
1	.92	.80	.89	1.04	1.16	1.20	1.03
2	1.16	(1.09)	.96	.78	.73	.74	0.91
3	.77	.98	.86	1.06	1.00	1.10	0.97
4	1.05	1.04	1.02	.99	.96	.94	1.00
5	.94	.85	.87	.88	1.07	1.11	0.95
6	1.11	1.14	1.09	1.11	1.16	1.18	1.10
7	1.12	1.16	1.24	1.21	1.23	1.21	1.19
8	1.19	1.17	1.23	1.24	1.25	1.22	1.21
9	1.16	1.19	1.10	1.14	1.06	1.08	1.13
10	1.10	1.04	1.11	1.13	1.15	1.16	1.12
11	1.14	1.17	1.20	1.19	1.19	1.14	1.16
12	1.13	1.19	1.36	1.36	1.40	1.49	1.33
13	1.55	1.58	1.60	1.66	1.65	1.60	1.59
14	1.44	1.62	1.70	1.66	1.66	1.68	1.67
15	1.65	1.74	1.74	1.78	1.70	1.83	1.70
16	1.58	1.56	1.51	1.50	1.50	1.44	1.54
17	1.46	1.48	1.43	1.40	1.37	1.34	1.42
18	1.34	1.40	1.38	1.35	1.34	1.30	1.35
19	1.30	1.31	1.33	1.26	1.22	1.19	1.28
20	(1.15)	(1.14)	(1.13)	(1.12)	(1.11)	(1.10)	1.18
21	1.10	1.10	1.16	1.18	1.18	1.17	1.14
22	1.16	1.24	1.29	1.26	1.23	1.11	1.22
23	1.10	1.16	1.19	1.18	1.14	1.16	1.17
24	1.20	1.22	1.30	1.25	1.23	1.17	1.24
25	1.16	1.13	1.10	1.05	1.15	1.14	1.15
26	1.24	1.31	1.34	1.66	1.40	1.36	1.34
27	1.43	1.45	1.42	1.44	1.34	1.32	1.40
28	1.30	1.35	1.30	1.10	1.09	1.00	1.10
29	.98	.98	1.00	1.00	1.00	1.01	0.98
30	1.04	1.07	1.10	1.13	1.14	1.19	1.11
31	1.13	1.19	1.20	1.19	1.14	1.18	1.16
Mean	1.194	1.223	1.229	1.225	1.230	1.222	30.223

June, 1858. 29 inches +. Mean Lat. 74°.8 N., Long. 60°.1 W.

Day.	4h.	8h.	Noon.	4h.	8h.	Midn't.	Mean.
1	1.09	1.10	1.09	1.05	1.08	1.05	1.07
2	.99	.83	.89	.93	.96	.88	0.89
3	.86	1.15	1.20	1.16	1.16	1.13	1.13
4	1.00	.94	.93	.93	1.03	1.16	0.99
5	1.25	1.24	1.30	1.33	1.34	1.29	1.29
6	1.21	1.25	1.28	1.25	1.25	1.25	1.25
7	1.24	1.31	1.34	1.29	1.25	1.26	1.29
8	1.25	1.29	1.34	1.30	1.18	1.14	1.25
9	1.12	1.10	1.00	1.06	1.00	.96	1.05
10	.94	.89	.90	.92	.96	.90	0.92
11	.97	.98	1.02	1.00	1.00	1.05	1.00
12	1.10	1.13	1.10	1.20	1.24	1.25	1.16
13	1.25	1.01	1.10	1.16	1.15	1.18	1.10
14	1.18	1.17	1.22	1.24	1.26	1.20	1.20
15	1.16	1.22	1.19	1.16	1.25	1.23	1.21
16	1.19	1.10	1.12	1.04	1.00	.90	1.07
17	.90	.84	.90	.90	1.00	1.04	0.97
18	.88	.90	1.01	.90	.87	.97	0.88
19	.84	.91	.81	.84	.97	.88	0.86
20	.84	.84	.81	.97	.88	.93	0.83
21	.85	.70	.83	.88	.81	.93	0.83
22	.91	.84	1.01	1.06	1.11	1.10	1.02
23	1.10	1.10	1.18	1.19	1.10	1.10	1.13
24	1.08	1.06	1.08	1.07	1.03	.86	1.03
25	.86	.89	.87	.88	.86	.73	0.80
26	.75	.74	.74	.65	.64	.50	0.70
27	.69	.43	.42	.53	.45	.57	0.51
28	.99	.68	.74	.79	.61	.84	0.73
29	.88	.61	1.00	1.08	1.20	1.14	1.02
30	1.30	1.20	1.20	1.20	1.21	1.18	1.22
Mean	29.996	30.014	30.030	30.032	30.030	30.025	30.015

READINGS OF ANEROID BAROMETER 1779(?) ON BOARD THE YACHT FOX.

July, 1858. 29 Inches +. Mean Lat. 74°.4 N., Long. 76°.6 W.

Day.	4h.	8h.	Noon.	4h.	8h.	Midn't.	Mean.
1	1.19	1.17	1.08	1.24	1.22	1.10	1.16
2	1.13	1.09	1.10	1.18	1.24	1.10	1.10
3	1.07	1.10	1.09	1.06	1.07	1.07	1.07
4	1.05	1.11	1.16	1.33	1.18	1.18	1.19
5	1.04	1.05	.94	.88	.66	.79	0.93
6	.73	.91	.86	.90	.80	.81	0.84
7	.74	.74	.84	.93	.80	.80	0.83
8	.78	.77	.76	.77	.77	.74	0.73
9	.74	.74	.70	.64	.69	.64	0.78
10	.64	.62	.68	.70	.71	.67	0.64
11	.70	.80	.69	.70	.73	.70	0.70
12	.69	.70	.68	.71	.76	.63	0.70
13	.65	.67	.56	.83	.80	.82	0.80
14	.66	.63	.56	.90	.73	.73	0.68
15	.79	.74	.73	.94	.68	.86	0.76
16	.80	.41	.84	.62	.78	.74	0.67
17	.79	.79	.84	.80	.90	1.73	0.85
18	1.26	1.23	1.24	1.24	1.27	1.29	1.23
19	1.30	1.30	1.30	1.40	1.44	1.42	1.39
20	1.42	1.44	1.44	1.42	1.46	1.46	1.44
21	1.46	1.50	1.49	1.46	1.46	1.44	1.47
22	1.44	1.47	1.40	1.40	1.45	1.42	1.40
23	1.40	1.37	1.30	1.30	1.20	1.16	1.32
24	1.14	1.20	1.12	1.10	1.06	1.03	1.10
25	.88	.87	.89	.98	.83	.90	0.88
26	.88	.96	.94	.94	.94	.91	0.92
27	.80	.80	.97	.81	.80	.89	0.80
28	.98	.84	.84	.94	.96	.88	0.88
29	.80	.83	.92	.91	.90	.80	0.92
30	.80	.80	.83	.79	.79	.79	0.83
31	.80	.81	.83	.80	.86	.84	0.84
Mean	29.943	29.961	29.965	29.971	29.974	29.960	29.961

August, 1858. 29 Inches +. Mean Lat. 73°.1 N., Long. 66°.5 W.

Day.	4h.	8h.	Noon.	4h.	8h.	Midn't.	Mean.
1	.80	.84	.89	.94	1.00	1.00	0.90
2	1.07	1.11	1.13	1.15	1.17	1.19	1.14
3	1.18	1.15	1.18	1.15	1.16	1.12	1.16
4	1.14	1.14	1.16	1.16	1.16	1.15	1.15
5	1.20	1.23	1.24	1.26	1.27	1.30	1.25
6	1.29	1.24	1.24	1.24	1.23	1.20	1.24
7	1.13	1.13	1.02	.96	.79	.72	0.95
8	.84	.84	.85	.69	.69	.62	0.56
9	.80	.62	.71	.72	.78	.80	0.72
10	.83	.42	.66	.90	.80	.80	0.67
11	.83	.73	.88	.95	.75	.99	0.87
12	.88	.93	.87	.87	.69	.83	0.87
13	.87	.93	.84	.83	.74	.76	0.83
14	.72	.70	.70	.72	.72	.74	0.72
15	.74	.74	.80	.88	.88	.88	0.87
16	.88	.96	1.10	1.10	.94	.78	0.98
17	.74	.89	.83	.89	1.04	1.04	0.90
18	.84	.88	.88	.88	.84	.84	0.89
19	.88	.91	.98	.94	1.20	.93	0.97
20	1.01	1.10	1.08	1.14	1.10	1.30	1.10
21	1.16	1.29	1.20	1.20	1.23	1.19	1.16
22	1.05	.96	.99	.97	.90	.66	0.92
23	.87	.88	.86	.98	.80	.87	0.83
24	.80	.66	.86	.80	.66	.64	0.69
25	.68	.69	.76	.61	.51	.76	0.73
26	.70	.84	.91	.80	.83	.86	0.67
27	.70	.70	.84	.94	.98	.73	0.96
28	.90	1.03	0.98	1.11	1.08	1.04	1.09
29	.98	.98	.90	1.06	1.03	1.06	1.00
30	1.07	1.15	1.15	1.14	1.14	1.20	1.12
31	1.19	1.19	1.13	1.14	1.36	1.16	1.16
Mean	29.917	29.921	29.941	29.943	29.949	29.947	29.944

Readings of Aneroid Barometer [illegible] on board the Yacht Fox.

September, 1858. 29 Inches +. Mean Lat. [illegible] N., Long. [illegible] W.

Day.	4h	8h	Noon.	4h	8h	Midn't.	Mean.
1	1.13	1.13	1.19	1.25	1.24	1.28	1.20
2	1.34	1.25	1.35	1.38	1.35	1.31	1.27
3	1.26	1.30	1.30	1.30	1.34	1.30	1.30
4	1.30	1.28	1.32	1.31	1.30	1.21	1.29
5	1.21	1.20	1.23	1.14	1.18	1.14	1.22
6	1.20	1.10	1.12	(1.18)	(1.00)	(0.96)	1.07
7	.95	.94	.92	.86	.93	.90	[illegible]
8	.80	.90	.96	.97	.96	.98	0.94
9	.97	1.03	1.10	1.16	1.11	1.18	1.09
10	1.19	1.30	1.30	1.28	1.34	1.23	1.21
11	1.30	1.10	1.30	1.30	1.24	1.34	1.31
12	1.16	1.13	1.11	1.17	1.17	1.16	1.16
13	1.13	1.13	1.18	1.17	1.16	1.32	1.16
14	1.30	1.26	1.26	1.20	1.23	1.23	1.24
15	1.30	1.25	1.29	1.29	1.34	1.37	1.30
16	1.27	1.31	1.31	1.30	1.13	1.30	1.31
17	1.35	1.30	1.21	1.30	1.25	1.19	1.24
18	1.14	1.16	1.12	1.10	1.30	1.13	1.15
19	1.10	1.14	1.18	1.30	1.10	1.19	1.16
20	1.00	1.08	1.08	.60	.96	.90	0.94
21	.72	.72	.74	.72	.78	.86	0.75
22	.90	1.00	1.74	1.03	.90	.76	0.93
23	.53	.33	.31	.26	.46	.40	0.44
24	.75	.90	.94	.90	.90	.90	0.91
25	.90	1.03	1.03	1.00	1.00	1.00	1.03
26	1.10	1.20	1.12	1.24	1.24	1.26	1.16
27	1.30	1.20	1.31	1.31	1.30	1.30	1.27
28	1.16	1.20	1.10	1.04	1.11	1.12	1.18
29	1.10	1.30	1.30	1.21	1.30	1.18	1.19
30	1.13	1.19	1.06	1.04	1.03	.90	1.06
Mean	30.094	30.105	30.110	30.110	30.127	30.107	30.104

October, 1858. 29 Inches +. Mean Lat. [illegible] N., Long. [illegible] W.

Day.	4h	8h	Noon.	4h	8h	Midn't.	Mean.
1	.88	.16	.56	.65	.80	.70	0.73
2	.64	.62	.73	.73	.73	.80	0.72
3	.64	.72	.71	.60	.80	.70	0.74
4	.91	.66	.93	.91	.96	1.01	0.93
5	1.10	1.23	1.30	1.35	1.43	1.44	1.31
6	1.44	1.56	1.60	1.63	1.68	1.64	1.56
7	1.66	1.64	1.70	.60	1.63	1.53	1.66
8	1.45	1.43	1.48	1.46	1.50	1.46	1.47
9	1.44	1.44	1.40	1.36	1.37	1.33	1.39
10	1.30	1.16	1.11	.74	.63	.46	[illegible]
11	.43	.45	.44	.41	.44	.47	0.43
12	.43	.50	.55	.57	.73	.75	0.60
13	.74	.76	.85	.86	.88	.86	0.84
14	.88	.97	1.04	1.09	1.16	1.25	1.04
15	1.19	1.34	1.25	1.11	1.10	.90	1.13
16	.83	.78	.73	.66	.66	.81	0.70
17	.56	.62	.60	.70	.73	.72	0.67
18	.53	.90	.90	.90	.93	.94	0.83
19	.78	.76	.70	.47	.60	.46	0.67
20	.39	.44	.46	.53	.66	.10	0.60
21	.80	.72	.81	.88	1.16	1.16	0.87
22	1.31	1.30	1.33	1.31	1.34	1.36	1.30
23	1.30	1.28	1.33	1.20	1.23	1.14	1.24
24	1.09	1.08	.18	.80	.78	.74	0.67
25	.72	.80	.96	1.24	1.14	1.24	0.96
26	1.24	1.33	1.60	1.36	1.37	1.36	1.36
27	1.34	1.48	1.45	1.40	1.43	1.34	1.42
28	1.26	1.36	1.21	1.16	1.23	1.18	1.21
29	1.10	1.10	1.04	1.04	1.03	1.00	1.06
30	.90	.90	.93	.90	.90	1.04	0.97
31	1.07	1.10	1.20	1.20	1.10	1.12	1.10
Mean	29.967	30.007	30.036	29.950	30.031	30.010	30.007

READINGS OF ANEROID BAROMETER 1701 ON BOARD THE YACHT FOX.

November, 1858. 29 inches +. Mean Lat. 72°.0 N., Long. 94°.8 W.

Day.	2h.	4h.	6h.	8h.	10h.	Noon.	2h.	4h.	6h.	8h.	10h.	Midn't.	Mean.
1	1.10	1.05	1.10	1.11	1.16	1.04	1.03	1.02	.99	.97	.94	.94	1.04
2	.94	.94	.95	.97	.98	1.00	1.05	1.14	1.10	1.14	1.16	1.20	1.03
3	1.34	1.26	1.24	1.26	1.34	1.24	1.34	1.34	1.40	1.40	1.34	1.30	1.32
4	1.22	1.23	1.12	1.14	1.16	1.16	1.18	1.22	1.24	1.29	1.20	1.24	1.18
5	1.13	1.16	1.14	1.15	1.23	1.23	1.16	1.16	1.16	1.18	1.18	1.18	1.17
6	1.13	1.16	1.25	1.24	1.26	1.28	1.28	1.34	1.32	1.36	1.34	1.30	1.27
7	1.34	1.37	1.33	1.34	1.37	1.36	1.42	1.40	1.46	1.48	1.50	1.50	1.40
8	1.44	1.44	1.46	1.50	1.50	1.44	1.48	1.50	1.52	1.52	1.52	1.52	1.50
9	1.58	1.48	1.48	1.60	1.50	1.54	1.56	1.60	1.60	1.62	1.60	1.60	1.58
10	1.63	1.63	1.66	1.63	1.64	1.66	1.64	1.66	1.66	1.66	1.64	1.65	1.64
11	1.67	1.58	1.56	1.54	1.52	1.50	1.44	1.46	1.45	1.46	1.46	1.46	1.50
12	1.46	1.46	1.45	1.43	1.50	1.44	1.49	1.47	1.47	1.46	1.40	1.40	1.46
13	1.44	1.40	1.34	1.42	1.37	1.33	1.32	1.32	1.26	1.16	1.16	1.11	1.31
14	1.09	1.06	1.02	1.07	1.06	1.10	1.09	1.10	1.18	1.26	1.22	1.24	1.12
15	1.36	1.36	1.34	1.33	1.34	1.36	1.36	1.38	1.44	1.44	1.36	1.42	1.37
16	1.56	1.55	1.52	1.47	1.46	1.52	1.50	1.42	1.40	1.44	1.30	1.20	1.47
17	1.29	1.14	1.10	1.16	1.16	1.14	1.22	1.22	1.20	1.20	1.16	1.15	1.16
18	1.10	1.10	1.06	1.08	1.12	1.14	1.13	1.15	1.16	1.16	1.16	1.16	1.12
19	1.17	1.17	1.17	1.20	1.16	1.16	1.16	1.18	1.16	1.16	1.14	1.14	1.17
20	1.08	1.06	1.01	1.03	1.00	1.00	.98	.99	1.00	1.03	1.04	1.06	1.03
21	1.10	1.10	1.09	1.14	1.13	1.14	1.10	1.14	1.14	1.12	1.13	1.11	1.12
22	1.12	1.15	1.16	1.19	1.16	1.22	1.24	1.28	1.29	1.30	1.34	1.34	1.23
23	1.32	1.31	1.30	1.36	1.35	1.39	1.36	1.46	1.46	1.46	1.50	1.50	1.40
24	1.60	1.60	1.63	1.63	1.64	1.63	1.64	1.66	1.60	1.66	1.63	1.64	1.62
25	1.60	1.57	1.58	1.59	1.54	1.63	1.64	1.60	1.58	1.60	1.57	1.54	1.57
26	1.56	1.54	1.56	1.60	1.54	1.36	1.54	1.52	1.52	1.44	1.40	1.40	1.52
27	1.33	1.28	1.24	1.26	1.20	1.10	1.05	1.06	1.03	1.02	.94	.91	1.12
28	.86	.80	.73	.75	.74	.74	.72	.70	.66	.66	.67	.69	0.73
29	.64	.65	.64	.73	.74	.74	.73	.74	.76	.80	.81	.81	0.74
30	.92	.94	.90	.97	.98	1.00	1.00	1.02	1.00	1.01	.96	1.00	0.96
Mean	1.263	1.231	1.226	1.263	1.273	1.270	1.263	1.260	1.274	1.283	1.270	1.264	30.261

December, 1858. 29 inches +. Mean Lat. 72°.0 N., Long. 94°.8 W.

Day.	2h.	4h.	6h.	8h.	10h.	Noon.	2h.	4h.	6h.	8h.	10h.	Midn't.	Mean.
1	1.03	.96	1.00	0.98	1.04	1.00	1.12	1.16	1.16	1.16	1.20	1.20	1.10
2	1.20	1.16	1.17	1.20	1.20	1.15	1.16	1.10	1.10	1.10	1.04	1.00	1.14
3	.96	.94	.96	1.00	1.03	1.05	1.12	1.02	1.04	1.01	.96	.97	1.00
4	.96	.94	.93	.98	.96	.96	1.00	1.01	1.04	1.08	1.09	1.10	1.00
5	1.10	1.10	1.12	1.12	1.12	1.12	1.12	1.10	1.18	1.14	1.15	1.16	1.14
6	1.16	1.12	1.11	1.16	1.16	1.13	1.13	1.10	1.08	1.05	1.09	.99	1.10
7	.94	.94	.92	.99	1.00	1.01	1.04	1.06	1.16	1.06	1.06	1.03	1.02
8	1.02	1.00	.98	1.00	1.00	1.00	1.00	1.01	1.04	1.05	1.09	1.00	1.03
9	1.09	1.06	1.09	1.12	1.16	1.04	1.04	1.06	1.01	.98	.98	.93	1.04
10	.90	.84	.80	.84	.82	.76	.74	.76	.74	.74	.79	.70	0.79
11	.80	.67	.80	.74	.73	.74	.74	.74	.74	.68	.92	.85	0.76
12	.74	.86	.91	.90	.90	.90	.67	.94	.94	.97	1.09	1.00	0.91
13	1.03	1.04	1.06	1.16	1.20	1.20	1.22	1.26	1.26	1.26	1.22	1.24	1.16
14	1.24	1.23	1.20	1.24	1.25	1.26	1.26	1.20	1.23	1.23	1.24	1.22	1.24
15	1.20	1.20	1.14	1.20	1.22	1.20	1.16	1.16	1.14	1.20	1.20	1.10	1.19
16	1.12	1.10	1.13	1.10	1.18	1.10	1.10	1.12	1.08	1.08	1.08	1.07	1.10
17	1.05	1.04	1.10	1.08	1.08	1.05	1.05	1.06	1.08	1.09	1.09	1.06	1.08
18	1.06	1.06	1.09	1.16	1.14	1.10	1.10	1.12	1.10	1.10	1.09	1.06	1.10
19	1.06	1.04	.99	1.02	1.01	.99	.95	1.00	1.01	1.00	1.00	1.00	1.01
20	.90	.84	.82	.86	.80	.66	.82	.79	.73	.85	.86	.84	0.81
21	.46	.65	.66	.56	.53	.56	.62	.66	.70	.76	.76	.80	0.61
22	.57	.74	.77	.89	.90	1.00	1.02	1.06	1.09	1.06	1.10	1.10	0.79
23	1.04	1.10	1.06	1.12	1.13	1.10	1.09	1.08	1.06	1.08	1.04	1.03	1.08
24	1.03	1.02	1.01	1.02	1.08	1.09	1.09	1.11	1.11	1.12	1.12	1.12	1.09
25	1.12	1.17	1.12	1.14	1.16	1.14	1.16	1.16	1.12	1.13	1.10	1.10	1.13
26	1.08	1.08	1.10	1.09	1.12	1.14	1.15	1.16	1.16	1.16	1.16	1.16	1.13
27	1.20	1.30	1.34	1.30	1.33	1.31	1.36	1.44	1.41	1.40	1.36	1.53	1.37
28	1.54	1.52	1.50	1.70	1.73	1.73	1.73	1.77	1.74	1.70	1.70	1.66	1.66
29	1.64	1.56	1.54	1.56	1.40	1.44	1.46	1.28	1.33	1.32	1.30	1.28	1.44
30	1.23	1.20	1.16	1.20	1.16	1.14	1.16	1.20	1.20	1.21	1.23	1.23	1.19
31	1.20	1.16	1.16	1.16	1.16	1.16	1.16	1.17	1.16	1.13	1.11	1.10	1.16
Mean	1.064	1.049	1.053	1.070	1.094	1.068	1.097	1.105	1.095	1.094	1.080	1.081	30.081

Readings of Aneroid Barometer 11701 on board the Yacht Fox.

January, 1858. 29 inches +. Mean Lat. 18°.0 N., Long. 94°.3 W.

Day.	2h.	4h.	6h.	8h.	10h.	Noon.	2h.	4h.	6h.	8h.	10h.	Midn't.	Mean.
1	1.04	1.04	.90	.85	.92	.92	.64	.83	.60	.60	.79	.76	0.80
2	.76	.77	.76	.76	.76	.80	.84	.84	.89	.92	.90	.90	0.83
3	.98	.98	.92	.94	1.02	1.02	1.04	1.08	1.08	1.03	1.06	1.04	1.01
4	1.06	1.00	1.00	1.02	1.03	1.00	.98	1.09	1.04	1.04	1.06	1.03	1.03
5	1.08	1.08	1.09	1.16	1.34	1.28	1.36	1.38	1.44	1.44	1.46	1.44	1.29
6	1.44	1.46	1.46	1.46	1.44	1.42	1.44	1.42	1.37	1.30	1.30	1.29	1.41
7	1.24	1.20	1.17	1.21	1.22	1.23	1.20	1.15	1.20	1.23	1.19	1.14	1.20
8	1.16	1.19	1.15	1.19	1.23	1.23	1.24	1.27	1.28	1.24	1.25	1.23	1.21
9	1.12	0.96	.84	.94	.91	.84	.84	.74	.84	.84	.84	.89	0.92
10	.90	.94	.96	1.00	1.13	1.10	1.30	1.22	1.24	1.30	1.30	1.36	1.14
11	1.23	1.27	1.33	1.30	1.43	1.42	1.40	1.43	1.46	1.46	1.44	1.46	1.40
12	1.44	1.40	1.34	1.32	1.41	1.34	1.38	1.37	1.37	1.38	1.35	1.33	1.37
13	1.23	1.24	1.25	1.28	1.18	1.20	1.20	1.20	1.20	1.19	1.16	1.19	1.22
14	1.15	1.20	1.08	1.15	1.13	1.14	1.16	1.15	1.18	1.21	1.20	1.23	1.19
15	1.24	1.28	1.23	1.26	1.32	1.24	1.34	1.38	1.31	1.30	1.40	1.42	1.32
16	1.41	1.38	1.42	1.30	1.36	1.34	1.34	1.34	1.34	1.34	1.33	1.30	1.36
17	1.26	1.24	1.24	1.27	1.29	1.30	1.27	1.29	1.26	1.26	1.24	1.24	1.27
18	1.21	1.19	1.17	1.21	1.15	1.16	1.13	1.10	1.13	1.15	1.10	1.10	1.16
19	1.10	1.10	1.14	1.21	1.20	1.21	1.16	1.23	1.22	1.03	1.02	1.10	1.10
20	1.09	1.04	.94	.98	.88	.98	.92	.93	.94	.94	.98	.90	0.97
21	1.00	.98	.97	1.03	1.02	1.00	1.00	1.03	1.03	1.00	.98	.95	1.00
22	.88	.80	.74	.73	.80	.97	.90	.88	.88	.88	.87	.90	0.86
23	.88	.91	.91	.90	.94	.94	.97	.99	1.07	1.05	1.03	1.04	0.95
24	1.06	1.04	1.06	1.10	1.15	1.07	1.10	1.14	1.17	1.16	1.15	1.10	1.13
25	1.14	1.19	1.10	1.20	1.33	1.34	1.35	1.36	1.30	1.30	1.30	1.34	1.24
26	1.16	1.33	1.26	1.34	1.36	1.30	1.33	1.33	1.31	1.32	1.30	1.30	1.32
27	1.28	1.26	1.31	1.30	1.33	1.33	1.30	1.34	1.34	1.36	1.30	1.35	1.30
28	1.35	1.38	1.35	1.39	1.43	1.32	1.33	1.33	1.36	1.38	1.40	1.41	1.37
29	1.41	1.42	1.40	1.40	1.44	1.44	1.43	1.44	1.43	1.40	1.40	1.40	1.42
30	1.50	1.38	1.40	1.43	1.48	1.48	1.44	1.50	1.51	1.46	1.53	1.52	1.46
31	1.50	1.50	1.50	1.54	1.54	1.49	1.56	1.52	1.53	1.55	1.54	1.56	1.53
Mean	1.173	1.158	1.146	1.160	1.187	1.180	1.192	1.200	1.207	1.200	1.204	1.200	29.190

February, 1858. 29 inches +. Mean Lat. 18°.0 N., Long. 94°.3 W.

Day.	2h.	4h.	6h.	8h.	10h.	Noon.	2h.	4h.	6h.	8h.	10h.	Midn't.	Mean.
1	1.46	1.47	1.46	1.48	1.46	1.43	1.40	1.38	1.30	1.04	1.27	1.22	1.40
2	1.23	1.20	1.15	1.20	1.20	1.19	1.17	1.13	1.00	1.06	.98	.92	1.15
3	.86	.81	.74	.80	.75	.72	.78	.68	.66	.63	.57	.60	0.73
4	.90	.90	.86	.73	.78	.94	.89	.92	.90	1.02	1.06	1.00	0.84
5	1.00	1.10	1.10	1.24	1.10	1.19	1.16	1.23	1.36	1.34	1.34	1.23	1.10
6	1.23	1.21	1.17	1.20	1.23	1.29	1.23	1.23	1.36	1.10	1.20	1.28	1.23
7	1.22	1.22	1.23	1.23	1.23	1.27	1.33	1.30	1.29	1.32	1.33	1.36	1.27
8	1.30	1.30	1.30	1.36	1.34	1.32	1.30	1.30	1.23	1.29	1.29	1.34	1.30
9	1.21	1.22	1.20	1.20	1.26	1.24	1.25	1.27	1.29	1.20	1.20	1.20	1.23
10	1.24	1.22	1.16	1.08	1.22	1.10	1.20	1.20	1.21	1.14	1.17	1.14	1.20
11	1.15	1.06	1.10	1.00	.94	.80	.80	.81	.76	.74	.78	.80	0.90
12	.64	.60	.58	.57	.53	.64	.65	.64	.40	.60	.66	.69	0.59
13	.65	.66	.69	.62	.69	.93	.63	.64	.56	.54	.68	.66	0.63
14	.60	.60	.67	.69	.70	.73	.76	.70	.82	.84	.84	.90	0.76
15	.89	.90	.80	.86	.99	1.00	1.04	1.04	1.00	1.03	1.10	1.05	0.99
16	1.04	1.07	1.07	1.10	1.13	1.12	1.14	1.10	1.10	1.15	1.15	1.19	1.12
17	1.19	1.10	1.21	1.23	1.28	1.26	1.23	1.30	1.31	1.32	1.34	1.35	1.27
18	1.32	1.32	1.30	1.30	1.41	1.46	1.47	1.51	1.51	1.52	1.53	1.54	1.45
19	1.52	1.46	1.46	1.52	1.51	1.50	1.52	1.50	1.50	1.47	1.49	1.48	1.49
20	1.40	1.38	1.31	1.30	1.37	1.38	1.34	1.38	1.35	1.35	1.39	1.39	1.32
21	1.35	1.35	1.35	1.38	1.34	1.35	1.39	1.40	1.43	1.44	1.45	1.44	1.39
22	1.40	1.37	1.38	1.44	1.44	1.46	1.44	1.46	1.44	1.46	1.45	1.44	1.44
23	1.44	1.44	1.42	1.51	1.56	1.55	1.50	1.50	1.50	1.50	1.54	1.51	1.50
24	1.46	1.46	1.55	1.49	1.50	1.47	1.45	1.44	1.44	1.40	1.36	1.33	1.46
25	1.37	1.34	1.30	1.28	1.37	1.34	1.23	1.23	1.34	1.36	1.34	1.35	1.34
26	1.28	1.25	1.31	1.30	1.29	1.29	1.30	1.30	1.31	1.31	1.30	1.26	1.29
27	1.21	1.15	1.10	1.13	1.10	1.08	0.94	.94	.97	.98	.93	.94	1.06
28	.53	.70	.75	.63	.63	.68	.91	.92	.84	.60	.58	.59	0.63
Mean	1.135	1.120	1.110	1.146	1.149	1.146	1.155	1.191	1.154	1.153	1.150	1.160	29.149

Readings of Aneroid Barometer 1770 on board the Yacht Fox.

March, 1859. 29 inches +. Mean Lat. 72°.0 N., Long. 94°.2 W.

Day.	2h.	4h.	6h.	8h.	10h.	Noon.	2h.	4h.	6h.	8h.	10h.	Midn't.	Mean.
1	.90	.92	.96	1.10	1.16	1.14	1.18	1.17	1.17	1.18	1.20	1.26	1.10
2	1.20	1.10	1.14	1.22	1.25	1.25	1.27	1.25	1.24	1.23	1.23	1.20	1.23
3	1.14	1.16	1.13	1.08	1.17	1.17	1.15	1.14	1.14	1.24	1.14	1.12	1.15
4	1.12	1.10	1.10	1.14	1.14	1.18	1.23	1.24	1.28	1.23	1.37	1.38	1.21
5	1.32	1.31	1.30	1.37	1.40	1.40	1.43	1.45	1.47	1.46	1.46	1.49	1.41
6	1.47	1.44	1.41	1.50	1.53	1.52	1.53	1.53	1.56	1.53	1.53	1.54	1.51
7	1.50	1.47	1.46	1.44	1.44	1.47	1.46	1.44	1.43	1.33	1.36	1.31	1.44
8	1.28	1.22	1.16	1.14	1.19	1.18	1.16	1.19	1.18	1.14	1.15	1.16	1.18
9	1.10	1.06	1.08	1.10	1.10	1.10	1.09	1.10	1.11	1.14	1.16	1.19	1.10
10	1.11	1.08	1.04	1.04	1.08	1.04	1.04	1.00	.96	.83	.01	.46	1.08
11	.62	.76	.94	.73	.80	.60	.79	.79	.79	.61	.62	.50	0.81
12	.96	.78	.81	.72	.93	.94	1.02	1.05	1.10	1.13	1.17	1.21	0.97
13	1.22	1.30	1.22	1.32	1.32	1.36	1.32	1.34	1.42	1.43	1.40	1.41	1.33
14	1.43	1.44	1.38	1.46	1.43	1.42	1.42	1.44	1.44	1.44	1.44	1.40	1.43
15	1.38	1.34	1.31	1.34	1.32	1.34	1.29	1.31	1.24	1.24	1.21	1.18	1.30
16	1.14	1.10	1.10	1.14	1.12	1.10	1.09	1.09	1.10	1.09	1.08	1.08	1.10
17	1.16	1.04	1.05	1.14	1.14	1.16	1.16	1.12	1.28	1.30	1.33	1.32	1.14
18	1.30	1.31	1.37	1.34	1.38	1.52	1.40	1.44	1.44	1.44	1.46	1.44	1.40
19	1.44	1.44	1.44	1.46	1.65	1.60	1.50	1.57	1.64	1.64	1.57	1.16	1.50
20	1.66	1.66	1.56	1.64	1.66	1.66	1.66	1.73	1.70	1.79	1.73	1.73	1.67
21	1.78	1.70	1.74	1.76	1.74	1.76	1.75	1.76	1.80	1.73	1.81	1.80	1.77
22	1.78	1.76	1.78	1.80	1.82	1.82	1.82	1.78	1.76	1.78	1.76	1.74	1.79
23	1.70	1.68	1.64	1.58	1.64	1.61	1.58	1.58	1.56	1.54	1.56	1.52	1.61
24	1.44	1.43	1.43	1.46	1.46	1.44	1.40	1.40	1.39	1.34	1.38	1.38	1.42
25	1.32	1.30	1.39	1.38	1.40	1.40	1.44	1.44	1.46	1.40	1.44	1.44	1.43
26	1.44	1.53	1.54	1.66	1.60	1.58	1.60	1.56	1.56	1.56	1.51	1.57	1.57
27	1.54	1.50	1.60	1.54	1.56	1.57	1.56	1.62	1.64	1.66	1.68	1.60	1.60
28	(1.60)	(1.70)	(1.71)	1.72	(1.70)	1.60	(1.63)	1.66	(1.64)	1.70	(1.67)	1.64	1.66
29	(1.56)	1.54	(1.56)	1.56	(1.58)	1.56	(1.56)	1.54	(1.64)	1.60	(1.69)	1.61	1.58
30	(1.69)	1.60	(1.62)	1.66	(1.66)	1.66	(1.68)	1.70	(1.70)	1.72	(1.72)	1.74	1.67
31	(1.73)	1.72	(1.73)	1.76	(1.76)	1.76	(1.72)	1.72	(1.71)	1.70	(1.67)	1.64	1.71
Mean	1.384	1.386	1.348	1.380	1.396	1.394	1.386	1.397	1.376	1.406	1.407	1.396	30.383

April, 1859. 29 inches +. Mean Lat. 72°.0 N., Long. 94°.2 W.

Day.	6h.	9h.	Noon.	6h.	8h.	11h.	Mean.
1	1.56	1.56	1.52	1.62	1.64	1.60	1.60
2	1.27	1.28	1.23	1.19	1.18	1.16	1.22
3	1.17	1.14	1.00	1.08	.90	.94	1.05
4	.87	.92	.94	1.00	1.03	1.04	0.97
5	1.07	1.08	1.07	1.02	1.10	1.10	1.07
6	1.07	1.08	1.02	1.07	1.08	1.02	1.06
7	.98	1.02	.96	1.00	1.06	1.07	1.01
8	1.07	1.12	1.14	1.16	1.25	1.27	1.17
9	1.37	1.44	1.46	1.53	1.61	1.62	1.47
10	1.67	1.62	1.76	1.80	1.94	1.91	1.78
11	1.88	1.70	2.02	2.07	2.11	2.11	1.98
12	2.16	2.16	2.27	2.24	2.27	2.26	2.23
13	2.17	2.17	2.16	2.14	2.18	2.11	2.16
14	2.04	2.07	2.04	2.01	1.99	1.86	2.02
15	1.87	1.76	1.66	1.50	1.62	1.46	1.65
16	1.27	1.37	1.37	1.36	1.33	1.27	1.33
17	1.28	1.29	1.27	1.27	1.34	1.32	1.30
18	1.17	1.18	1.10	1.11	1.10	1.12	1.13
19	1.27	1.36	1.42	1.46	1.54	1.53	1.42
20	1.17	1.47	1.60	1.63	1.68	1.61	1.58
21	1.57	1.57	1.54	1.60	1.28	1.18	1.41
22	.97	1.03	.90	.97	.83	.88	0.93
23	1.08	1.17	1.14	1.16	1.10	1.03	1.11
24	1.07	1.09	1.16	1.17	1.23	1.20	1.16
25	1.17	1.17	1.10	1.10	1.10	1.04	1.13
26	.97	1.02	1.10	1.17	1.26	1.28	1.14
27	1.27	1.27	1.34	1.33	1.34	1.39	1.32
28	1.37	1.36	1.40	1.47	1.41	1.45	1.43
29	1.47	1.47	1.46	1.46	1.44	1.43	1.45
30	1.37	1.37	1.41	1.43	1.43	1.40	1.43
Mean	1.376 (1.3[illegible]) At 6h.	1.407	1.395	1.396	1.403	1.381 (1.374) At 11h.	30.391 30.380

Readings of Aneroid Barometer 1701 on board the Yacht Fox.

May, 1859. 29 inches +. Mean Lat. 18°.0 N., Long. 94°.8 W.

Day.	6h.	9h.	Noon.	3h.	6h.	11h.	Mean.
1	1.27	1.30	1.40	1.45	1.29	1.31	1.30
2	1.27	1.29	1.37	1.30	1.34	1.33	1.32
3	1.30	1.37	1.30	1.28	1.34	1.33	1.30
4	1.29	1.30	1.28	1.25	1.29	1.24	1.27
5	1.17	1.22	1.25	1.27	1.25	1.23	1.22
6	1.20	1.24	1.28	1.28	1.27	1.28	1.26
7	1.28	1.27	1.30	1.30	1.37	1.27	1.30
8	1.30	1.23	1.30	1.28	1.23	1.16	1.27
9	1.16	1.17	1.25	1.26	1.21	1.29	1.20
10	1.19	1.22	1.23	1.22	1.23	1.16	1.21
11	1.26	1.13	1.20	1.08	1.07	1.06	1.08
12	.96	.97	1.08	1.08	1.17	1.01	1.03
13	1.00	1.02	1.10	.97	1.01	.96	1.00
14	.80	.83	.85	.95	.97	.90	0.86
15	.74	.77	.83	.80	.90	.41	0.83
16	.72	.83	.84	.63	.83	.91	0.81
17	.78	.75	.72	.82	.87	.85	0.81
18	.80	.85	.90	.97	1.03	1.04	0.93
19	1.03	1.09	1.14	1.19	1.24	1.27	1.17
20	1.25	1.29	1.33	1.32	1.34	1.33	1.31
21	1.30	1.29	1.26	1.23	1.23	1.25	1.26
22	1.13	1.15	1.17	1.20	1.23	1.22	1.19
23	1.20	1.23	1.28	1.29	1.31	1.32	1.27
24	1.26	1.23	1.33	1.30	1.34	1.31	1.32
25	1.25	1.29	1.30	1.30	1.25	1.34	1.29
26	1.28	1.25	1.33	1.33	1.30	1.28	1.29
27	1.19	1.19	1.28	1.30	1.25	1.37	1.26
28	1.29	1.30	1.36	1.41	1.42	1.40	1.37
29	1.30	1.43	1.47	1.48	1.54	1.36	1.41
30	1.53	1.56	1.53	1.64	1.65	1.66	1.62
31	1.65	1.65	1.75	1.70	1.70	1.70	1.69
Mean	1.199 (1.175) At 6h.	1.200	1.230	1.233	1.245	1.235 (1.231) At 10h.	29.227 29.226

June, 1859. 29 inches +. Mean Lat. 19°.0 N., Long. 94°.2 W.

Day.	6h.	9h.	Noon.	3h.	6h.	11h.	Mean.
1	1.49	1.45	1.70	1.49	1.67	1.35	1.46
2	1.52	1.40	1.44	1.36	1.29	1.21	1.30
3	1.15	1.15	1.23	1.27	1.22	1.33	1.26
4	1.23	1.24	1.30	1.29	1.30	1.40	1.27
5	1.44	1.46	1.01	1.55	1.54	1.50	1.51
6	1.54	1.58	1.60	1.62	1.64	1.63	1.60
7	1.54	1.64	1.56	1.52	1.62	1.43	1.53
8	1.36	1.21	1.29	1.34	1.19	1.36	1.30
9	1.09	1.19	1.13	1.14	1.22	1.28	1.19
10	1.16	1.23	1.24	1.28	1.25	1.22	1.23
11	1.19	1.18	1.20	1.30	1.23	1.21	1.22
12	1.11	1.10	1.00	1.09	1.14	1.10	1.09
13	1.00	1.00	1.01	1.01	1.03	1.03	1.00
14	.88	1.01	1.00	1.00	1.00	.94	0.98
15	.85	.94	.94	.43	.98	.86	0.88
16	.85	.93	.94	.90	.73	.91	0.86
17	.73	.80	.86	.86	.84	.61	0.86
18	.76	.73	.63	.73	.61	.63	0.77
19	1.02	1.00	1.06	1.00	1.14	1.10	1.08
20	1.19	1.20	1.16	1.15	1.07	1.16	1.15
21	1.16	1.16	1.10	1.03	.99	.98	1.08
22	.98	1.02	1.03	1.04	1.04	1.06	1.03
23	1.06	1.03	1.08	1.01	.99	.99	1.01
24	1.01	1.04	1.02	1.06	.98	.93	1.00
25	.93	.92	.86	.86	.94	.94	0.96
26	.75	.76	.71	.79	.77	.71	0.76
27	.74	.79	.80	.85	.83	.82	0.81
28	.83	.91	.97	1.14	1.11	1.10	1.00
29	1.10	1.11	1.04	1.01	1.06	1.06	1.07
30	1.14	1.13	1.18	1.18	1.09	1.04	1.18
Mean	1.114 (1.111) At 6h.	1.123	1.133	1.131	1.120	1.101 (1.100) At 10h.	29.124 29.123

READINGS OF ANEROID BAROMETER 17701 ON BOARD THE YACHT FOX.

July, 1859. 29 inches +. Mean Lat. 75°.0 N., Long. 94°.8 W.

Day.	2h.	4h.	6h.	8h.	9h.	10h.	Noon.	2h.	4h.	6h.	8h.	10h.	11h.	Midnt.	Mean.
1	(1.00)	(0.96)	.95	(.83)	.90	(.90)	.92	(.93)	.89	(.94)	1.00	(.98)	.97	(.97)	0.95
2	(.96)	(.85)	.85	(.95)	.85	(.85)	.94	(.97)	1.01	(1.03)	1.04	(1.04)	1.06	(1.08)	0.99
3	(1.07)	(1.09)	1.10	(1.11)	1.12	(1.10)	1.07	(1.05)	1.04	(1.02)	1.00	(1.00)	.99	(.97)	1.05
4	(.98)	(.98)	.98	(.98)	.90	(.97)	.85	(.84)	.83	(.83)	.80	(.80)	.88	(.85)	0.94
5	(.83)	(.80)	.79	(.79)	.78	(.77)	.79	.74	.75	.74	.74	.74	(.73)	.72	0.78
6	.70	.70	...	.70	.74	.80	.80	.88	.84	.88	.93	.98	---	1.00	0.83
7	.96	.99	...	1.01	1.02	1.04	1.04	1.04	1.10	.99	.93	.90	...	.97	1.00
8	.79	.91	...	.67	.76	.78	.76	.76	.72	.60	.67	.62	...	.58	0.69
9	.58	.47	...	.43	.42	.39	.30	.34	.32	.29	.33	.31	...	.30	0.38
10	.28	.29	...	.05	.04	.00	.00	*.98	*.99	*.97	*.98	.00	...	.03	0.06
11	.16	.29	...	.14	.34	.30	.36	.43	.46	.50	.53	.60	...	.65	0.36
12	.66	.70	...	.73	.79	.72	.63	.65	.68	.65	.69	.64	...	.75	0.67
13	.74	.74	...	.73	.70	.70	.66	.66	.60	.68	.62	.69	...	.69	0.68
14	.65	.83	...	.68	.85	.63	.76	.77	.77	.77	.70	.73	...	.73	0.69
15	.72	.71	...	.70	.70	.70	.70	.74	.72	.74	.72	.72	...	.73	0.72
16	.73	.74	...	.69	.62	.64	.68	.62	.69	.78	.76	.70	...	.76	0.73
17	.76	.79	...	.66	.63	.66	.60	.62	.79	.79	.71	.71	...	.69	0.70
18	.63	.67	...	.64	.66	.67	.68	.69	.70	.76	.74	.75	...	.74	0.70
19	.76	.74	...	.78	.80	.86	.96	1.02	1.00	1.04	1.03	1.03	...	1.02	0.90
20	1.02	1.04	...	1.06	1.12	1.14	1.10	1.23	1.17	1.19	1.14	1.12	...	1.11	1.12
21	1.10	1.13	...	1.14	1.22	1.19	1.28	1.34	1.30	1.34	1.34	1.34	...	1.34	1.26
22	1.34	[illegible]	...	1.39	1.46	1.50	1.57	1.58	1.50	1.48	1.51	1.44	...	1.42	1.46
23	1.42	1.41	...	1.45	1.46	1.40	1.40	1.19	1.40	1.46	1.40	1.30	...	1.30	1.40
24	1.36	1.30	...	1.36	1.42	1.45	1.46	1.44	1.42	1.34	1.34	1.31	...	1.30	1.36
25	1.34	1.30	...	1.25	1.26	1.26	1.25	1.26	1.20	1.20	1.19	1.14	...	1.14	1.23
26	1.12	1.11	...	1.13	1.10	1.12	1.17	1.10	1.14	1.00	1.06	.98	...	.96	1.09
27	.92	.90	...	.90	.90	.92	.94	.98	.91	.94	.94	.93	...	.91	0.92
28	.91	.91	...	.95	1.14	1.00	1.12	1.14	1.12	1.10	1.08	1.00	...	1.10	1.04
29	1.07	1.08	...	1.03	1.06	1.10	1.16	1.13	1.13	1.12	1.18	1.13	...	1.06	1.10
30	1.16	1.19	...	1.14	1.19	1.20	1.20	1.18	1.20	1.18	1.19	1.17	...	1.13	1.16
31	1.19	1.12	...	1.15	1.19	1.17	1.15	1.12	1.12	1.10	1.08	1.08	...	1.08	1.11
Mean	0.979	0.945	—	0.957	0.912	0.924	0.933	0.949	0.940	0.930	0.936	0.903	—	0.932	29.917

August, 1859. 29 inches +. Mean Lat. 71°.9 N., Long. 19°.8 W.

Day.	6h.	9h.	Noon.	3h.	9h.	Midn't.	Mean.
1	.99	1.06	1.04	1.06	1.10	1.02	1.03
2	1.02	1.10	1.00	.96	.94	.80	0.95
3	.84	.81	.83	.86	.69	.79	0.83
4	.73	.78	.80	.83	.90	.99	0.85
5	.85	.96	.84	.83	.91	.91	0.83
6	.84	.89	.84	.80	.84	.78	0.83
7	.74	.74	.75	.79	.80	.81	0.77
8	.83	.86	.84	.80	.91	.79	0.83
9	.74	.73	.85	.94	.95	.96	0.87
10	.97	1.00	1.10	1.12	1.04	1.06	1.06
11	1.09	1.18	1.11	1.19	1.08	.98	1.10
12	.94	.96	.93	.93	.94	.90	0.93
13	.93	.93	.94	.94	.83	.91	0.93
14	.60	.74	.73	.68	.67	.68	0.71
15	.79	.74	.87	1.02	1.10	1.18	0.93
16	1.14	1.13	1.15	1.12	1.07	1.03	1.10
17	.94	.92	.80	.84	.73	.64	0.84
18	.70	.64	.66	.64	.64	.53	0.65
19	.59	.56	.41	.53	.50	.41	0.51
20	.59	.60	.44	.53	.55	.41	0.54
21	.53	.64	.44	.70	.57	.64	0.65
22	.51	.56	.64	.80	.80	.70	0.68
23	.83	.90	1.12	1.21	1.20	1.29	1.13
24	1.26	1.22	1.20	1.16	1.10	1.06	1.19
25	1.08	1.07	1.10	1.15	1.15	1.13	1.11
26	1.12	1.14	1.15	1.10	1.12	1.10	1.13
27	1.10	1.10	1.13	1.13	1.19	1.20	1.14
28	1.21	1.30	1.26	1.35	1.40	1.42	1.30
29	1.48	1.47	1.46	1.45	1.40	1.40	1.45
30	1.44	1.30	1.27	1.23	1.22	1.22	1.29
31	1.22	1.23	1.25	1.24	1.23	1.24	1.23
Mean	0.936	0.940	0.951	0.963	0.962	0.944	29.950

* Refers to 29 inches.

READINGS OF ANEROID BAROMETER 11701 ON BOARD THE YACHT FOX.
September, 1859. 29 Inches +. Mean Lat. 68°.9 N., Long. 46°.9 W.

DAY.	4h.	8h.	Noon.	4h.	8h.	Midnight.
1	1.24	1.28	1.27	1.28	1.31	1.29
2	1.18	1.18	1.29	1.30	1.30	1.16
3	1.16	1.15	1.26	1.04	.66	.80
4	.90	.79	.77	.70	.61	.60
5	.78	.74	.65	....	....	....
6	.70	.65	.66	.56	.70	.73
7	.78	.83	.61	.57	.58	.80
8	.87	.85	.66	.58	.66	.80
9	.75	.80	.63	.60	.84	.84
10	.81	.73	.90	.91	.85	.74
11	.80	.81	.90	.81	.84	.99
12	.88	.93	.78	.84	.76	.96
13	.91	.75	.91	.88	.86	.86
14	.93	.90	.93	.93	.93	.90
15	.99	.92	.90	1.00	1.01	1.02
16	1.05	1.15	1.10	1.24	1.30	1.30
17	1.30	1.32	1.33	1.30	1.30	1.30
18	1.33	1.28	1.22	1.20	1.18	1.18

Additional Readings of the Marine Mercurial Barometer, between September, 1857, and April, 1858.

A description of the Marine Barometer adopted by Her Majesty's government, on the recommendation of the Kew Observatory Committee of the British Association for the Advancement of Science, will be found in the appendix to the fourth number of meteorological papers, published by authority of the Board of Trade. London, 1860.

READINGS OF THE MARINE MERCURIAL BAROMETER, ADIE No. 263, ON BOARD THE YACHT FOX.
Height of cistern above the level of the sea, 4 feet.
September, 1857. 29 Inches +. Mean Lat. 75°.2 N., Long. 65°.3 W.

DAY.	4h. Bar.	4h. Th.	8h. Bar.	8h. Th.	Noon. Bar.	Noon. Th.	4h. Bar.	4h. Th.	8h. Bar.	8h. Th.	Midnight. Bar.	Midnight. Th.	Mean. Bar.	Mean. Th.	Mean at 32°.
	Inch.	°	Inch.	°	Inch.	°	Inch.	°	Inch.	°	Inch.	°	Inch.	°	Inch.
20	[illegible]	[illegible]	[illegible]	[illegible]	[illegible]	[illegible]	[illegible]	[illegible]	[illegible]	[illegible]	[illegible]	[illegible]	[illegible]	[illegible]	[illegible]
21	[illegible]	[illegible]	[illegible]	[illegible]	[illegible]	[illegible]	[illegible]	[illegible]	[illegible]	[illegible]	[illegible]	[illegible]	[illegible]	[illegible]	[illegible]
22	[illegible]	[illegible]	[illegible]	[illegible]	[illegible]	[illegible]	[illegible]	[illegible]	[illegible]	[illegible]	[illegible]	[illegible]	[illegible]	[illegible]	[illegible]
23	[illegible]	[illegible]	[illegible]	[illegible]	[illegible]	[illegible]	[illegible]	[illegible]	[illegible]	[illegible]	[illegible]	[illegible]	[illegible]	[illegible]	[illegible]
24	[illegible]	[illegible]	[illegible]	[illegible]	[illegible]	[illegible]	[illegible]	[illegible]	[illegible]	[illegible]	[illegible]	[illegible]	[illegible]	[illegible]	[illegible]
25	[illegible]	[illegible]	[illegible]	[illegible]	[illegible]	[illegible]	[illegible]	[illegible]	[illegible]	[illegible]	[illegible]	[illegible]	[illegible]	[illegible]	[illegible]
26	[illegible]	[illegible]	[illegible]	[illegible]	[illegible]	[illegible]	[illegible]	[illegible]	[illegible]	[illegible]	[illegible]	[illegible]	[illegible]	[illegible]	[illegible]
27	[illegible]	[illegible]	[illegible]	[illegible]	[illegible]	[illegible]	[illegible]	[illegible]	[illegible]	[illegible]	[illegible]	[illegible]	[illegible]	[illegible]	[illegible]
28	[illegible]	[illegible]	[illegible]	[illegible]	[illegible]	[illegible]	[illegible]	[illegible]	[illegible]	[illegible]	[illegible]	[illegible]	[illegible]	[illegible]	[illegible]
29	[illegible]	[illegible]	[illegible]	[illegible]	[illegible]	[illegible]	[illegible]	[illegible]	[illegible]	[illegible]	[illegible]	[illegible]	[illegible]	[illegible]	[illegible]
30	[illegible]	[illegible]	[illegible]	[illegible]	[illegible]	[illegible]	[illegible]	[illegible]	[illegible]	[illegible]	[illegible]	[illegible]	[illegible]	[illegible]	[illegible]
Mean.	.715	36.6	.704	39.6	.753	43.0	.736	39.0	.720	37.9	.724	40.3	.723	34.2	
At 32°.	29.685		29.657		29.697		29.673		29.666		29.640		29.684		29.654

The column for 4h A. M. was obtained by interpolation, the difference in the aneroid readings of 4h and 8h was applied to the reading of the marine barometer at 8h to get the value for 4h.

The reduction to 32° was effected by means of Table XVII., C., of Guyot's Meteorological Tables (Edition of 1858).

The reading for 4 A. M., between October 1 and 20, being wanting, they were supplied by means of differences of the aneroid readings, as stated above.

Readings of the Marine Mercurial Barometer, Adie No. 308, on board the Yacht Fox.
October, 1857. 29 Inches +. Mean Lat. 73°.8 N., Long. 67°.9 W.

Day.	4h. Bar.	Th.	8h. Bar.	Th.	Noon. Bar.	Th.	4h. Bar.	Th.	8h. Bar.	Th.	Midnight. Bar.	Th.	Means. Bar.	Th.	Mean.
	Inch.	°	Inch.	°	Inch.	°	Inch.	°	Inch.	°	Inch.	°	Inch.	°	Inch.
1	(.420)	(60)	.872	46	.596	56	.908	[illegible]	.858	54	.790	50	.638	50	.330
2	(.454)	(40)	.308	40	.480	54	.431	45	.347	52	.550	54	.419	47	.455
3	(1.001)	(41)	.349	51	1.008	47	1.126	51	1.138	58	1.079	56	1.012	52	.969
4	(.794)	(44)	.815	45	.892	49	.900	49	.390	52	.631	53	.600	48	.546
5	(.960)	(41)	.730	45	.248	50	.673	48	.278	52	.510	52	.557	49	.466
6	(.484)	(42)	.494	47	.450	49	.369	49	.729	54	.397	41	.804	49	.397
7	(.746)	(47)	.249	42	.254	45	.248	44	.813	48	.518	51	.742	47	.712
8	(.762)	(40)	.912	49	.511	53	.961	49	.997	51	.930	48	.828	48	.610
9	(.981)	(49)	.988	45	1.076	50	1.138	50	1.161	53	1.131	50	1.079	49	1.025
10	(1.118)	(47)	1.012	47	.961	45	.946	42	.867	46	.816	45	.941	44	.924
11	(.692)	(50)	.872	47	.898	44	.851	46	.856	49	.509	51	.872	44	.738
12	(.781)	(39)	.619	39	.819	48	.440	43	.544	50	.519	50	.914	42	.443
13	(.580)	(47)	.631	47	.615	50	.561	48	.400	51	.496	53	.515	50	.468
14	(.262)	(52)	.392	50	.290	53	.344	51	.480	50	.417	47	.348	54	.327
15	(.452)	(51)	.418	54	.430	53	.319	51	.613	54	.591	50	.800	54	.463
16	(.388)	(51)	.498	56	.695	55	.546	56	.750	56	.587	49	.465	54	.414
17	(.609)	(47)	.482	57	.614	56	.641	51	.640	58	.396	49	.967	59	.473
18	(.806)	(52)	.460	52	.679	58	.640	59	.772	52	.900	56	.818	58	.742
19	(.618)	(57)	.810	53	.296	56	.649	53	.497	57	.694	59	.654	54	.491
20	(.896)	(50)	.079	50	.390	56	.782	54	.753	59	.738	59	.769	54	.663
21	.702	50	.709	56	.750	54	.752	56	.529	55	.340	60	.961	56	.541
22	.718	60	.400	59	.316	55	.375	56	.462	50	.420	56	.294	53	.314
23	.566	60	.564	56	.586	53	.852	57	.831	57	.652	58	.519	54	.540
24	.906	44	.750	46	.896	48	1.090	47	1.136	42	1.271	45	.887	52	.954
25	1.369	41	1.398	41	1.362	44	1.396	40	1.424	40	1.401	43	1.358	46	1.271
26	1.560	46	1.452	42	1.509	45	1.136	47	1.546	47	1.500	50	1.521	46	1.477
27	1.516	43	1.276	44	1.356	44	1.176	38	1.564	38	1.492	50	1.144	46	1.342
28	.962	42	.612	45	.962	46	1.019	54	1.464	36	1.444	51	1.006	47	.972
29	1.086	49	1.542	42	1.990	48	.812	59	.680	58	.770	58	.842	49	.949
30	.670	44	.564	44	.497	53	.560	54	.640	55	.510	54	.600	51	.566
31	.438	41	.460	40	.734	43	.541	39	.726	56	.720	50	.483	33	.534
Means	.754	47	.800	47	.892	46	.832	50	.856	54	.851	54	.662	50.5	
At 32°	29.131		29.714		29.748		29.714		29.700		29.700		29.751		29.754

November, 1857. 29 Inches +. Mean Lat. 74°.8 N., Long. 69°.1 W.

Day.	4h. Bar.	Th.	8h. Bar.	Th.	Noon. Bar.	Th.	4h. Bar.	Th.	8h. Bar.	Th.	Midnight. Bar.	Th.	Means. Bar.	Th.
	Inch.	°	Inch.	°	Inch.	°	Inch.	°	Inch.	°	Inch.	°	Inch.	°
1	.752	52	.797	52	.751	56	.774	58	.446	58	.758	50	0.756	50.7
2	.464	53	.634	49	.709	58	.742	58	.696	59	.671	58	0.694	55.7
3	.596	54	.620	56	.494	56	.794	52	.456	57	.813	56	0.748	55.2
4	.929	52	.991	(54)	1.027	51	1.049	57	1.190	61	1.099	54	1.021	54.8
5	1.098	53	1.108	49	1.169	53	1.163	58	1.172	59	1.268	62	1.161	54.2
6	1.094	54	1.170	51	1.135	52	1.085	52	.926	58	.961	51	1.037	53.7
7	.794	52	.733	51	.820	54	.794	54	.946	57	.920	59	0.901	55.6
8	.814	53	.893	51	.823	59	.849	54	1.060	57	1.011	58	0.893	53.6
9	1.176	51	1.133	51	1.139	56	.616	51	.672	55	.667	58	0.948	56.7
10	.932	54	1.028	57	1.034	52	1.074	53	1.039	56	1.003	58	1.011	55.8
11	.820	53	.980	50	.902	56	.829	54	.414	55	.580	55	0.768	54.3
12	.541	50	.494	57	.799	56	.796	54	.750	58	.714	58	0.664	52.6
13	.530	55	.562	56	.792	54	.478	53	.546	56	.574	57	0.556	52.8
14	.616	55	.554	54	.560	56	.490	56	.653	58	.850	58	0.465	52.8
15	.692	57	.414	59	.632	59	.634	59	.274	58	.159	59	0.470	53.9
16	.122	54	.134	56	.476	57	.680	56	.823	55	.382	53	0.369	55.6
17	.143	56	.356	56	.158	58	.450	57	.470	55	.687	55	0.379	55.3
18	.594	57	.792	45	.370	58	1.062	58	1.090	57	1.093	58	0.663	53.7
19	1.044	52	1.033	55	1.022	56	1.049	57	1.088	53	1.024	56	1.032	54.5
20	.900	56	.798	52	.948	52	.976	54	.956	56	.660	52	0.854	55.5
21	.930	56	.796	50	.440	56	.439	58	.825	50	.444	57	0.743	54.3
22	.545	56	.387	56	.230	50	.224	57	.294	56	.362	57	0.396	51.3
23	.518	56	.538	56	.794	53	.730	56	.383	52	.324	52	0.492	52.2
24	.734	56	.754	56	.764	56	.624	56	.678	52	.580	54	0.407	52.8
25	.862	56	.662	56	.380	56	.857	56	*.990	57	.804	56	0.778	54.8
26	*.956	56	*.099	52	*.976	52	*.986	54	.979	59	.150	58	0.469	54.3
27	.584	56	.154	54	.250	52	.244	57	.381	53	.184	58	0.201	55.2
28	.460	56	.530	51	.370	50	.560	57	.568	58	.500	56	0.573	58.3
29	.718	59	.811	59	.967	56	.970	57	1.050	59	1.001	59	0.900	54.3
30	1.090	55	1.254	56	1.154	52	1.254	55	1.250	58	1.242	54	1.198	55.2
Means	0.679	55.9	0.697	52.3	0.737	55.2	0.747	56.0	0.760	57.4	0.722	57.2	0.734	55.5
At 32°	29.631		29.654		29.662		29.674		29.674		29.647		29.656	

* Refers to 28 inches.

Readings of the Marine Mercurial Barometer, Adie No. [illegible], on board the Yacht Fox.

December, 1857. 29 inches +. Mean Lat. 74°.3 N., Long. 67°.4 W.

Day.	4h. Bar.	4h. Th.	8h. Bar.	8h. Th.	Noon. Bar.	Noon. Th.	4h. Bar.	4h. Th.	8h. Bar.	8h. Th.	Midnight. Bar.	Midnight. Th.	Mean. Bar.	Mean. Th.
	Inch.	°	Inch.	°	Inch.	°	Inch.	°	Inch.	°	Inch.	°	Inch.	°
1	1.029	57	1.233	49	1.236	53	1.271	47	1.141	49	1.110	50	1.083	50.3
2	1.095	44	1.040	45	.979	52	.925	51	.905	63	.853	57	0.959	52.3
3	.7[illegible]	46	.763	49	.766	61	.666	63	.532	62	.520	60	0.649	50.0
4	.570	43	.623	43	.491	41	.524	61	.534	62	.478	47	0.520	47.0
5	.450	37	.410	49	.332	47	.291	63	.142	66	.147	54	0.340	49.0
6	.110	41	.103	41	.140	58	.104	55	.274	61	.374	62	0.196	49.0
7	.479	43	.473	41	.712	49	.778	60	.847	61	.863	51	0.707	47.2
8	[illegible]	45	[illegible]	46	.954	51	.964	54	1.023	64	1.045	50	0.948	51.5
9	1.391	45	1.112	50	1.134	52	1.156	56	1.123	55	1.150	55	1.117	53.9
10	1.060	46	1.022	45	1.084	53	1.127	57	1.126	54	1.160	55	1.094	53.0
11	1.163	45	1.100	48	1.165	50	1.241	65	1.143	55	.999	56	1.145	61.1
12	.791	45	.812	32	.413	50	.394	56	.339	59	.241	69	0.467	52.3
13	.150	46	.099	46	.190	49	.169	51	.190	57	.254	54	0.163	51.7
14	.274	50	.311	47	.421	57	.469	56	.402	56	.499	56	0.410	53.6
15	.619	46	.610	46	.570	54	.597	56	.411	58	.505	60	0.569	53.8
16	.683	49	.543	47	.544	51	.518	56	.630	59	.518	58	0.604	54.8
17	.656	41	.620	46	.624	54	.672	57	.651	60	.653	60	0.621	52.5
18	.631	47	.636	46	.649	59	.663	61	.664	60	.650	61	0.650	55.6
19	.637	51	.643	52	.774	59	.722	60	.878	56	.620	59	0.710	56.3
20	.669	48	.692	50	.365	54	.636	60	.630	51	.569	62	0.607	54.5
21	.511	50	.550	50	.500	56	.713	55	.738	59	.510	59	0.670	55.9
22	.530	46	.676	47	.641	56	.655	60	.622	60	.515	60	0.633	56.0
23	.735	48	.716	52	.732	56	.716	59	.624	59	.569	54	0.709	56.0
24	.669	40	.846	49	.930	57	.900	59	.946	65	.941	63	0.911	56.3
25	.733	51	.614	52	.591	53	.544	49	.644	65	.541	56	0.606	56.6
26	.494	47	.494	49	.349	51	.490	56	.345	56	.252	52	0.472	51.0
27	.154	44	.044	46	.061	56	*.030	59	*.961	58	*.946	51	0.014	53.9
28	*.845	50	*.922	46	*.490	64	*.454	58	*.976	61	*.930	59	*0.961	54.7
29	*.680	47	*.912	45	*.954	56	.050	49	.223	59	.254	64	0.041	55.3
30	.350	50	.473	45	.464	56	.460	60	.646	62	.794	61	0.563	56.2
31	.763	49	.743	46	.774	60	.801	64	.838	61	.774	60	0.771	56.5
Mean	0.645	48.9	0.612	44.4	0.617	53.8	0.633	60.1	0.640	56.9	0.633	57.9	0.630	53.0
At 32°	29.540		29.544		29.530		29.554		29.544		29.560		29.545	

January, 1858. 29 inches +. Mean Lat. 73°.8 N., Long. 63°.7 W.

Day.	4h. Bar.	4h. Th.	8h. Bar.	8h. Th.	Noon. Bar.	Noon. Th.	4h. Bar.	4h. Th.	8h. Bar.	8h. Th.	Midnight. Bar.	Midnight. Th.	Mean. Bar.	Mean. Th.
	Inch.	°	Inch.	°	Inch.	°	Inch.	°	Inch.	°	Inch.	°	Inch.	°
1	.746	42	.712	45	.540	52	.434	58	.468	63	.460	63	0.535	54.0
2	.341	48	.341	48	.419	60	.416	60	.314	60	.301	63	0.327	54.0
3	.151	48	*.984	48	*.836	50	*.764	63	*.754	63	*.771	64	*0.801	57.0
4	*.716	61	*.792	65	*.644	60	*.646	56	*.944	[illegible]	.620	60	*0.675	63.5
5	.100	49	.148	47	.172	65	.137	60	.960	61	.976	64	0.116	63.5
6	.012	61	*.906	51	*.902	56	*.846	60	*.974	50	*.950	58	*0.979	54.5
7	*.928	47	*.942	46	.979	52	.074	57	.130	60	.100	51	0.041	52.6
8	.100	46	.141	47	.146	53	.132	65	.161	51	.310	56	0.134	52.0
9	.060	46	.099	48	.127	56	.157	61	.191	51	.272	72	0.141	56.0
10	.243	51	.250	50	.320	56	.377	65	.451	56	.475	65	0.266	56.0
11	.413	46	.542	46	.412	52	.431	59	.467	59	.526	60	0.614	53.7
12	.543	46	.614	42	.702	56	.713	54	.714	56	.530	56	0.621	54.2
13	.843	46	.818	48	.625	52	.791	41	1.041	60	1.020	63	0.791	57.0
14	1.040	53	1.472	46	1.310	49	1.420	65	1.254	56	1.000	60	1.344	56.2
15	1.000	47	.730	49	.544	59	.915	56	.416	60	.900	66	0.906	57.4
16	.766	52	.656	46	.424	49	.721	50	.447	63	.671	61	0.677	56.0
17	.766	48	.720	46	.730	59	.767	55	.966	60	1.014	68	0.800	56.0
18	1.057	43	1.062	46	1.043	55	1.069	60	1.041	63	1.054	56	1.005	56.4
19	1.033	47	1.063	45	1.200	54	1.200	59	1.140	58	1.055	61	1.074	56.6
20	.971	46	.190	45	.710	54	.610	56	.419	56	.363	58	0.627	53.1
21	.660	44	.610	46	.101	50	.314	56	.841	60	.191	61	0.611	53.4
22	.770	49	.775	45	.451	54	.768	65	.941	66	.411	63	0.710	51.7
23	.364	45	.449	49	.189	53	.710	55	.730	67	.764	56	0.370	56.7
24	.605	43	.621	41	.444	61	.313	63	.134	60	.056	53	0.341	49.2
25	.074	49	.052	48	.070	50	.000	64	*.947	68	*.912	53	0.016	50.2
26	*.926	44	.092	43	.125	53	.169	52	.104	56	.123	61	0.097	50.0
27	.075	44	.134	42	.300	53	.450	56	.844	54	.730	60	0.348	51.2
28	.772	45	.866	43	.900	52	.957	63	1.013	63	1.049	56	0.920	50.8
29	1.120	44	1.175	42	1.223	51	1.642	57	1.330	56	1.428	56	1.374	51.0
30	1.445	44	1.759	44	1.540	51	1.951	57	1.945	56	1.507	61	1.548	52.4
31	1.800	50	1.722	49	1.630	57	1.423	61	1.236	56	1.130	56	1.346	55.0
Mean	0.541	47.6	0.656	45.8	0.685	54.6	0.684	57.4	0.697	59.0	0.699	58.0	0.347	54.0
At 32°	29.631		29.510		29.621		29.527		29.530		29.519		29.520	

* Refers to 28 inches.

Readings of the Marine Mercurial Barometer, Adie No. 909, on board the Yacht Fox.

February, 1858. 29 Inches +. Mean Lat. 71°.5 N., Long. 60°.9 W.

Day.	4h.		8h.		Noon.		4h.		8h.		Midnight.		Mean.	
	Bar.	Th.	Bar.	Th.	Bar.	Th.	Bar.	Th.	Bar.	Th.	Bar.	Th.	Bar.	Th.
	Inch.	°	Inch.	°	Inch.	°	Inch.	°	Inch.	°	Inch.	°	Inch.	°
1	1.047	45	.948	46	1.027	54	1.010	54	.938	54	.830	52	0.974	52.0
2	.760	41	.648	46	.607	54	.612	54	.671	56	.640	54	0.653	52.5
3	.816	47	.500	49	.617	54	.673	60	.606	59	.640	59	0.618	54.8
4	.507	47	.423	49	.321	52	.376	56	.423	58	.416	62	0.444	55.7
5	.640	52	[illegible]	49	.500	53	.674	58	.502	50	.600	61	0.545	55.3
6	.387	50	.372	50	.310	59	.321	59	.379	62	.718	63	0.417	57.7
7	.570	51	.618	51	.536	54	.609	62	.602	56	.714	60	0.564	56.0
8	.742	49	.712	56	.672	59	.646	61	.962	62	.924	64	[illegible]	58.3
9	.870	49	.840	62	.940	62	.781	60	.806	63	.833	67	0.757	58.5
10														
11														
12														
13														
14														
15														
16														
17	.612	51	.655	52	.752	58	.754	59	.730	59	.752	67	0.576	57.5
18	[illegible]	52	.612	53	.530	60	.474	59	.750	58	[illegible]	76	[illegible]	59.3
19	.152	50	.054	52	.640	55	.253	53	.452	59	[illegible]	60	0.253	55.7
20	[illegible]	52	.482	53	.374	56	.311	59	.249	61	.377	56	0.331	57.9
21	.400	55	.471	56	.614	56	.791	54	.161	64	[illegible]	62	0.644	59.3
22	[illegible]	56	.902	50	.946	12	.919	63	[illegible]	72	.778	61	[illegible]	[illegible]
23	.646	54	.842	54	.671	61	.623	63	[illegible]	59	.641	60	0.624	56.5
24	.647	51	.316	51	.100	58	.041	61	.414	61	.234	57	[illegible]	56.2
25	.253	53	.274	51	.044	59	.644	65	.154	61	.513	62	0.404	59.5
26	.540	57	.530	56	.504	64	.771	62	.316	59	[illegible]	63	0.504	59.3
27	.662	61	.911	62	.914	56	.932	71	.971	60	1.027	59	0.914	64.3
28	.930	49	.973	51	1.041	59	1.044	60	.981	53	.923	60	0.970	56.7
Mean	0.622	51.7	0.645	52.8	0.651	57.7	0.657	60.4	0.651	59.4	0.645	60.2	0.640	56.9
At 32°	29.5[illegible]		29.5[illegible]		29.574		29.573		29.550		29.5[illegible]		29.565	

March, 1858. 29 Inches +. Mean Lat. 69°.6 N., Long. 59°.1 W.

Day.	4h.		8h.		Noon.		4h.		8h.		Midnight.		Mean.	
	Bar.	Th.	Bar.	Th.	Bar.	Th.	Bar.	Th.	Bar.	Th.	Bar.	Th.	Bar.	Th.
	Inch.	°	Inch.	°	Inch.	°	Inch.	°	Inch.	°	Inch.	°	Inch.	°
1	.920	44	.742	50	.793	56	.799	60	.731	61	.643	56	0.773	55.7
2	.695	49	[illegible]	57	.674	61	.614	62	.614	63	.962	54	0.579	54.5
3	1.154	49	1.252	55	1.310	60	1.030	56	[illegible]	61	.814	57	0.947	56.0
4	.518	48	.682	53	.686	62	1.164	54	1.300	59	1.300	58	0.937	57.7
5	1.000	51	1.400	56	1.376	64	1.342	56	1.444	58	1.476	63	1.303	57.5
6	1.474	54	1.500	56	.622	60	1.710	60	1.740	62	1.703	62	1.472	58.2
7	1.620	53	1.716	65	1.725	56	1.640	60	1.796	59	1.510	54	1.643	57.3
8	1.413	54	1.364	61	1.419	55	1.430	57	1.412	58	1.430	63	1.413	58.3
9	1.330	54	1.290	61	1.230	53	1.170	50	1.010	57	.904	55	1.159	54.2
10	.744	47	.650	56	.760	57	.316	54	.060	61	*.550	61	0.770	55.1
11	*.772	52	*.710	57	*.772	56	*.[illegible]	60	*.[illegible]	60	*.[illegible]	61	*0.794	57.3
12	*.307	53	*.550	53	.600	63	.140	60	.337	60	.500	60	0.110	57.7
13	.350	50	.353	54	.501	64	[illegible]	61	.377	61	.424	57	0.346	59.7
14	.400	54	.474	53	.624	60	[illegible]	63	.449	60	.644	54	0.460	57.7
15	.843	47	.470	46	.770	66	[illegible]	56	.675	61	.800	64	0.745	55.3
16	.952	50	1.700	57	1.010	64	1.002	56	1.110	54	1.120	61	1.046	57.0
17	1.000	48	1.096	54	1.130	63	1.100	57	1.103	58	1.043	54	1.043	54.6
18	.868	50	.898	64	.900	65	.770	53	.769	56	.674	56	0.810	51.0
19	[illegible]	49	.618	60	.631	61	[illegible]	54	.720	55	.763	57	[illegible]	52.9
20	.748	47	.312	61	.715	54	[illegible]	59	.610	56	.672	54	0.672	54.3
21	.431	54	.759	54	.663	56	[illegible]	54	.510	56	.407	56	0.523	56.0
22	.416	47	.410	53	.476	57	.164	57	.404	56	.502	54	0.412	54.8
23	[illegible]	56	.854	48	.715	56	.777	49	1.070	63	1.215	63	[illegible]	[illegible]
24	1.454	50	1.776	53	1.723	60	1.556	60	1.344	60	1.041	56	1.318	57.6
25	1.352	49	1.343	50	1.390	56	1.271	57	1.303	56	1.370	54	1.303	54.3
26	1.377	47	1.458	63	1.560	53	1.610	57	1.640	63	1.563	59	1.479	52.0
27	1.400	48	1.414	50	1.163	53	1.390	51	1.525	53	1.344	50	1.313	50.7
28	1.423	44	1.342	41	1.376	49	1.350	54	0.779	51	1.310	41	1.331	47.0
29	1.343	43	1.485	53	1.480	51	1.400	55	1.489	53	1.410	45	1.433	53.0
30	1.353	43	1.290	54	1.163	53	1.174	55	1.111	50	1.124	57	1.170	53.7
31	1.163	49	1.099	51	1.150	49	1.063	47	1.064	53	1.066	53	1.063	50.5
Mean	0.934	48.9	0.934	52.3	0.941	55.5	0.971	57.4	0.970	56.3	0.900	56.1	0.943	55.1
At 32°	29.8[illegible]		29.873		29.8[illegible]		29.9[illegible]		29.9[illegible]		29.8[illegible]		29.8[illegible]	

* Refers to 28 inches.

Readings of the Marine Mercurial Barometer, Adie No. [illegible], on board the Yacht Fox. April, 1858. 29 inches +. Mean Lat. [illegible]°.9 N., Long. [illegible]°.8 W.

Days.	6h.		9h.		Noon.		3h.		6h.		Midnight.		Mean.	
	Bar.	Th.	Bar.	Th.	Bar.	Th.	Bar.	Th.	Bar.	Th.	Bar.	Th.	Bar.	Th.
	Inch.	°	Inch.	°	Inch.	°	Inch.	°	Inch.	°	Inch.	°	Inch.	°
1	[illegible]	47	[illegible]	[illegible]	[illegible]	54	[illegible]	[illegible]	[illegible]	[illegible]	[illegible]	[illegible]	[illegible]	[illegible]
2	[illegible]	[illegible]	[illegible]	[illegible]	[illegible]	[illegible]	[illegible]	[illegible]	[illegible]	[illegible]	[illegible]	[illegible]	[illegible]	[illegible]
3	[illegible]	[illegible]	[illegible]	[illegible]	[illegible]	[illegible]	[illegible]	[illegible]	[illegible]	[illegible]	[illegible]	[illegible]	[illegible]	[illegible]
4	[illegible]	[illegible]	[illegible]	[illegible]	[illegible]	[illegible]	[illegible]	[illegible]	[illegible]	[illegible]	[illegible]	[illegible]	[illegible]	[illegible]
5	[illegible]	[illegible]	[illegible]	[illegible]	[illegible]	[illegible]	[illegible]	[illegible]	[illegible]	[illegible]	[illegible]	[illegible]	[illegible]	[illegible]
6	[illegible]	[illegible]	[illegible]	[illegible]	[illegible]	[illegible]	[illegible]	[illegible]	[illegible]	[illegible]	[illegible]	[illegible]	[illegible]	[illegible]
7	[illegible]	[illegible]	[illegible]	[illegible]	[illegible]	[illegible]	[illegible]	[illegible]	[illegible]	[illegible]	[illegible]	[illegible]	[illegible]	[illegible]
8	[illegible]	[illegible]	[illegible]	[illegible]	[illegible]	[illegible]	[illegible]	[illegible]	[illegible]	[illegible]	[illegible]	[illegible]	[illegible]	[illegible]
9	[illegible]	[illegible]	[illegible]	[illegible]	[illegible]	[illegible]	[illegible]	[illegible]	[illegible]	[illegible]	[illegible]	[illegible]	[illegible]	[illegible]
10	[illegible]	[illegible]	[illegible]	[illegible]	[illegible]	[illegible]	[illegible]	[illegible]	[illegible]	[illegible]	[illegible]	[illegible]	[illegible]	[illegible]
11	[illegible]	[illegible]	[illegible]	[illegible]	[illegible]	[illegible]	[illegible]	[illegible]	[illegible]	[illegible]	[illegible]	[illegible]	[illegible]	[illegible]
12	[illegible]	[illegible]	[illegible]	[illegible]	[illegible]	[illegible]	[illegible]	[illegible]	[illegible]	[illegible]	[illegible]	[illegible]	[illegible]	[illegible]
13	[illegible]	[illegible]	[illegible]	[illegible]	[illegible]	[illegible]	[illegible]	[illegible]	[illegible]	[illegible]	[illegible]	[illegible]	[illegible]	[illegible]
14	[illegible]	[illegible]	[illegible]	[illegible]	[illegible]	[illegible]	[illegible]	[illegible]	[illegible]	[illegible]	[illegible]	[illegible]	[illegible]	[illegible]
15	[illegible]	[illegible]	[illegible]	[illegible]	[illegible]	[illegible]	[illegible]	[illegible]	[illegible]	[illegible]	[illegible]	[illegible]	[illegible]	[illegible]
16	[illegible]	[illegible]	[illegible]	[illegible]	[illegible]	[illegible]	[illegible]	[illegible]	[illegible]	[illegible]	[illegible]	[illegible]	[illegible]	[illegible]
Means	[illegible]	[illegible]	[illegible]	[illegible]	[illegible]	[illegible]	[illegible]	[illegible]	[illegible]	[illegible]	[illegible]	[illegible]	[illegible]	[illegible]
At 32°	[illegible]		[illegible]		[illegible]		[illegible]		[illegible]		[illegible]		[illegible]	

First Year.—Recapitulation of Mean Readings from the preceding record of the Aneroid Barometer, No. [illegible], from September, 1857, to September, 1858.

Position.		1857.	2h.	4h.	6h.	8h.	10h.	Noon.	2h.	4h.	6h.	8h.	10h.	Mid't.	Mean.
N. Lat.	W. Long.														
[illegible]	[illegible]	Sept.	[illegible]	[illegible]	[illegible]	[illegible]	[illegible]	[illegible]	[illegible]	[illegible]	[illegible]	[illegible]	[illegible]	[illegible]	[illegible]
[illegible]	[illegible]	Oct.	[illegible]	[illegible]	[illegible]	[illegible]	[illegible]	[illegible]	[illegible]	[illegible]	[illegible]	[illegible]	[illegible]	[illegible]	[illegible]
[illegible]	[illegible]	Nov.	[illegible]	[illegible]	[illegible]	[illegible]	[illegible]	[illegible]	[illegible]	[illegible]	[illegible]	[illegible]	[illegible]	[illegible]	[illegible]
[illegible]	[illegible]	Dec.	[illegible]	[illegible]	[illegible]	[illegible]	[illegible]	[illegible]	[illegible]	[illegible]	[illegible]	[illegible]	[illegible]	[illegible]	[illegible]
[illegible]	[illegible]	1858, Jan.	[illegible]	[illegible]	[illegible]	[illegible]	[illegible]	[illegible]	[illegible]	[illegible]	[illegible]	[illegible]	[illegible]	[illegible]	[illegible]
[illegible]	[illegible]	Feb.	[illegible]	[illegible]	[illegible]	[illegible]	[illegible]	[illegible]	[illegible]	[illegible]	[illegible]	[illegible]	[illegible]	[illegible]	[illegible]
[illegible]	[illegible]	March	[illegible]	[illegible]	[illegible]	[illegible]	[illegible]	[illegible]	[illegible]	[illegible]	[illegible]	[illegible]	[illegible]	[illegible]	[illegible]
[illegible]	[illegible]	April	[illegible]	[illegible]	[illegible]	[illegible]	[illegible]	[illegible]	[illegible]	[illegible]	[illegible]	[illegible]	[illegible]	[illegible]	[illegible]
[illegible]	[illegible]	May		[illegible]		[illegible]		[illegible]		[illegible]		[illegible]		[illegible]	[illegible]
[illegible]	[illegible]	June		[illegible]		[illegible]		[illegible]		[illegible]		[illegible]		[illegible]	[illegible]
[illegible]	[illegible]	July		[illegible]		[illegible]		[illegible]		[illegible]		[illegible]		[illegible]	[illegible]
[illegible]	[illegible]	Aug.		[illegible]		[illegible]		[illegible]		[illegible]		[illegible]		[illegible]	[illegible]
[illegible]	[illegible]		[illegible]	[illegible]	[illegible]	[illegible]	[illegible]	[illegible]	[illegible]	[illegible]	[illegible]	[illegible]	[illegible]	[illegible]	[illegible]

Second Year.—Recapitulation of Mean Readings from the preceding record of the Aneroid Barometer, No. [illegible], from September, 1858, to September, 1859. At Port Kennedy: Lat. [illegible]°.0 N., Long. [illegible]°.2 W.

1858.	2h.	4h.	6h.	8h.	10h.	Noon.	2h.	4h.	6h.	8h.	10h.	Midn't.	Mean.
Sept.		[illegible]		[illegible]		[illegible]		[illegible]		[illegible]		[illegible]	[illegible]
Oct.		[illegible]		[illegible]		[illegible]		[illegible]		[illegible]		[illegible]	[illegible]
Nov.	[illegible]	[illegible]	[illegible]	[illegible]	[illegible]	[illegible]	[illegible]	[illegible]	[illegible]	[illegible]	[illegible]	[illegible]	[illegible]
Dec.	[illegible]	[illegible]	[illegible]	[illegible]	[illegible]	[illegible]	[illegible]	[illegible]	[illegible]	[illegible]	[illegible]	[illegible]	[illegible]
1859, Jan.	[illegible]	[illegible]	[illegible]	[illegible]	[illegible]	[illegible]	[illegible]	[illegible]	[illegible]	[illegible]	[illegible]	[illegible]	[illegible]
Feb.	[illegible]	[illegible]	[illegible]	[illegible]	[illegible]	[illegible]	[illegible]	[illegible]	[illegible]	[illegible]	[illegible]	[illegible]	[illegible]
March	[illegible]	[illegible]	[illegible]	[illegible]	[illegible]	[illegible]	[illegible]	[illegible]	[illegible]	[illegible]	[illegible]	[illegible]	[illegible]
April		[illegible]		[illegible]		[illegible]		[illegible]		[illegible]		[illegible]	[illegible]
May		[illegible]		[illegible]		[illegible]		[illegible]		[illegible]		[illegible]	[illegible]
June		[illegible]		[illegible]		[illegible]		[illegible]		[illegible]		[illegible]	[illegible]
July	[illegible]	[illegible]	[illegible]	[illegible]	[illegible]	[illegible]	[illegible]	[illegible]	[illegible]	[illegible]	[illegible]	[illegible]	[illegible]
Aug.		[illegible]		[illegible]		[illegible]		[illegible]		[illegible]		[illegible]	[illegible]
	[illegible]	[illegible]	[illegible]	[illegible]	[illegible]	[illegible]	[illegible]	[illegible]	[illegible]	[illegible]	[illegible]	[illegible]	[illegible]

Recapitulation of Mean Readings from the preceding records of the Marine Mercurial Barometer, Adie No. [illegible], on board the Yacht Fox.

The readings are reduced to the temperature 32°. The cistern is 4 feet above the level of the sea.

Thermom. D. Bulb	Thermom. W. Bulb	1857.	4h.	8h.	Noon.	4h.	8h.	Midnight.	Mean.
			Inches.	Inches.	Inches.	Inches.	Inches.	Inches.	Inches.
[illegible]	[illegible]	September	[illegible]	[illegible]	[illegible]	[illegible]	[illegible]	[illegible]	[illegible]
[illegible]	[illegible]	October	[illegible]	[illegible]	[illegible]	[illegible]	[illegible]	[illegible]	[illegible]
[illegible]	[illegible]	November	[illegible]	[illegible]	[illegible]	[illegible]	[illegible]	[illegible]	[illegible]
[illegible]	[illegible]	December	[illegible]	[illegible]	[illegible]	[illegible]	[illegible]	[illegible]	[illegible]
[illegible]	[illegible]	1858, January	[illegible]	[illegible]	[illegible]	[illegible]	[illegible]	[illegible]	[illegible]
[illegible]	[illegible]	February	[illegible]	[illegible]	[illegible]	[illegible]	[illegible]	[illegible]	[illegible]
[illegible]	[illegible]	March	[illegible]	[illegible]	[illegible]	[illegible]	[illegible]	[illegible]	[illegible]
[illegible]	[illegible]	April	[illegible]	[illegible]	[illegible]	[illegible]	[illegible]	[illegible]	[illegible]

Comparison of the Readings of the Aneroid and Mercurial Barometers.

The preceding tabular results furnish the means of comparing the two barometers, and of deducing a correction to the indications of the aneroid barometer, in order to give the readings obtained from the mercurial barometer, referred to 32° of temperature. This correction is necessarily independent of the temperature, there being no thermometric readings in connection with the aneroid: any constant correction for difference of level between the two instruments is included. The following table contains the corresponding readings at the same days and hours, each being the mean of six observations a day.

Table of comparison of corresponding mean readings of the mercurial and the aneroid barometer, and resulting correction to the latter.

Date.	Mercurial.	Aneroid.	M − A = Δ
	Inches.	Inches.	Inch.
1857, September	[illegible]	29.874	−0.221
October	29.744	29.957	−0.213
November	[illegible]	[illegible]	[illegible]
December	29.555	29.774	−0.221
1858, January	[illegible]	[illegible]	[illegible]
February	[illegible]	[illegible]	[illegible]
March	[illegible]	[illegible]	−0.224
April	[illegible]	30.245	[illegible]
Mean	—	Δ =	−0.22[illegible]

These differences appear remarkably regular, and show that the mean monthly readings of the aneroid may be relied on to one-hundredth of an inch. There appears to be no tendency of a change of Δ depending on the higher or lower reading of the barometer, nor is there any variation due to changes in temperature. The correction to the aneroid readings to refer them to the corresponding readings

[a] The mean of 11 days, from Sept. 20th to 30th.
[b] The mean of 21 days, from Feb. 1st to 9th, and from Feb. 17th to 28th.
[c] The mean of 16 days, from April 1st to 16th.

of the mercurial barometer is, therefore, — 0.22 inches. This quantity, strictly speaking, is composed of two parts; the first, the true index error of the aneroid, and the second, the specific difference of the two instruments in different latitudes, the mercurial barometer (weighing a mass of mercury against a mass of air) being independent of a change of gravity, whereas the aneroid barometer is sensible to any increase of gravity as we proceed to the northern high latitudes. Within the limits of latitudes 66°.0 N. and 75°.3 N. this variation amounts to 0.014 inches; and its greatest difference from the mean, say in latitude 72°.0 N., is, therefore, + 0.008 inches. This quantity being smaller than the uncertainty of the results by the aneroid, I have considered it as a correction that can safely be neglected. The formula $b = b_{45} (1 - 0.0026 \cos 2 \phi)$ shows the variation for any latitude ϕ.

North of latitude 45° the aneroid gives the higher readings.

Resulting mean 4-hourly and mean monthly readings of the mercurial barometer in the months of September, 1857, *and February and April*, 1858.—The results for these months, given above, require a small correction to refer them from part of the month to the whole month; this was obtained by means of the known aneroid readings for the interval when the mercurial barometer was not read, the index correction — 0^{in}.22 having first been applied. We find—

Referred mean readings of the mercurial barometer for the full months of September, February, and April, of the first year:—

Average N. Lat.	Average W. Long.	Month.	6h.	9h.	Noon.	6h.	9h.	Midn't.	Mean.
75 .3	62 .0	1857, September	29.797	29.718	[illegible]	29.725	[illegible]	[illegible]	[illegible]
71.3	[illegible]	1858, February	29.[illegible]	29.[illegible]	29.[illegible]	29.[illegible]	29.[illegible]	29.[illegible]	29.[illegible]
65.0	57.7	1858, April	29.[illegible]	29.[illegible]	29.[illegible]	29.[illegible]	29.[illegible]	29.[illegible]	29.[illegible]

The following comparisons were made for the purpose of ascertaining how near the mean of 6 and 12 observations a day approximate to the true daily mean as derived from hourly observations. The following mean hourly readings, taken for 16 days between January 6 and January 22, 1858, are taken from the record; also the means for 7 days in January, 1859, and for 15 days in July, 1859. (Of these observations I find only the results recorded.)

JANUARY, 1858. FOR 13 DAYS.

Hour A. M.	Bar.	Hour A. M.	Bar.	Hour P. M.	Bar.	Hour P. M.	Bar.
1	29.741	7	29.697	1	29.776	7	29.763
2	.733	8	.695	2	.767	8	.757
3	.724	9	.706	3	.748	9	.758
4	.716	10	.723	4	.754	10	.763
5	.710	11	.731	5	.774	11	.776
6	.709	Noon	.737	6	.776	Midn't	.752

Mean of 24 observations a day . . . 29.746
" " 12 " " . . . .744 From the even hours,
" " 6 " " . . . .744 " " " "
including noon and midnight,
and at equal intervals.

JANUARY, 1859. FOR 7 DAYS.

Hour A. M.	Bar.	Hour A. M.	Bar.	Hour P. M.	Bar.	Hour P. M.	Bar.
1	30.057	7	30.059	1	30.040	7	30.051
2	.057	8	.047	2	.036	8	.050
3	.051	9	.069	3	.043	9	.049
4	.043	10	.053	4	.051	10	.079
5	.048	11	.044	5	.053	11	.046
6	.043	Noon	.040	6	.051	Midn't	.043

Mean of 24 observations a day . . . 30.048
" " 12 " " . . . .050 From the even hours,
" " 6 " " . . . .041 " " " "
and at equal intervals.

JULY, 1859. FOR 15 DAYS.

Hour A. M.	Bar.	Hour A. M.	Bar.	Hour P. M.	Bar.	Hour P. M.	Bar.
1	30.012	7	30.047	1	30.087	7	30.050
2	.012	8	.061	2	.090	8	.046
3	.011	9	.071	3	.094	9	.053
4	.018	10	.072	4	.080	10	.054
5	.021	11	.073	5	.071	11	.022
6	.024	Noon	.064	6	.063	Midn't	.013

Mean of 24 observations a day . . . 30.049
" " 12 " " . . . .049 From the even hours,
" " 6 " " . . . .047 " " " "
and at equal intervals.

The results show conclusively that the hourly and bi-hourly series give the same mean, and that the mean, deduced from six observations a day, does not materially differ from either; no correction need therefore be applied to daily means derived from readings at intervals of two and four hours.

Diurnal Variation of the Atmospheric Pressure.

The diurnal variation, which is almost vanishing in the higher latitudes of the Arctic regions, can only be satisfactorily traced by means of a combination of a great number of observations; it is also frequently masked by the great irregular fluctuations in the atmospheric pressure. The observations were, therefore, grouped, the first part comprising the results in Baffin Bay, from September, 1857, to August, 1858, inclusive, and the second part, the results at Port Kennedy, from September, 1858, to August, 1859, inclusive.

For greater convenience the results by the aneroid have been reduced to the results by the mercurial barometer, by the application of the correction — 0in.221.

The readings for the hours 4, 8, 12, A. M. and P. M., for the first eight months between Sept. and April, were taken from the preceding abstract of the mercurial barometer (the readings in Sept. February, and April from the table containing the referred means). All tabular numbers for the same eight months, at the hours 2, 6, 10, A. M. and P. M., are derived from the readings of the aneroid barometer by interpolation by means of differences; thus to obtain the reading at 10 A. M., in September, we have—

Aneroid reading at 10 A. M. 0.013 greater than at 8 A. M. Mercurial barometer reading at 8 A. M. = 29.715, hence at 10 A. M. = 29.728; again, aneroid at 10 A. M. 0.003 smaller than at noon. Mercurial barometer at noon 29.727, hence at 10 A. M. = 29.724, and the resulting mean from the comparison of the preceding and following hour becomes 29.726 as given in the table.

The annual mean for the hours 2, 6, 10, A. M. and P. M. is obtained in a similar manner; thus, for 10 A. M. we have: From 8 months, Sept. to April, mean at 10 A. M., the reading 0.020 greater than at 8 A. M. or = 29.731 + 0.020; it is also 0.006 greater than at noon or = 29.743 + 0.006; the mean of the two values is 29.750 as given in the table.

Diurnal variation of the atmospheric pressure during the year from September, 1857, to August, 1858, in mean latitude 72°.6 N., and mean longitude 63°.8 W.; nearly in the centre of Baffin Bay. 29 inches is to be added to the tabular numbers.

Hours.	2h.	4h.	6h.	8h.	10h.	Noon.	2h.	4h.	6h.	8h.	10h.	Midn't.
1857, Sept.	.713	.707	.710	.715	.726	.727	.730	.732	.730	.725	.727	.726
Oct.	.737	.734	.760	.714	.742	.748	.750	.746	.762	.760	.753	.750
Nov.	.628	.631	.614	.626	.621	.629	.614	.674	.600	.671	.647	.647
Dec.	.565	.560	.567	.544	.558	.552	.551	.558	.544	.566	.564	.554
1858, Jan.	.567	.611	.576	.610	.599	.621	.524	.627	.533	.630	.528	.619
Feb.	.625	.671	.614	.660	.644	.646	.644	.657	.658	.658	.646	.672
Mar.	.874	.880	.876	.912	.887	.900	.880	.894	.870	.901	.890	.861
April	.931	.930	.920	.922	.920	.922	.920	.922	.925	.919	.900	.914
May		.971		1.063		1.079		1.046		1.010		1.002
June		.743		.763		.818		.812		.819		.813
July		.725		.741		.735		.751		.754		.729
Aug.		.697		.711		.721		.743		.764		.737
Mean		.730		.731		.743		.763		.756		.743
Completed means	.723		.726		.750		.745		.746		.763	

The table of bi-hourly means for the second group was obtained from the general recapitulation of result, by subtracting 0.221 from each mean to reduce it to the reading of the standard marine barometer, and by referring the incomplete means at the hours 2, 6, 8, A. M. and P. M., to their corresponding value for a complete series of 12 values by a process similar to that explained in case of the preceding table.

Diurnal variation of the atmospheric pressure during the year from September, 1858, to August, 1859, at Port Kennedy, in latitude 72°.0 N., and longitude 94°.2 W. 29 inches is to be added to the tabular numbers, which, as well as the preceding tabular numbers for 1857–8, should be considered as reduced to the temperature 32° (Fahr.).

Hours.	2h.	4h.	6h.	8h.	10h.	Noon.	2h.	4h.	6h.	8h.	10h.	Midn't.
1858, Sept.		[illegible]		.9[illegible]4		[illegible]		.671		.9[illegible]		[illegible]
Oct.		.746		.7[illegible]		[illegible]		.777		.810		.725
Nov.	1.022	1.010	1.003	1.042	1.032	1.042	1.042	1.059	1.052	1.063	1.049	1.043
Dec.	.941	.82[illegible]	.872	[illegible]	.873	[illegible]	.871	[illegible]	.874	.873	[illegible]	[illegible]
1859, Jan.	.951	.917	.927	[illegible]	.974	[illegible]	.971	[illegible]	[illegible]	[illegible]	[illegible]	.979
Feb.	.914	[illegible]	[illegible]	.925	[illegible]	.925	.924	.920	[illegible]	.911	.927	.919
Mar.	1.131	1.114	1.124	1.150	1.166	1.165	1.165	1.116	1.179	1.1[illegible]	1.1[illegible]	1.173
April		1.1[illegible]		1.1[illegible]		1.1[illegible]		1.173		1.1[illegible]		1.153
May		[illegible]		[illegible]		1.0[illegible]		1.012		1.02[illegible]		1.010
June		[illegible]		.901		[illegible]		.910		[illegible]		[illegible]
July	.628	[illegible]	.666	.691	.702	.712	.727	.719	.709	[illegible]	.692	.611
Aug.		.715		.719		.730		.715		.741		.723
Mean		.851		.923		.933		.928		.943		.923
Completed Mean	[illegible]		[illegible]		.935		.936		.940		.934	

These results, when expressed analytically by means of Bessel's form of periodic functions with application of the method of least squares, become—

1. For Baffin Bay, 1857–1858—

$$b = \overset{\text{Inches.}}{29.743} + 0.013 \sin(\theta + 5°) + 0.004 \sin(2\theta + 159°)$$

2. For Port Kennedy, 1858–1859—

$$b = \overset{\text{Inches.}}{29.925} + 0.021 \sin(\theta + 22°) + 0.009 \sin(2\theta + 150°)$$

3. For Van Rensselaer Harbor, 1853–54–55, for comparison—

$$b = \overset{\text{Inches.}}{29.765} + 0.003 \sin(\theta + 290°) + 0.003 \sin(2\theta + 201°)$$

In which expressions the angle θ counts from noon at the rate of 15° an hour.

The comparison of the observations with the values deduced by the formulæ is shown in the following two diagrams, in which the observed values are indicated by dots.

DIURNAL VARIATION OF ATMOSPHERIC PRESSURE IN BAFFIN BAY.
Latitude 72°.5 N.

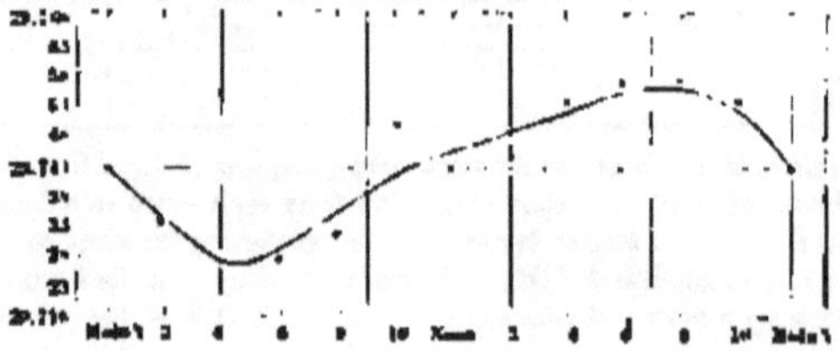

Diurnal Variation of Atmospheric Pressure at Port Kennedy.
Latitude 72°.0 N.

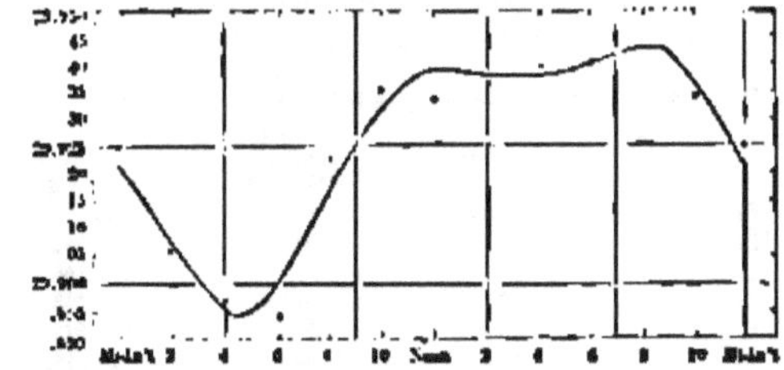

These curves have in common a maximum at about 7½ P. M., and a minimum at about 4½ A. M.; the hour of maximum at Van Rensselaer Harbor was 10 P. M., whereas a minimum at 4 A. M. is hardly perceptible at this place. A secondary maximum is plainly indicated at Port Kennedy about noon, and a secondary minimum about 2½ P. M., which secondary minimum seems to correspond with the principal minimum at Van Rensselaer Harbor at 1½ P. M.

The range of the diurnal fluctuation of the barometer is as follows:—

1. In Baffin Bay . . . . . 0.038 inches.
2. At Port Kennedy . . . . . 0.048 "
3. At Van Rensselaer Harbor . . . 0.010 "

Hence, between latitudes 72°.2 and 78°.6, there is a diminution in range of 0.028 inches; at this rate, the diurnal fluctuation would become insensible (be less than 0.001) in about 81° north latitude.

The following table of observed bi-hourly means is added for convenience of reference and for comparison:—

Hour.	Baffin Bay. Lat. 72 .5	Port Kennedy. Lat. 72 .0.	Van Rensselaer. Lat. 78 .6.
2	29.733	29.906	29.765
4	.739	.901	.766
6	.736	.924	.766
8	.731	.923	.762
10	.750	.925	.761
Noon	.743	.923	.762
2	.745	.936	.759
4	.753	.939	.762
6	.756	.940	.767
8	.758	.943	.769
10	.753	.934	.771
Midn't	.743	.925	.765
Mean . . .	29.743	29.925	29.765

Annual Variation of the Atmospheric Pressure.

The mean monthly height of the barometer is obtained directly from the preceding tables, showing the diurnal fluctuation, by applying to the monthly mean the correction for index, +0.007, and the reduction to the level of the sea, +0.005. To the table I have added for comparison the values for Van Rensselaer Harbor (also referred to the level of the sea by applying +0.005).

MONTHLY MEAN READINGS OF THE BAROMETER AT THE LEVEL OF THE SEA, AND AT 32° FAHR.

Month.	1857–8. Baffin Bay. Lat. 72°.6.	1858–9. Port Kennedy. Lat. 72°.0.	1853, '54, '55. Van Rensselaer. Lat. 78°.6.
January	29.532	29.970	29.778
February . . .	29.619	29.933	.846
March	29.823	30.178	.750
April	29.940	*30.179	.903
May	*30.014	30.010	*.942
June	29.817	29.918	.719
July	29.753	29.764	.741
August . . .	29.734	29.741	.694
September . . .	29.725	29.899	.659
October . . .	29.754	29.798	.735
November . . .	29.645	30.052	.768
December . . .	29.570	29.878	29.753
Mean . . .	29.753	29.938	29.775

It should be remembered that the monthly means in the first column were obtained while the ship was drifting and sailing in Baffin Bay, on which account the annual fluctuation may not appear as plainly as if the ship had been stationary in the middle latitude 72°.6 N.

The maximum in each series has been marked with an asterisk (*); it occurs either in April or May. The occurrence of the minimum does not agree at these stations; in Baffin Bay it occurred in January, at Port Kennedy in July, and at Van Rensselaer Harbor in September—showing plainly that more observations are required to fix the season or month in which it takes place on the average.

The preceding monthly values are represented by the formulæ:—

1. For Baffin Bay, 1857–8—

$$B = 29.756 + 0.155 \sin(\theta + 304°) + 0.113 \sin(2\theta + 230°)$$

(Greatest difference between an observed and computed value = 0.04 inches).

2. For Port Kennedy, 1858–59—

$$B = 29.938 + 0.137 \sin(\theta + 17°) + 0.106 \sin(2\theta + 232°)$$

(Greatest difference between observed and computed values; in October, —0.13, in November, +0.11).

3. For Van Rensselaer, 1853, '54, '55—

$$B = 29.775 + 0.079 \sin(\theta + 4°) + 0.044 \sin(2\theta + 194°)$$

Expressed in inches, and θ counting from January 1st, and at a rate of 30° a month.

The computed annual range, or the difference between the highest and lowest monthly mean, is as follows:—

Baffin Bay . . .	0.44 inches.
Port Kennedy . .	0.41 "
Van Rensselaer . .	0.31 "

Taking the mean of the expressions for the three stations, the following formulæ furnish the type-curve for lat. 74°.4 N., and long. 77°.0 W., for the *diurnal* and *annual* variation of the atmospheric pressure:—

$$h = \overset{\text{Inches}}{29.823} + 0.012 \sin(\theta + 340°) + 0.005 \sin(2\theta + 171°)$$
$$B = 29.823 + 0.124 \sin(\theta + 348°) + 0.088 \sin(2\theta + 221°)$$

Diurnal Extremes.

The irregular oscillations from day to day are subject to an annual variation, as exhibited in the following table of average differences in the atmospheric pressure on consecutive days. The daily changes were made out, irrespective of sign, and were obtained from the comparison of the daily means of the aneroid readings.

To the two localities—Baffin Bay and Port Kennedy, I have added, for comparison, Van Rensselaer Harbor, and also a column for a mean of the three localities.

	1857–8. Baffin Bay. 73°.5 N. Lat.	1858–9. Port Kennedy. 72°.0 N. Lat.	1853, '54, '55. Van Rensselaer. 78°.6 N. Lat.	Mean.
September . . .	0.17 inches.	0.12 inches.	0.11 inches.	0.13 inches.
October . . .	0.19	0.21	0.16	0.18
November . . .	0.22	0.14	0.17	0.15
December . . .	0.21	0.18	0.28	0.19
January . . .	0.28	0.31	0.17	0.18
February . . .	0.20	0.16	0.25	0.21
March . . .	0.22	0.12	0.17	0.17
April . . .	0.19	0.16	0.13	0.16
May . . .	0.10	0.07	0.14	0.10
June . . .	0.12	0.10	0.10	0.10
July . . .	0.08	0.14	0.09	0.10
August . . .	0.11	0.12	0.10	0.10
Mean . .	0.17	0.19	0.15	0.16

In Baffin Bay the progression is more regular than at Port Kennedy; the mean from the two stations compares very favorably with the result deduced from Dr. Kane's observations. The oscillations in the winter months are twice as great as those in the summer months.

The larger variations in the atmospheric pressure have already been noticed in the discussion of particular storms in the preceding part of the paper.

Monthly and Annual Extremes.

The following table contains the observed maxima and minima of the atmospheric pressure in each month, as observed by or referred to the mercurial marine barometer. (At 32° Fahr.)

Month.	Baffin Bay, 1857-58.			Port Kennedy, 1858-59.			For comparison: Van Rensselaer Harbor, 1853, '54, '55.		
	Max.	Min.	Range.	Max.	Min.	Range.	Max.	Min.	Range.
September	30.34	29.12	1.22	30.12	29.06	1.06	30.15	29.04	1.11
October	30.50	28.98	1.52	30.88	29.16	1.72	30.33	29.05	1.28
November	30.18	28.81	1.38	30.46	29.42	1.04	30.33	29.03	1.30
December	30.19	28.72	1.47	30.55	29.23	1.32	30.42	28.96	1.46
January	30.92	28.61	2.31	30.34	29.51	0.83	30.44	29.09	1.35
February	30.30	29.00	1.30	30.38	29.23	1.15	30.45	29.04	1.41
March	30.78	28.63	2.15	30.60	29.57	1.03	30.49	29.14	1.35
April	30.40	29.19	1.21	31.08	29.64	1.61	30.37	29.28	1.09
May	30.34	29.31	1.03	30.50	29.54	0.96	30.48	29.18	1.30
June	30.12	29.20	0.92	30.64	29.43	1.21	30.13	29.39	0.74
July	30.26	29.34	0.92	30.34	29.53	0.81	29.97	29.40	0.57
August	30.05	29.31	0.74	30.27	29.20	1.07	30.05	29.22	0.83
Mean	30.40	29.04	1.36	30.47	29.32	1.15	30.31	29.14	1.17

The monthly range is greatest in winter and least in summer in Baffin Bay and at Van Rensselaer Harbor; at Port Kennedy the amount of range is rather irregularly distributed over the year.

Absolute observed maxima and minima and extreme range (corrected for index error and referred to the level of the sea by the addition of 0.01).

Locality.	Max.	Date.	Min.	Date.	Range.
Baffin Bay	30.94	Jan. 30, '58.	28.64	Mar. 11, '58	2.30
Port Kennedy	31.14	April 12, '59.	28.74	July 10, '58.	2.40
Van Rensselaer Harbor.	30.57	Jan. 23, '55.	28.44	Feb. 19, '54.	2.13

Relation of the Atmospheric Pressure to the Direction of the Wind.

In this investigation the aneroid readings alone have been employed. For this purpose the daily readings at the hours 6 A. M. and 6 P. M., and at noon and midnight, were compared with the corresponding mean of five days (two days before and two days after the day in question). This substitution of the pentemera for the monthly means, as normals, was considered a desirable improvement. Each difference was inserted in the column for the respective wind (eight in all with a column for calms). In the exceptional case, where no observation was made at one or the other of the above hours, the observation at the nearest hour adjacent was substituted. A + sign indicates a pressure higher than the mean, a — sign a pressure lower than the mean. The following table contains the results arranged for two localities of one years' observations for each (commencing with September); the results at Port Kennedy for the S. E., S., and S. W. winds, are contracted in one mean on account of the scarcity of wind from these directions. The results for Van Rensselaer[1] have been added for comparison.

[1] Exchanging the magnetic for the true direction, on page 111 of Dr. Kane's meteorological record and discussion; a correction already referred to before.

Direction from of the wind.		1857-59. Baffin Bay. Lat. [illegible]	1858-59. Port Kennedy. Lat. 72 [illegible]	1853-4-5. Van Rensselaer Lat. 78 [illegible]
N.	.	+ 0.031 inches.	+ 0.004 inches.	— 0.025 inches.
N. E.	.	+ 0.009	— 0.024	} — 0.016
E.	.	+ 0.001	— 0.016	
S. E.	.	— 0.036	} + 0.015	0.000
S.	.	— 0.005		+ 0.025
S. W.	.	— 0.007		+ 0.045
W.	.	— 0.010	+ 0.005	— 0.021
N. W.	.	— 0.023	+ 0.003	— 0.031
Calm .	.	+ 0.035	+ 0.013	+ 0.005

The maximum effect of any one wind (or calm) does not exceed 0.04 of an inch, and, considering the short period of observation, and the probable irregularity in the phenomenon itself, the above figures for any one locality show a tolerable degree of progression. During calms the barometer is higher on the average 0.017 inch.

The above tabular quantities (after omitting the calms and making the algebraic sum of the results for each place equal zero) are contained in the expressions—

Inches.

For Baffin Bay $\beta = + 0.015 \; sin \; (\theta + 27°)$

For Port Kennedy $\beta = + 0.015 \; sin \; (\theta + 181)$

For Van Rensselaer $\beta = + 0.018 \; sin \; (\theta + 240)$,

The angle θ counting from the north. These expressions give nearly the same amount (0.016 inches) of elevating and depressing effect of the winds on the average, but do not correspond in the direction; thus, in Baffin Bay, according to the above, the barometer is higher with the wind from the N., N. E., and E., and lower with the wind from the S. W., W., and N. W.; whereas, at Port Kennedy, where the wind is much subject to local influences, nearly the opposite law would hold good.

The changes in the atmospheric pressure during the more violent storms have already been noticed, and were illustrated with diagrams.

APPENDIX.

APPENDIX.

Record of the Weather kept on board the Yacht "Fox," from July 2, 1857, to September 19, 1859; with Notes on the Specific Gravity of Sea Water, on the State of the Ice, Appearance of Animals, etc. etc.; on the Aurora Borealis and Atmospheric Phenomena.

The state of the weather is indicated by the following letters (Beaufort's notation):—

b	Blue sky.	*p*	Passing showers.
c	Clouds (detached).	*q*	Squally.
d	Drizzling rain.	*r*	Rain.
f	Foggy.	*s*	Snow.
g	Gloomy.	*t*	Thunder.
h	Hail.	*u*	Ugly (threatening) appearance.
l	Lightning.	*v*	Visibility, objects at a distance unusually visible.
m	Misty (hazy).	*w*	Wet (dew).
o	Overcast.	*s*	Snow drift.

A bar (—) or a dot (.) under any letter augments its signification.

The sign ("), in the record of the state of the weather, indicates the same entry as that of the hour immediately preceding.

The position of the vessel is given in the preceding record. The specific gravity of sea water was determined by Twaddel's hydrometer, that of distilled water being 1.000. The temperature of sea water and atmospheric pressure have already been stated.

The specific gravity of sea water, in the last column, is given in units of the fourth place of decimals, as indicated by the heading of the table.

For reasons stated by A. Mitchell, A. M., M. D., in the July number, 1860, of the Edinburgh New Philosophical Journal, it has not been deemed advisable to publish the observations for amount of ozone in the atmosphere. It is evident that the amount of discoloration of the papers exposed depends, in a great measure, on the air passed over, and, therefore, presents the combined effect of the quantity of ozone and the strength of the wind.

July, 1857. Record of the Weather kept on board the Yacht Fox, with general remarks.

Day.	4h.	8h.	Noon.	4h.	8h.	Midnight.	Specific Gravity of Sea Water, 1.0
1	b	m	m	m	c	m	—
2	o	o	o	m	o	r	[illegible]
3	c	m	m	m	o	o	[illegible]
4	o	o	m	m	o	o	[illegible]
5	c	o	b c	m	o	b	[illegible]
6	c	b c	c	b m	o	m	[illegible]
7	b c	o	b	b c	o	o	[illegible]
8	o	o	c o	o	o	c m p	—
9	p	c m p	c m	m o	m	f	[illegible]
10	d m	m o r	o r	m	r m	b m	[illegible]
11	b	m	m o	r	c d	o f	[illegible]
12	m r q	b c	b	b r	m	o	[illegible]
13	b	o	o	c	m	b c	—
14	b m	f	r m	o	d	c	[illegible]
15	r	d	m f	m	b r	f	[illegible]
16	m	c d	m o	m	o	f	[illegible]
17	d	f	o	o	m	o	—
18	f	o	m	m	c	b g	[illegible]
19	b	. . .	. . .	g r	b	m	—
20	r	c	b c	m	m	m	—
21	m	m	b m	o	f	m	—
22	f	o	o	o	b	o	[illegible]
23	b	o	m	o	o	o	—
24	b	c	o	f	g	c	[illegible]
25	b r	o	o	o	o	b	[illegible]
26	b	o	b c	o	o	m	[illegible]
27	b	g	o	c	o	c	[illegible]
28	q	c	r	p	m	o f	[illegible]
29	r f	c	o	c p	c	m	[illegible]
30	b r	o	o	m	m	m	[illegible]
31	b c	c	m	o	o	o	[illegible]

NOTES TO JULY RECORD.

1st. Aberdeen.

7th. Porpoises going east; a shearwater and two terns seen; fulmar petrels constantly in sight.

8th. A shearwater, an Arctic tern, and several fulmar petrels seen.

9th. A whale seen.

11th. Fulmar petrels constantly in sight.

12th. Mountains of South Greenland seen; Cape Farewell, N. 66°, W. 74'; fulmar petrels, kittiwake gulls, also strange petrels in sight.

14th. Fulmar and strange petrels, and kittiwakes in sight; several hours in sight of the ice.

16th. Loons are not uncommon.

17th. Sailing through heavy pack ice.

18th. Sailing through heavy pack ice.

19th. At noon in harbor of Frederickshaab.

22d. Anchored at 1h. 30m. P. M. in Fiskernaes Harbor.

25th. Hove to off Godhavn 8 A. M.

26th. One rorqual seen, mollymauks, and an occasional glaucous gull.

27th. Mollymauks as usual.

29th. A glaucous gull shot; considerable number seen; one black whale seen. Specific gravity of water in 110 fathoms 1.0275, temperature 31°.5; at surface 1.0215, temperature 31°.8.

31st. In Lievely Harbor.

August, 1857. RECORD OF THE WEATHER KEPT ON BOARD THE YACHT FOX, WITH GENERAL REMARKS

Date.	4h.	[illegible]	Noon.	4h.	[illegible]	Midnight.	Spec. Gravity of Sea Water, 1.0
1	r	m	m	bc	m	r	[illegible]
2	r	m	m	oc	c	bc	[illegible]
3[1]	f	o	m	bc	c	o	[illegible]
4	r	cqr	prq	pr	rp	bcq	[illegible]
5	bc	m	m	m	c	o	[illegible]
6	c	m	m	o	cm	g	[illegible]
7	or	o	f	bc	m	f	[illegible]
8	f	o	or	o	cm	r	[illegible]
9	bc	o	or	c	o	or	[illegible]
10[2]	r	bc	o	mr	f	m	[illegible]
11	f	b	m	m	m	m	[illegible]
12	b	o	m	m	m	m	[illegible]
13	b	m	m	bc	m	m	[illegible]
14[3]	bc	m	m	m	b	m	[illegible]
15	bc	m	m	o	m	m	[illegible]
16	bc	m	m	m	f	m	[illegible]
17	f	m	m	md	m	or	[illegible]
18	o	mo	cm	m	m	m	[illegible]
19	cm	o	m	m	mo	o	[illegible]
20	cm	o	o	cm	mo	r	[illegible]
21	o	o	f	gr	f	mo	[illegible]
22	mo	m	bc	d	m	c	[illegible]
23	ro	o	m	m	c	bc	[illegible]
24	bc	b	m	bc	c	o	[illegible]
25	c	o	mbi	mor	r	d	[illegible]
26	d	bc	m	f	c	o	[illegible]
27	c	or	c	bc	c	o	[illegible]
28	o	f	m	mo	o	g	[illegible]
29	bc	m	b	bm	b	m	[illegible]
30	bc	o	ocq	f	pmo	m	[illegible]
31	oc	o	r	b	m	m	[illegible]

NOTES TO AUGUST RECORD.

1st. In Disco Fiord; eider ducks abundant.

2d. One black whale and several rorquals seen.

3d. Off Innog Point; immense flocks of ducks.

4th. At Ritenbenk.

5th. A few rotchies seen.

6th. Off Upernavik; took on board six dogs at Proven, and fourteen at Upernavik.

7th. Several rotchies seen.

9th. Sailing amongst loose ice.

10th. Off the Devil's Thumb.

12th. Steaming through ice.

13th. Specific gravity of fresh water on the iceberg, 1.001.

14th. At midnight (14th to 15th) fast to a berg south of Brown's Island.

16th. Running through lanes in the pack.

17th. Running through lanes in the pack and beset.

18th. Beset in Melville Bay.

---

[1] Specific gravity of sea water marked with an asterisk (*), taken from the fourth number of Meteorological Papers, published by the Board of Trade. London, 1858. At 6 P.M. at anchor in 7 fathoms water, one-third of a mile off shore; bad holding ground; coaling at Ritenbenk.

[2] The specific gravity of the surface water fell from 1.0270 on the 9th, to 1.0238 on the 10th. The yacht is said to have been off the glacier, and was surrounded by bergs, the fresh water from which probably caused the diminution in the specific gravity at the surface. The specific gravity of the fresh water on a berg was 1.0010.

[3] Specific gravity in 314 fathoms	1.026	Temperature	30°.0
" " " 50 "	1.025	"	29.5
" " " 25 "	1.024	"	31.5

[4] Cape Walker, N. 60° E. (true); Cape Melville, N. 15° W. (true).

20th. Three seals seen.
21st. Two seals shot.
24th. One seal shot.
26th. Two glaucous gulls shot.
27th. Three seals and a turnstone shot; warping through the ice; ship nipped.
28th. Two seals shot.
29th. Cape Melville N. 8° 14' W. (true).
30th. Cape Melville N. 10° 30' W. (true).

September, 1857. RECORD OF THE WEATHER KEPT ON BOARD THE YACHT FOX, WITH GENERAL REMARKS.

DAY.	4h.	8h.	Noon.	4h.	8h.	Midnight.	Specific Grav. of Sea Water, 1.0
1	b	bc	m	m	m	c	
2	f	m	m	m	m	m	[illegible]
3	f	bf	f	fo	mo	f	[illegible]
4	f	mo	m	o	m	f	[illegible]
5	o	f	ro	c	o	c	[illegible]
6	f	ms	m	c	bc	o	[illegible]
7	c	co	m	oo	o	m	
8	ob	co	o	f	c	o	
9	f	fs	ro	m	m	frs	
10	o	f	m	o	mo	o	
11	os	m	rs	fs	o	f	
12	f	m	bc	f	m	m	
13	bc	m	m	m	fo	f	
14	fs	f	o	m	m	b	
15	bc	m	m	m	m	m	
16	o	c	ro	o	m	c	
17	b	m	m	m	m	m	
18	b	m	m	m	m	m	
19	b	m	m	m	m	m	
20	b	m	m	m	m	m	
21	b	m	m	m	bc	m	
22	c	m	bc	o	bc	c	
23	f	bc	b	bc	c	m	
24	b	bc	b	m	bc	b	
25	c	b	bc	b	f	m	
26	b	m	m	m	m	m	
27	o	m	bc	o	o	f	
28	f	bc	o	c	o	s	
29	f	m	bcm	c	f	m	
30	f	r	cm	c	m	bs	

NOTES TO SEPTEMBER RECORD.

1st. Four seals shot; beset in Melville Bay.
2d. Three seals shot.
3d. Three seals shot.
4th. Two seals shot.

---

[1] Specific gravity of sea water, from record in fourth number of Meteorological papers, Board of Trade.
[2] Specific gravity of sea, at surface . . . . 1.0265. Temperature 29.6
" " " " at 35 fathoms . . . 1.0261 " 29.0
" " " " " 90 " . . . 1.0272 " 29.0
" " " " " 98 " . . . 1.0262 " 29.6
[3] Cape Melville, N. 51° 40' E. (true); two black whales seen; four seals shot.
[4] A slight swell perceptible; 6 seals shot; a young burgomaster and a kittiwake seen; also several mollymokes.
[5] Two burgomaster gulls shot; a white falcon seen.
[6] At 2 A.M., dry bulb, 29°.3, wet, 29°.5; five seals and a burgomaster shot; at 10 P.M., dry bulb, 32°.8, wet bulb, 32°.5.
[7] Snow buntings seen; a ring seal shot.
[8] Snow shoals; wet bulb, 30°, dry bulb, 29°; at 4 A.M., dry bulb, 29°.9, wet bulb, 29°.0; a seal and a burgomaster shot.

5th. A black whale seen; sounded in 69 fathoms; yellowish mud; six seals obtained.
6th. Soundings in 85 fathoms; yellowish mud.
7th. A *Tringa* shot.
8th. Soundings in 86 fathoms; same bottom.
9th. Soundings in 94 fathoms; mud, shells, and stones.
10th. Soundings in 88½ fathoms; stones and mud.
11th. Soundings in 83 fathoms; stones and mud.
12th. Soundings in 80 fathoms; soft mud.
13th. Strong refraction in N. W.; three ravens, one burgomaster, and one turnstone seen.
14th. Soundings in 74 fathoms; a sea snipe shot; dry bulb 29°.0, wet 29°.8 at 9 A. M.
15th. Soundings in 78 fathoms; two ravens, a few snow buntings, and a burgomaster seen.
16th. Soundings in 69 fathoms; stones.
17th. Soundings in 51 fathoms; mud.
18th. Longitude by Jupiter's first satellite 65° 5′ W.
19th. Faint aurora at 2 A. M.; sounded in 114 fathoms; stones and mud.
21st. No bottom with 120 fathoms; wet bulb 25.5, dry bulb 29.5.
22d. Sounded in 125 fathoms; sand and mud; two bears seen.
23d. Sounded in 130 fathoms; soft mud.
24th. Specific gravity of surface of sea 1.0250, at 29° temperature; two bears seen; faint aurora in the N. E.
25th. Faint aurora from N. N. W. to S. S. W.; two seals and a glaucous gull seen
26th. A raven shot.
27th. A raven seen; at 2 A. M. a slight aurora in the E. S. E.
28th. No bottom with 140 fathoms.
29th. Two bears seen.
30th. Many shooting stars at midnight (30th to 1st).

October, 1857. Record of the Weather kept on board the Yacht Fox, with general remarks.

Day.	2h.	4h.	6h.	8h.	10h.	Noon.	2h.	4h.	6h.	8h.	10h.	Mid't.
1	o	m	f	m	m	m v	c	[illegible]	o	m	o	m
2	c	m	m	m	c	o	m c	f	m	m	o	m
3	f	m	m	m	b c	b c m	b	m	m	m	v	m
4	b	m	m	c	m	m	m	m	o	m	c	b c
5	c	m	b c	m	m	m	b	m	m	m	m	m
6	b	m	c	m	b c	m	c	m	b c	o	b c v	b
7	m	m	m	b m	b c m	m	b c	m	f	m	c	m
8	b c	c	f	m	c m	m	m	c	m	m	f	c
9	o	m	m	v	o	m	o	m	c	b c	b	m
10	b o	m	m	b m	b	m	m	f	m	m	f	m
11	f	o	m	b m	m	m	b c	m	m	b	m	c m
12	f	o	b	[illegible]	m v	m	c	v	m	m	b m	f
13	f	m	o	m	m	m c	f	o	o	c c	m	m
14	c c	m	m	m	c m	m	m	b c m	o	b m	m o	m
15	o	o c	m	m	m	m	o	m	m	o	m	m
16	c	m	m	o	m	o	o	o	m	c	c s	m
17	o	c	b	b c	c	b c	m	c	o	c	m	o
18	c	m	m	m	m	m o	m	m	m	m	m	m
19	m	m	m	c	m	m	m	f	m	m	m	m
20	o	m	v	m	o	m	m	o	m	m	m	m
21	f	m	m	o	b c	g m	o	m	m	o	m	m
22	m	v	m	m	m	m	m	m	m	m	m	m
23	o	v	m	m	b c	o	m	m	m	m	b	m
24	m	o	m	o	b	m	m	m	v	c	b c	m
25	v	m	b c	o	m	c m	m	m	o	o	m	m
26	m	m	m	c	b c	m	m	m	o	m	m	m
27	m	c	m	m	b c	m	m	m	m	b m	m	m
28	b m	m	m	m	m	o	b c	m	m	o	c	b c
29	o	m	m	m	m	o	c	m	c	b	m	m
30	b c	o	o	m	b c	o	m	m	b	o	m	m
31	c	m	c	m	b c	m	m	m	o	c	m	m

NOTES TO OCTOBER RECORD.

1st. Ice drift N. W.; a ptarmigan caught by the dogs; a flock of eider-ducks and a raven seen.

2d. Dusk at 7^h.

3d. Dawn at 5^h 10^m; dusk at 7^h.

4th. Dusk at 6^h 30^m; at 11 P. M. an aurora in W. N. W.

5th. Dawn at 5^h 30^m, dusk at 6^h 30^m; at midnight longitude by chronometer and Jupiter 69° 45′ W.

6th. Dawn at 5^h 20^m; tried for soundings with 140 fathoms; dusk at 6^h 20^m.

7th. Dawn at 5^h 35^m, dusk at 6^h 15^m; two bear tracks near the ship.

8th. Dawn at 5^h 35^m, dusk at 6^h 10^m.

9th. 2 A. M. aurora seen from S. S. E. to E. S. E.; dawn at 5^h 30^m; a raven seen; dusk at 6^h 0^m.

10th. Dawn at 5^h 35^m, dusk at 5^h 55^m.

11th. Dawn at 6^h 0^m, dusk at 5^h 10^m.

12th. Dawn at 5^h 30^m, dusk at 5^h 40^m; a flock of eider-ducks passed to the southward; fox and bear tracks seen; between 8 and 10 P. M. some shooting stars.

13th. Dawn at 5^h 35^m, dusk at 5^h 30^m.

14th. Dawn at 6^h 0^m, dusk at 5^h 30^m; the young ice opened for some miles in length; a slight swell observed.

15th.[1] Dawn at 5^h 30^m, dusk at 5^h 30^m.

16th. Dawn at 6^h 30^m; dusk at 5^h 30^m; seals in the lane of water; tried for soundings with 185 fathoms.

17th. Dawn at 6^h 15^m, dusk at 5^h 15^m; high land seen from north to N. E. by E. (true); seals in the lane of water, also narwhals; thickness of young ice one month old, 1 foot 3.8 inches; overlying snow, 2½ inches.

18th. Dawn at 6^h 30^m, dusk at 5^h 0^m.

19th. Dawn at 6^h 45^m, dusk at 4^h 30^m.

20th. Dawn at 6^h 50^m, dusk at 4^h 25^m.

21st. Dawn at 6^h 50^m, dusk at 4^h 15^m; distant land bearing E. N. E., true; a large seal seen.

22d. Dawn at 6^h 45^m, dusk at 4^h 10^m.

23d. Dawn at 7^h 0^m, dusk at 4^h 35^m; a fox track near the ship, and a seal seen.

24th. Dawn at 7^h 0^m, dusk at 4^h 30^m.

25th. Dawn at 6^h 35^m, dusk at 4^h 20^m.

26th. Dawn at 7^h 30^m; dusk at 4^h 15^m; Cape York N. 3° E. (true); Cape Dudley Digges N. 50° E. (true).

27th. Dawn at 7^h 0^m, dusk at 4^h 30^m.

28th. Dawn at 7^h 15^m; dusk at 4^h 15^m; the ice opening and in motion near the ship.

29th. Daylight at 7^h 30^m; a lane of water crossing the bows and distant two hundred yards; a long lane on port beam distant one mile, and extending east and west two or three miles; dusk at 4^h.

30th. Ice movement and pressure all preceding night within two hundred yards of the ship; at 4^h 30^m A. M. slight aurora from S. to S. S. E. (true); dawn at 7^h 15^m, dusk at 4^h 0^m; at 10 P. M. ice in motion.

31st. Dawn at 7^h 30^m; wide lane of water, covered with thin bay ice in all directions; dusk at 3^h 40^m; ice in motion and water space increasing.

---

[1] Thickness of snow falling during three or four weeks, 2½ inches; thickness of ice one month old, 15.5 inches.

November, 1857. RECORD OF THE WEATHER KEPT ON BOARD THE YACHT FOX, WITH GENERAL REMARKS.

DAY	2h.	4h.	6h.	8h.	10h.	Noon.	2h.	4h.	6h.	8h.	10h.	Mid't.
1	c	o	b c	o	b c m	m c	s	s	o	o	o	b
2	m	c	c	b c	o	m	o	o	b c	m	o	c
3	b c	b	o	c	m	o	m	o	m	o	o	c
4	m	o	o	o	o	m c	o	o	c	o	o	c m
5	c	b c	o	o	c	o	o	m	o	m	o	o
6	c	o	c m	b c	o	o	m	c	m s	o	o	o
7	m s	o	o	o	b c	b c	o	c	m	o	c	o
8	m	o	m s	o	c m s	c	o	c m	c	m	o	m s
9	m s	c	o	m	m	c m	m	c	m	o	m	b c
10	o	c	c	m	m	o	o	c	o	m	c	o
11	m	f	m	o	b c	o	o	o	c	c	c	m
12	m	o	c	b c	o	o	m	b	m	o	b	m
13	m	o	m s	o	o	o	m	o	c m s	m s	o	c m
14	m c	o	c o	m	c s s	o	o	m s	o	o	m o s	o
15	m o s	o	o	o	m	c o	o	o	o	m	o	o
16	c c	o	m o	o	o	o	o	m s	o	o	s s	o
17	c s	o	o	o	c s	o	o	o	c m	o	m	o
18	m o	o	o	b c	c	o	m o	o	o	o	m	o
19	m	o	f	b c	o	c	m	o	o	o	o	o
20	m s	s	o	m	c	c m	b c	m	o	m	m	o
21	m	o	o	s	c	o	b c	c m	o	c s	o	o
22	m o s	m s	o	o	m o s	o	o	o	o	m	m	o
23	s s	o	b c	o	o	o	c	o	b c	b	b c	o
24	c	m	c	o	b c	o	o	o	b	o	b	b c
25	b c	o	m	o	c	o	b s	m	b s	o	o	o
26	b c	b c	c	o	c	b c	b s	c	o	o	o	b m
27	b s	o	b c	o	o	o	o	b	b p	o	o	b c
28	c	o	c m	o	b c	o	o	o	b	s	o	o
29	c c	o	b s	o	o	o	b	o	b c	c	b	o
30	b o	o	o	o	o	o	o	o	o	o	o	o

NOTES TO NOVEMBER RECORD.

1st. Dawn at 7^h 30^m, dusk at 3^h 50^m.

2d. Dawn at 7^h 40^m, dusk at 3^h 30^m; 8 P. M. a bear came to the ship and was shot; length 7 feet 3 inches.

3d. Dawn at 7^h 50^m, dusk at 3^h 30^m.

4th. Dawn at 8^h 0^m, dusk at 3^h 15^m.

5th. Dawn at 7^h 30^m, dusk at 3^h 15^m.

6th. Dawn at 7^h 45^m, dusk at 3^h 15^m; ice in motion; lanes of water in the S. W. and N. W.; two seals seen.

7th.[1] Dawn at 7^h 45^m, dusk at 3^h 15^m; lanes of water in all directions; two dovekies shot; slight streak of aurora near horizon in the S. E. after 6 P. M.

8th. Dawn at 8^h 10^m, dusk at 3^h 0^m; several seals seen; 8 P. M. faint aurora in the W. N. W.

9th.[2] Dawn at 8^h 30^m, dusk at 2^h 55^m; ice in motion, opening and closing; several seals seen; at 10 P. M. several shooting stars, and a faint lunar rainbow.

10th. 3 A. M. faint streaks of aurora from south to west, near horizon; dawn at 8^h 30^m, dusk at 2^h 55^m; several seals seen.

---

[1] Notices of aurora inclosed within brackets were taken from the fourth number of Meteorological Papers of the Board of Trade.

[7th, midnight. Faint in S. W. (true) horizon, 25° in breadth, and about 20° in extent, of a pale yellow color at times, oscillating and decreasing in extent to 10°; again on following night in N. N. W. horizon.]

[2] [9th, midnight. In south to east (true) pale yellow to pale green, with rays streaming towards the zenith, about 7° above horizon, and being apparently just above a bank of fog, which gradually overcame and obscured it. There were no vibrations or scintillations, but at times it appeared broken up to detached pieces. It continued for an hour and a quarter.]

11th.[1] A dovekie seen; two seals shot; dusk at 2^h 50^m; 8 P. M. slight aurora in S. W.; several falling stars.

12th. Dawn at 8^h 50^m, dusk at 2^h 40^m; a dovekie seen; three seals shot.

13th. Dawn at 8^h 45^m, dusk at 2^h 35^m; motion perceptible in the ice; a few seals and a dovekie seen.

14th. Dawn at 8^h 50^m; ice in motion, the old ice crushing up the new ice; dusk at 2^h 22^m.

15th. Dawn at 9^h 15^m; ice moving; several large pools of water; a narwhal and many seals seen, one shot; dusk at 2^h 30^m.

16th. Dawn at 9^h 15^m; a seal shot and a dovekie seen; dusk at 2^h 15^m.

17th. Dawn at 9^h 20^m, dusk at 2^h 0^m.

18th. Dawn at 9^h 35^m, dusk at 2^h 5^m; a few seals and narwhals seen.

19th. Dawn at 9^h 50^m, dusk at 2^h 0^m; two or three seals seen.

20th. Dawn at 9^h 45^m, dusk at 2^h 0^m; one seal seen.

21st. Dawn at 9^h 45^m, dusk at 2^h 15^m.

22d. Dawn at 9^h 50^m, dusk at 1^h 50^m.

23d.[2] Dawn at 9^h 45^m; one seal seen; 8 P. M. aurora near the horizon in the S. E.; at midnight, aurora from N. W. to S. W. and S. E.

24th. 9 A. M. aurora at the S. E. horizon; dusk at 1^h 45^m.

25th. Dawn at 9^h 50^m, dusk at 1^h 40^m; a small lane of water near the ship; only one seal seen.

26th. Dawn at 9^h 50^m, dusk at 1^h 35^m.

27th. Dawn at 10^h 0^m, dusk at 1^h 30^m.

28th. Dawn at 10^h 5^m, dusk at 1^h 25^m.

29th. Dawn at 10^h 0^m, dusk at 1^h 35^m.

30th. Dawn at 10^h 15^m, dusk at 1^h 10^m.

December, 1857. RECORD OF THE WEATHER KEPT ON BOARD THE YACHT FOX, WITH GENERAL REMARKS.

DAY.	2^h	4^h	6^h	8^h	10^h	Noon.	2^h	4^h	6^h	8^h	10^h	Mid't.
1	b c	[illegible]	[illegible]	[illegible]	[illegible]	[illegible]	[illegible]	[illegible]	[illegible]	[illegible]	[illegible]	[illegible]
2	b c	[illegible]	[illegible]	[illegible]	[illegible]	[illegible]	[illegible]	[illegible]	[illegible]	[illegible]	[illegible]	[illegible]
3	b v	[illegible]	[illegible]	[illegible]	[illegible]	[illegible]	c m	[illegible]	[illegible]	[illegible]	[illegible]	b v
4	b v	[illegible]	[illegible]	[illegible]	[illegible]	[illegible]	[illegible]	[illegible]	[illegible]	[illegible]	[illegible]	m c
5	b v	[illegible]	[illegible]	[illegible]	[illegible]	[illegible]	b v	[illegible]	m s	[illegible]	[illegible]	[illegible]
6	m s	[illegible]	c m s	[illegible]	c m	[illegible]	[illegible]	[illegible]	[illegible]	[illegible]	[illegible]	[illegible]
7	c m	[illegible]	[illegible]	[illegible]	[illegible]	[illegible]	b c	[illegible]	[illegible]	b c	[illegible]	[illegible]
8	b v	b c	c m	[illegible]	[illegible]	b c	c	c m	[illegible]	[illegible]	b v	[illegible]
9	b v	[illegible]	[illegible]	b v	[illegible]	[illegible]	b	b v	[illegible]	[illegible]	c	b c
10	b	b v	[illegible]	[illegible]	b c	b	[illegible]	[illegible]	[illegible]	b v	b m	[illegible]
11	[illegible]	[illegible]	[illegible]	[illegible]	b c	[illegible]	b c	b	b c	b	[illegible]	b v
12	[illegible]	[illegible]	c s	[illegible]	[illegible]	[illegible]	[illegible]	m s	[illegible]	[illegible]	[illegible]	[illegible]
13	m s	[illegible]	[illegible]	[illegible]	[illegible]	b m s	b m	b	[illegible]	[illegible]	b c	[illegible]
14	c	c m	m	[illegible]	b	b v	c	b	[illegible]	[illegible]	[illegible]	[illegible]
15	c	[illegible]	b	[illegible]	b c	[illegible]	[illegible]	[illegible]	[illegible]	[illegible]	[illegible]	[illegible]
16	[illegible]	[illegible]	c	b	[illegible]	[illegible]	c	[illegible]	[illegible]	[illegible]	[illegible]	[illegible]
17	[illegible]	[illegible]	[illegible]	b m	[illegible]	[illegible]	b c	[illegible]	[illegible]	b v	[illegible]	b c
18	b c	c	[illegible]	b v	[illegible]	b c	[illegible]	[illegible]	b	b v	[illegible]	[illegible]
19	b v	[illegible]	[illegible]	[illegible]	c	[illegible]	b c	b v	[illegible]	[illegible]	m	[illegible]
20	[illegible]	[illegible]	[illegible]	c	[illegible]	[illegible]	[illegible]	[illegible]	[illegible]	[illegible]	m c	[illegible]
21	[illegible]	s c	m s	[illegible]	m	[illegible]	[illegible]	[illegible]	[illegible]	[illegible]	b c	[illegible]
22	[illegible]	[illegible]	[illegible]	[illegible]	[illegible]	c	m	[illegible]	m s	[illegible]	[illegible]	[illegible]
23	[illegible]	[illegible]	[illegible]	[illegible]	[illegible]	m s	[illegible]	[illegible]	m	c	[illegible]	[illegible]
24	[illegible]	[illegible]	c	m	c m	[illegible]	[illegible]	b v	[illegible]	b c	c	[illegible]
25	[illegible]	[illegible]	[illegible]	[illegible]	[illegible]	b m	c m	b m	b v	[illegible]	[illegible]	m
26	b v	m	[illegible]	[illegible]	b s	[illegible]	[illegible]	[illegible]	[illegible]	[illegible]	b v	b m
27	[illegible]	[illegible]	[illegible]	[illegible]	m s	[illegible]	m c s	[illegible]	[illegible]	[illegible]	[illegible]	[illegible]
28	[illegible]	[illegible]	m v	[illegible]	[illegible]	[illegible]	[illegible]	c s	b v	m v	c	m v
29	m v	v s	c s	[illegible]	[illegible]	[illegible]	b	m	b v	[illegible]	b v	[illegible]
30	m	[illegible]	b v	[illegible]	[illegible]	[illegible]	b c	b c v	[illegible]	b v	[illegible]	[illegible]
31	b v	b v	b	[illegible]	b c	b c	[illegible]	b v	[illegible]	[illegible]	[illegible]	[illegible]

[1] [11th, midnight. Bright in S. E. (true).]

[2] [23d, midnight. Very bright till 2 A. M. in N. W. to S. E. (true).]

[On the 16th, the thickness of ice 5 feet 1 inch; increase since last month, 6 inches.—B. of T. Papers.]

NOTES TO DECEMBER RECORD.

1st. Dawn at 10^h 30^m, dusk at 1^h 5^m; ice crushing up at the edges of the floe.

2d. Dawn at 10^h 30^m, dusk at 1^h 10^m

3d. Dawn at 10^h 30^m, dusk at 1^h 0^m

4th. Dawn at 11^h 0^m; a well-marked halo and several paraselenæ, 7^h to 10^h P. M., consisting of five false moons, three arcs of halos, and a horizontal belt of light round the heaven and passing through the moon

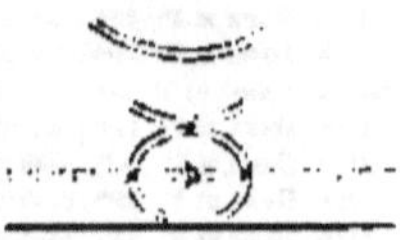

5th. Dawn at 10^h 30^m, dusk at 0^h 50^m

6th. Unable to read by light of the sky.

7th. Dawn at 11^h 0^m; several cracks near the ship; one seal seen.

8th. Dawn at 11^h 0^m; dusk at 0^h 30^m; the cracks nearly closed.

9th. Dawn at 11^h 5^m; dusk at 0^h 45^m; midnight (9th to 10th), aurora from E. N. E. to E. S. E. (true), also several shooting stars.

10th. Dawn at 11^h 0^m, dusk at 1^h 20^m; 9 P. M., faint aurora in the south, streaming towards the zenith.

11th. Dawn at 11^h 30^m, dusk at 0^h 30^m

12th. Dawn at 11^h 15^m, dusk at 0^h 20^m; [2 A. M., slight aurora to southward;] 10 P. M., faint aurora in N. W.

13th. Dawn at 11^h 0^m, dusk at 0^h 50^m; 6 P. M., bright aurora in S. E; 10 P. M., aurora from the S. E. to N. E. [part of an arc], with rays shooting up towards the zenith.

14th. 2 A. M., faint aurora towards the southern horizon; dawn at 11^h 10^m, dusk at 0^h 15^m; found a perceptible divergence in the gold leaves of an electrometer when attached to a insulated wire and passed down to the sea; 9 P. M., faint aurora in the N. E. (true).

15th. Dawn at 11^h 10^m, dusk at 0^h 30^m; several shooting stars between 5 and 6 P. M.; midnight (15th to 16th), faint aurora to southward. [Thickness of ice 3 feet 0 inches; increase since last month 11½ inches.—B. of T. Papers.*]

16th. No daylight. [6 P. M., aurora slight from E. to N. E., and at 10 P. M. bright from S. to N. E., continuing till 10 A. M. next day, at 6 P. M. again for one hour, across the zenith from E. to W. and N. W.; the electrometer was sensibly affected.]

17th. Dawn at 11^h 30^m, dusk at 0^h 30^m; 6 P. M., slight aurora E. to N., 10 P. M., bright aurora S. to N. E.

18th. Thickness of September ice 3 feet 0 inches, overlying closely packed snow 8½ inches; 4 A. M. aurora still visible, 0^h 15^m A. M. aurora disappeared; dawn at 11^h 15^m, dusk at 0^h 30^m; 4 P. M., faint aurora from E. to W. and N. W., passed through the zenith; 10 P. M., aurora S. S. E. to S. S. W., near horizon.

19th. Dawn at 11^h 45^m, dusk at 0^h 25^m; a wide crack, N. W. and S. E., half a mile from the ship.

20th. No daylight.

21st. Daylight at 11^h 45^m, dusk at 0^h 15^m

22d. No daylight.

23d. No daylight.

24th. Dawn at 11^h 15^m, dusk at 0^h 20^m; narrow lane of water recently opened to the S. W. and N. W. of the ship, and distant from one-quarter to one mile.

25th, 26th, 27th. No daylight.

28th. Dawn at 11^h 25^m, dusk at 0^h 45^m

29th. Dawn at 11^h 0^m, dusk at 11^h 45^m; small lanes of water, and several fresh cracks near the ship.

30th. Dawn at 11^h 15^m, dusk at 0^h 45^m

31st. Dawn at 10^h 35^m, dusk at 0^h 50^m [No birds seen and only one seal.—B. of T. Papers.]

* Hard packed snow 6½ inches thick.

January, 1858. RECORD OF THE WEATHER KEPT ON BOARD THE YACHT FOX, WITH GENERAL REMARKS.

Day.	2h	4h	6h	8h	10h	Noon.	2h	4h	6h	8h	10h	Mid'n.
1	b c	[illegible]	[illegible]	[illegible]	[illegible]	[illegible]	b	[illegible]	[illegible]	[illegible]	[illegible]	b
2	b c	[illegible]	[illegible]	[illegible]	b c	[illegible]	[illegible]	[illegible]	b c	[illegible]	[illegible]	[illegible]
3	b c	[illegible]	[illegible]	[illegible]	b c	[illegible]	b c	[illegible]	[illegible]	[illegible]	[illegible]	[illegible]
4	b c	[illegible]	[illegible]	[illegible]	[illegible]	[illegible]	[illegible]	m c	[illegible]	[illegible]	[illegible]	[illegible]
5	o c	[illegible]	[illegible]	m o	[illegible]	[illegible]	c m	[illegible]	b c	b	[illegible]	b c
6	c m	b	b o	b c	b	b s	b c	[illegible]	[illegible]	[illegible]	[illegible]	b c
7	b c s	[illegible]	[illegible]	[illegible]	[illegible]	[illegible]	[illegible]	m c	[illegible]	[illegible]	[illegible]	[illegible]
8	m c	[illegible]	[illegible]	[illegible]	[illegible]	[illegible]	[illegible]	[illegible]	[illegible]	[illegible]	[illegible]	[illegible]
9	o c	[illegible]	[illegible]	[illegible]	b m	b c m	b m	b c	[illegible]	[illegible]	[illegible]	[illegible]
10	b c	[illegible]	[illegible]	[illegible]	[illegible]	[illegible]	[illegible]	b c	b c	b c m	[illegible]	[illegible]
11	[illegible]	[illegible]	m c	[illegible]	[illegible]	b c	m c	[illegible]	[illegible]	b c	[illegible]	[illegible]
12	[illegible]	[illegible]	[illegible]	[illegible]	m c	[illegible]	b c	[illegible]	[illegible]	[illegible]	[illegible]	[illegible]
13	[illegible]	[illegible]	[illegible]	b c	[illegible]	[illegible]	[illegible]	[illegible]	[illegible]	[illegible]	[illegible]	[illegible]
14	b c	[illegible]	[illegible]	b c	b c	[illegible]	[illegible]	[illegible]	[illegible]	[illegible]	[illegible]	[illegible]
15	o s	[illegible]	[illegible]	[illegible]	[illegible]	[illegible]	[illegible]	[illegible]	[illegible]	b c	[illegible]	[illegible]
16	o c	[illegible]	[illegible]	[illegible]	m c	[illegible]	[illegible]	[illegible]	[illegible]	[illegible]	[illegible]	[illegible]
17	o o	[illegible]	[illegible]	[illegible]	[illegible]	b c	b c s	[illegible]	[illegible]	[illegible]	[illegible]	[illegible]
18	b c	[illegible]	[illegible]	[illegible]	b c	[illegible]	[illegible]	[illegible]	b	[illegible]	[illegible]	[illegible]
19	b c	[illegible]	[illegible]	[illegible]	c	[illegible]	b c	[illegible]	[illegible]	[illegible]	m c	[illegible]
20	o c	[illegible]	[illegible]	[illegible]	[illegible]	[illegible]	[illegible]	[illegible]	m s	[illegible]	m c	[illegible]
21	m c	[illegible]	[illegible]	[illegible]	[illegible]	m c s	o c	[illegible]	[illegible]	[illegible]	[illegible]	[illegible]
22	[illegible]	[illegible]	[illegible]	b c	[illegible]	[illegible]	[illegible]	[illegible]	b o	[illegible]	[illegible]	b c
23	m c	. . .	m c s	o s	[illegible]	[illegible]	[illegible]	b c	b	[illegible]	[illegible]	[illegible]
24	b c	[illegible]	[illegible]	b c	[illegible]	[illegible]	[illegible]	[illegible]	[illegible]	[illegible]	[illegible]	[illegible]
25	[illegible]	[illegible]	o c	[illegible]	[illegible]	[illegible]	[illegible]	[illegible]	b c	m s	[illegible]	[illegible]
26	[illegible]	[illegible]	[illegible]	o c	[illegible]	[illegible]	[illegible]	[illegible]	o c	[illegible]	[illegible]	[illegible]
27	m c	[illegible]	[illegible]	[illegible]	b c	[illegible]	[illegible]	[illegible]	[illegible]	b c	[illegible]	[illegible]
28	b c	[illegible]	b	[illegible]	b c	b	b c	[illegible]	[illegible]	[illegible]	[illegible]	[illegible]
29	b c	[illegible]	[illegible]	[illegible]	[illegible]	[illegible]	[illegible]	[illegible]	b c	b c	[illegible]	[illegible]
30	b c	[illegible]	[illegible]	[illegible]	[illegible]	[illegible]	[illegible]	[illegible]	[illegible]	[illegible]	[illegible]	[illegible]
31	b c	[illegible]	b c	b c	b c	[illegible]	b c	[illegible]	b c	[illegible]	[illegible]	[illegible]

NOTES TO JANUARY RECORD.

1st. Dawn at $10^{h}\ 45^{m}$, dusk at $1^{h}\ 0^{m}$; temperature in snow-hut −15°.

2d. Dawn at $10^{h}\ 30^{m}$, dusk at $1^{h}\ 30^{m}$.

3d. Dawn at $11^{h}\ 10^{m}$.

4th. Dawn at $11^{h}\ 10^{m}$, dusk at $0^{h}\ 35^{m}$.

5th. Dawn at $11^{h}\ 15^{m}$, dusk at $1^{h}\ 15^{m}$; a lane of water in the west extending N. E. and S. W. (true); one seal seen.

6th. Dawn at $10^{h}\ 45^{m}$, dusk at $1^{h}\ 15^{m}$.

7th. Dawn at $10^{h}\ 45^{m}$, dusk at $1^{h}\ 30^{m}$.

8th. Dawn at $10^{h}\ 35^{m}$, dusk at $1^{h}\ 50^{m}$.

9th. Dawn at $10^{h}\ 15^{m}$; at 9 P. M. bright aurora from west to east (magnetic) passing through west; 10 P. M., slight aurora occasionally visible round the horizon; 11 P. M., same.

10th. Dawn at $10^{h}\ 5^{m}$, dusk at $1^{h}\ 15^{m}$.

11th. Dawn at $10^{h}\ 50^{m}$, dusk at $2^{h}\ 30^{m}$; aurora near the S. W. horizon at 9 P. M.

12th. Dawn at $10^{h}\ 50^{m}$, dusk at $1^{h}\ 45^{m}$; at 8 P. M. a patch of aurora 8° above horizon S. by E. (true).

13th. Dawn at $9^{h}\ 50^{m}$, dusk at $2^{h}\ 10^{m}$.

14th. Daylight at $9^{h}\ 40^{m}$, dusk at $2^{h}\ 5^{m}$.

15th. Dawn at $10^{h}\ 15^{m}$, dusk at $2^{h}\ 10^{m}$.

16th. Dawn at $10^{h}\ 0^{m}$, dusk at $2^{h}\ 0^{m}$.

17th. Dawn at $9^{h}\ 50^{m}$, dusk at $2^{h}\ 30^{m}$; a bear supposed to have alarmed the dogs; 8 P. M., aurora near horizon bearing N. and E. from 8 until midnight.

18th. Dawn at $9^{h}\ 15^{m}$, dusk at $2^{h}\ 40^{m}$.

19th. Dawn at $9^{h}\ 40^{m}$, dusk at $2^{h}\ 45^{m}$.

20th. Dawn at $9^{h}\ 30^{m}$, dusk at $2^{h}\ 45^{m}$; temperature in snow-hut, 6 hours after it was built, 7° above the external temperature; three huts were built by 8 men in 45 minutes.

21st. Dawn at 9h 30m, dusk at 3h 0m

22d. Dawn at 9h 10m, dusk at 3h 15m; much refraction in the S. E.

23d. Dawn at 9h 20m, dusk at 3h 0m

24th. Dawn at 9h 0m, dusk at 3h 15m

25th. Dawn at 9h 0m, dusk at 3h 15m; a halo round the moon at 1h P. M.

26th. Dawn at 9h 0m, dusk at 3h 30m

27th. Dawn at 8h 45m, dusk at 3h 30m

28th. Dawn at 8h 15m; sun's upper limb appeared at 11h 25m; refraction 59' 55'', neglecting the height of the eye (5 feet); sun's upper limb disappeared at 1h 0m m. t.; dusk at 3h 45m.

29th. Dawn at 8h 15m; sun's upper limb appeared at 11h 10m m. t., disappeared 1h 25m; dusk at 3h 45m; 10 men built two houses in 30 minutes; mercury froze at about —41°.

30th. Dawn at 8h 30m; sun's upper limb appeared at 10h 50m, disappeared at 1h 50m; dusk at 3h 50m. Two seals and a dovekie seen in a large crack three or four miles east of the ship.

31st. Dawn at 8h 15m; sun's upper limb appeared at 10h 40m; a seal and several dovekies seen in a lane of water; sun's upper limb disappeared at 2h 0m; dusk at 4h 0m

February, 1858. Record of the Weather kept on board the Yacht Fox, with general remarks.

Day.	2h.	4h.	6h.	8h.	10h.	Noon.	2h.	4h.	6h.	8h.	10h.	Midt.
1	b c	[illegible]	[illegible]	[illegible]	[illegible]	b c	b c	b c	[illegible]	[illegible]	[illegible]	[illegible]
2	b c	[illegible]	[illegible]	[illegible]	[illegible]	[illegible]	[illegible]	m s	m s	[illegible]	b m	[illegible]
3	b c	[illegible]	[illegible]	[illegible]	[illegible]	[illegible]	[illegible]	[illegible]	[illegible]	b m	[illegible]	b c
4	b m	[illegible]	[illegible]	b c	[illegible]	[illegible]	[illegible]	[illegible]	b	b c	[illegible]	[illegible]
5	b c	[illegible]	b c	[illegible]	[illegible]	[illegible]	[illegible]	[illegible]	[illegible]	[illegible]	[illegible]	[illegible]
6	m	[illegible]	o s	[illegible]	[illegible]	[illegible]	[illegible]	[illegible]	[illegible]	[illegible]	[illegible]	[illegible]
7	b c	[illegible]	b	b c	[illegible]	[illegible]	[illegible]	[illegible]	[illegible]	[illegible]	[illegible]	[illegible]
8	m	[illegible]	b c	[illegible]	b o	[illegible]	[illegible]	[illegible]	[illegible]	[illegible]	b m	[illegible]
9	b m	[illegible]	b c	[illegible]	[illegible]	[illegible]	b c s	b m s	[illegible]	[illegible]	b c s	[illegible]
10	b m s	[illegible]	[illegible]	[illegible]	[illegible]	[illegible]	c m s	[illegible]	[illegible]	m s	c m	[illegible]
11	m	c m	b c s	b c	b c s	b c	[illegible]	[illegible]	[illegible]	c m s	[illegible]	[illegible]
12	c m s	c s	[illegible]	c m	b c	[illegible]	[illegible]	[illegible]	b	b m	[illegible]	[illegible]
13	b m	[illegible]	b c	[illegible]	[illegible]	[illegible]	[illegible]	[illegible]	b m	b c	b m s	[illegible]
14	b c	[illegible]	[illegible]	[illegible]	[illegible]	[illegible]	b c s	[illegible]	[illegible]	[illegible]	[illegible]	[illegible]
15	b c s	[illegible]	[illegible]	b s	[illegible]	[illegible]	b c	b c s	[illegible]	[illegible]	[illegible]	[illegible]
16	b c	b c s	[illegible]	[illegible]	[illegible]	[illegible]	b s	[illegible]	[illegible]	[illegible]	b c s	[illegible]
17	b c	[illegible]	b c	[illegible]	b c s	[illegible]	[illegible]	[illegible]	[illegible]	[illegible]	[illegible]	[illegible]
18	b c s	[illegible]	[illegible]	b s	[illegible]	[illegible]	b c s	[illegible]	[illegible]	[illegible]	[illegible]	[illegible]
19	m s	b c s	[illegible]	c s	[illegible]	[illegible]	[illegible]	m s	[illegible]	[illegible]	b c	[illegible]
20	b c	[illegible]	[illegible]	[illegible]	m s	m s	c o s	[illegible]	b c s	[illegible]	c m s	m c
21	m c s	[illegible]	o s	[illegible]	c s	b c	[illegible]	[illegible]	[illegible]	[illegible]	[illegible]	[illegible]
22	b c	[illegible]	[illegible]	[illegible]	[illegible]	[illegible]	[illegible]	[illegible]	[illegible]	[illegible]	b c s	[illegible]
23	b c s	[illegible]	[illegible]	[illegible]	[illegible]	[illegible]	[illegible]	[illegible]	[illegible]	[illegible]	[illegible]	[illegible]
24	b c s	[illegible]	[illegible]	[illegible]	[illegible]	[illegible]	[illegible]	- - -	- - -	o m s	o q m s	[illegible]
25	o q m r	[illegible]	[illegible]	o m s	[illegible]	[illegible]	c m s	[illegible]	[illegible]	[illegible]	b c s	b c
26	c m s	[illegible]	[illegible]	o m s	o m s	[illegible]	[illegible]	[illegible]	m s	[illegible]	b c	b
27	b c	[illegible]	[illegible]	c	b c	[illegible]	[illegible]	o s	b c s	b c	s c	m s
28	m s	b p s	[illegible]	[illegible]	s s	b c	[illegible]	[illegible]	[illegible]	b c	[illegible]	[illegible]

NOTES TO FEBRUARY RECORD.

1st. Dawn at 8h 0m; sun's upper limb appeared at 10h 25m m. t.; a sooty fox shot, small and fat, weight 7 lbs.; sunset at 2h 5m, dusk at 4h 10m

2d. Dawn at 8h 0m; sun's upper limb appeared at 10h 10m; no sounding with 170 fathoms; several new cracks; cirro-stratus moving to S. E.; dusk at 4h 10m; 9 P. M. aurora faint in the S. E. horizon for about ten minutes; 10 P. M. an auroral arch in the S. E., visible for one hour, faint from S. E. to E. N. E., the extremities of the arch touching the horizon; the S. E. extremity was the brightest, with an occasional stream towards the zenith.

3d. Dawn at 7h 50m; sun's upper limb appeared at 10h 5m; dusk at 4h 20m; at 11 P. M. an arch of an aurora from S. E. (true) horizon to the zenith; ice in motion.

4th. Dawn at $7^h 50^m$; the ice has opened in several places; some seals and dovekies seen; dusk at $4^h 30^m$; 8 until 10 P. M. ice in motion near the ship.

5th. Dawn at $7^h 50^m$; sun's upper limb appeared at $10^h 5^m$ a. m.; six dovekies shot, a few seals seen; at 3 P. M. the floe cracked ten yards astern of the ship, many cracks running N. E. and S. W., and considerable motion in the ice; built snow huts in 40^m.

6th. Dawn at $7^h 45^m$, dusk at $4^h 30^m$; 11 P. M. a slight aurora to the N. E. [Thickness of old floe ice 4 feet 6 inches.]

7th. Dawn at $7^h 50^m$; sun's upper limb disappeared at $2^h 40^m$; dusk at $4^h 30^m$; $11^h 15^m$ P. M. until midnight pale streaks and patches of aurora near horizon between S. S. E. and north (true).

8th. Dawn at $7^h 50^m$, dusk at $4^h 40^m$.

9th. Dawn at $7^h 55^m$, dusk at $4^h 40^m$; at 11 A. M. a faint parhelion; 10 P. M. aurora from N. E. to S. E.

10th. 3 A. M. slight aurora from N. to S., passing through the zenith; dawn at $7^h 30^m$, dusk at $4^h 45^m$.

11th. Dawn at $7^h 20^m$, dusk at $4^h 50^m$; a broad line of water one mile astern of the ship running E. N. E. and W. S. W.

12th. Dawn at $7^h 20^m$, dusk at $5^h 0^m$.

13th. 4 A. M. a slight aurora in the west; dawn at $7^h 15^m$; prismatic halo round the sun; several seals seen; dusk at $5^h 10^m$; 11 P. M. aurora near horizon between S. S. E. and E., with vertical rays or streamers half way up to the zenith, arch about 14° above the horizon.

14th. Dawn at $7^h 5^m$; two dovekies seen; $1^h 30^m$ P. M. an ill-defined halo about 18° diameter, its extremities at the horizon prismatic; ice opening in a lane two miles N. W. from ship; dusk at $5^h 20^m$.

15th. Dawn $7^h 0^m$; an imperfect double halo around the sun, diameter about 16° and 28°; dusk at $5^h 30^m$; 7^h to 9^h P. M. pale aurora near horizon between S. S. E. and E. N. E., with vertical rays towards the zenith, arch 4° above horizon.

16th. Dawn $6^h 50^m$; an imperfect halo slightly prismatic; dusk at $5^h 30^m$; at 8 P. M. bright, pale yellow aurora along the horizon between S. E. and N. N. E., with vertical streamers towards zenith, forming at times an arc, double and even treble, from 4° to 8° above horizon.

17th. Aurora continued until 5 A. M., when it disappeared; thickness of ice 3 feet 9 inches, of snow 9½ inches; dawn at $6^h 45^m$; at noon imperfect prismatic halo, diameter 45°, luminous spots at horizon 22° E. and W. of the sun; several seals seen; dusk at $5^h 30^m$; halo round the moon, diameter 46°; 10 P. M. aurora near the south horizon, arc from S. S. W. to N. N. E. about 4° above horizon.

18th. Midnight until 4 A. M. aurora between S. W. and E.; dawn at $6^h 50^m$, dusk at $5^h 35^m$; $8^h 30^m$ P. M. several arcs about 15° above horizon, between S. S. E. and E.; 10 P. M. aurora ceased.

19th. Dawn at $6^h 40^m$, dusk at $5^h 35^m$; at midnight (19th—20th) arch of aurora 5° above horizon, between S. S. E. and N. E.

20th. Dawn at $6^h 40^m$; a wide lane of water two miles north from the ship, and extending E. N. E. and W. S. W., the terminations not visible; 6 P. M. prismatic halo round the moon, diameter 4° 30′.

21st. Dawn at $6^h 30^m$, dusk at $5^h 50^m$.

22d. Dawn at $6^h 30^m$; tried for soundings with 100 fathoms; several seals and dovekies seen in wide lane to the north of the ship, also a bear; dusk at $5^h 40^m$; at midnight (22d—23d) halo round the moon.

23d. Dawn at $6^h 15^m$, dusk at $6^h 0^m$.

24th. Dawn at $6^h 10^m$, dusk at $6^h 0^m$.

25th. Dawn at $6^h 0^m$, dusk at $6^h 0^m$.

26th. Dawn at $6^h 0^m$, dusk at $6^h 10^m$.

27th. Dawn at $5^h 55^m$ dusk at $6^h 15^m$; snow melted against ship's side in the sun at 9 A. M., temperature in shade −22°; a seal shot; dovekies seen; at noon black bulb thermometer −7°, in shade −17°.5.

28th. Dawn at $6^h 0^m$; no water in sight; dusk at $6^h 15^m$; midnight (28th—1st) halo round the moon, diameter 43°; altitude of moon 19½°.

March, 1858. RECORD OF THE WEATHER KEPT ON BOARD THE YACHT FOX, WITH GENERAL REMARKS.

DAY.	2h.	4h.	6h.	8h.	10h.	Noon.	2h.	4h.	6h.	8h.	10h.	Midt.
1	m	m	co	m	bc	m	m	o	ms	m	bcs	m
2	cs	bcs	ms	s	co	m	o	bc	c	bc	m	s
3	bc	m	m	s	ms	m	m	m	co	mss	m	bms
4	ms	bcs	ms	m	m	bcs	m	bc	m	m	b	m
5	bc	m	m	m	m	b	bc	m	s	b	bo	m
6	bc	m	m	b	m	m	s	bc	m	m	m	m
7	bc	m	m	m	bs	bm	bc	b	bc	b	bc	m
8	bc	m	m	s	m	s	m	m	m	m	m	s
9	bc	m	m	m	co	m	bc	m	m	m	m	m
10	m	bc	ms	m	m	m	co	m	s	ms	m	m
11	ms	m	m	m	ms	m	m	cm	bc	m	m	m
12	bc	cm	bc	cs	ms	m	co	cms	ms	m	ms	m
13	ms	m	m	m	bc	cm	ms	m	bc	m	m	m
14	bc	b	bo	m	m	m	m	m	o	m	m	m
15	b	bc	m	m	m	bcs	m	m	m	m	m	m
16	bcs	m	bc	m	m	m	m	m	m	m	m	m
17	bc	o	m	m	m	c	bc	c	m	bc	bo	bc
18	bc	m	m	b	m	m	m	m	m	m	m	bc
19	bc	m	m	s	b	m	m	s	m	m	m	m
20	bc	m	m	fo	m	f	m	bc	m	m	m	b
21	b	m	bc	m	bo	m	bc	m	f	o	m	m
22	f	co	o	m	cs	m	m	f	fo	fo	mo	m
23	ms	m	m	m	ms	m	m	m	f	ms	m	m
24	m	m	mc	ms	co	ms	m	bc	m	m	ms	bcs
25	bcs	o	m	m	co	bcs	m	m	cs	m	m	m
26	co	ms	bcs	m	m	m	m	m	m	m	m	m
27	bs	m	m	m	m	m	m	m	m	m	m	m
28	bo	bcs	m	bc	m	m	m	m	m	m	m	m
29	b	bc	bcs	b	bc	m	m	m	m	m	m	ms
30	cms	m	m	m	m	m	m	m	m	ms	bcs	m
31	bcs	m	m	bs	b	m	m	m	bcs	bc	b	m

NOTES TO MARCH RECORD.

1st. Noon tried for soundings with 130 fathoms.

2d. A large lane of water opened E. N. E. and W. S. W. about one mile south of the ship; several seals seen and five shot; aurora visible between S. W. by S. and east from 10.30 P. M. until 2h 30m A. M. (3d) (patches, arches and streamers).

3d. Several lanes and cracks in the ice north of the ship, in which some narwhals and dovekies and several seals were seen; hail fell from 10 P. M. until 11.

4th. 10 P. M. Auroral arch in the N. E. at a low altitude. [A broad arch reaching nearly to the zenith.]

5th. At noon, black bulb thermometer in the sun zero, temperature in shade, —18°; at 3 P. M. the ice suddenly detached itself from the ship's bows and sides allowing her to rise eleven inches forward. 9 P. M. Aurora in clouds and streamers between N. W. and S., visible throughout the night; the sound of crushing or cracking ice distinctly heard during the night.

6th. 9 P. M., bright aurora between S. S. W. and E. from 5° to 60° above horizon, ceased at 10h 30m. [Bands and arches with streamers towards the zenith.]

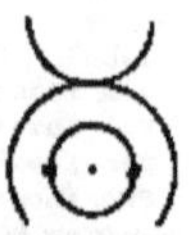

7th. 9 A. M., appearance of high land supposed to be Disco bearing east (true); from 11 A. M. until 2 P. M. a double prismatic halo (red external) about the sun, diameters 45° and 90° nearly; horizontal parhelia on inner halo in same altitude as the sun; a portion of inverted arch above outer halo; sun's altitude 18°.

8th. At daylight appearance of land bearing E. by N.; a lane of water northwest of the ship in which seals and narwhals were seen; 10 P. M., faint aurora in S. E.

9th. A bear passed near the ship; many seals, some dovekies, and a black whale seen.

10th. Two small seals shot and some narwhals seen; several lanes and pools of water to the northward.

11th. Ice much broken up, also lanes and small pools of water northward of the ship.

12th. Water in lanes and pools in sight all around; a slight swell perceptible in the lanes and cracks.

13th. A seal shot.

14th. Several small lanes and pools to the northward.

15th. At 10h 30m P. M. a band of aurora between S. and S. E. (true) about 8° elevation, with occasional vertical streamers ascending.

16th. Ice 4 feet 3½ inches thick, increase for the month 6½ inches; snow 9½ inches, no increase; ice opened 120 yards west of the ship and a wide lane of water formed, extending N. and S.; its extremes not visible; 8 P. M., aurora from S. W. to N. E. near the horizon and with vertical streamers (lasted till midnight).

17th. Several seals seen, three dovekies shot; the ice much broken up and wide lanes of water running N. and S.; 10 P. M., bright aurora between S. W. and E. N. E.

18th. A seal shot; the ice closing; the tracks of three bears seen; 4h 30m P. M. ice crushing up with great force, that in which the ship is frozen appears setting southward of the western ice; 11 P. M., aurora between S. with E. N. E. (10° above horizon with streamers towards zenith); the ice opening.

19th. Several seals and dovekies seen; at noon, a faint halo with parhelia; 6 P. M. ice in motion, afterwards stationary.

20th. Sounded in 150 fathoms, soft mud.

21st. Noon, the lane opened to the westward of the ship.

22d. A seal shot; six dovekies shot; 10h 30m P. M., the ice detached itself from the ship and she heeled over to the gale.

23d. A seal and a dovekie shot; a large pool of water 60 yards west of the ship; much water in sight to the southward; many narwhals seen swimming northward.

24th. The ice apparently drifting southward and opening in different directions; 10 P. M., ice in motion and pressing against the floe edge 10 yards west of the ship.

25th. 1h 45m A. M., ice slacked off and the crack opened; from 4 until 8 P. M. the ice in motion and crushing up with great pressure in the crack W. of the ship.

26th. 9 P. M., halo around the moon, diameter about 44°; altitude moon's centre 23°; slight motion in the ice.

27th. 8 P. M., ice opened in lane W. 50 yards from ship.

29th. 8 A. M., got bottom with 150 fathoms, mud, supposed depth 170 fathoms.

30th. Two seals and two dovekies shot; 11 P. M., Paraselenæ on each side and above the moon, distant about 23°, moon's altitude 11°.

31st. Three seals shot; a fresh bear track close to the ship.

April, 1858. Record of the Weather kept on board the Yacht Fox, with general remarks.

Day.	2h.	4h.	6h.	8h.	10h.	Noon.	2h.	4h.	6h.	8h.	10h.	Mid't.
1	bc	[illegible]	[illegible]	[illegible]	[illegible]	[illegible]	[illegible]	[illegible]	[illegible]	[illegible]	[illegible]	[illegible]
2	b	[illegible]	[illegible]	[illegible]	bc	[illegible]	[illegible]	[illegible]	[illegible]	b	[illegible]	[illegible]
3	bc	[illegible]	bcq	cmq	bms	[illegible]	[illegible]	[illegible]	cbs	[illegible]	ms	[illegible]
4	qms	[illegible]	ms	[illegible]	[illegible]	[illegible]	qms	[illegible]	[illegible]	[illegible]	[illegible]	[illegible]
5	qmr	[illegible]	[illegible]	[illegible]	[illegible]	[illegible]	[illegible]	[illegible]	[illegible]	ms	[illegible]	[illegible]
6	ms	ms	[illegible]	bc	[illegible]	[illegible]	[illegible]	[illegible]	[illegible]	b	bc	co
7	c	bc	ms	[illegible]	[illegible]	[illegible]	bc	cm	ms	[illegible]	msi	[illegible]
8	msb	[illegible]	[illegible]	[illegible]	qmos	[illegible]	[illegible]	bcms	b	[illegible]	[illegible]	[illegible]
9	b	bc	b	bc	[illegible]	[illegible]	[illegible]	[illegible]	[illegible]	[illegible]	[illegible]	[illegible]
10	bc	[illegible]	[illegible]	[illegible]	[illegible]	[illegible]	[illegible]	[illegible]	[illegible]	[illegible]	[illegible]	[illegible]
11	bc	[illegible]	[illegible]	[illegible]	[illegible]	[illegible]	[illegible]	[illegible]	[illegible]	[illegible]	os	bc
12	bc	[illegible]	[illegible]	[illegible]	[illegible]	[illegible]	[illegible]	[illegible]	[illegible]	[illegible]	[illegible]	[illegible]
13	bc	[illegible]	[illegible]	[illegible]	[illegible]	[illegible]	[illegible]	[illegible]	[illegible]	[illegible]	[illegible]	[illegible]
14	bc	[illegible]	[illegible]	[illegible]	[illegible]	[illegible]	[illegible]	[illegible]	[illegible]	[illegible]	[illegible]	[illegible]
15	bc	[illegible]	[illegible]	[illegible]	[illegible]	[illegible]	[illegible]	[illegible]	[illegible]	[illegible]	[illegible]	[illegible]
16	bcs	[illegible]	[illegible]	[illegible]	[illegible]	bc	bcq	[illegible]	[illegible]	bqs	[illegible]	[illegible]
17	bqs	[illegible]	[illegible]	[illegible]	[illegible]	[illegible]	[illegible]	[illegible]	bcq	[illegible]	[illegible]	[illegible]
18	...	bmq	...	bqs	...	[illegible]	...	[illegible]	...	cms	...	[illegible]
19	...	mcs	...	[illegible]	...	[illegible]	...	ms	...	bc	...	bcm
20	...	bc	...	[illegible]	...	[illegible]	...	[illegible]	...	[illegible]	...	[illegible]
21	...	bc	...	[illegible]	...	[illegible]	...	[illegible]	...	bp	...	[illegible]
22	...	bp	...	[illegible]	...	[illegible]	...	[illegible]	...	[illegible]	...	b
23	...	bc	...	bo	...	[illegible]	...	bq	...	[illegible]	...	co
24	...	c	...	co	...	[illegible]	...	ms	...	[illegible]	...	co
25	...	bc	...	cms	...	bms	...	mc	...	co	...	c
26	...	bm	...	ms	...	bc	...	[illegible]	...	[illegible]	...	[illegible]
27	...	co	...	c	...	[illegible]	...	co	...	ms	...	co
28	...	c	...	[illegible]	...	[illegible]	...	[illegible]	...	os	...	c
29	...	bc	...	b	...	[illegible]	...	bc	...	[illegible]	...	co
30	...	o	...	co	...	[illegible]	...	[illegible]	...	ms	...	mos

NOTES TO APRIL RECORD.

1st. A wide lane opening two miles N. E. of the ship; 9 P. M. a streak of aurora 8° above horizon between S. S. E. and N. W., with streamers towards the zenith.

2d. Two black whales seen.

4th. At noon our old floe cracked in a N. N. E. and S. S. W. line about thirty yards from the ship; it widens to about sixty yards.

5th. At 8h 30m the old floe cracked in line with ship, that on the port side drifted off about fifty yards; secured ship to fast ice, head to wind.

6th. A whale and many narwhals seen; four seals shot.

7th. Tried for soundings with 170 fathoms.

8th. Ice quiet, but drifting rapidly before the wind.

9th. A walrus seen; before sunset the western land became visible, supposed Cape Dyer, S. 48° W. (true); 11 P. M. aurora between E. and N., and from 10° elevation stretching up to the zenith.

10th. A large iceberg bearing E. (true); tried for soundings with 180 fathoms; Cape Dyer visible S. 69° W.; another cape S. 62° W.; midnight faint aurora from S. to E. (true).

11th. A bear's track within eighty yards of the ship; a fog bank in S. E.; 9 to 12 P. M. a pale aurora between E. and S. E.

12th. A lane of water opened astern in the direction of a large berg in the E. N. E.; much mist and vapour in the S. E.; eight dovekies shot; 11 P. M. aurora to the southward between E. and W. S. W. (about 15° above horizon, with streamers towards zenith, and numerous nebular spots of light at intervals in arch).

13th. 6 P. M. distant land seen, bearing S. W. ½ W. (true); 11 P. M. aurora similar to last night.

14th. A large flock of ducks flying N. W.; tried for soundings with 170 fathoms; 10 P. M. a bright aurora in the east (true); midnight, faint to the southward at 15° elevation.

15th. 1h 30m A. M. a bear came close to the ship; thickness of ice 3 feet 11 inches, increase for the month 1 foot 2¼ inches; snow 10½ inches, increase 1¾; a number of mollymauks seen; 10h 30m P. M. aurora to the southward, appearing over a fog bank (afterwards forming an arch from E. to S., disappeared at midnight).

16th. At 8 P. M. ice cracked and opened alongside; secured ship by the stern with three hawsers.

17th. Pieces of our floe began to break off, and at 11 A. M. the ship went adrift with them; 3 P. M. shipped rudder and stood to the eastward under double reefed mainsail and flying staysail.

18th. The ice closed about the ship at 8 A. M.; sludge and bay ice only visible; several bergs in sight; at 6 P. M. ship fast in young ice; many mollymauks about, and a snow bunting seen.

19th. Three bears seen; several bergs in sight.

20th. A considerable swell; unshipped rudder at 8 A. M.; the lofty clouds going to the westward at P. M.; a bear and a seal killed; several small bergs in sight.

21st. Tried for soundings with 170 fathoms.

22d. Many small bergs near; they change rapidly their bearings, as if the ship and pack were drifting past them to the S. W.; experienced a S. W. current.

23d. A large black whale seen, also a seal; experienced a westerly set; several large seals lying on the ice.

24th. 8 P. M. a swell from the S. E., and ice commenced to break up.

25th. Swell rapidly increasing; ice striking against the ship; proceeded under sail and steam to the eastward: noon, swell ten feet high; ship receiving very violent and frequent shocks, and proceeding, head to swell, through close heavy ice; 6 P. M. swell thirteen feet high, ice less close, shocks still more violent; 8 P. M. cleared the ice, stopped engine, and made sail.

26th. Mollymauks and kittiwakes abundant.

27th. 7 A. M. saw the land about Sukkertoppen N. E. by N. (true).

28th. Anchored at Holsteinsborg at 7h. 30m. P. M. in seventeen fathoms water, secured with hawsers to the rocks.

29th and 30th. In the harbor of Holsteinsborg.

[Specific gravity of sea-water:—

On the 7th,	in 110 fathoms,	1.0275	(temp. 34°);	in 5 fathoms,	1.0275	(temp. 30°).
" 10th,	" 100	" 1.0280	" 34°;	" 4	" 1.0275	" 30°.
" 16th,	" 110	" 1.0310	" 31°;	" 4	" 1.0310	" 30.5°.
" 21st,	" 110	" 1.0280	" 31.5°.]			

May, 1858. Record of the Weather kept on board the Yacht Fox, with general remarks.

DAY.	4h.	8h.	Noon.	4h.	8h.	Midnight.
1	m o s	m	b	m	m	c o
2	c	m	b c	m	m	o
3	b c	m	b	m	m	m
4	c	c	m s	m	m	m
5	m o s	m	m	b c	m	m
6	m s	b c	c	m	m	m
7	m s	b c	c	m	m	c
8	b c	c	c g s	c	c m	b
9	c m	...	b c	m s	p m s	m
10	b c	b m	b m s	m s	m p s	s
11	m o s	m s	b c m	b c	m	c
12	b c	m	m s	c s	m	o
13	b c	m	m	m	m	m
14	b	m	m	m	m	c
15	b	b f	f	m	b f	b m
16	b	m	m	b c	f	b
17	f s	m	b m	m	f	b
18	f	b m	b c	b	m	o
19	f	m	b m	b	m	m
20	b m	b	m	m	m	m
21	b	m	m	b c	m	m
22	b c	m	c o	m	b c	m
23	b	b c	o	m	b	b c
24	b c	c	c	b f	m	m
25	b	m	o	b c	b	c s
26	c s	m	b c	o	m	b
27	c	b c	m	b	m	m
28	b	m	m	m	m	m
29	b c	m	m	b c	m	b m
30	f	m	m	m	b m	f
31	m s	m	m	c s	m	f s

NOTES TO MAY RECORD.

1st. At Holsteinborg.

8th. Sailed from Holsteinborg at 1h A. M.

9th. Much ice about; white whale seen; specific gravity of sea water, surface, 1.0270.

10th. Midnight (9th—10th) off Northstrom Fiord; icebergs and ice about; noon, off Rifkol; at 7h 15m, when 8 miles from Godhavn, stopped by ice extending in to the land; thick fog and snow came on; very narrowly escaped running on the N. W. of the Whalefish Islands. [Passed more than 400 bergs.]

11th. Anchored at Whalefish Islands in 12½ fathoms.

15th. 6 P. M., prismatic halo around sun about 45° diameter, two lateral parhelia, some polarization; also an arch 15° above horizon, apparently of a circle of same diameter as halo, opposite the sun.

16th. Godhavn Harbor and entrance filled with packed ice.

17th. 7h 30m P. M., anchored in Upernavik, Back Bay, in 10½ fathoms.

24th. Left Upernavik, and steamed to Godhavn.

25th. Steamed out of Godhavn at 4h 30m A. M.

26th. 6 A. M., entered the Waigat; 4h 30m, anchored off the coal seam in 7 fathoms; one-third of a mile off shore.

27th. Proceeded under steam northward at 11h 50m P. M.

28th. Passed out of the Waigat, steering for Black Hook.

29th. At 5h 30m P. M. off Black Hook, Sanderson's Hope ahead; many bergs in sight.

31st. 7 A. M., hove to off Sanderson's Hope; 10h 30m A. M., bore up for Upernavik.

JUNE, 1858. RECORD OF THE WEATHER KEPT ON BOARD THE YACHT FOX, WITH GENERAL REMARKS.

Day.	4h.	8h.	Noon.	4h.	8h.	Midnight.	Specific Grav. of Sea Water, 1.0
1	bc	co	c	bc	m	m	
2	bc	m	m	m	m	m	
3	c	cm	m	m	bc	m	
4	b	bc	m	m	cmo	mod	
5	mos	co	c	co	c	m	
6	bc	m	ms	c	co	m	
7	bc	o	co	bc	b	bc	
8	bc	b	m	bc	m	m	
9	b	m	bq	bc	m	m	
10	b	f	m	m	fm	m	
11	fs	m	m	c	m	m	
12	c	cf	cm	bm	f	m	
13	f	m	m	m	bcf	bc	
14	bc	b	m	m	bc	o	
15	c	bc	m	m	b	m	
16	b	bf	m	bc	m	m	265
17	f	d	df	f	m	cm	268
18	co	c	co	f	m	m	272
19	bc	m	b	bc	m	b	273
20	b	m	m	m	m	f	263
21	f	m	bm	bc	b	m	265
22	b	m	c	bc	c	m	270*
23	co	m	c	c	co	c	275
24	co	m	m	m	bc	m	260
25	bc	b	m	m	bc	m	273
26	oc	o	m	o	cd	pr	275
27	op	cqr	mm	fm	m	mo	270
28	o	fc	mm	m	bcm	mo	
29	f	m	cm	co	m	oc	276
30	f	co	c	bm	f	m	260

* At 1½ fathoms, 273.

NOTES TO JUNE RECORD.

4th. Started under steam at 5^h 30^m A. M.; west point of Great Duck Island (Narsak), north one and a half mile; 3^h 30^m P. M., made fast to land ice in a bay on south side of Upernavik Island; the ice closed in and beset the ship.

6th. Started under steam at 5^h 30^m A. M.; at 10^h 30^m made fast to a grounded berg in 25 fathoms, half a mile west of a rugged island having a large cairn on the summit of its S. W. extreme; Buchan Island west three and a half or four miles.

7th. Passed north of Buchan Island, and close along its west side; at 8^h 30^m A. M. struck and remained fast on a reef of rocks, tide falling; extremes of Buchan Island S. 36° W. and S. 15° E., distant about one mile; at 1^h 30^m P. M. low water.

8th. At 11^h 40^m A. M. observed a rock above water bearing from noon position S. 25° E. (true) three miles; passed inside Horse's Head; 3^h 10^m passed another rock; Horse's Head N. 15° E; Cape Shackleton (North Bluff) N. 40° E. (true).

9th. Steamed at intervals for about three hours.

11th. Made fast one mile N. of the Duck Islands.

12th. Tried to reach a lead close to Cape Wilcox but failed and returned; new moon at 2 P. M., high water at 11^h 6^m A. M.; rise 8 feet 3 inches; flood sets N. N. W., ebb sets S. S. E., about 2' an hour between the islands.

16th. At 10^h 40^m P. M. steamed to the northward, and made fast to land ice; 4' N. ½ W. from Eastern Duck Island.

17th. 4 P. M. saw the Sabine Islands bearing N. E. (true), and distant seven miles.

18th. Passed through and steamed along the land ice.

19th. Made fast at a nip; four bears seen, many seals and birds; 10 A. M., until 3^h 30^m P. M., under sail, working to westward; unable to distinguish the land ice from the loose ice.

22d. Advanced one mile to the N. W.; progress impeded by nips.

23d. At 9 P. M. got through the nip and made sail to the N. W.; three bears seen.

24th. At 11 A. M. came up to a nip and made fast; about 300 little auks shot.

25th. Nip opened; proceeded under steam and sail; two bears seen; at 4^h 30^m P. M. stopped at a nip; 8' S. E. of Bushnan Island.

26th. 1 P. M. made fast to land ice; **Cape York N. W. 6'; 9 P. M. proceeded to the westward;** shot a walrus.

27th. Blowing strong and very thick; 3^h 15^m P. M. made fast to a floe; when clear saw Conical Island N. W. 15' or 20'; off shore six miles.

28th. Find the floe is held fast by grounded bergs near us; 42 fathoms; mud and **stones; shot** rotchies; many rotchies' eggs picked up.

29th. The ship in a large space of water; no land visible; considerable movement in the loose ice caused by current and wind.

30th. 6 A. M. lying to a floe three miles off shore.

[The specific gravity of the surface water is copied from the fourth number of the *Board of Trade Papers.*]

July, 1858. RECORD OF THE WEATHER KEPT ON BOARD THE YACHT FOX, WITH GENERAL REMARKS.

Day.	4h.	8h.	Noon.	4h.	8h.	Midnight.	Specific Gravity of Sea Water, 1.0
1	f	m	fo	bc	f	bm	265
2	bc	bcm	bm	f	bm	oc	275
3	mc	m	fo	f	m	m	270
4	f	m	o	m	m	bc	270
5	bc	m	m	co	m	oc	275
6	oc	m	oc	m	c	f	275
7	o	c	m	cm	bc	m	
8	b	bc	m	m	m	m	
9	b	m	m	bc	m	m	270
10	b	bc	m	m	m	m	
11	b	bc	m	m	m	m	270
12	b	bc	oo	m	m	m	
13	oqo	m	cos	co	os	m	
14	os	co	c	os	cm	m	275
15	c	co	m	cqr	c	c	
16	c	cr	of	bc	f	bc	270
17	c	b	m	bc	b	m	273
18	f	bc	b	bc	f	m	
19	f	b	m	bc	m	m	
20	b	m	m	bs	m	[illegible]	
21	bc	b	m	bc	b	bc	273
22	bc	m	m	b	m	m	
23	bc	m	m	m	m	c	
24	bc	m	m	m	m	m	273
25	bc	m	m	m	m	m	265
26	bc	m	m	f	bc	c	
27	bc	m	m	m	m	m	
28	bc	m	m	m	co	bc	
29	co	or	m	co	bc	m	280
30	mo	fr	c	mc	cm	m	
31	cmq	co	mor	co	m	or	

NOTES TO JULY RECORD.

1st. Noon, the ship received a considerable nip, the floes being checked by a grounded berg; rudder damaged.

2d. Several large seals on the ice; 4 P. M., water visible, started under steam and reached at 6 P. M.; made all sail; midnight lost sight of the pack.

3d. Passing through loose ice; a seal shot.

4th. At midnight (4th–5th) fog cleared off, the pack close to leeward of us.

5th. Sailing along the pack edge. 9 P. M., about 15 miles from Conical Island; bore up through lanes in the pack.

6th. Sailing through heavy ice, thick fog at midnight.

7th. Lying fast to a large floe in a confined space of water; Cobourg Island visible to the northward.

8th. Noon, steamed about four miles to the west; land visible from E. N. E. to N. ½ W. (magnetic.)

9th. From 6 P. M. until 7 P. M. working through nips.

10th. Noon, Cobourg Island in the N. W. 15' or 18'; a seal shot.

11th. 8 A. M., reached a large space of water with ice in shore; no ice in sight towards Jones' Sound; found the pack to rest against the land; a black whale seen; 11 P. M., rounded Cape Horsburg two miles off shore.

12th. Made fast to land ice off [illegible] Island and communicated with natives; proceeded four miles further into a large space of water; found ice all around; kept ship between the pack and the land westward of Cape Osborne.

13th. At 9h 30m A. M., made fast to land ice ½ mile off shore in seven fathoms water; the pack fast driving up the sound and closing in.

14th. The pack in the offing moving with the wind and tide; found above high water mark, a piece of an oaken ship's timber 7 x 8 inches, with three nails and an iron bolt through it, much bleached.

15th. Proceeded to Cape Warrender; ice all round.

16th. Lying to in a space of water off Cape Warrender.

17th. The ice is very loose; stopped when within four miles of Cape Hay; many narwhals and two black whales seen.

20th. Commenced boring through the pack to the S. E.

21st. Attempted to bore through the pack; a seal shot.

22d. Attempted to bore through the pack; a very large bear shot.

24th. Steaming through loose ice from 7 until 10 P. M.; 8 P. M., off Possession Bay.

25th. Made fast to the land ice; a bear seen.

26th. 4 A. M., ship drifted to a loose floe in order to drift to the southward with it.

27th. Made fast to land ice off Button Point; at noon one mile off shore; shooting party brings back 318 loons.

28th. Captain and interpreter left the ship to visit the natives up the inlet; shooting party returns with 201 loons.

29th. The ice in the inlet broke up; shifted ship to the land ice 1½ mile N. E. of Button Point; Captain and party returned.

30th. 9 P. M., commenced steaming up Pond's Inlet with two natives on board.

31st. 8 A. M., made to fast ice 12 miles up the inlet, found it too weak to make fast to; a strong ice current.

(Numerous icebergs were seen this month.)

[Notes on specific gravity of sea water are from the 4th paper of the Board of Trade.]

August, 1858. RECORD OF THE WEATHER KEPT ON BOARD THE YACHT FOX, WITH GENERAL REMARKS.

DAY.	4h.	8h.	Noon.	4h.	8h.	Midnight.	Specific Grav. of Sea Water, 1.0
1	o g	c	m	c o	b c q	b c	
2	c o g	b c	m	m	m	m	
3	b c	b	m	b c	m	o	
4	c	c m	b c	m	m	c r	
5	b c	c	m	m	b c	m	
6	b	m	m	o	b c	b	
7	b	b c	m	b c q	o q	m q r	
8	m o g	m	m o r	m o q	r o g	c o	
9	m c	m	o	m o	m	m	
10	o s	f	m o	m	f	m	253
11	f	o	m	b c	m	m	
12	b c	m	m	c	m	m	
13	c	b c	m	c	m	m	276
14	c o	c	b c	m	m	o	
15	c	m	m	o	b c	m	[illegible]
16	c	b m	b f	b m	f o	f g	
17	f g	b c	b m	b c	c o	m	[illegible]
18	c m	c	b c	b c	c o c	c o m	[illegible]
19	o o	b c	m	m	c	c o	[illegible]
20	c s	m	c g o	b c	b c s	c	210
21	b c	m	m	m	c s	m	
22	c o	m	m	m o	o	m o	
23	f	m	c o	m	m	m	
24	c o	o	b c	c o	b c	m	
25	b c	m	m	o	o q	m	
26	c q	b c q	b c	c o	m	m	
27	o	o g	c	c o	m	c o o	233
28	c o	m	m	m	m	m	
29	c f o	m s	b c	c o	m	m	
30	c m	m	b c	m	m	o	
31	c o	m	o	m	m	m	

NOTES TO AUGUST RECORD.

1st. 9h 15m A. M., Captain and party left the ship to visit the natives at Kaparoktalik; many seals were seen; ice broke adrift; got the ship clear when within her own length of a rock

2d. Beating to the westward through drifting ice; 6 P. M., Captain and party returned; bore up to the eastward.

3d. Midnight (2–3) four natives came on board; endeavoring to beat out of Pond's Bay.

4th. Found the current to set westward along the north shore; whales seen.

5th. Steaming from 4 until 7 P. M.; then made fast to land ice, three miles southeast of Cape Graham Moore; whale seen.

7th. A bear shot.

8th. A heavy gale with very heavy sea.

10th. Many walrus seen; passed through a few streams of ice; 9 P. M., rounded Cape Hurd in thick fog; grounded in the mouth of Rigby Bay; floated off; a bear shot.

11th. A bear shot; anchored inside Cape Riley and commenced taking on board coals.

12th. Loose ice in motion with the tide; coaling from C. Riley and receiving stores from Beechey Island.

14th. Proceeded to Beechey Island; anchored off the house in five fathoms.

16th. Sailed for Cape Hotham at 6 A. M., at 7h 30m off Cape Hotham depot, landed and brought off two whale boats; proceeded to the westward.

17th. Steered for Peel Sound 9 P. M., Cape Granite N. 73° E., and Cape Lyons N. 56° W.; observed fast ice extending across the straits from about Cape Briggs to McClure Bay; bore up for Narrow Straits.

18th. At 9h 15m A. M., passed Limestone Island; 4 P. M., off Cape McClintock; 9 P. M., steaming against a head-wind round N. E. cape; midnight anchored in Port Leopold in seven fathoms; 1' N. N. W. of Whaler Point.

19th. Examining stores on Whaler Point; 5h 30m P. M. made sail to the southward.

20th. 10h 20m A. M., passed Fury Point in a snow shower; 4 P. M., off Cape Garry; 6h 30m, rounded the north point of Brentford Bay; observed a small cairn upon it; 10h 15m, anchored in a bay four miles farther west.

21st. A bear shot; made an attempt to pass through Bellot Straits, found it full of loose ice in rapid motion with a very strong tide; returned to Depot Bay; erected a cairn and landed a depot of 15 days provisions.

22d. A bearded seal shot.

23d. Made another attempt to pass through Bellot Straits, found it choked; ran to the southward until stopped by fast ice; anchored in a harbor on east side of Levesque Island at 4 P. M; a herd of reindeer seen on north shore of Bellot Straits, and two seen on shore here.

24th. Made another attempt to penetrate Bellot Straits; anchored in a small bay on the north shore, about half way through at 11h 15m P. M., a very unsafe position.

25th. At 9h 30m A. M., left anchorage and steamed west 4', but being unable to get farther returned to Depot Bay and anchored there at 9 P. M.

26th. At 9 A. M., ran to the southward, anchored in Stillwell Bay? 7 fathoms soft mud; landed 120 rations in casks in lat. 71° 21' N.; heavy streams of ice in the offing.

27th. 9 A. M., made sail for Depot Bay; working to windward between the streams of ice in the offing and the land.

28th. Very little ice seen this day.

29th. Noon, anchored in Depot Bay in 10 fathoms water.

30th. At 5 A. M. steamed into Bellot Straits, finding it still full of loose ice; anchored in a harbor at the head of Port Kennedy at 10h 30m A. M. in 11 fathoms; at 4 P. M. Captain and boat party left the ship to examine the ice in Victoria Strait from the western hills; a herd of deer seen and a bearded seal shot.

31st. Several deer seen inland.

[Several Brent geese and Peregrine falcons shot on the 23d and 29th; from the 1st to the 5th whales were very numerous.—*H. of T. Papers.*]

September, 1858. RECORD OF THE WEATHER KEPT ON BOARD THE YACHT FOX, WITH GENERAL REMARKS.

DAY.	4h	8h	Noon.	4h	8h	Midnight.
1	b	b c	b	m	b c	o
2	b c	m	m	o	b	m
3	m	r	b c	m	m	m
4	c	s	b c	m	m	m
5	b c	c	m	b c	m	m
6	c	r o	m	m	m	m
7	r o	m	m	r	r o	m
8	r o	m	m	s	o c	c
9	m c	o	b c	m	m	b
10	c m	c	b c	r m	r	m
11	c o	b c m	m	o	o c	m
12	c	m	o	c	m	m
13	b c	b	m	m	b c	b
14	b c	m	m	m	m	o
15	o	d g	c	o	o s	b c
16	c o	s	m	m	m	m
17	m d	m	c	c o	d	o
18	c	b c	o	c o	c	o
19	c	m	m	s	m	m
20	f s	c	m	c m	o c	m
21	o s	m	m	m	m	c o
22	c o	m	b c	m	o	m
23	o	m	m	m d	m	b
24	c	b c	m	c	b c	c o
25	c o s	m	m	m	m	m
26	o c	m	m	m	c o	o
27	b c	m	m	c	m s	c
28	c	m	m	m	m	c o
29	c	c o	m	m	c	m
30	c	c o s	c s	o s	o	m

NOTES TO SEPTEMBER RECORD.

1st. One reindeer shot.

2d. Captain Young and boat party left to explore the S. W. part of Brentford Bay.

5th. Party returned; several deer seen.

6th. 6 A. M. steamed into Bellot Straits; high water at 11h A. M.; found tide running east; 1h 30m P. M. passed into the western sea; found the main pack resting upon Capes Bird and Hopkins, and extending as far west as visible; made fast to the edge of the ice; 1' south of Cape Bird.

10th. Two seals shot.

11th. Returned to Port Kennedy and anchored in the entrance in 10 fathoms; a few deer seen, and a hare shot.

12th. A hare shot.

13th. [Observed a comet.]

18th. Steamed through Bellot Straits and made fast to the ice near Pemmican Rock; sent an officer and dog-sledge to examine the ice between us and Separation Island.

20th. At 8h 15m P. M. a vivid flash of sheet lightning was observed.

21st. Dogs and parties carrying provisions to the southward.

23d. 8 P. M. observed the comet, increased in brilliancy.

25th. Lieut. Hobson and parties started with thirteen days' provisions to carry out southern depots; placed a boat and gear upon Pemmican Rock.

27th. Placed a depot of 100 rations on Pemmican Rock; cast off at noon and steamed for Port Kennedy; when 4½ miles within western end of Bellot's Straits, sounded in 76 fathoms; rock and sand; tide about to commence setting west; boring through young ice, and sledge ran into the fast ice in the entrance of Port Kennedy at 10 P. M., and, being unable to penetrate further, made fast; 18 fathoms water; off shore one-fourth of a mile; 12 fathoms at Winter Quarters.

29th. Two reindeer shot; their weights, exclusive of the entrails, are 154 and 139 lbs.

30th. Reindeer seen.

[Specific gravity of sea water 7th, 1.0315; on the 27th, 1.0230; at 65 fathoms, 1.0310; temp. 31°. — *B. of T. Report.*]

October, 1858. RECORD OF THE WEATHER KEPT ON BOARD THE YACHT FOX, WITH GENERAL REMARKS.

DAY.	4h	8h	Noon.	4h	8h	Midnight.
1	c	o	m	s	m	m
2	m s	c s	o	m	m s	o
3	s	m s	o m s	c s	q s	m
4	o q s	c b	b s	m s	m	m
5	m s	c	m	o	m s	o
6	c o	c	o	m	c	m
7	c	c m	b c	o s	s	m
8	b c	b	m	m	m	m
9	b	m	m	m	m	m
10	b	f	m	f s	o	m
11	s	m s	o m s	m s	m	m
12	m s	c	b c	b	b c	b
13	b c	m	m	m	m	m
14	b c	m	m	m	m	m
15	b c	m	m	m	m	o
16	m s s	o s	m	o s s	m	o s
17	o s	b	m	m	m	m
18	m s	o	b c	m	m	m
19	m s	o s	m	m	m	m
20	s	c	b c	b	o	m
21	m s	b c s	m s s	m s	c s	b c
22	b s	o	m	b c	m	m
23	b m	o m s	m s	m	m	o s
24	o	o	o s	m s	o s	m
25	m	b c	b c	m	m	m
26	b m s	m	m	b c s s	b c s	m
27	b c	m	m	m	m	m
28	s	m	m	m	m	m
29	b c	m	m	m	m	m
30	b c	m s	m	m f s	m s	m q s
31	m s	m	m	m s	m	m

NOTES TO OCTOBER RECORD.

1st. Four reindeer seen; 8 P. M., the crack running up the harbor widened; hove the ship eighty yards further ahead.

2d. Two small herds of deer seen.

3d. 10h 30m P. M. lightning observed.

4th. Three ptarmigan seen.

5th. Two herds of deer seen.

6th. Reindeer seen.

7th. A few reindeer and ptarmigan seen.

8th. A reindeer shot; 10 P. M. comet visible.

9th. 10 P. M. comet visible.

10th. Four reindeer seen.

12th. One reindeer seen.

13th. Built an ice-house for magnetic observatory.

15th. Thickness of ice formed since the third, 9¾ inches.

19th. Lieut. Hobson and party started to carry depot down the west coast of Boothia at 9 A. M.

20th. A hare shot; many seals seen in the open water in the straits; 8 P. M. halo round the moon, diameter about 45°.

22d. 8 P. M. Prismatic halo around the moon.

24th. 8 P. M. aurora in the S. E. [about 20° above the horizon].

27th. From 8 P. M. until midnight, faint aurora between S. and N. W. [about 25° above the horizon, the extremities being joined by a narrow band stretching across the zenith.—*D. of T. Papers.*]

30th. A hare shot, two deer seen; 8 P. M. faint aurora in the S. W.

31st. Two ptarmigan shot; 10 P. M. faint aurora in the N. W.

November, 1858. Record of the Weather kept on board the Yacht Fox, with general remarks.

Day.	2h.	4h.	6h.	8h.	10h.	Noon.	2h.	4h.	6h.	8h.	10h.	Mid't.
1	m s	m	m b	o	m	m	m	m	b c	m	m	o
2	m	m s	m s	b c	m	m	m	b c s	o	m	m	m
3	b c s	m	m	m	m	m	m	o	b c	m	m	b c s
4	b c	m	m	m	m	b m s	m	m s	b m s	m	b m	o
5	b m	m	m	m	m	m	b m s	m	m	b m	m	o
6	b m	m	m	o	b c m	m	m	m	m s	m s	m	m
7	m s	m	m	o	m	m	b m	m	m	m	m	o
8	b c	m	m	m	m	m	b c s	b c	m	m	m	m
9	b c m	m	m	m	m	m	m	m	m	b	m	m
10	b	m	b c m	b	b m	m	m	m	m	m	m	m
11	b m	m	b c	o s	b c	o	m	m	m	b c m	m	b m
12	b m	m	m	o	m	m	m	m	o	m	b	m
13	b	b m	b c	m s	m	m	s	m s	m	m	o	m
14	m s	m	m	m	m s	m	m s	o	b c s	b m s	m s	m
15	m s	b m s	m	m	m	m	b c	m	b m	m	b c m	m
16	b c m	m	m	m	m	m s	m	m c s	m s	m	m c s	m
17	m s	m	m	b	m	m	b	m	b c	m s	m o s	m
18	m o s	m	m	o	m	m	m s	c s	b c	m	b c m	o
19	b c m	m	m s	c m	m	m	m	m	m	c m s	b c m	m
20	b c m	m	m	m s	s	m s s	m	m	m s	b m	m	m
21	m s	m	m	m	m s s	c m	b c m	c m	o	m	c m s	c m
22	b c m	m	m	m	m	m	m	m	m	b m	m	o
23	b m	m	b c m	m	m	m	o	o	b m	b	m	b m
24	b m	m	m	b c m	m	m	m	b	b c	o	m	m
25	b	b c m	b m	m s	m	b m s	m	m	b s	m	m	m
26	b c	m	m	m	m	m	m	m	m	b m c	o	m
27	m s	b c	m	m s	b c	m	m	m	m	m	m	m
28	m s	m	m	m	m	m	m	m	m	m	b m s	m
29	b m s	o	o	m	o	m	m	m	m	m	m	m
30	m s s	m	m	o	m	m	m	m	b m s	b m	m	b c

NOTES TO NOVEMBER RECORD.

4th. Lieut. Hobson and party returned; a recent deer track seen.

6th. [10 P. M. faint aurora from S. by E. to W. S. W.]

7th. and 8th. [10 P. M. aurora faint in S. W.]

9th. Faint aurora between S. and W. 10° above horizon, 10 P. M.

12th. 10 P. M. a pale streak from the northern horizon to the zenith.

14th. 10 P. M. faint aurora between S. W. and W. N. W.

16th. A deer came near the ship; three ptarmigan seen; [thickness of ice 1 foot 9½ inches.]

21st. A ptarmigan seen.

23d. 10 P. M. a halo around the moon.

24th. Three ptarmigan seen.

26th. 5 P. M. several willow grouse seen; two deer seen.

December, 1858. RECORD OF THE WEATHER KEPT ON BOARD THE YACHT FOX, WITH GENERAL REMARKS.

DAY.	2h.	4h.	6h.	8h.	10h.	Noon.	2h.	4h.	6h.	8h.	10h.	Midt.
1	b c	[illegible]	[illegible]	[illegible]	b	[illegible]	[illegible]	[illegible]	[illegible]	[illegible]	[illegible]	[illegible]
2	b c	[illegible]	[illegible]	[illegible]	[illegible]	b m	[illegible]	...	b c	[illegible]	b	[illegible]
3	b	b c	[illegible]	[illegible]	m s	[illegible]	b m s	[illegible]	[illegible]	[illegible]	[illegible]	[illegible]
4	b m c	[illegible]	[illegible]	[illegible]	b c	[illegible]	[illegible]	[illegible]	[illegible]	[illegible]	[illegible]	[illegible]
5	b c	[illegible]	[illegible]	[illegible]	[illegible]	[illegible]	b c	[illegible]	[illegible]	b	[illegible]	[illegible]
6	b c	[illegible]	[illegible]	[illegible]	[illegible]	[illegible]	[illegible]	b	[illegible]	b m s	[illegible]	[illegible]
7	b c s	[illegible]	m	b	[illegible]	[illegible]	[illegible]	[illegible]	[illegible]	[illegible]	[illegible]	[illegible]
8	b	[illegible]	[illegible]	[illegible]	[illegible]	[illegible]	b m	m	m s	b m s	[illegible]	[illegible]
9	b m	[illegible]	[illegible]	[illegible]	b	[illegible]	b m	[illegible]	[illegible]	[illegible]	[illegible]	[illegible]
10	b c	b c m	[illegible]	c m	b c m	b m s	[illegible]	[illegible]	[illegible]	[illegible]	[illegible]	m s
11	m	b m	[illegible]	[illegible]	[illegible]	[illegible]	[illegible]	[illegible]	[illegible]	[illegible]	[illegible]	[illegible]
12	b c	[illegible]	b m	b c	[illegible]	[illegible]	[illegible]	[illegible]	b c s	[illegible]	b m	[illegible]
13	b	[illegible]	[illegible]	[illegible]	[illegible]	[illegible]	b s	b m s	[illegible]	[illegible]	[illegible]	[illegible]
14	b	[illegible]	[illegible]	[illegible]	[illegible]	[illegible]	[illegible]	[illegible]	[illegible]	b c	b c	[illegible]
15	b c s	[illegible]	[illegible]	b c	m s	[illegible]	b s	b m s	[illegible]	b m	[illegible]	[illegible]
16	b m s	[illegible]	[illegible]	[illegible]	[illegible]	b c s	[illegible]	[illegible]	[illegible]	b c	[illegible]	[illegible]
17	b	b c	b m	[illegible]	m	...	b c	[illegible]	b m	[illegible]	[illegible]	[illegible]
18	m	c m	[illegible]	[illegible]	[illegible]	[illegible]	b c	[illegible]	[illegible]	[illegible]	[illegible]	[illegible]
19	b c	[illegible]	[illegible]	m s	m	b c m	[illegible]	[illegible]	[illegible]	b	[illegible]	[illegible]
20	b s	[illegible]	[illegible]	b c s	c m s	[illegible]	[illegible]	[illegible]	[illegible]	[illegible]	m s	[illegible]
21	m s	[illegible]	b m c	[illegible]	[illegible]	[illegible]	[illegible]	m	[illegible]	b m	[illegible]	b
22	m s	[illegible]	m	[illegible]	[illegible]	[illegible]	[illegible]	[illegible]	m s	m	m s	[illegible]
23	m s	[illegible]	[illegible]	g m	[illegible]	[illegible]	[illegible]	b m	[illegible]	[illegible]	[illegible]	[illegible]
24	b c	[illegible]	[illegible]	[illegible]	b c m	c m	b c	[illegible]	[illegible]	b c m	[illegible]	[illegible]
25	b c	[illegible]	[illegible]	b c	b c	b m	[illegible]	m	b m g	[illegible]	b m c	[illegible]
26	m s	[illegible]	m	m c	b s	[illegible]	[illegible]	[illegible]	b c s	m c	[illegible]	b m c
27	m s	[illegible]	[illegible]	[illegible]	[illegible]	[illegible]	[illegible]	b m s	[illegible]	[illegible]	[illegible]	[illegible]
28	b c s	b m s	[illegible]	[illegible]	b m	[illegible]	[illegible]	[illegible]	[illegible]	b m s	[illegible]	[illegible]
29	b	[illegible]	b c	[illegible]	b m	b c	[illegible]	[illegible]	[illegible]	b	[illegible]	[illegible]
30	b c	[illegible]	b	[illegible]	b m	b c	[illegible]	b m	b c	[illegible]	[illegible]	[illegible]
31	b c	[illegible]	[illegible]	[illegible]	[illegible]	[illegible]	m	b m s	[illegible]	[illegible]	m s	[illegible]

NOTES TO DECEMBER RECORD.

1st. Four ptarmigan seen.

3d. 11 P. M., pale aurora in S. W. (true), about 18° above horizon.

4th. 10 P. M., aurora in S. W. [Bright from E. to W. N. W. (through south), about 25° above the horizon.—*B. of T. Papers.*]

5th. A ptarmigan seen; from 6 P. M. until midnight aurora from horizon between S. E. and W., extending upwards nearly to the zenith. [6 to 7h. 30m. P. M., flashing from S. E. to N. W. across the zenith; at 10 P. M. faint in the westward, and at midnight in W. N. W. and across zenith from N. W. to S. E.—*B. of T. Papers.*]

6th. 8 until 9 P. M., pale aurora between W. and S. E., about 25° above horizon.

8th. A fox caught; 6 P. M., aurora in the S. E. [about 40° above horizon].

9th. A fox caught.

10th. A fox caught.

11th. 10 P. M., several shooting stars.

12th. 6 to 7 P. M., bright aurora between E. by S. and N. W. [Bright from N. W. to S. E. (through S.) about 60° above horizon.—*B. of T. Papers.*]

13th. 6 to 7 A. M., light aurora between S. E. and N.; 9 P. M., aurora from S. S. E. to W. N. W., about 20° above the horizon [and continuing until midnight]; several ptarmigan seen.

14th. 6 A. M., bright aurora from S. W. through E. to N. W.; 10 P. M., aurora between S. E. and S. W. near the horizon. [20° above horizon.—*B. of T. Papers.*] Ptarmigan seen.

16th. 5 to 6 A. M.; bright aurora from E. through S. to N. W. [30° above horizon.—*B. of T. Papers.*]

18th. 9 P. M., a lunar halo, diameter about 45°. [Thickness of ice, 6 feet 1 inch.]

19th. A covey of ptarmigan seen.

20th. 9 P. M., a lunar halo, diameter 45°.

22d. A ptarmigan seen.

24th. 11 P. M., bright aurora all over the heavens (causing the magnetometer to oscillate considerably.—B. of T. Papers).

25th. Aurora between S. S. E. and W. by N., about 20° above the horizon.

29th. A ptarmigan, and the recent track of a deer, and one or two hares seen.

30th. 6 P. M., aurora to the southward, about 35° above the horizon.

31st. A ptarmigan seen.

January, 1859. Record of the Weather kept on board the Yacht Fox, with general remarks.

Day.	2h.	4h.	6h.	8h.	10h.	Noon.	2h.	4h.	6h.	8h.	10h.	Mid't.
1	m c	b m	b	o	b c	o	b c s	b c	b m r	b m	b c s	b c
2	b m	m s	[illegible]	c s	[illegible]	[illegible]	b c s	m	m	b c	b	[illegible]
3	b c	m	o	[illegible]	o	m	b m c	b c	m	[illegible]	m	m
4	b c	[illegible]	b	m	b s	b c r	[illegible]	m	[illegible]	m	[illegible]	b c
5	b c	o	b m	b m s	[illegible]	[illegible]	b	[illegible]	b m	b	b m	[illegible]
6	b m	b c	b m	[illegible]	[illegible]	b m	[illegible]	b m s	m	[illegible]	[illegible]	[illegible]
7	b m s	b c	[illegible]	m	[illegible]	b m	[illegible]	b m s	m	b	b m s	[illegible]
8	b m s	[illegible]	m	[illegible]	[illegible]	[illegible]	b m	[illegible]	b	m	m	[illegible]
9	b	b m	[illegible]	[illegible]	b c	[illegible]	m	[illegible]	b c	b	[illegible]	[illegible]
10	b	[illegible]	[illegible]	[illegible]	[illegible]	[illegible]	[illegible]	[illegible]	[illegible]	[illegible]	[illegible]	[illegible]
11	b	[illegible]	[illegible]	[illegible]	m c	[illegible]	m	[illegible]	m s	[illegible]	b m	[illegible]
12	m	[illegible]	b m	[illegible]	[illegible]	[illegible]	b c	[illegible]	[illegible]	b m r	c m	b c
13	b c	[illegible]	c	c m	c m s	[illegible]	m c	[illegible]	[illegible]	[illegible]	[illegible]	[illegible]
14	m s	[illegible]	[illegible]	[illegible]	b m	m s	[illegible]	[illegible]	m r	o	b c	o
15	b	[illegible]	b c s	[illegible]	[illegible]	[illegible]	[illegible]	m s	b m s	b m	[illegible]	[illegible]
16	b m s	[illegible]	b	[illegible]	b m	b c	o	[illegible]	[illegible]	b c m	[illegible]	[illegible]
17	b m	[illegible]	b c	[illegible]	c m s	m r	c m	[illegible]	[illegible]	b c m	b c m s	[illegible]
18	b m s	o	[illegible]	[illegible]	o	[illegible]	m o	[illegible]	[illegible]	b c m	[illegible]	o
19	b c	[illegible]	b m	b	b m	[illegible]	b	[illegible]	b m	o	[illegible]	o
20	m s	[illegible]	[illegible]	b m s	b	b c	[illegible]	[illegible]	b m	m	b	o
21	b	o	b m	o	[illegible]	[illegible]	[illegible]	[illegible]	[illegible]	[illegible]	[illegible]	o
22	b m	[illegible]	[illegible]	o	m	m s	[illegible]	o	[illegible]	o	[illegible]	o
23	b m	[illegible]	[illegible]	b c	o	b m	[illegible]	[illegible]	b	b c	[illegible]	o
24	b	[illegible]	b s	b m s	[illegible]	[illegible]	[illegible]	[illegible]	[illegible]	[illegible]	[illegible]	[illegible]
25	b m s	[illegible]	[illegible]	m	[illegible]	[illegible]	[illegible]	[illegible]	[illegible]	[illegible]	[illegible]	[illegible]
26	b m s	m	[illegible]	[illegible]	m	b	[illegible]	[illegible]	[illegible]	m	[illegible]	[illegible]
27	b	m	[illegible]	b m	[illegible]	[illegible]	[illegible]	[illegible]	b m s	o	[illegible]	m s
28	b m r	m	[illegible]	b m	b m s	m r	[illegible]	b m s	[illegible]	m	b s	[illegible]
29	b m s	[illegible]	b m	[illegible]	b	b m	[illegible]	[illegible]	[illegible]	[illegible]	[illegible]	b
30	b	b m	[illegible]	[illegible]	[illegible]	[illegible]	[illegible]	[illegible]	b	[illegible]	[illegible]	o
31	b	m	o	o	[illegible]	[illegible]	[illegible]	[illegible]	[illegible]	o	b m	[illegible]

NOTES TO JANUARY RECORD.

1st. 6 P. M. aurora from S. to W. about 40° above the horizon.

2d. 6 P. M. faint aurora in the S. W. about 40° above horizon, just above fog bank.

3d. 5 P. M. faint aurora in the east from horizon to zenith; 11 P. M. narrow band of aurora from S. S. E. to zenith.

5th. 10 P. M. faint aurora between S. E. and W. S. W. near the horizon.

9th. 6 to 7 A. M. bright aurora between W. and N. W; 10h 30m P. M. a narrow band of aurora from S. to W., passing through the zenith.

10th. 5 to 7 A. M. slight aurora from S. E. through S. to N. W.; 9 P. M. until midnight, strong auroral bands from S. to N. through the zenith.

11th. 9 P. M. until midnight, aurora between S. E. and W. about 15° above horizon.

12th. Some ptarmigan seen.

13th. A ptarmigan seen.

14th. 10 P. M. a lunar halo, diameter 45°.

16th. A ptarmigan shot.

17th. A fox caught; 4 P. M. a lunar halo.

18th. A fox caught; 6 P. M. a bear's track seen in Depot Bay.
19th. A hare shot; 10 P. M. a halo round the moon.
21st. A ptarmigan shot, and a hare seen.
22d. A raven seen.
26th. Sun's upper limb appeared at 11 A. M.; fresh tracks of two reindeer seen.
30th. Three ptarmigan shot, 8 A. M.
31st. 8 A. M. bright aurora between S. E. and N. W., passed through S. W.; 6 P. M. pencils of auroral rays from horizon to zenith between S. E. and W.; electrometer strongly affected; two ptarmigan shot.

February, 1859. RECORD OF THE WEATHER KEPT ON BOARD THE YACHT FOX, WITH GENERAL REMARKS.

DAY	2h.	4h.	6h.	8h.	10h.	Noon.	2h.	4h.	6h.	8h.	10h.	Mid't.
1	b	m	c	c	c	c	c	c	b m	b	c	b s
2	b m s	c	c	c	m	c	c	c	c	m s	m	c
3	m	c	b c	c	b c s	b c	c	b m s	b m	b m s	c	c
4	m s	c	c	m	b s	b c s	b c m s	c	m s	b	b m	c
5	b m s	b m	c	c	m	b m	b	b m	c	m	c	m
6	b m s	b m	b m s	c	c	c	m s	c	b m	c	b m s	c
7	b s	c	b c	c	c	b c s	b c	b c s	b m s	b c	b	c
8	b	c	c	b m	b	c	b s	c	b m	b s	c	b
9	b s	b m	c	b c	c	b	m	c	c	c	c	c
10	b m	m	c	c	m s	b m	b c	b m	b	c	b m	c
11	b s	c	c	c	b c s	b c	b	b s	c	b c	b c	c
12	b	c	c	b c	c	c m	m s	m	b c	c	b	c
13	b	c	b c	b c m	b m	c	c	c	c	c	b c	c
14	b c	c	c	b m	b c q	c	b c m	b c	b m	c	c	b
15	b m	b c	c	m s	b c s	c	b m s	c	c	b m	c	b m s
16	b c	b m	c	c	b m s	b m	b m s	c	b m	c	c	c
17	b	b m	m s	c	c	c	b m	b c	b m	c	c	b c q
18	b s	b m	m s	c	b s	b m	c	m	c	b m	m	b m
19	b m	m q	m s	b m s	c	b m	c	m	c	c	c	c
20	b c	c	c	b m	b c	b c s	b s	b	c	c	b m	c
21	m	c	b	b m	b	c	c	c	c	c	b s	c
22	b c	b m s	b s	c	c	c	b c s	m	c	b s	c	c
23	b	c	c	b m	m	b s	b m	m	c	c	c	c
24	m	b m	m	m s	b m	c	m	m	c	c	b	b m
25	b m s	m s	b m s	m	m s	b	m s	m	c	b m	c	c
26	b m	c	m s	b m	c	m	c	m	b c m	b m	c	b
27	b	c	c	b m s	c	c	c	m	c	c	b s	b m s
28	m s	m	b m s	c	c	b s	m	c	c	c	b q s	c

NOTES TO FEBRUARY RECORD.

1st. 8 A. M. aurora between S. E. and N. W., passing through south.
2d. A ptarmigan shot.
3d. Two reindeer seen; ascertained the water space in Bellot Straits for one mile east and west.
4th. A seal and a dovekie seen in the open water.
8th. 6 P. M. aurora in the S. W.
9th. Some ptarmigan seen.
12th. Two reindeer and several ptarmigan seen; a sooty fox caught; halo round the moon.
16th. Two ptarmigan seen; halo round the moon.
17th. 8 A. M. the early travelling parties left the ship; fifteen ptarmigan shot.
19th. 10 P. M. aurora from south to north through the zenith.
20th. Nine ptarmigan shot; 11 P. M. faint aurora from south to zenith.
21st. Thermometer against a black surface exposed to the sun showed zero; (exposed against the ship's side, —0.5°.)
23d. 2 A. M. very bright aurora from N. E. to S. W.; at 4 A. M. slight aurora to the east; four ptarmigan shot; one white fox caught.
24th. Two white foxes caught.
25th. A white fox caught.
26th. A hare seen; 11 P. M. until midnight, aurora from north to south through zenith.
27th. A fox caught.

March, 1859. RECORD OF THE WEATHER KEPT ON BOARD THE YACHT FOX, WITH GENERAL REMARKS.

Day.	2h.	4h.	6h.	8h.	10h.	Noon.	2h.	4h.	6h.	8h.	10h.	Midt.
1	[illegible]	[illegible]	[illegible]	[illegible]	[illegible]	[illegible]	[illegible]	[illegible]	[illegible]	[illegible]	[illegible]	[illegible]
2	[illegible]	[illegible]	[illegible]	[illegible]	[illegible]	[illegible]	[illegible]	[illegible]	[illegible]	[illegible]	[illegible]	[illegible]
3	[illegible]	[illegible]	[illegible]	[illegible]	[illegible]	[illegible]	[illegible]	[illegible]	[illegible]	[illegible]	[illegible]	[illegible]
4	[illegible]	[illegible]	[illegible]	[illegible]	[illegible]	[illegible]	[illegible]	[illegible]	[illegible]	[illegible]	[illegible]	[illegible]
5	[illegible]	[illegible]	[illegible]	[illegible]	[illegible]	[illegible]	[illegible]	[illegible]	[illegible]	[illegible]	[illegible]	[illegible]
6	[illegible]	[illegible]	[illegible]	[illegible]	[illegible]	[illegible]	[illegible]	[illegible]	[illegible]	[illegible]	[illegible]	[illegible]
7	[illegible]	[illegible]	[illegible]	[illegible]	[illegible]	[illegible]	[illegible]	[illegible]	[illegible]	[illegible]	[illegible]	[illegible]
8	[illegible]	[illegible]	[illegible]	[illegible]	[illegible]	[illegible]	[illegible]	[illegible]	[illegible]	[illegible]	[illegible]	[illegible]
9	[illegible]	[illegible]	[illegible]	[illegible]	[illegible]	[illegible]	[illegible]	[illegible]	[illegible]	[illegible]	[illegible]	[illegible]
10	[illegible]	[illegible]	[illegible]	[illegible]	[illegible]	[illegible]	[illegible]	[illegible]	[illegible]	[illegible]	[illegible]	[illegible]
11	[illegible]	[illegible]	[illegible]	[illegible]	[illegible]	[illegible]	[illegible]	[illegible]	[illegible]	[illegible]	[illegible]	[illegible]
12	[illegible]	[illegible]	[illegible]	[illegible]	[illegible]	[illegible]	[illegible]	[illegible]	[illegible]	[illegible]	[illegible]	[illegible]
13	[illegible]	[illegible]	[illegible]	[illegible]	[illegible]	[illegible]	[illegible]	[illegible]	[illegible]	[illegible]	[illegible]	[illegible]
14	[illegible]	[illegible]	[illegible]	[illegible]	[illegible]	[illegible]	[illegible]	[illegible]	[illegible]	[illegible]	[illegible]	[illegible]
15	[illegible]	[illegible]	[illegible]	[illegible]	[illegible]	[illegible]	[illegible]	[illegible]	[illegible]	[illegible]	[illegible]	[illegible]
16	[illegible]	[illegible]	[illegible]	[illegible]	[illegible]	[illegible]	[illegible]	[illegible]	[illegible]	[illegible]	[illegible]	[illegible]
17	[illegible]	[illegible]	[illegible]	[illegible]	[illegible]	[illegible]	[illegible]	[illegible]	[illegible]	[illegible]	[illegible]	[illegible]
18	[illegible]	[illegible]	[illegible]	[illegible]	[illegible]	[illegible]	[illegible]	[illegible]	[illegible]	[illegible]	[illegible]	[illegible]
19	[illegible]	[illegible]	[illegible]	[illegible]	[illegible]	[illegible]	[illegible]	[illegible]	[illegible]	[illegible]	[illegible]	[illegible]
20	[illegible]	[illegible]	[illegible]	[illegible]	[illegible]	[illegible]	[illegible]	[illegible]	[illegible]	[illegible]	[illegible]	[illegible]
21	[illegible]	[illegible]	[illegible]	[illegible]	[illegible]	[illegible]	[illegible]	[illegible]	[illegible]	[illegible]	[illegible]	[illegible]
22	[illegible]	[illegible]	[illegible]	[illegible]	[illegible]	[illegible]	[illegible]	[illegible]	[illegible]	[illegible]	[illegible]	[illegible]
23	[illegible]	[illegible]	[illegible]	[illegible]	[illegible]	[illegible]	[illegible]	[illegible]	[illegible]	[illegible]	[illegible]	[illegible]
24	[illegible]	[illegible]	[illegible]	[illegible]	[illegible]	[illegible]	[illegible]	[illegible]	[illegible]	[illegible]	[illegible]	[illegible]
25	[illegible]	[illegible]	[illegible]	[illegible]	[illegible]	[illegible]	[illegible]	[illegible]	[illegible]	[illegible]	[illegible]	[illegible]
26	[illegible]	[illegible]	[illegible]	[illegible]	[illegible]	[illegible]	[illegible]	[illegible]	[illegible]	[illegible]	[illegible]	[illegible]
27	[illegible]	[illegible]	[illegible]	[illegible]	[illegible]	[illegible]	[illegible]	[illegible]	[illegible]	[illegible]	[illegible]	[illegible]
28	...	[illegible]	...	[illegible]	...	[illegible]	...	[illegible]	...	[illegible]	...	[illegible]
29	...	[illegible]	...	[illegible]	...	[illegible]	...	[illegible]	...	[illegible]	...	[illegible]
30	...	[illegible]	...	[illegible]	...	[illegible]	...	[illegible]	...	[illegible]	...	[illegible]
31	...	[illegible]	...	[illegible]	...	[illegible]	...	[illegible]	...	[illegible]	...	[illegible]

NOTES TO MARCH RECORD.

2d. Seven ptarmigan and one hare shot.

3d. Noon, Captain Young and party returned.

4th. Twelve ptarmigan shot.

5th. Frost smoke in Prince Regent's Inlet.

6th. A white fox caught, a reindeer seen, a ptarmigan shot; 9 P. M. a narrow band of aurora from N. N. W. to S. S. E. through zenith—a well-marked divergence of leaves of gold electrometer.

10th. Nine ptarmigan shot; one hare seen.

14th. Noon, Captain McClintock and party returned.

16th. 3 A. M. a lunar halo; two ptarmigan shot.

18th. 9 A. M. Captain Young with two dog sledges left for Fury Beach; 1 P. M. Dr. Walker with a party started to bring in depot from Cape Airy.

19th. Two bears seen, and two ptarmigan shot.

20th. A hare seen; a white fox caught.

21st. A hare seen.

22d. A hare seen and a white fox caught; several ptarmigan seen.

23d. A hare seen and a ptarmigan shot; a lemming caught; Bellot's Straits entirely free from vapor.

24th. A ptarmigan shot; a white fox caught; a bear seen.

25th. 10 A. M. Dr. Walker and party returned.

26th. Two hares seen.

28th. A hare and a ptarmigan shot; 6 P. M. Captain Young and party returned from Fury Beach.

30th. A parhelion on each side of the sun; a ptarmigan shot and a hare seen; at midnight aurora seen between land to W. and S. W. and observer.

31st. 11 P. M. aurora in west seen between land and observer.

April, 1859. RECORD OF THE WEATHER KEPT ON BOARD THE YACHT FOX, WITH GENERAL REMARKS.

DAY.	4h	8h	Noon.	4h	8h	12h
1	b c	m	b c	b c s	b g s	m
2	b g c	b s	b	o	m	o
3	b s	b	b c	c	c m s	m
4	c m s	c s	m	c	m	b c
5	c m	m	b c	b	m	b c
6	b s	b c	b c s g	b c	m	m
7	b c	m	m	b	m	m
8	b c	b	m	b c	m	b
9	m	q m	b c	m	m s	m
10	c	b c	b s	b c q	b c	b
11	b	m	m	m	m	m
12	b	m	m	m	m	m
13	b	m	m	m	m	m
14	o c	m	b c	m	b	b c
15	b c	m	m	c	m	b
16	b	m	m	c	b s	m
17	m	m	c s	m	m c	m s
18	m s	o s g	m c s	m s g	b c s g	o s
19	o	b s	b c	b	m c	m
20	m s	b	b c	m	m	o s
21	o	m	m	b c	b c s	o c
22	m	b	m s	m	m	b
23	o	b	b c	b s	b c s	b m s
24	b s	m	o c s	o	b c	b m
25	b m	b s	b	b o	m	m
26	o	m	m	b	b o c	o c
27	b	m c	b c	o	o c s	o c
28	m s	m	o c	b c	o c s	m s
29	b c	b	b c	m	o c m	m
30	m s	m	m	m	m o c s	m

NOTES TO APRIL RECORD.

1st. A fox caught; 10h 20m P. M.; Captain McClintock and party left the ship, also Lieutenant Hobson and party for long spring journey to the southward.

4th. A white wolf prowling about the ship.

5th. Travelling party detained by weather.

7th. A hare seen; 9 A. M.; Captain Young and party left ship for search of Prince of Wales' land; a lemming caught.

8th. A hare seen; Bellot Straits quite free from vapour; two ptarmigan shot.

9th. Noticed a second space of water in Bellot Straits, smaller and about two miles farther west than first.

10th. A hare seen.

11th. A hare seen; thickness of ice formed since Oct. 3d, 6 feet 2 inches.

13th. A raven seen.

15th. Bellot Straits entirely free from vapour throughout the day.

20th. A hare seen.

21st. A hare seen; prismatic parhelion and part of halo on each side of the sun distant about 22° 30'.

22d. A raven seen.

25th. Two hares seen.

27th. A hare seen.

29th. A bear and two cubs seen.

[No aurora reported.]

May, 1859. Record of the Weather kept on board the Yacht Fox, with general remarks.

Date.	4h.	8h.	Noon.	4h.	8h.	12h.
1	[illegible]	[illegible]	[illegible]	[illegible]	[illegible]	[illegible]
2	[illegible]	[illegible]	[illegible]	[illegible]	[illegible]	[illegible]
3	[illegible]	[illegible]	[illegible]	[illegible]	[illegible]	[illegible]
4	[illegible]	[illegible]	[illegible]	[illegible]	[illegible]	[illegible]
5	[illegible]	[illegible]	[illegible]	[illegible]	[illegible]	[illegible]
6	[illegible]	[illegible]	[illegible]	[illegible]	[illegible]	[illegible]
7	[illegible]	[illegible]	[illegible]	[illegible]	[illegible]	[illegible]
8	[illegible]	[illegible]	[illegible]	[illegible]	[illegible]	[illegible]
9	[illegible]	[illegible]	[illegible]	[illegible]	[illegible]	[illegible]
10	[illegible]	[illegible]	[illegible]	[illegible]	[illegible]	[illegible]
11	[illegible]	[illegible]	[illegible]	[illegible]	[illegible]	[illegible]
12	[illegible]	[illegible]	[illegible]	[illegible]	[illegible]	[illegible]
13	[illegible]	[illegible]	[illegible]	[illegible]	[illegible]	[illegible]
14	[illegible]	[illegible]	[illegible]	[illegible]	[illegible]	[illegible]
15	[illegible]	[illegible]	[illegible]	[illegible]	[illegible]	[illegible]
16	[illegible]	[illegible]	[illegible]	[illegible]	[illegible]	[illegible]
17	[illegible]	[illegible]	[illegible]	[illegible]	[illegible]	[illegible]
18	[illegible]	[illegible]	[illegible]	[illegible]	[illegible]	[illegible]
19	[illegible]	[illegible]	[illegible]	[illegible]	[illegible]	[illegible]
20	[illegible]	[illegible]	[illegible]	[illegible]	[illegible]	[illegible]
21	[illegible]	[illegible]	[illegible]	[illegible]	[illegible]	[illegible]
22	[illegible]	[illegible]	[illegible]	[illegible]	[illegible]	[illegible]
23	[illegible]	[illegible]	[illegible]	[illegible]	[illegible]	[illegible]
24	[illegible]	[illegible]	[illegible]	[illegible]	[illegible]	[illegible]
25	[illegible]	[illegible]	[illegible]	[illegible]	[illegible]	[illegible]
26	[illegible]	[illegible]	[illegible]	[illegible]	[illegible]	[illegible]
27	[illegible]	[illegible]	[illegible]	[illegible]	[illegible]	[illegible]
28	[illegible]	[illegible]	[illegible]	[illegible]	[illegible]	[illegible]
29	[illegible]	[illegible]	[illegible]	[illegible]	[illegible]	[illegible]
30	[illegible]	[illegible]	[illegible]	[illegible]	[illegible]	[illegible]
31	[illegible]	[illegible]	[illegible]	[illegible]	[illegible]	[illegible]

NOTES TO MAY RECORD.

1st. Prismatic parhelion and part of halo on each side of the sun, distant about 22°.

2d. Two ravens seen. The water space in Bellot Strait much increased in extent.

4th. A white wolf seen.

5th. Parhelion and part of halo on each side of sun.

6th. Prismatic parhelion and part of halo on each side of sun distant 22° 30' (observed).

9th. Two hares seen; also recent tracks of a small herd of deer.

10th. Five hares seen.

11th. Ice formed since Oct. 3d, 1858, 5 feet 4 inches; several hares seen.

12th. Four hares seen. Two small pools of water noticed in the strait between Fox Island and south shore.

13th. Two hares seen; 8 P. M., fine snow falling.

14th. A young bear shot; tip to tip 6 feet 1 inch.

15th. Two hares seen.

16th. Two hares seen; part of Captain Young's party returned.

17th. Two hares seen and two snow buntings shot.

18th. Two hares and some buntings seen.

19th. Three seals and one wolf seen.

21st. A snow bunting seen; a long lane of water seen to the E. N. E. in Regent's Inlet.

22d. Ice loosened from ship's sides, allowing her to rise 3 feet 4 inches forward and 8 inches aft; two hares seen; also recent tracks of seven deer going northward.

24th. A deer seen; two others crossing ice to northward.

25th. A fox seen; also several buntings shot; three burgomasters seen flying north.

26th. One bunting seen, one finch shot; four men and sledge started for Pemmican Rock to join Captain Young.

June, 1859. RECORD OF THE WEATHER KEPT ON BOARD THE YACHT FOX, WITH GENERAL REMARKS.

DAY.	4h.	8h.	Noon.	4h.	8h.	12h.
1	o m s	[illegible]	o m s	m	f c m	b c m s
2	m	m o s	b c s	m	m	o r
3	o c	m	b c	m	m	m
4	b c	m	m	b	b c	m
5	m	m	b c	b	m	m
6	o	b c	o c	b c	b o	m
7	b o	b	o c	m	o	b c
8	b c	m	m	m	o c g	m o g
9	b c	o	b c	m c	m o r	b c
10	b c	m	m	m	b	m
11	b c	m	m	o	b c g	b c q g
12	b	m	b c	m	m	b
13	b	m	b c	b	m	m
14	b	m	m	m	m	m
15	b	m	m	m	o c	m o f
16	o	m	m	m	m	b c
17	b	m	b c	b	o f	m
18	o	o c	c c	m	m o c	b c
19	b c	m	o c	o f r	b c	m
20	m	m	b c	m r	m	m
21	o	m	m	c	m o c	c
22	b c	m	o c	b c	m	o c
23	o c	b c	m o g	m	m	b c s
24	b c	o m	b c	m	m	o c
25	b c	m	m	m	m	m
26	b c	m	m	m	m	m
27	o c	m	m	b c	m	m
28	b c	m	b	m	m	m
29	b c	o	o c s	o c	b c	m
30	b c	o	m	m	m	m

NOTES TO JUNE RECORD.

2d. A bunting seen.

3d. Some gulls, a bunting, and a raven seen; black bulb thermometer in sun's rays, 93° in maximo.

4th. Some geese, gulls, and bunting seen; a bear came near the ship; a fox shot alongside.

5th. Some bunting and a gull seen; some small pools of water to eastward of Fox Island, in the centre of current of straits; several pools of water to E. N. E. and N. E. in Regent's Inlet.

6th. Measured height of mountain ahead of harbor—11[illegible] feet (aneroid); a small cairn on top.

7th. Captain Young returned on board; a raven, several ducks, and bunting seen; three reindeer crossing the ice to northward; remainder of Captain Young's party returned.

9th. A deer, a hare, and a fox seen; also some buntings and sandpipers.

10th. A deer, some gulls, buntings, and sandpiper seen; some buntings and sandpiper shot; Captain Young and party left the ship.

11th. Several buntings and gulls seen.

12th. Two sandpipers shot.

13th. First plant in flower (*Saxifraga oppositifolia*); a fox caught, and some buntings shot; a deer, a hare, some geese, gulls, and duck seen; ice formed since Oct. 8, 4 feet 6 inches.

14th. Lieut. Hobson and party returned on board, bringing documents and relics of Franklin's expedition from west side of King William's Land; some duck and sandpipers seen.

15th. Maximum, black bulb thermometer in sun's rays, 96°.5; three sandpipers shot; some gulls seen.

16th. Two long-tailed ducks and two sandpipers shot; some ducks and gulls seen.

17th. Many ducks and gulls seen, also one seal; one king and two long-tailed ducks shot.

18th. Several ducks and one seal seen.

19th. Captain McClintock and party returned on board, bringing relics of Franklin's expedition obtained from natives on east coast of King William's Land, and picked up on Montreal Island and south shore of King William's Land; a bear, seal, and some duck seen.

20th. Two ducks shot.
21st. One seal shot.
22d. Twelve ducks and one hare shot; seal seen.
23d. Five ducks and one red-throated diver shot; a seal seen.
24th. Four ducks and four deer seen.
25th. One duck and one diver shot.
26th. One duck shot.
27th. One duck and one plover shot; two deer seen.
28th. Four plover shot.
29th. One deer seen; two ducks shot; one ermine caught.
30th. Several geese seen, and a duck shot.

July, 1859. RECORD OF THE WEATHER KEPT ON BOARD THE YACHT FOX, WITH GENERAL REMARKS.

DAY.	2h.	4h.	6h.	8h.	10h.	Noon.	2h.	4h.	6h.	8h.	10h.	Midt.
1	...	o m	...	o c	...	b c	...	m	...	b	...	b c
2	...	b c	...	m	...	b	...	b	...	b c	...	m
3	...	o	...	b c	...	m	...	b	...	m	...	m
4	...	b	...	b c	...	m	...	b	...	m	...	m
5	...	o m	...	b c	...	m	m	m	m	m	m	m
6	c	o c	o c	m	c	b c	m	o c	o c	o c r	b c	m
7	b c	o c	m	m	m	m	b c	m	o c r	o m r	o m	m
8	o m s	m	o c	b s	o c	m	c	o f	m f	m	o c	o f
9	o c	o c	m	c	o c	b c	m	m	m	m	m	m
10	c	m	o c	m	m	o r q	o c q r	m	m	m	m	m
11	o r r	b c	m	o c	m	m	m	m	m	f c	m	m
12	b c	m	m	m	m	o c	m	m	m	o c	o m f	m f
13	b c	m	o c	m	m	c	o c	m	m	m	m	c
14	c	b c	m	m	m	m	m	m	m	m	o c	m
15	b c	m	o c	m	m	m	b c	m	m	m	m	m
16	b c	m	m	m	b c o	b c	m	m	m	m	m	m
17	b c	m	m	m	m	m	m	m	m	c	b c	m
18	m s	c	o c	m	o c q r	o m s	o c	m	m	f c	m	o r r
19	s m r q	o c q	o c	m	b c	m	m	m	b	b c	m	m
20	b c	c	b c	m	m	m	b	b c	m	m	b	b c
21	b c	m	m	m	m	m	m	m	m	m	b	m
22	b	m	m	m	m	m	m	m	m	m	m	m
23	b	m	m	b m	m	m	m	m	m	m	m	m
24	b c	b	b m	b	m	m	b c	m	m	m	m	m
25	b c	b	m	m	b c	m	b	m	m	b c	m	m
26	b c	m	m	m	m	m	m	m	c	c	m	m
27	c	o c	b c	m	m	m	m	m	m	m	m	m
28	b c	m	m	m	m	b	m	m	b c	m	m	m
29	b c	m	m	m	m	m	m	m	m	m	m	m
30	b c	m	m	m	b	m	b c	m	m	b	b c	m
31	b c	m	b	m	b c	m	m	m	c	m	m	m c

NOTES TO JULY RECORD.

2d. Two ducks and two divers shot.
3d. Four ducks and two gulls shot.
4th. Three ducks and one seal shot.
5th. Commenced tide observations; one duck, one diver, and a silvery gull shot; an ermine seen.
6th. Two hares seen.
7th. A gull shot and lemming caught; several seals seen on the ice.
11th. A seal and a duck shot; the water has much increased in Bellot Straits.
12th. Several lanes of water seen in Regent's Inlet; two seals shot.
13th. One seal shot.
14th. One hare shot, and an ermine seen.
15th. Three seals shot.
16th. Two ducks shot.

17th. A fox seen.

18th. A seal shot, and another taken from a bear; a gull and a duck shot.

20th. An auk seen.

25th. Several flocks of ducks flying eastward.

26th. Bellot Straits clear of ice as far as Western Head.

27th. Ice breaking up around the ship; 13 gulls shot.

28th. A large extent of harbor ice commenced driving out.

29th. Drifted with harbor ice, to which the ship is attached, between the Fox Island and the main, until 2 A. M., when the ice was brought up by the land and shoals; 4 A. M., western current ceased; 5 A. M., ice commenced drifting eastward; 9 A. M., made sail to a light S. W. breeze; 9^h 45^m got clear of the ice, and proceeded into Port Kennedy; 11 A. M., anchored in 6½ fathoms off Observation Point.

30th. Ice breaking away from head of harbor; outer harbor almost clear; 11^h 30^m, harbor ice drifted foul of the ship; several gulls shot.

31st. Two gulls and one duck shot.

August, 1859. RECORD OF THE WEATHER KEPT ON BOARD THE YACHT FOX, WITH GENERAL REMARKS.

DAY.	4^h	8^h	Noon.	4^h	8^h	Midnight.
1	m c	m	o	m	m	m
2	c o	o r	o m r	m r	m	o r
3	o r	r	m r	m	m	b r
4	o c	b c	m	m	m	b
5	b	m	o c	m	b c	b
6	b c	b	b c	m	m	c
7	o c	c	o c	b c	m	m
8	o c	m	b	m	m	m
9	m c	o	b c	b c m	o	m r
10	o c r	c	o m	b c	o	o r
11	o	o	o c	c	o c	o c r
12	o c r	m	b c	o c q r	o c	m
13	o c q	m q	m	m	o	o c q
14	o r	o c	m	m r	f	m r
15	m	o c q	o c q	b c q	m	b q
16	b	c	b c	f	m c	f
17	f	b	o	m	o	m
18	b	o	m	f	b m	b
19	b m	b c	o	b	b m	o
20	o c	b c	o	f c	m r	m
21	o c	m	c	o c	o m	o m
22	o c	c	b	b c	o	o
23	b c	m	m	m	m	o
24	b c	m	m	b m	c r	m r c
25	b c	m	m	c	o m r	o r c
26	o f	o c	b c	m	b	m
27	b	m	m	m	b c	m
28	b c	b	o	b c	m	m
29	b c	m	m	m	b	m
30	b	m	b c	m	b	m
31	b	m	m	m	m	m

NOTES TO ABSTRACT RECORD.

1st. One seal and fifteen ducks shot; also two gulls.

2d. 4^h 30^m A. M., thunder.

4th. Bellot Straits and Port Kennedy clear of ice.

5th. A seal shot.

6th. A deer and two seals shot.

7th. Harbor full of drift ice.

8th. Ice stationary; 8 P. M., ice setting into the harbor.

9th. 10h 20m A. M., weighed and proceeded out of the harbor under sail and steam; noon, passing south end of Long Island; 1h, passed between Brown's Island and off Lying Islet southeastward; 2h 30m, off Hazard Islet; 8h, off Mt. Oliver; 8 to 12, steering between pack and land.

10th. 4 A. M., steaming past Cape Garry; Creswell Bay clear of ice; 11h 30m A. M., made fast to grounded ice in 8 fathoms, 3 cable lengths off shore of Adelaide Bay; Fury Point S. E. by E. (true); a seal and several dovekies shot; white whales, ducks, and mollymauks seen; pack closing in; low water 3 P. M.; ebb sets to S. W. along land; high water near midnight; rise 7½ feet.

11th. A white whale shot, 13 feet 8 inches long; pack closing in Creswell Bay.

12th. Ice driving to southwestward; no water visible in Creswell Bay or in N. E.; a seal seen; tide flowed until midnight; water rose 10 feet.

13th. Pack is slowly drifting southwestward; (4 A. M.) no water visible from mast-head, except inside the space into which we are lying; a small seal and some dovekies shot; many king ducks flying northward; high water at 12h 30m.

14th. 4 A. M., pack driving to southwestward; many ducks flying northward.

15th. Tide flowed until about 1h 30m A. M.; at 5h 45m P. M. Fury Beach bore W. (true) three miles distant.

16th. 2h 40m A. M., off Batty Bay, free from ice; 9 A. M., off Elwin Bay; 8h 30m P. M., Cape Sepping N. W. ½ W., distant 8'; ice seen extending from Leopold Island eastward.

17th. A black whale and some narwhals seen; Barrow Strait clear of ice as far as visible; 4 P. M., passed a small stream of ice.

18th. Many narwhals about the ship; passing stream of loose ice; 7h 30m P. M., passing Admiralty Inlet; some pack or stream ice seen in shore.

19th. 4 A. M., two miles off Wollaston Island; passing among loose ice; midnight (19–20), passing round Cape Byam Martin, distant 4'.

20th. Noon, off Cape Hatton, distant 1½'; a bear and two cubs shot; 5 P. M., off Cape Graham Moore.

21st. No floe ice visible.

22d. Some rotches seen; passed several bergs.

23d. 75 bergs in sight; saw some stream ice to eastward.

24th. A few bergs in sight; 9 P. M., saw the land about Svarte Huk.

25th. A finback whale seen; rotches seen.

26th. Saw the land about Mellem Fiord; 4 P. M., off Disco Fiord.

27th. 2 A. M., anchored in Godhavn Harbor in 7½ fathoms.

Specific gravity of sea water—

21st. 1.0275.	24th. 1.0270.
22d. 1.0275.	25th. 1.0265.
23d. 1.0260.	26th. 1.0275.

31st. [Aurora slight in S. W. (true) at 11 P. M.—*B. of T. Papers.*]

September, 1858. Record of the Weather kept on board the Yacht Fox, with general remarks.

Day.	4h	8h	Noon.	4h	8h	Midnight.	Specific gravity of Sea Water, 1.0
1	b c	[illegible]	b	b c	[illegible]	c	[illegible]
2	o r	c	b c	m	m	d	[illegible]
3	o r	[illegible]	b c	o c	o m	o c	[illegible]
4	o	o c	m	m d	m	m	[illegible]
5	b s	o c	m	m	b q	b	[illegible]
6	c m	o c	o c f	o c q	b c	m	[illegible]
7	p	o	m	b r	m	m	[illegible]
8	b c	m	m	m	c	b c	[illegible]
9	m c d	r	b c	c	b c	m	[illegible]
10	b c d	[illegible]	[illegible]	m	b c	m	[illegible]
11	b r	b c d	m	m	b d	b	[illegible]
12	o r	o c q	m	o m	m	b c	[illegible]
13	o f	o f r	f	f r	o f r	f c	[illegible]
14	o f r	[illegible]	m	o m	[illegible]	c m	[illegible]
15	o c	c	b c	[illegible]	o c q	b c	[illegible]
16	b c q	b c	m r	b c	[illegible]	b c	[illegible]
17	c m	o c	m	[illegible]	c	m r	
18	m s	m c	m	c m r	m c q	m c	

NOTES TO SEPTEMBER RECORD.

1st. Proceeded out of Godhavn; two whales seen.
2d. Passed several bergs.
3d. Bergs seen.
4th to 5th. Midnight; six bottle-nosed whales seen.
6th. Bergs in sight; passed a drift pine log; midnight, slight aurora in S. E.
7th. Bergs passed; a fulmar seen; midnight, aurora in S. W.
8th. Bottle-nosed whale seen.
9th. Passed piece of drift pine.
10th. [Aurora, 10 P. M., in N. E.—*B. of T. Papers.*]
15th. Porpoises seen.
18th. 8 P. M., sounded in 68 fathoms.

TABULATION OF AURORAS, WITH OBSERVATIONS AND NOTES, BY DR. DAVID WALKER.
(Copied from the log-book.)

Date.		True Direction of Aurora.	Date.		True Direction of Aurora.	Date.		True Direction of Aurora.
			1858.			1858.		
1857.			March	3	* N. W. by N. to E.	Dec.	6	N. W'd.
Oct.	30	S. to S. S. E.		4	N. to W. N. W.		18	* N. W. to S. E. through S.
Nov.	7	* S. E.		5	S. W. by N. to N. W.			
	8	N. N. E. to E. N. W.		8	N. W. to E.		13	* N. N. E. to W. N. W.
	9	* E. to E.		9	S. E.		14	* E. N. E. to N. W.
	9	N. E.		16	* N. by W. to N. E.		15	N. W. through N. to E.
	11	* N. W. to S. E.		17	* S. W. to E. N. E.		24	All over the heavens.
Dec.	9	N. N. E. to E. S. E.		18	* N. by E. to E. N. E.		29	* W. by N. to S. S. E.
	10	N. to zenith.	April	9	* E. to N.		30	E'd.
	11	N. W.		10	* S. to E.	1859.		
	12	N. E. to S. E.		11	* E. to S. E.	Jan.	1	* W. to N.
	14	E. to N. E.		12	* E. by S. to W. S. W.		2	* N. W'd.
	16	E'd.		13	* E. to W. S. W.		3	N. E'd.
	17	* E. to N. E. and E. to N.		14	* E. to E.		8	W. N. W. to N. E.
	19	E. to W.		15	* E. to E.		9	* W. to N. W.
1858.							9	N. to S. through zenith.
Jan.	9	N. W. to S. E. and all round horizon.	Oct.	28	* S. to W.		18	* N. W. to S. E. by S.
				29	* N. S. E. to W. N. W.		20	N. to S. through zenith.
	11	S. W.		30	* S. W'd.		21	* N. N. to W.
	13	S. to E.		31	* N. W'd.		31	* N. W. to N. E. by E.
	17	S. to E.	Nov.	8	N. by E. to W. N. W.		31	W. to S. E. to zenith.
Feb.	2	* S. E. to E. N. E.		7	* N. W.	Feb.	1	* N. W. to S. E. by S.
	3	N. E. to zenith.		8	* S. W.		5	* S. W'd.
	7	* S. S. E. to N.		9	* N. to W.		19	N. to S. through zenith.
	8	* N. E. to S. E.		13	N. to zenith.		20	S. to zenith.
	13	S. S. E. to E.		14	* N. W. to W. N. W.		23	N. E. to S. W.
	15	S. S. E. to E. N. E.	Dec.	3	* S. W'd.		28	N. to S. through zenith.
	16	S. E. to N. N. E.		4	E. through S. to W. N. W.	March	6	N. N. W. to S. S. E. through zenith.
	17	S. S. W. to E. S. E.						
	18	S. S. E. to E.		5	* N. E. to N. W.		30	* W. to N. W.
	19	S. S. E. to N. E.		8	* S. E. to W.		31	* W.

* During our drift down Baffin's Bay and Davis' Straits (1857–'8) the aurora was noticed on 48 nights; of these, 16—marked with an asterisk—were observed in a direction where water or water sky had been seen during the day. The general direction of the remainder was between N. E. and S. E. None were particularly bright but two or three, and even these scarcely equalled the brilliancy of those seen at times in the north of Scotland. On some occasions the aurora was from horizon to zenith, but generally from 10° to 40° above the horizon, with occasional streamers; these latter were generally present towards the zenith, but only sometimes reaching so far. At times pulsations were noticed in the patches and bands of light; these were often contrary to the surface wind. On the whole stars of all magnitudes were dimmed when viewed through the aurora, but only those of small magnitude

were rendered invisible. Once only was there noticed a connection between cirrous clouds and the aurora.

"Of the 42 auroras observed during our winter at Port Kennedy (1858-'9) 24—marked with an asterisk—were in a direction of a space of water, open throughout the winter, or of the vapor rising from it. More than this number might be traced to it, but of these 24 I am certain. On the nights of the 20th and 21st March, 1859, I noticed the aurora between myself and the land; the patches of light could plainly be seen a few feet above the small mass of vapor arising from the water. The opposite land was from two and a half to three miles distant, and I am confident, if this land had been sufficiently high, the most of these 24 auroras would have been seen suspended but a short distance above the surface of the water or ice. On five occasions the aurora was observed to cause agitation of the magnetic needle; on one of these, Dec. 21, 1858, I noticed a vibration of 10°; on the other four times the vibration was not much more than a degree; four of these five occurred when the aurora was from south to north, passing through the zenith. A fine wire was attached to the fore yard-arm by insulated supports and led to a snow house with a connection through the floe to the water beneath. Here the gold leaf electroscope was at times applied, and I was enabled to observe the presence of the electricity in the atmosphere and also the influence of the aurora on the instrument. There appeared to occur two periods of minimum electric intensity about 9 P. M. and noon; the instrument not being sufficiently delicate I could not be satisfied about the time of the maximum. On the whole there seemed to be more free electricity present in the air at Port Kennedy than Baffin's Bay or Davis' Strait. On six occasions in 1857-'8 I observed a well-marked effect on the electroscope by the presence of aurora, the gold leaves diverging with greater force and remaining so for a longer time than usual. On three occasions at Port Kennedy, when the aurora was from horizon to zenith, the electroscope was strongly affected; on all these occasions the electricity was positive."

[D. W.]

PUBLISHED BY THE SMITHSONIAN INSTITUTION,
WASHINGTON CITY,
MAY, 1862.

www.ingramcontent.com/pod-product-compliance
Lightning Source LLC
Chambersburg PA
CBHW020553270326
41927CB00006B/818

* 9 7 8 3 7 4 1 1 4 4 5 5 4 *